160X

✳ AMERICAN WRITERS SERIES ✳

Volumes of representative selections, prepared by American scholars under the general editorship of Harry Hayden Clark, University of Wisconsin. Volumes now ready are starred.

AMERICAN TRANSCENDENTALISTS, *Raymond Adams, University of North Carolina*

*WILLIAM CULLEN BRYANT, *Tremaine McDowell, University of Minnesota*

*JAMES FENIMORE COOPER, *Robert E. Spiller, Swarthmore College*

*JONATHAN EDWARDS, *Clarence H. Faust, University of Chicago, and Thomas H. Johnson, Hackley School*

*RALPH WALDO EMERSON, *Frederic I. Carpenter, Harvard University*

*BENJAMIN FRANKLIN, *Frank Luther Mott and Chester E. Jorgenson, University of Iowa*

*ALEXANDER HAMILTON AND THOMAS JEFFERSON, *Frederick C. Prescott, Cornell University*

BRET HARTE

*NATHANIEL HAWTHORNE, *Austin Warren, Boston University*

OLIVER WENDELL HOLMES, *Robert Shafer, University of Cincinnati*

*WASHINGTON IRVING, *Henry A. Pochmann, Mississippi State College*

HENRY JAMES, *Lyon Richardson, Western Reserve University*

ABRAHAM LINCOLN

*HENRY WADSWORTH LONGFELLOW, *Odell Shepard, Trinity College*

JAMES RUSSELL LOWELL, *Norman Foerster, University of Iowa, and Harry H. Clark, University of Wisconsin*

HERMAN MELVILLE, *Willard Thorp, Princeton University*

JOHN LOTHROP MOTLEY

THOMAS PAINE, *Harry H. Clark, University of Wisconsin*

FRANCIS PARKMAN, *Wilbur L. Schramm, University of Iowa*

*EDGAR ALLAN POE, *Margaret Alterton, University of Iowa, and Hardin Craig, Stanford University*

WILLIAM HICKLING PRESCOTT, *Claude Jones, Johns Hopkins University*

*SOUTHERN POETS, *Edd Winfield Parks, University of Georgia*

SOUTHERN PROSE, *Gregory Paine, University of North Carolina*

*HENRY DAVID THOREAU, *Bartholow Crawford, University of Iowa*

*MARK TWAIN, *Fred Lewis Pattee, Rollins College*

*WALT WHITMAN, *Floyd Stovall, University of Texas*

JOHN GREENLEAF WHITTIER

*

AMERICAN WRITERS SERIES
*
HARRY HAYDEN CLARK
General Editor

*

*Pen drawing by Kerr Eby, after
a portrait by John W. Jarvis*

JAMES FENIMORE COOPER

ÆT. 33

James Fenimore Cooper

REPRESENTATIVE SELECTIONS, WITH
INTRODUCTION, BIBLIOGRAPHY, AND NOTES

BY

ROBERT E. SPILLER

Professor of English
Swarthmore College

AWS

AMERICAN BOOK COMPANY
New York · Cincinnati · Chicago
Boston · Atlanta

PREFACE

The selection of representative passages from the work of a novelist is always difficult. Parts of novels are rather disjointed, especially if brief, and whole novels are too long. The difficulty is unusually great in Cooper's case because of his prolix style and his leisurely method of developing action, characters, and ideas. It is better, if one may read only one of his books, to limit oneself, for example, to *The Spy, The Pioneers, The Red Rover, The Pathfinder,* or *Satanstoe.*

But no one of these books will give the reader a full and critical view of Cooper's ideas of art and life, or of his place in the history of American literature and thought. For these ends one must turn to the critical prose, of which there is more and better than is usually believed. Not only do his ideas stand out in sharper statement on these pages than in his fictional work, but his writing is freed from many of its worst defects. His descriptions of people, places, and events are often more vivid; his characters, because they are individuals rather than types, are more believable; his action is frequently swifter and more direct; and his style inclines to be less pompous and wordy.

Cooper's chief contribution to our literature lies, of course, in his work as a novelist, but his importance as a social critic must be recognized, and an understanding of the relationship of his criticism to his fiction is essential to an appreciation of his art. This volume is therefore restricted to the critical prose in order that the student may, by means of it, gain a knowledge of the mind of one of the first authors to give form and direction to American literature.

The text of the passages from critical works is a faithful reproduction, with the correction of a very few and minor typographical errors, of that of the first American editions.

v

That of the prefaces and introductions to the novels is taken
from the Townsend-Darley collected edition of 1859-1861,
which is the earliest to include all of Cooper's revisions and
annotations, and may therefore be considered as authoritative.

I am indebted to Mr. Joseph Coppock for aid in preparing
this volume, and to innumerable others who made possible my
earlier studies of Cooper, of which this is an immediate product.

                                                              R. E. S.

CONTENTS

JAMES FENIMORE COOPER

I. THE PROBLEM

With Cooper's first half-dozen novels, American literature came into its own. By 1829, they had all been republished in England and translated into French and German. Several had also found translators in Italy, Sweden, Denmark, and probably in other European countries. A writer in the London *Athenaeum* in that year linked Cooper's name with those of Irving and Channing as the only American writers who were generally known abroad.[1] At home, *The Spy* was appearing in its seventh edition, *The Pioneers* in its sixth.

Cooper did not yet fully believe in himself as a literary man, and he was not at first so considered by others. Samuel Knapp, the first historian of our literature,[2] does not mention him, and only two years later he stated his primary purpose in succinct terms: "Her [his country's] mental independence is my object, and if I can go down to the grave with the reflection that I have done a little towards it, I shall have the consolation of knowing that I have not been useless in my generation."[3]

Moral rather than aesthetic purpose motivated his work as it did his character. Primarily a man of action rather than of mind, he absorbed the thought currents of his day and of his inheritance with eager enthusiasm, and he spoke for his cause with the energetic dogmatism of American vitality. Whether or not we attribute this moral enthusiasm to his Quaker inheri-

[1] *Athenaeum*, II, 637 (Oct. 14, 1829).

[2] S. L. Knapp, *Lectures on American Literature* (New York, 1829).

[3] *Correspondence of James Fenimore-Cooper*, ed. by J. F. Cooper (New Haven, 1922), I, 227. He himself summarized the problem of an emergent American literature in *Notions of the Americans* (Philadelphia, 1828), II, 431–453, and of an emergent American language in *The American Democrat* (Cooperstown, 1838), pp. 117–124.

tance,[4] we can find a source for it in the blind optimism and vital energy which are natural products of frontier conditions and unfolding civilization. He lived at a time when American culture had sent down its first firm roots into the new soil, but was still uncertain as to what fruits it might bear. It was Cooper's task to profit by the autonomy which political independence had brought and to enlarge the spirit of independence to include the sense of security which only self-knowledge can produce. Never a man of the frontier himself, he was a product of frontier conditions. Literature to him was merely the expression of opinions in accord with actual conditions. "It is high time," he wrote in 1837, "not only for the respectability, but for the *safety* of the American people, that they should promulgate a set of principles that are more in harmony with their facts."[5] This was the basic motive for his writing. The form which that writing took was largely accidental. Fortuitous circumstances determined his choice of theme for *Precaution, The Spy, The Pioneers*, and *The Pilot*, the novels which determined the material for most of his later work: society, American history, the backwoods, and the sea. He fell into the forms of the domestic novel of manners and the romantic tale of adventure because they were easy and familiar to him, not because he cared deeply about their artistic requirements and uses. The literary principles which he gradually evolved from his experience were not narrowly aesthetic, nor were his social principles the results of disciplined thinking or formulated doctrine.

A codified analysis of his position would therefore be fruitless. Rather we must follow him through the stages of his development as a moving, growing, vital, and expressive force in the evolution of American culture at a period of stumbling self-realization.

[4] H. S. Canby, *Classic Americans* (New York, 1931), pp. 97–142. Cf. p. lxiii below.

[5] *Gleanings in Europe: England*, ed. by R. E. Spiller (New York, 1930), p. 153.

II. NATIONALISM AND ROMANTICISM

Cooper thought of himself always as the defender of "American principles" or "American opinions," and of the mission of American literature as the defending and propagating of an apparently unified doctrine. Even a cursory examination of American thought in the early years of national life reveals no such unity. Politically, Americans were first divided between loyalists and rebels, later between federalists and republicans.[6] Socially and economically, practically all class conflicts and divergencies of the old country were reproduced in various patterns in the new, from aristocratic New York and Virginia to democratic Massachusetts and Pennsylvania.[7] In the religious war between Calvinism and Deism, almost all sects were represented, and all were subject to schisms no less disrupting than the Unitarian break with Congregationalism.[8] Philosophically, materialism and idealism existed side by side, often in the same mind, unaware of their constitutional antipathy. Obviously, if a unity of American principles existed, as Cooper so confidently believed, it must be sought in some synthesizing force underlying these divergencies.

But even in cases where analysis seems to reveal little more than a confusion of conflicting factors, unity may be observed in general trends of thought and feeling exhibiting themselves as moral forces. Such a force was the "revolutionary spirit" which originated in France in the eighteenth century, swept that nation into temporary chaos, determined the issue of American independence, and worked itself out in England in

[6] R. G. Adams, *Political Ideas of the American Revolution* (Durham, N. C., 1922), pp. 15–39, 153–181.

[7] C. A. and M. R. Beard, *The Rise of American Civilization* (New York, 1927), I, 124–145.

[8] I. W. Riley, *American Thought* (New York, 1915), pp. 1–18, 54–95. See also G. A. Koch, *Republican Religion: The American Revolution and the Cult of Reason* (New York, 1933), and H. M. Morais, *Deism in Eighteenth Century America* (New York, 1934).

terms of reform legislation. No single definition of this spirit, except perhaps as a desire to be done with the old social order, would satisfactorily embrace all of these developments. Neither can it be attributed wholly to rationalism in philosophy, the naturalism and humanitarianism of Rousseau, the Utilitarianism of Bentham and Mill, the laissez faire economics of Adam Smith and Ricardo, deism and the rise of religious tolerance, or the literary romanticism of Goethe or Wordsworth. Yet it was in terms of this revolutionary spirit that colonial America drew herself together and created a new nation.

To the French, America appeared as the embodiment of a moral ideal, an "agricultural, philosophical, tolerant, pious, reasoning, and happy nation." [9] It remained for the half century following the Revolution to demonstrate whether or not this ideal had sufficient power to become a social order and to subdue the conflicting elements of which the new nation was composed. Political independence opened rather than closed the issue.

An American citizen of these years could scarcely avoid being influenced by the process of unfolding civilization, however much or little he were given to reading and thinking in politics, religion, economics, philosophy, or social theory. He might believe in a centralized or a distributive government for the new nation, in property rights or communism, in Unitarianism or Anglicanism, in materialism or idealism, but he must agree with his fellows that in America old wrongs were to be righted by a simple belief in the integrity of man and the impulse to work. Without revelation of its origin, the following comment of Hamilton might well be attributed to his antagonist Jefferson: "That Americans are entitled to freedom is incontestable on every rational principle. All men have one common original: they participate in one common nature, and consequently they

[9] B. Faÿ, *The Revolutionary Spirit in France and America* (New York, 1927), p. 23.

have one common right. No reason can be assigned why one man should exercise any power or preëminence over his fellow creatures more than another; unless they have voluntarily vested him with it." [10] In a strong nationalism on the moral plane, differences in opinion on other levels were resolved. When Lafayette wrote in 1777, "The happiness of America is ultimately bound up with the happiness of humanity. She is going to become a cherished asylum of virtue, of tolerance, of equality and of peaceful liberty," [11] he was expressing a belief which was held by conservatives and radicals alike. The Declaration of Independence had "proclaimed not only war with England, but a civil war between the Whigs and Tories in America." [12] Its successful outcome was a victory for the Whig philosophy, and, with the treaty of 1783, the shape of the American mind, whatever its variety of contents, was cast in the mold of an ideal of liberty of state and person. Political in origin and in its first form, this ideal permeated all other aspects of American thought and was translated into as many idioms as there are fields of human activity. The process took a half century or more, but when Cooper was a boy and a young man, the problem foremost in the public mind concerned not the validity of this central doctrine but the details of its application. With the doctrine itself his whole consciousness was permeated.

During the first half century of independence, there seems to have been implicit in this doctrine the concept of an aristocracy of worth. Jefferson, supposedly the most ardent advocate of democratic principles in his day, accepts it without qualification. "I agree with you," he writes to John Adams on October 28, 1814, "that there is a natural aristocracy among men. The

[10] A. Hamilton, "A Full Vindication" (1774), in *Works*, ed. by H. C. Lodge (New York, 1885), I, 5–6.
[11] Letter to his wife, June 7, 1777, quoted in B. Whitlock, *Lafayette* (New York, 1919), I, 67.
[12] C. H. Van Tyne, *The American Revolution, 1776–1783* (New York, 1905), p. 87.

grounds of this are virtue and talents." [13] But with the election of Andrew Jackson to the Presidency in 1828, the term "democracy" gained a new meaning in which aristocracy of any kind had no part. "The possessors of property and the aristocrats of intellect had been the only classes with whom the politicians had concerned themselves," writes Claude G. Bowers. "Respectability sternly set itself against the presumptuous ambitions of what it conceived to be a rough, illiterate representative of the 'mob.'" [14] Immediately the old party lines and the solidarity of "American principles" were threatened. As the earlier ideal of democracy had worked its way from a political theory into an all-embracing social philosophy, so once again a political attitude became the determinant of the social. Equalitarianism gained a new meaning and the radicals of a previous generation were forced to decamp or to reassert the old moral principles, now as the voice of conservatism.

Cooper and other members of the landed class in his generation never accepted the new doctrine. It matters little to which part in the new alignment they gave their allegiance; the issue which they believed to be of primary consequence was not expressed in terms of party lines. "Here, in our view," he wrote, virtually on his deathbed in 1851, "is the great danger to the country—which is governed, in fact, not by its people, as is pretended, but by factions that are themselves controlled most absolutely by the machinations of the designing. . . . Party is the most potent despot of the times." [15]

A definition of "American principles," as Cooper used the term, may therefore be reduced to a belief in liberty as a moral force, a social structure with small property ownership at its base, an aristocracy of worth, and a strong sense of nationality. Beyond this, the essentials of the doctrine do not go; incon-

[13] *Writings*, ed. by P. L. Ford (New York, 1892), IX, 425.
[14] C. G. Bowers, *Party Battles of the Jackson Period* (Boston, 1922), p. 31.
[15] *New York* (New York, 1930), pp. 38–39.

sistencies in detail or in application are of little relevance. The moral force which united Adams and Jefferson in their efforts to establish and sustain the new nation was the heritage of Americans of the privileged classes in the following generation. They built their imperfect culture upon it at the very moment when the new concepts and practices of equalitarian political doctrine were threatening to rob them of it.

American literature emerged during this period as a result of social stability attained and as an answer to the plea for an application of national independence wider than the political. It was therefore motivated primarily by a belief in the principles which had established the social order. The logic of the argument is unassailable: We have gained our political independence, let us now free our minds as well as our government of European domination, and develop our culture as an expression of our national autonomy. The idea is repeated many times over in the periodicals and books of the day, but always with the same moral enthusiasm, irritation at delay, and optimism for the future. "It is not merely that since 1783 we have sought to declare our literary independence of Great Britain," writes Howard Mumford Jones, "it is the finding of ways by which we might express our independence that is the heart of the problem." [16] The declaration of cultural independence implicit in American writers from Freneau to Emerson is the mainspring of our romantic movement as well as the primary cause of our having a literature at all. The culture of which it is the expression was restless, still relatively insecure, and in a state of rapid development. Most of it bears the stamp of what Cooper calls "American principles" in some respect. The ideal of liberty furnishes its dominant theme, of nationalism its reason for being, and of aristocracy the sense of privilege necessary to the cultivation of the amenities of life. Its central prob-

[16] H. M. Jones, *America and French Culture* (Chapel Hill, N. C., 1927), pp. 7–8.

lem is the reconciliation of the imported traditions necessary to
it as an art with the requirements of native ideals and materials.

The first stage in the emergence of our literature was one of
imitation of English classic and contemporary models. Timo-
thy Dwight's

> Fair Verna! loveliest village of the west;
> Of every joy, and every charm possess'd; [17]

is distinguishable from Goldsmith's

> Sweet Auburn! loveliest village of the plain,

chiefly in the loss of poetic power. Such efforts of the native
muse led Freneau to lament the paucity of western genius and
to advise such American authors as there were to graft their
despised profession upon some lucrative trade.[18] He was himself more original, writing poetry to which Coleridge and
others of the English romantics owed a debt. But with the
exception of an occasional flash of such genius, most of the
writing of the day was neither "classic" nor "romantic"; it
was imitative of English models of both species. John Trumbull used an American theme in classic meter;[19] Brockden
Brown wrote of Indians in a forest that might have existed in
almost any part of the world;[20] Francis Hopkinson described
the domestic agonies of the annual American "whitewashing"
in a facile Addisonian manner;[21] and Royall Tyler placed his
pseudo-Sheridan comedy of American manners on the Battery
and in the drawing rooms of New York.[22] There were many

[17] *Greenfield Hill* (New York, 1794), Part II, ll. 1–2.
[18] "Advice to Authors, by the late Mr. Robert Slender," *Miscellaneous
Works* (Philadelphia, 1788), pp. 42–48.
[19] *M'Fingal* (Philadelphia, 1775).
[20] *Edgar Huntly* (Philadelphia, 1799). See Ernest Marchand's "The
Literary Opinions of Charles Brockden Brown," *Studies in Philology*,
XXXI, 541–566 (Oct., 1934).
[21] "A Letter from a Gentleman in America," *Pennsylvania Packet*, June
18, 1785.
[22] *The Contrast* (Philadelphia, 1790).

others with a spot of originality here and there in their work, the chief literary inspiration for which was imported.

To this literary temper, the spirit of nationalism contributed a fresh creative urge. At first, it was sporadic in its appearance, lacking integration in the whole process. The conception of literature as something apart from life, as *belles-lettres*, pervaded it still. A fiery tirade against political despotism could find no expression other than the stark prose of the controversial pamphlet or the creaking forms of borrowed literary tradition. A flash of appreciation of American scenery or the quaint originality of the Yankee character asserted themselves in settings of Gothic romance or London society. Obviously the assertion of American nationality must strike deeper.

The War of 1812 seems to have had at least some part in awakening the needed national pride. Immediately after the victory of the *Constitution*, periodicals like the *Port Folio*, *Niles's Register*, and the *Portico* began publishing articles in which naval power and the need for a national literature were linked themes;[23] and at least one of Cooper's earliest incentives toward patriotism was born of his experience in the Navy.

Among the many contemporary expressions of this type, Bryant's review of American poetry in 1818 is notable for its judgment.[24] Recognizing the need for an American spirit in poetry, he warned against that form of patriotism which could not distinguish artistic worth from loyalty to the national cause. At the same time, he inveighed against the "sickly and affected imitation of the peculiar manner of some of the late popular poets of England." In the poems written before 1818, he discovered little of genuine worth, but he took hope in the good taste of the American reading public. In his own early verse he kept his mind on the immediate response which he felt to the

[23] J. C. McCloskey, "The Campaign of Periodicals after the War of 1812 for National American Literature," *Publications of the Modern Language Association*, L, 262–273 (March, 1935).
[24] *North American Review*, VII, 198–211 (July, 1818).

beauties of the Berkshire Hills, and on the religious moods which he had inherited. Here, to be sure, was a deeper and more genuine form of nationalism, determined by his being American rather than by his affiliation with a political party.

The campaign for a national literature in this sense raged through the periodical press for the next two decades, much of it provoked by British criticism and by the writings of English travelers in America. Whereas French commentators like Chateaubriand[25] and De Tocqueville[26] tended to preserve the romantic ideal of an American Utopia, the English, from whatever causes of jealousy or of accuracy of observation, kept their eyes on the crudities of facts and their minds in a state of hostility. Six months after the appearance of Bryant's essay, Sydney Smith published his classic review of three such volumes of travel, in which he announced: "Literature the Americans have none—no native literature we mean. . . . Prairies, steamboats, grist-mills, are their natural objects for centuries to come."[27] Many Americans were willing to accept this as their destiny. On October 18, 1823, Charles J. Ingersoll delivered before the American Philosophical Society in Philadelphia, "A Discourse Concerning the Influence of America on the Mind," in which he recognized excellence in practical affairs rather than in philosophical or literary interpretation as the peculiar genius of Americans.[28] In his satirical travel book, *Inchiquin, the Jesuit's Letters, during a Late Residence in the United States of America* (New York, 1810), he had praised his countrymen for these virtues, but had been equally ready to acclaim such monstrosities as Barlow's *Columbiad*. Evidence of this kind serves to support Bryant's thesis that uncritical patriotism was the worst foe of national attainment in letters.

Ingersoll's *Discourse* provoked the sanest and most pene-

[25] *Travels in America and Italy* (London, 1828).
[26] *Democracy in America* (1835–1840), (New York, 1904).
[27] *Edinburgh Review*, XXXI, 132–150 (Dec., 1818).
[28] *A Discourse . . .* (Philadelphia, 1823).

trating review of the problem to appear before Emerson's *American Scholar* (1837). William Ellery Channing replied to the pamphlet in an essay entitled *The Importance and Means of a National Literature* (1830). "By a national literature," he writes, "we mean the expression of a nation's mind in writing. ... It will be seen, that we include under literature all the writings of superior minds, be the subjects what they may." [29]

It was impossible for America to have a romantic movement of her own until she had thus related her literature to her national mind; and the driving force of that national mind was the revolutionary ideal of liberty which had given the nation its political independence. The political basis of the movement was therefore inevitable; the assertion of mental independence preliminary to all else. Yet it was not only in America that the break with a literary past depended upon political doctrine at this time. "Almost to a man," writes Crane Brinton, "the English romanticists were actively interested in politics. ... It is seldom—and this in itself is a significant fact—that a whole generation devotes itself to politics as fervently as did that of 1800 in England. Indeed, among the romantics Lamb and Keats alone seem to have escaped the contagion." [30] The causes are not far to seek. The breakdown of the old order and the individualism of the new, raised political idealism to an ethical, almost a religious plane.

This link between politics and literature was all very well as long as the high level was maintained. But with the English reviewers the connection became a bond, coercing literature to a political conformity. "The Edinburgh review," wrote Francis Jeffrey, "it is well known, aimed high from the beginning:—And, refusing to confine itself to the humble task of pronouncing on the mere literary merits of the works that

[29] *Works* (Boston, 1841–1843), I, 243.
[30] C. Brinton, *The Political Ideas of the English Romantics* (Oxford, 1926), p. 4.

came before it, professed to go deeply into *the Principles* on which its judgments were to be rested." [31] So much fire has been directed at Jeffrey's confusion of "principles" with "political bias" in his famous condemnations of *Endymion* and *The Excursion* that the liberalizing influence of his work has been forgotten. In the revolt against eighteenth-century classicism and the isolation of literature in a vacuum, men of relatively small mind like himself, Smith, Gifford, and the other editors, confused political theory with party loyalty. "It [the *Edinburgh Review*] was political," writes Hugh Walker, "which it had every right to be, and it carried politics into literature, and pronounced critical judgment not solely according as books were good or bad, but partly as they were Whig or Tory, which it had no right to do. . . . Unfortunately for English literature, the evil was combated, not by the establishment of a disinterested organ, but by setting up another partisan one [the *Quarterly Review*]." [32] On the other hand, the doctrine, when divorced from partisan bias, was a necessary liberation for the literature which had been so completely divorced from life. At the root of the revolt of both the romantic poets and the reviewers lay the doctrine of Taine "that a literary work is not a mere individual play of imagination, the isolated caprice of an excited brain, but a transcript of contemporary manners, a manifestation of a certain kind of mind." [33] This doctrine, in its application to the principles of American nationalism, rather than to those of party affiliation, was at the heart of the pleas of Channing, Cooper, and Emerson. They comprehended it with varying degrees of success, but they were at one in theory.

When Cooper turned his attention to the problem, the old distinction between literature as *belles-lettres* and as political

[31] F. Jeffrey, *Contributions to the Edinburgh Review* (New York, 1860), p. v.

[32] H. Walker, *The English Essay and Essayists* (New York, 1915), p. 206.

[33] H. Taine, *Histoire de la littérature anglaise* (Paris, 1863), I, iii (translated).

propaganda had pretty well broken down. Political patriotism had expanded to include the entire life of thought; literature had left its alcove and was ready to attempt an expression of the entire American experience. The point was merely underscored, not invented, by Emerson.

Examination of such evidence as this helps to establish an intelligent approach to the writings of Cooper and to explain his lifelong search for a literary form in which he might comprehend the American personality, critically and as a whole. He absorbed his theory of "American principles" emotionally rather than by analysis; it dominated his literary expression by moral enthusiasm rather than by logic; he accepted the patriotic view of the purpose of literature in terms broader than those of earlier writers; and, perhaps more than anyone else in his day, he gave impetus to a romantic movement in our letters by centering his attention on an ideal and comprehensive nationalism rather than upon its derivatives.

III. INHERITANCE

Born in 1789, Cooper published nothing until 1820. In the early years, his character and his dominant ideas were molded by his inheritance, by the influence of his father, his home, and his father's friends, and by the post-pioneer conditions in central New York State, as well as by the more highly cultivated society of New York City and the settlements along the lower Hudson and the Sound.

All that Cooper himself has to say about this first and unliterary period was written in later years and is strongly colored by his developed personality and doctrines. Much light is thrown upon it, however, by the writings of his father and his daughter, and by what we know from other sources of the circumstances of his childhood and youth.[34]

[34] William Cooper, *A Guide in the Wilderness* (Dublin, 1810); Susan Fenimore Cooper, "Small Family Memories," *Correspondence of J. F. Cooper,*

The first fact to be borne in mind is that he was *not* a pioneer, even though he wrote so extensively of the pioneers and of life on the frontier. His childhood was formal, in a closely-knit home life in a settled community, and his own moves were always toward the east and its culture rather than toward the western fringe of civilization.

His father, although a pioneer of the homesteading generation, was a Federalist in politics and had many of the attributes of the aristocrat in his social thinking. The Cooper family life was shaped on the patriarchal model. The elder Mrs. Cooper devoted herself to her home and her children, who grew up with strong feeling for family integrity and loyalty, and attachment to place.

Compared to the Dutch patroons and the English patentees of northern New York, however, William Cooper's theories of property rights, suffrage, liberty, equality, and other "American opinions" were liberal and democratic. His political and social theory was firmly founded on his theory of land settlement, outlined in his *Guide*. His principles were few: (1) Buy large tracts and sell (not rent or give) them to settlers of all classes, but preferably to artisans and farmers, buying more as fast as these were sold; (2) live and work with the settlers, joining with them in such community enterprises as roads and bridges; (3) develop such industries as sugar and potash, as well as the more obvious lumbering and farming; and (4) keep in mind the commercial development of the nation as a whole, working for such improvements as trade highways and canals. "The mirror of partisan perfection as a Federalist squire," [35] he appeared to his son as a democratic gentleman, privileged because of his business sagacity and his control of his fellows. Cooperstown

---

I, 9–72; *idem, Pages and Pictures from the Writings of James Fenimore Cooper* (New York, 1861); and *idem*, prefaces to fifteen of the novels (New York, 1876, 1881–1884).

[35] D. R. Fox, *The Decline of Aristocracy in the Politics of New York* (New York, 1919), p. 136.

was named after him, developed by his theories, and shaped around his personality. The "Mansion House," later replaced by Otsego Hall, a large structure at the foot of the lake, was Cooper's boyhood home, the embodiment of his father's directness and power. All about this industrious squirearchy were the neobaronial tracts of the Dutch patroons, who rented their land to farmer-tenants, and beyond them was the unsettled and wooded wilderness; while sixty miles to the east was the town of Albany, capital of an agrarian aristocracy. The picture is vividly painted in *The Pioneers.* "There existed," writes Henry Cabot Lodge, "in New York an upper class, stronger and better defined than in any northern province . . . and closely allied to the ruling class in Virginia."[36] The Cooper home was in accord with this tradition.

When Cooper and his brothers were sent to Yale and Princeton for the education which their father lacked, they went, therefore, with an assurance that they would be permitted, both by him and by the society of which they were a part, to use their intellectual powers to build on the material foundations of family stability which their father had laid. To Cooper, there was nothing inconsistent with democracy in this assumption, as his later attitude toward his own children demonstrates. Furthermore, when he married into one of the Tory families of New York, he adopted and carried on its traditions as he accepted that part of its holdings in land which came to him. He may, therefore, be considered in these early years as an aristocrat in the social sense, as a man who accepted an unequal society and his own place of priority in it.

Life at Yale and in the Navy were, of course, important to Cooper's development, but they did little to alter his basic attitudes. His marriage, on the other hand, was a profoundly significant influence. Susan Augusta De Lancey was the grand-

[36] H. C. Lodge, *A Short History of the English Colonies in America* (rev. ed., New York, 1881), p. 327.

daughter of James De Lancey, Chief Justice and Governor of
New York, and leader of the Loyalists in that state during the
Revolution.[37]   There were, in Colonial times, two parties
distinguishable in the political life of the state, although their
names frequently changed.   One represented the shopkeepers,
small farmers, sailors, shipwrights, poor traders, and artisans;
the other the patroons, rich fur traders, merchants, crown
officers, and English landowners.   The differences between
them were more than political.   Social prominence, economic
superiority, and loyalty to the Church of England were identified with loyalty to the King; and wealth, particularly in land,
determined economic, social, and religious positions.

The De Lanceys lost their power with their land after the
Loyalist cause was defeated, but Mrs. Cooper inherited a share
of the holdings of the Heathcote family at Mamaroneck through
descent from James De Lancey's wife, Anne Heathcote.   Cooper
was married at Heathcote Hall, and his new home, Angevine
Farm, a few miles inland, symbolized an acceptance of the
family tradition.   His seeming uncertainty as to whether he
wished to settle his family at Cooperstown or in Westchester
County is symptomatic of the conflict between the extreme
conservatism of the De Lancey tradition and the modified conservatism of his own.   Not until his new profession of novelist
took him to New York City was the issue finally resolved.   But
if we wish deep-rooted causes for his religious leanings in the
last years of his life, for his social conservatism, for his belief
in property rights, for his tolerance of slavery, for his lifelong
antipathy to middle-class New Englanders, and for many other
aspects of his character and point of view, we cannot neglect
the fact that he married a De Lancey.   The social novels of his
later years present us with perhaps the best picture we have of
life as James De Lancey must have known it, modified by the

[37] A. C. Flick, *Loyalism in New York during the American Revolution*
(New York, 1901), pp. 13–16.

ideals of William Cooper, and seen through the prism of Jeffersonian liberalism.

IV. SOCIAL CRITICISM IN THE NOVELS, 1820–1828

When Cooper began to write novels, therefore, he was firmly established in his own privileged place in a stable society. As yet he took no deep interest in social or political causes. He looked about him with an observant rather than a philosophical eye, and he believed in his country and in the principles of its constitution because he had nothing to complain of in his own lot. Never a wide reader, he drew his conclusions from the facts immediately about him and from the opinions of such friends and relatives as Judge William Jay, Governor Clinton, and Bishop De Lancey. He worshipped at an Episcopal Church, joined the local agricultural society and the state militia, built a house on a hill overlooking his land and the distant sea, and brought up his family of daughters in all the proprieties and accomplishments of women of the day. Like the Squire of Bracebridge Hall, he steeped himself in local tradition and history, and he was interested in the characters of the people about him.

In the novels written before 1828, his attitude is that of the observer and moralizer rather than that of the analytical critic. In his first, *Precaution*, the moralizer alone is present. It is significant, in the light of his later work, that Sir Edward Moseley "was descended from one of the most respectable of the creations of his order by James, and had inherited, with many of the virtues of his ancestor, an estate which placed him among the greatest landed proprietors of the country," [38] and that his wife was "a woman of many valuable and no obnoxious qualities, civil and attentive by habit to all around her, and perfectly disinterested in her attachments to her own family." [39]

[38] *Precaution* (New York, 1861), p. 51.
[39] *Ibid.*, p. 52.

The life at Moseley Hall and in the rectory was presumably English, but Cooper had never, up to this time, left his native shore. The details were gleaned from his reading, but the social pattern was far from alien to his temperament and to the comparatively crude approximations of aristocracy which he had experienced on the fringe of the wilderness.

Cooper's turn to American material in *The Spy* and *The Pioneers* was deliberate, but his social ideals were not materially altered, nor did he immediately become more critical. Judge Temple, in the latter novel, is the prototype of the American gentleman to be developed in theory later and illustrated more fully in the Littlepage novels of 1845–1846. The social scene is now faithful to the author's experience, but the landed proprietor still speaks in the person of William Cooper, dead now more than a decade. The ancestor of Marmaduke Temple "became the master of many thousands of acres of uninhabited territory, and the supporter of many a score of dependents." [40] The friend of his son, Edward Effingham, was a member of "one of the few families then resident in the colonies, who thought it a degradation to its members to descend to the pursuits of commerce." [41] Here, similarly, speaks James De Lancey, although the novelist has chosen his material because it is familiar and congenial to him rather than because of a wish to illustrate or to satirize an ideal. Even the name Heathcote appears in *The Wept of Wish-ton-Wish*. Yet social generalizations from the facts are comparatively rare. The change in Cooper's attitude between 1821 and 1831 is clearly illustrated by his revision of *The Spy* in the latter year for its inclusion in Bentley's "Standard Novels" series. An example is his description of a dinner-table conversation. When the party is assembled, the discussion withholds interest from the food. The worry of the Negro, Caesar, is described objectively in the first version: "The black

[40] *The Pioneers* (New York, 1859), p. 29.
[41] *Ibid.*, p. 30.

well knew the viands were getting cold, and felt his honour concerned in the event." [42] In the revision, this sentence reads: "The black well knew the viands were not improving; and though abundantly able to comprehend the disadvantage of eating a cold dinner, it greatly exceeded his powers of philosophy to weigh all the latent consequences to society which depend on social order." [43] The phrase, "all the latent consequences to society," although ironic, indicates clearly the drift of Cooper's mind from the fact to the cause. The verbosity of the second version reveals a development not so fortunate.

The appeal of a settled, though unequal, social order rested for Cooper on its maintenance of moral security. Its ideals of character and conduct were clearly defined and codified by manners and religious practices. The Anglican Church translates into religious custom the codes of English aristocratic and agrarian conventions. Without inquiry, Cooper accepted this whole structure, with a resultant emphasis on conventional morality, manners, and Christian character, whether in the woods or in the drawing room.

There is comparatively little treatment in these early novels of the cosmopolitan society of New York City, which was satirized by Halleck, Tyler, Paulding, and the other "Knickerbockers," and which Cooper later attacked directly in *Home as Found.* He keeps his characters in the simple surroundings which he knew and admired. "The youth of Frances," he tells us in *The Spy,* "when she left the city, had prevented her sacrificing, in conformity to the customs of that day, all her native beauties on the altar of fashion." [44] Human nature, in its more nearly unsullied manifestations, was to be his topic.

[42] *The Spy* (fifth American ed., Philadelphia, 1827), I, 217.
[43] *The Spy* (New York, 1859), p. 186. Tremaine McDowell has pointed out that these revisions reveal a growing sense of literary art as well as of social consciousness. ("James Fenimore Cooper as Self-Critic," *Studies in Philology,* XXVII, 508–516, July, 1930.)
[44] *The Spy* (New York, 1859), p. 79.

Two primitive characters that represent his types of ideal conduct appear first in these early novels: the noble and stoical Indian, Chingachgook, and the man of nature, Natty Bumppo. In the third chapter of *The Last of the Mohicans*, these two meet on the banks of a small but rapid stream. Each presents to the other the chief point in his philosophy of life, and they find in each other a deep and primitive sympathy, although the issue of their debate, whether or not the white man has a right to the new lands, is not resolved. Racial traditions contain all the philosophy of the Indian. He believes only what Nature and his fathers have told him: "The land we had taken like warriors we kept like men." But to the trapper, "everything depends on what scale you look at things."[45] Because he rejects the sophistications of his people, can shoot to the mark, and can respect honesty and courage in his fellows of whatever color, he feels himself on a par with the red man. The right of the intruders to the land depends on their superiority as men, their justice, and their humanity. The scale which Bumppo supplies to enlarge the Indian's is that of the Bible as interpreted in Protestant tradition. Under Christian influence, the red warrior forsakes his inhuman ways, his brutality, and his ignorance, to rely upon justice and charity. Cooper's primitivism is in no sense pagan; it is a complete acceptance of Protestant ethical tradition, qualified by a rejection rather than by a reform of the social sophistications and corruptions which had resulted in the three centuries of evolution in that tradition. It has been commonly assumed that Cooper, like Chateaubriand and others of the day, identified the Indian with the "noble savage" ideal and may therefore be classified as a follower of Rousseau and

---

[45] *The Last of the Mohicans* (New York, 1859), pp. 33–39. Gregory L. Paine has pointed out that Cooper's treatment of the Indians began with a reliance on his sources rather than on first-hand knowledge, and that in his later novels, a tendency to idealize the red man grew upon him. ("The Indians of the Leather-stocking Tales," *Studies in Philology*, XXIII, 16–39, Jan., 1926.)

writes in his *Gleanings*, "is sure of having that of his own country, and he who is abused by England will be certain of being abused at home." [50] The American character and American manners had reached a low ebb in the English mind, and the American mind in its turn was habitually deferential to English opinion. Cooper addressed his book to both peoples, hoping that a fair and sympathetic picture of America might influence the English, and indirectly raise the level of self-respect in America itself. It was an ambitious undertaking, certain of failure in immediate effect, although undoubtedly of ultimate influence. Cooper adopted a semi-fictional formula, representing the book as having been written by an English gentleman who was guided in his travels and in his observations by a New York aristocrat. His readers on both sides of the water misunderstood his intentions and were irritated rather than soothed by the parts which they fully understood. He offended both the English sense of superiority and the American spirit of democracy. The book had a small sale in comparison with that of his novels.

Cooper was careful in his facts and studied reliable sources in preparation. He was one of the best informed men of his time on social conditions in his own New York State, and he tended to generalize for the nation in terms of the particular locale which he knew. This prejudice somewhat detracts from his reliability; but the more serious bias was his deliberate intention to present things in their most favorable light. The book may be accepted, however, not only for the value of its opinions, but for the light it throws on actual social conditions.

The presumed author is an enlightened Englishman, a man of sound learning and aristocratic taste, but broad in his sympathies, a character familiar in various guises throughout Cooper's novels and easily to be identified with his own ideal conception of himself. He is a member of a club of such gentlemen of

[50] *England* (New York, 1930), p. 228.

various nations, all of them fictional: Sir Frederick Waller, Bart., the Baron von Kemperfelt, the Comte Jules de Béthizy, the Abbate Giromachi, and others. Bachelors all, these gentlemen devote their time to travel in various parts of the world to learn what they can of man in his social being as expressed in the ideals and manners of civilized peoples. The supposed author has undertaken a study of America, and he addresses his first letter from Liverpool on July 22, 1824, from which port he is on the point of sailing with a letter of introduction to John Cadwallader of Cadwallader, New York. Cadwallader later qualifies for election to the club, in spite of the objection of some of its members that democratic society makes the development of the true gentleman impossible.

Cooper adopted in this work for the first time the epistolary form so common in eighteenth-century English novels. He did so, he says in his preface, because "a close and detailed statistical work on the United States of America could not keep its place as authority for five years." [51] Rather he prefers to emphasize "the principles of government and the general state of society," which are not so readily subject to change. An informal method was therefore necessary. After a dignified expression of thanks in a dedication to the imaginary Cadwallader, the narrative proceeds in a succession of letters to various members of the club.

It is easy to trace the line of travel of the bachelor. His third letter is dated from New York and describes his arrival, which was soon followed by that of Lafayette on his triumphal and final visit to his foster fatherland. The American reception of this honored guest furnishes a theme for the entire book and serves to show off the national character in a favorable light. The letters of the first volume find the bachelor for the most part in or near New York City. From this center, he makes trips to inland New England and to Cadwallader's (Cooper's) home in central New York State. In the second volume, we

[51] *Notions* (Philadelphia, 1828), I, vii.

find him in Washington observing the operations of the government and making a hurried tour of the Southern states. He finally returns to New York and concludes his tour with a visit to Boston. The journey itself, however, is comparatively unimportant. Its purpose is to provide the writer with observations from which he may generalize.

During the months—one might almost say years—of preparation of the *Notions*, Cooper had been gradually clarifying his ideas about America. The discrepancies between her principles, as he defined them, and her practices had not yet become apparent to him, but his experience with European society was providing him with an admirable background for judgment. As his mind developed, he came to identify conventional ethics and etiquette with political idealism, and he wove them all into a social philosophy which he preached in novel after novel and tract after tract without pause. This integration of his morality and his historical sense took place during his European years when he observed antithetical political ideals in open conflict. The code which he had at first applied only to individuals he gradually came to apply to society as a whole.

The early years of his residence abroad, however, did little to bring him into wide and varied contact with the life about him. He was concerned almost wholly with the two purposes which had taken him from home: the education of his daughters and young son, and the business arrangements for publishing and translating which he hoped would secure his financial independence as a writer. He did not believe in the use of letters of introduction, and Mrs. Cooper had no interest in receptions or social calls. Gradually, however, his presence was discovered by Lafayette, Scott, the Princess Galitzin (a Russian emigrée), the American envoy James Brown, and others of liberal political sympathies.[52] During 1827 he began to go to

[52] See Mrs. Cooper's letter to her father, Paris, March 23, 1827, in *Correspondence of J. F. Cooper*, I, 126.

affairs of a social nature by himself, a habit which was confirmed by his visit to London in the spring of the next year when he entered freely into the Whig society which gathered about Samuel Rogers, Lord Lansdowne, and Earl Grey. Unfortunately his personal letters of this year have been lost, but those in answer from Charles Wilkes [53] indicate a growing ability to discuss world affairs. While he was writing novels in the familiar romantic mode, he was thinking politically and socially.

France and England were then testing political liberalism as a means of avoiding the extremes of revolution and the old order. France had tried reaction in the restoration of the Bourbons Louis XVIII and Charles X, [54] and England was on the eve of the overthrow of her Tory government. [55] When Cooper arrived, both countries were still at the right; during his residence both swung to a hypothetical middle ground with the July Revolution of 1830 in the former and the passage of the Reform Bill of 1832 in the latter. Cooper took part in the discussions which preceded these changes, and sharpened his political wits. In the main, he was in sympathy with the turn of events, but he was intensely critical of compromise. His was a *via media* in its own right.

The longer he remained in Europe the firmer his friendship with Lafayette became and the more definitely the latter molded his opinions. Lafayette was, for a brief moment in July, the deciding voice in the affairs of France. It was he who made the gesture of the award of the throne to Louis Philippe, of the collateral Orléans dynasty, instead of to the legitimate and reactionary Bourbon who would have become Henry V. But after Louis became king, he proved to be more reactionary than Lafayette expected, and the latter found himself the leader of the Opposition to the *juste milieu* in the Chamber of Deputies.

[53] *Ibid.*, I, 144–147, 150–154.
[54] E. Bourgeois, *Modern France* (Cambridge, England, 1922), I, 87.
[55] C. Seymour, *Electoral Reform in England and Wales* (New Haven, 1915), pp. 7–103.

Cooper shared with him the feeling of disgust with government measures which were marked as liberal, but which seemed to the Opposition to be reactionary in the extreme. It was this stand which drew him into the finance controversy of 1831–1832 and into active aid of the cause of Polish freedom during the same years. In both instances, he felt that he was defending the theory and practice of the United States government against, in the first, a direct criticism, and in the second, a tyranny in another country from which the Constitution protected American institutions.[56]

The finance controversy was Cooper's initiation into the workings of European political machines. As in many of his other activities, his participation was the result of circumstance rather than of plan. On October 9, 1831, Lafayette sent him several articles by M. Saulnier, a writer in the employ of the government, which had appeared in the *Revue Britannique*,[57] asking for an expression of his opinion.[58] Lafayette's formal letter of November 22, probably a mere introduction to the pamphlet, states his challenge to the American: "It belongs to you, in vindication of republican institutions, to correct certain allusions published in the enclosed Britannic Revue. Besides our common American interest in this matter, I am anxious to undeceive those of my French colleagues who might, with safe consciences, oppose reductions in the ensuing budget, under the mistaken notion that taxation, in this country, falls short of the expenses of federal and state governments in the United States."[59] Cooper answered the challenge immediately, and his

[56] R. E. Spiller, "Fenimore Cooper and Lafayette: The Finance Controversy of 1831–1832," *American Literature*, III, 28–44 (March, 1931); and "Friends of Polish Freedom, 1830–1832," *American Literature*, VII, 56–75 (March, 1935).

[57] *Revue Britannique*, N. S. VI, 272–324 (June, 1831); VIII, 195–260 (Oct., 1831); and IX, 164–194 (Nov., 1831). Internal evidence suggests that the dates of issue were three months earlier than those of announced publication.

[58] *Correspondence of J. F. Cooper*, I, 245–246.

[59] *Letter to Gen. Lafayette* (Paris, 1831), p. 3.

pamphlet was used by Lafayette in the session of January, 1832. His subsequent letters in the Paris *National* (February 25–March 7, 1832) were replies to attacks upon his statements and opinions.

At the start of the controversy, Cooper's attitude was one of reluctant participation. "No American can," he says, "with propriety, withhold from you any information of this nature he may happen to possess," [60] and he concludes: "I have no desire to compare these facts with the charges sustained by France." [61] But his knowledge of European politics was becoming more acute. To Samuel Rogers in London, he had written on January 19, 1831: "Here we have just got out of the *provisoire*. The *furor* of moderation is likely enough, I think, to put us all back again. . . . The intentions of the 'juste milieu' are obviously to make the revolution a mere change of dynasties, while the people have believed in a change of principles. Could the different sections of the Opposition unite, the present state of things would not endure a month." [62] These are not profound opinions, but they reveal an increasing tendency to relate "principles" critically to "facts" in a specific political situation.

Meanwhile Cooper's intimacy with Lafayette was increasing, and he was led to frequent conversations on American principles and the facts of French political dissension. Before the close of the year, he wrote to Charles Wilkes: "The French ministry have preserved the peace by cheating France out of her institutions, but it will not do . . . . It is impossible to do as much for free institutions as has been done in France, and then go back, as is evidently the wish of the Aristocratic party." [63]

While engaged in this controversy, he was observing the lands which Scott had depicted in the glory of Feudalism, perhaps the worst tyranny (in the eye of the American) which his-

---

[60] *Ibid.*, p. 5.   [61] *Ibid.*, p. 49.
[62] P. W. Clayton, *Rogers and His Contemporaries* (London, 1889), II, 12–18.
[63] "New Letters," *American Literature*, I, 147 (May, 1929).

tory had recorded, and he had learned from Scott's own lips Tory theories which were hostile to those which he and Lafayette felt so strongly to be true. What could be more natural for him than to turn the white light of American liberalism on these dark corners of the past? "I had in view," he writes of *The Bravo*, "to exhibit the action of a narrow and exclusive system, by a simple and natural exposure of its influence on the familiar interests of life." [64] The same motive provoked the other novels of the European trilogy, *The Heidenmauer* and *The Headsman*. "To this tradition—true or false—we attach no importance," he wrote at the conclusion of *The Heidenmauer*. "Our object has been to show, by a rapidly-traced picture of life, the reluctant manner in which the mind of man abandons old, to receive new, impressions." [65] This, he felt, Scott had failed to do. "These very works of Sir Walter Scott," he wrote in the *Gleanings*, "are replete with one species of danger to the American readers; ... The bias of his feelings, of his prejudices, I might almost say of his nature, is deference to hereditary rank. I do not mean that deep feeling, which, perhaps, inevitably connects the descendant with the glorious deeds of the ancestor, and which every man of sentiment is willing to admit, as it is a beautiful feature in the poetry of life, but the deference of mere feudal and conventional laws, which have had their origin in force, and are continued by prejudice and wrong." [66]

The result was the trio of European novels, all of which were written and published in the latter days of his residence abroad. The scenes were laid in Italy, Switzerland, and the valley of the Rhine, where he had seen for himself surviving monuments of the middle ages in the forms of palaces, castles, and monasteries. Contrasting the liberal governments and societies of the Swiss cantons and the Italian free cities with their respective pasts, he

[64] *A Letter to His Countrymen* (New York, 1834), p. 12.
[65] *The Heidenmauer* (New York, 1861), p. 464.
[66] *England* (New York, 1930), p. 153.

drew his own moral, quite a different one from that of his rival in romance.

A Letter to His Countrymen was Cooper's first publication after his return to America on November 5, 1833. It reveals his dismay at conditions of society and politics as he found them, as well as his irritation at the criticism which was already being directed toward him by the press. It marks in many ways the principal turning point in his literary career. His disillusionment is extreme in contrast to his mood five years earlier when he wrote the *Notions*, but for the first time he attempts to reduce his political theories to a generalized statement in other than fictional form.

The immediate provocation for the tract was its author's desire to defend his personal reputation against the attacks of the reviewers. Edward Sherman Gould had contributed to the *New York American*, on June 7, 1832, a criticism of *The Bravo*, in which he not only attacked the social implications in the novel, but expressed the opinion that Cooper had written himself out and was now merely producing romances for the financial return they might bring. The review was sent to Cooper, who answered it in violent mood in the *Albany Daily Advertiser* for April 2, 1833. His resentment was justified, but its expression was tactless and its form irritating. The New York *Courier and Enquirer* and other American journals took up the quarrel. Finally, Cooper decided to review the whole case in a pamphlet. *A Letter to His Countrymen* announced Cooper's retirement as a novelist, and for six years he held to his resolution, devoting his attention to critical prose and social satire. As a document in the history of his literary reputation, the *Letter* is of only ephemeral value. Its facts and conclusions are heavily weighted with injured pride, and its issues are of little consequence. As the opening shot in his war with the press, it has importance for the historical aspect of our libel laws. But the parts of the pamphlet which deal with issues of a more theoretical nature are as good controversial prose as Cooper ever wrote. In order to defend himself, he had to restate and to justify his theories of democratic society and to demand America's independence from the dominance of European opinion. His experience in Europe had given him perspective on these issues and his position was at last clearly defined. Popular sovereignty, firm adherence to the Constitution, a union in which the central authority was checked in its assumption of the rights of the states, and a democratic society in which the freedom of the individual was balanced by a recognition of worth in leadership—these were a few of the principles which he here laid down and hereafter adhered to. "The inference that I could wish to draw from this brief statement," he writes, "is the absolute necessity of construing the Constitution of the United States on its own principles; of rigidly respecting the spirit as well as the letter of its provisions; and of never attempting to avert any evil which may arise under the practice of the government, in any other manner than that which is pointed out by the instrument itself." [67] With what seemed to him then to be his failure to promote this cause successfully by the writing of novels, he was ready to retire. "I came before you as a writer," he concludes, "when the habit of looking to others for mental aliment most disqualified the public to receive a native author with favor. It has been said lately that I owe the little success I met with at home, to foreign approbation. This assertion is unjust to you. Accident first made me a writer, and the same accident gave a direction to the subject of my pen. Ashamed to have fallen into the track of imitation, I endeavored to repair the wrong done to my own views, by producing a work that should be purely American, and of which love of country should be the theme. This work most of you received with a generous welcome that might have satisfied anyone that the heart of this great community is sound. It was only at a later

[67] *A Letter to His Countrymen*, p. 69.

day, when I was willing more obviously to substitute American *principles* for American *things*, that I was first made to feel how far opinion, according to my poor judgment, still lags in the arrear of facts. The American who wishes to illustrate and enforce the peculiar principles of his own country, by the agency of polite literature, will, for a long time to come, I fear, find that *his* constituency, as to all purposes of distinctive thought, is still too much under the influence of foreign theories, to receive him with favor. It is under this conviction that I lay aside the pen." [68]

But the pen was laid aside only in that it was devoted to purposes other than the writing of romances. The following years produced the five volumes of travel, published under the titles of *Gleanings in Europe* and *Sketches of Switzerland* (1836–1838) and *The American Democrat* (1838). In the order of the journey they describe rather than that of publication, the travels are: *France* (1837), *England* (1837), *Sketches of Switzerland* (1836), *Italy* (1838), and *Sketches of Switzerland, Part II* [Paris, Switzerland, and the Rhine] (1836). They are ostensibly made up of letters to friends, named in *France* and *England*, anonymous in the others; but they are actually short topical discussions, of loose unity, presumably based on notes taken during his residence abroad, but later so drastically expanded and amended that no passages from the books can be taken as indicative of Cooper's opinions at the time of his observations. His first plan was to write a volume on Europe which might serve as a companion to the *Notions*. "The fragments of travels that are here laid before the reader," he states in the preface to *Switzerland*, "are parts of a much more extensive work, that it was, originally, the intention of the writer to publish." [69] This work was never written. Instead, the travel letters followed each other in haphazard order.

[68] *Ibid.*, p. 98.
[69] *Switzerland* (Philadelphia, 1836), I, 7.

There is reason to believe that the epistolary form of these volumes was again a mere fictional device, a supposition supported by the total disappearance of the personal letters upon which the text is based, if any such letters ever existed. The published *Correspondence* contains no originals, nor have any personal letters more than remotely related to those in the volumes ever yet been discovered. The only extant notes upon which the text could have been based are far briefer than the parallel passages in the *Gleanings*.[70] The record of facts seems to bear the earlier dates of Cooper's travels (1826–1833); the expression of opinions is for the most part of the dates of writing (1836–1838).

France carries the narrative from the date of leaving New York, June 1, 1826, to February 17, 1828. The earlier letters describe the ocean passage and a hurried trip up to London to consult with Miller, Colburn, and Murray, English publishers with whom Cooper hoped to arrange terms. The remainder of the book forsakes the time sequence and records first impressions of Paris in the final days of the Restoration. The point of view is that of an outside observer. Only Lafayette, the American envoy James Brown, Scott, and the Princess Galitzin stand out in any detail as personalities.

England covers the period from February 17 to the last week of May, 1828, during which time Cooper, with his wife, son, and nephew-secretary, lived at 33 St. James's Place, London. The purpose of the trip was the publication of the *Notions*, but a chance meeting with the fashionable but impecunious Williams Spencer, youngest grandson of the third Duke of Marlborough, had prepared Cooper's social path. Spencer wrote letters to his friends in London announcing Cooper's arrival, and the American soon found himself drawn into the social life of the respectable poets and liberal statesmen aligned in the Whig

[70] "Fragments from a Diary," *Putnam's Magazine*, N. S. I, 167–172 (Feb., 1868), and N. S. I, 730–737 (June, 1868).

cause. Among these were Samuel Rogers, connoisseur and survival of eighteenth-century poetic traditions, William Sotheby, one of those many English poets who have made a highly respectable bid for fame by translating Homer, J. G. Lockhart, son-in-law and biographer of Scott, Lord Holland, and many others. At the breakfast and dinner tables of these gentlemen, Cooper met Coleridge, Scott again, Earl Grey, Sydney Smith, Tom Moore, and Sir James Mackintosh.

Switzerland and *Italy* record an extended trip to the south, starting in May, 1828, and concluding with a return to Paris in the fall of 1830. The summer of 1828 was spent on the out-skirts of Berne, with excursions to almost all accessible parts of the Confederation, and Cooper's comments are devoted to natural scenery rather than to people. In Florence the following winter, the Americans were drawn into the group of liberal expatriates of all nations that gathered about the hospitable Duke, among them the members of Napoleon's family who had survived their regal depositions. The summer of 1829 was spent in the Casa detta del Tasso at Sorrento on the Bay of Naples, after a trip down the coast in a Genoese felucca, and the following winter in Rome. During this period, Cooper again kept largely to himself, although he had occasional opportunities for conversations with men like the American sculptor, Horatio Greenough, the Polish refugee, Adam Mickiewicz, and Prince Aldobrandini. The return to Paris was made by way of the Rhine, Dresden (where Cooper paused long enough to see *The Water-Witch* through the press in September), and Frankfurt.

The final volume of the series is made up of miscellaneous notes on the trips to Switzerland and the Rhine valley which furnished material for *The Heidenmauer* and *The Headsman*, and the conversations with Lafayette in Paris during the period of the July Revolution which had such profound and lasting effects on Cooper's political and social views.

His main thesis throughout the series is that stated in *A*

Letter to His Countrymen: that an examination of European institutions reveals differences between them and American principles which make direct imitation of the utmost danger to the integrity of the new country. The works themselves are mere narratives of travel interspersed with comments pointing to this danger. Although the principles are themselves political, Cooper's interest in them lies almost wholly in their social applications.

Even through the veil of opinions added at a later date, we may trace the slow development of Cooper's doctrines in terms of his experiences. He shows little sympathy for the tottering Bourbon king in 1827. When, as part of the populace, he attended a dinner at which the royal family was on display, he noted the unpopularity of the king. "The catastrophe is to come," he concludes. "The instant the King's back was turned, the gallery became a scene of confusion." [71] He objects to conscription on the grounds of injustice,[72] he finds the speaking in the Chamber of "a dull, monotonous character," [73] but he appreciates the latitude of interpretation allowed in the French charter.[74] Such comments are not profound. They reveal only a superficially inquiring mind in matters of political theory and practice.

In England, however, Cooper's contact with leaders of the Whig cause gave him more grounds for his political opinions. Comparison of the British parliament with the American congress leads directly to theorizing on the bases of representative government. "The only power in England," he writes, "that can resist parliament is the body of the nation. . . . In England, the right of petition is the only regular mode by which the body of the nation can at all enter into the councils of the nation." [75] This situation he finds to be a potential danger to freedom of

---

[71] *France* (New York, 1928), p. 174.
[72] *Ibid.*, p. 153.   [73] *Ibid.*, p. 320.   [74] *Ibid.*, p. 326.
[75] *England* (New York, 1930), pp. 141–145.

thought. But even in England his mind was concerned more with social than with political matters, with problems of social priority and the rules of etiquette in the upper classes.

To the Swiss government he gave little critical attention in 1828. He objects to the appearance of the authorities of Vaud wearing the decorations of foreign orders as inconsistent with their professions of democracy,[76] and he is occasionally prompted to a comment on his "American principles," but for the most part he concerns himself with the scenery and history of the country. In Italy, likewise, he seemed little aware of the political structure behind social appearances, even to the point of being willing to "separate the absolute sovereign from the individual" [77] in a conversation with the Duke.

The visit to Lafayette, recorded in Part II of *Switzerland*, provokes one of his few generalizations on a purely political problem, a statement of the forms of government which he considers suitable to conditions in France. "I would establish a monarchy," he says, "and Henry V should be the monarch. I would select him on account of his youth, which will admit of his being educated in the notions necessary to his duty; and on account of his birth, which would strengthen his nominal government; for, I believe, that, in their hearts, and not withstanding the professions to the contrary, nearly half of France would greatly prefer the legitimate line of their ancient kings to the actual dynasty. This point settled, I would extend the suffrage as much as the facts would justify: certainly so as to include a million or a million and a half of electors. All ideas of the *representation* of property should be relinquished, as the most corrupt, narrow and vicious form of polity that has ever been devised, invariably tending to array one portion of the community against another, and endangering the very property it is supposed to protect. A moderate property *qualification* might

[76] *Switzerland* (Philadelphia, 1836), I, 155.
[77] *Italy* (Philadelphia, 1838), I, 71.

be adopted, in connexion with that of intelligence. The present scheme in France unites, in my view of the case, precisely the two worst features of admission to the suffrage that could be devised. The qualification of an elector is a given amount of direct contribution. This *qualification* is so high as to amount to *representation*, and France is already so taxed as to make a diminution of the burdens one of the first objects at which a good government would aim; it follows that as the ends of liberty are attained, its foundation would be narrowed, and the *representation* of property would be more and more assured. A simple property qualification would, therefore, I think, be a better scheme than the present.

"Each department should send an allotted number of deputies, the polls being distributed on the American plan. Respecting the term of service, there might arise various considerations, but it should not exceed five years, and I would prefer three. The present house of peers should be converted into a senate, its members to sit as long as the deputies. I see no use in making the term of one body longer than the other, and I think it very easy to show that great injury has arisen from the practice among ourselves. Neither do I see the advantage of having a part go out periodically; but, on the contrary, a disadvantage, as it leaves the representation of old, and, perhaps, rejected opinions, to struggle with the opinions of the day. Such collisions have invariably impeded the action and disturbed the harmony of our own government. I would have every French elector vote for each senator; thus the local interests would be protected by the deputies, while the senate would strictly represent France. This united action would control all things, and the ministry would be an emanation of their will, of which the king should merely be the organ.

"I have no doubt that the action of our own system would be better, could we devise some plan by which a ministry should supersede the present executive. . . . France has all the machinery of royalty, in her palaces, her parks, and other appliances of the condition; and she has, moreover, the necessary habits and opinions, while we have neither. There is, therefore, just as much reason why France should not reject this simple expedient for naming a ministry, as there is for our not adopting it. Here, then, would be, at once, a 'throne surrounded by republican institutions,' and, although it would not be a throne as powerful as that which France has at present, it would, I think, be more permanent than one surrounded by bayonets, and leave France, herself, more powerful, in the end." [78]

This passage, the main features of which were probably sketched as early as 1832 or 1833, indicates more careful thought than Cooper had previously given to the problems of government. His acceptance of royalty in France and his rejection of it in America were based on practical recognition of traditional patterns rather than on an ideal. In essence, he would have the two countries follow the same political doctrine, but he would have them adapt the details to the social patterns already existent. Politics to Cooper were significant only in so far as they provided theoretical bases for social procedure. His keener observations always derive from the morals, manners, and etiquette of the resultant society. The social problem to which he devoted his most nearly constant attention was the comparative study of conditions in England and in America, with collateral reference to those in France, Switzerland, and Italy.

At the time that he was traveling and first making his observations he was in the process of formulating his convictions with reference to the justification for an aristocracy of worth in a democracy, and its bearing on problems of property rights, law, suffrage, representation, and the conduct of social relationships. He therefore observed very closely the status of the aristocracy in the countries of his visit in order to distinguish the differences between American and European social ideals

[78] *Switzerland, Part II* (Philadelphia, 1836), I, 36–38.

in spite of many similarities in superficial facts. Because England was most persistently the model for America in such matters, his attention was directed primarily to her, and *England* is the key volume to the series.

"It seems to me," he writes, "that there is a singular conformity between English opinions and English institutions. The liberty of the country consists in franchises, which assure a certain amount of personal rights, and not in a broad system, which shall insure the control of numbers."[79] In this principle of privilege he finds the root of all English institutions. Yet there would seem to be no lasting security for the aristocracy in a society so arbitrarily divided into classes. "The danger," he feels, "comes equally from the rich and the poor: from the rich, because they are excluded from power by the action of the borough system; and from the poor, because they are reduced to the minimum of physical enjoyments, and are formidable by numbers, as well as by their intelligence."[80] Whig liberalism, by undermining the authority of the House of Lords, was, he felt, striking at the root evil of the situation, which lay in a political fallacy. "There exists," he believes, "a radical fault in the theory of the British government, which supposes three estates, possessed of equal legislative authority. Such a condition of the body politic is a moral impossibility. Two would infallibly combine to depose the other, and then they would quarrel which was to reap the fruits of the victory."[81]

The social effects of the English order seemed to him to provide a sharp contrast to those of the American. "The immediate tendency of the English system is to create an extreme deference in all the subordinate classes for their superiors, while that of the American is to run into the opposite feeling. . . . In England, the disaffected to the government are among precisely those who most sustain government in America."[82]

---

[79] *England* (New York, 1930), p. 199.
[80] *Ibid.*, pp. 188–189.   [81] *Ibid.*, p. 173.   [82] *Ibid.*, p. 376.

Yet the traditional formula maintains a stable society in spite of these theoretical weaknesses because "here all depends on men; on combinations, management, forethought, care, and policy. With us, the young Hercules is stripped of his swaddlings, and his limbs and form are suffered to take the proportions and shape of nature." [83]

With the cultural amenities of an aristocratic society, Cooper is in entire sympathy. "The English gentlemen," he finds, "have the merits of courage, manliness, intelligence, and manners. . . . They are our superiors in manners and in intelligence; they are our superiors in all that manliness which is dependent on opinion. . . . The masculine properties of the English aristocracy (I include the gentry, you will remember) have deservedly given them favour with the nation." [84] Yet all these virtues fail to make them admirable because of the fallacious and fraudulent principles upon which the whole social system is founded. "The consideration of these truths," he concludes, "suggest several useful heads of reflection. In the first place, they show us, if not the absolute impossibility, the great improbability, that the civilization, refinement, knowledge, wealth and tastes of even the best portions of America can equal those of this country, and suggest the expediency of looking to other points for our sources of pride. I have said, that the two countries act under the influence of moral agencies that are almost the converse of each other. The condensation of improvement and cultivation is so great here, that even the base of society is affected by it, even to deportment; whereas, with us, these properties are so dispersed, as to render it difficult for those who are lucky enough to possess them, to keep what they have got, in face of the overshadowing influence of a lower school, instead of being able to impart them to society. Our standard, in nearly all things, as it is popular, is necessarily one of mediocrity; a highly respectable, and, circumstances con-

[83] *Ibid.*, pp. 329–330.   [84] *Ibid.*, pp. 192–194.

sidered, a singularly creditable one, but still a mediocrity; whereas, the condition of these people has enabled them to raise a standard, which, however much it may be and is wanting in the better elements of a pure taste, has immensely the advantage of our own, in most of the obvious blandishments of life. More than half of the peculiarities of America, peculiarities for which it is usual to seek a cause in the institutions, simply because they are so peculiar themselves, are to be traced to facts like these; or, in other words, to the disproportion between surface and numbers, the want of any other than commercial towns, and our distance from the rest of the world." [85] The obvious task of America in the years to come, thought Cooper, was to realize that English amenities were the results, not of a particular political system, but of a close accord between opinions and facts, leading to a stable social situation. America might have a different but equally stable situation when her opinions caught up with her facts and her facts really expressed her opinions.

Continental society was to Cooper as pleasant and as fallacious a model for America as was English. In Paris, polished manners and social graces caught his eye, and he moved with genuine enjoyment in circles which he did not theoretically approve. His first impressions are not profound: "The perfect good taste and indifference which the French manifest concerning the private affairs, and concerning the mode of living, of one who is admitted to the *salons*, has justly extorted admiration, even from the English. . . . The great tact and careful training of the women serve to add very much to the grace of French society." [86] On the other hand, French morals were disturbing: "It is a melancholy admission, but it is no less true, that good breeding is sometimes quite as active a virtue as good principles. How many more of the company present were born about a year after their fathers were beheaded, I have no means of knowing." [87] His conclusion is that "the French have had to struggle through their apprenticeship in political rights, by the force of discussions and appeals to reason, and theory is still too important to be entirely overlooked." [88] Again the virtue in the situation lay in the correlation between facts and opinions rather than in the nature of either.

It was not until 1832 that Cooper attacked the bases of French society theoretically and found the three-estates conception as its fallacious substructure. [89] Whatever political accord there might be between America and France on the ideals of liberty and equality, a society based on fixed class distinctions could never be sound according to Cooper's interpretation of American principles. The social system of the *ancien régime* should, he felt with Lafayette, be modified to a state governed by "a monarchy with republican institutions." [90] "If England can have a throne, then, surrounded by aristocratical institutions, what is there to prevent France from having a throne 'surrounded by republican institutions?' The word 'Republic,' though it does not exclude, does not necessarily include the idea of a democracy. . . . It merely means a polity, in which the predominant idea is the 'public things,' or common weal, instead of the hereditary and inalienable rights of one. It would be quite practicable, therefore, to establish in France such an efficient constituency as would meet the latter conditions, and yet to maintain the throne, as the machinery necessary, in certain cases, to promulgate the will of this very constituency." [91] In this conception of the relationship of government to society in France, obviously derived from his conversations with Lafayette, Cooper moved one more step toward the clarifica-

[87] *Ibid.*, p. 313.   [88] *Ibid.*, p. 357.
[89] "Point de Bateaux à Vapeur," *Le Livre de Cent-et-Un* (Paris, 1832), IX, 221–250.
[90] *Switzerland, Part II*, I, 310.
[91] *Ibid.*, II, 34–35.

tion of his idea of an American democracy which would allow distinction.

In no other European societies except those of Florence and Rome was Cooper privileged to observe manners and morals at first hand and to relate them to political systems; and in these two cities the emigré groups in which he moved were hardly to be distinguished from those of Paris which he knew so much better. His criticism of European society, including the English, reduces itself to a simple formula. European liberal political ideals had advanced far beyond contemporary manners, but the manners themselves had the advantage of tradition and were therefore stable enough for the development of culture. In America, the reverse was the case. Whereas European customs must, thought Cooper, eventually be modified to conform to the new ideas, in America well formulated principles were not yet understood by the mass of the nation and there was no native tradition upon which to build. His two attacks, on the false principles underlying a comfortable and well-ordered society in Europe, and on the tardiness of America in recognizing her principles and applying them to her facts, spring from the same source.

It became his obvious duty, therefore, to attempt a logical formulation of ideal social standards for America in terms of what he believed to be basic American principles. This aim furnished the inspiration for *The American Democrat*.

This work is Cooper's most direct and comprehensive formulation of his social and political creed. In it, he defines his matured theory of the American democratic principle, and applies his definition to a variety of American institutions, both in themselves and in comparison with those of Europe. It is presented in the form of an elementary text, but it rests on no authority other than the opinions of the writer. The central principle is the belief in liberty for the individual within a society in which common rights are adequately protected by constitutional checks and balances. The republican form of government, as illustrated in the American system and compared with the monarchical and aristocratic forms of European countries, is analyzed and related to limited ideals of liberty and equality; then the following institutions are discussed: the press, suffrage, slavery, party, and formal religion. The whole is an admirable study, not so much of the then existing order as of Cooper's interpretation of the ideals underlying the original order of American society and government.

American principles are first defined in political terms. America is a confederated republic in which sovereignty is vested in the states. A republic is defined as "a government in which the pervading acknowledged principle is the right of the community as opposed to the right of the sovereign." [92] But because the governments of the states vary, there is no method of administering popular sovereignty. The national government, therefore, derives its power from the states as such, through representation, instead of directly from the people. "It follows, that the constitution of the United States was formed by the states, and not by the people of the entire country, as contended." [93] The states have conceded, through the Constitution, "most of the higher attributes of sovereignty." [94]

The most distinctive American political principle is the theory of political power as a public trust, granted by the constituent to the representative. This power is divided into three branches: the executive, the legislative, and the judicial, which operate according to the system of checks and balances. [95]

But America is not only a republic like France; it is a democracy. Before proceeding to a definition of this term, however, Cooper finds it necessary to correct two false notions: equality, instead of being absolute, "means equality of rights rather than of condition"; [96] and liberty merely means that "the body of the

---

[92] *The American Democrat* (Cooperstown, N. Y., 1838), p. 10.
[93] *Ibid.*, p. 21.   [94] *Ibid.*, p. 25.   [95] *Ibid.*, p. 34.   [96] *Ibid.*, p. 42.

The remainder of *The American Democrat* is an attempt to apply these principles to various other American institutions. Cooper's thought on social theory never went beyond this point.

Of the other critical prose of the period, the *History of the Navy of the United States of America* (1839) alone demands mention here. Cooper was definitely a "big navy" man, and his history was undertaken in the interest of this cause. He believed that America's sense of national being would not be appreciated either at home or abroad until she could build on the foundation of her scattered naval triumphs a strong and regular naval force. As a historian, however, he was no respecter of persons; he told his story as the facts seemed to him to require. Several controversies were the result of his honesty, and served, with those on the libel issue, to cloud his latter years. Whether or not the *Lives of Distinguished American Naval Officers* (1846) was prepared to state his final position on these issues, or was merely a convenient second use of old material, it is unnecessary to decide. The *History* had been told as a narration of events. He now singled out the most important actors in the drama and retold their stories. Most of the essays are elaborations of passages in the earlier book.

During this period of critical prose, Cooper wrote only three novels, all of them fictional treatments of his newly formulated doctrines. The first was *The Monikins* (1835), a satirical allegory in which he stressed the main theme of his estimate of the contrasting civilizations of two hemispheres. Again the fictional veil is thin. Monkeys or men, these Monikins are Americans, Englishmen, and Frenchmen. European civilization fails, he explains, because of caste, corruption, and insusceptibility to social change; American because of party, vulgarity, and money-madness. But as yet his denunciation of his own countrymen is mild compared to that of the Europeans; at heart he still finds America at least theoretically sound.

The other two novels of these years are really one, *Homeward Bound* and *Home as Found* (1838), the one a romance of the sea, the latter a portrait of Cooperstown very different from that presented in *The Pioneers*. With a long sheet of foolscap in front of him and his pen in hand, he sat down to tell a story in which he planned to record the observations of an American gentleman (himself) on his return with his family from a long residence abroad. The crudities of American society and the purity of American ideals which had been so violated were to be the substance of the tale. But he made the mistake of setting his opening scene on shipboard as the party set sail from England, and a typical romance of chase, escape, and adventure had to be worked out of his system before the real business of the day could be undertaken in the sequel. It was the second novel, not the first, that he had planned to write, as it was always into social criticism that he threw his most deliberate creative effort.

The close of the period 1828–1840 finds Cooper the author of extensive treatises on the national characters of America, England, and certain other European countries, a man with a definite social and political creed. His novels had long since lost primary interest for him; his mission in life seemed rather the reform of the American mind by the rediscovery of national traditions and the battling with what seemed to him the forces of disintegration in the political and social structure of his country. The result was an involvement in controversies on all sides and an expenditure of prodigious effort in libel trials, most of which brought him little more than personal vindication on specific points. That he was right on most issues seems little to have mattered; his popularity shrank to a fraction of its former strength, and with it his income. He never regained what he lost in formulating his theories and applying them to the civilization of which he was a part.[104]

[104] T. R. Lounsbury gives an account of these trials, which is still just,

VI. SOCIAL CRITICISM IN THE NOVELS, 1840–1850

"The utilitarian school, as it has been popularly construed," wrote Cooper in 1837, "is not to my taste, either, for I believe that there is great utility in the grace and elegance of life, and no one would feel more disposed to resist a system, in which these essential properties are proscribed." [105] It was against Utilitarianism, as he thus conceived it to be, that Cooper devoted the energies of the final decade of his life.

In 1840, he became once more primarily a novelist, and in eleven years produced eighteen works of fiction, approximately half of his total output. A number of them were primarily romances, written skilfully but with an eye to the market, and containing only incidental comments on society and government. Two groups, however, stand out as social documents: the land-problem group and the religious group. The first, consisting of the two parts of *Afloat and Ashore* and the three parts of the "Littlepage Manuscripts," is by far the more significant and might be taken as the logical climax of the forces which had shaped his career. The second, although containing some excellent work, is less well integrated and reveals a decline in power.

Between 1844 and 1846, Cooper published his five novels dealing with his theory of property rights as the basis of American civilization. His approach was historical, but he no longer thought of American history as merely a romantic past. He turned to the early days of settlement and of the war for independence in order to reveal the roots of contemporary society. He had settled his family in the scenes of his boyhood, repaired the old house, and established himself as prototype of a patrician order. In *Home as Found* he had described the con-

in his *James Fenimore Cooper* (Boston, 1882), pp. 171–230; that of E. R. Outland, *The "Effingham" Libels on Cooper* (Madison, Wis., 1929), is fuller and better documented, but not as satisfactory in its judgments.

[105] *England* (New York, 1930), p. 382.

dition of society which he had found at Templeton (Cooperstown) by dividing its development into three stages: the
first, that of settlement in which "the gentleman, even while he
may maintain his character and station, maintains them with
that species of good-fellowship, that marks the intercourse
between officer and soldier in an arduous campaign"; the second,
in which "we see the struggles for place, the heart-burnings and
jealousies of contending families, and the influence of mere
money"; the third, in which "men and things come within the
control of more general and regular laws." [106] Cooperstown, in
William Cooper's day, was in the first stage; his son found it
in the second and hoped to move with it into the third. To
illustrate this process he took typical landed families of the
early days and attempted to tell their histories through several
generations.

Afloat and Ashore, with its sequel, is the story of Miles
Wallingford, a member of a family that had held Clawbonny,
a modest estate on the Hudson, since 1707. Miles succeeded to
the property in 1794 at the age of eleven. The "afloat" part of
the tale, a good half, is a typical romance of the sea in Cooper's
best manner, but the "ashore" part strikes a new note. Without
the asperity of *Home as Found*, it is a more probing study of
the ideals, manners, and morals of a type of New York land-
owner. The plot concerns the courtship of Miles and Lucy
Hardinge, member of a neighboring family with slightly more
aristocratic pretensions than those of the Wallingfords. It is
not hard to read into this romance the social factors which must
have operated in the Cooper-De Lancey romance of 1811; and
Miles, with his blunt honesty and forthrightness, his recognition
of social differences without snobbery or false humility, his love
of the sea, and his love for Lucy, is a fair portrait of the youthful
Cooper as seen by the elderly. This part of the story is a
representation of the ideals expressed in *The American Democrat*.

[106] *Home as Found* (New York, 1860), pp. 187–189.

The Littlepage novels, *Satanstoe*, *The Chainbearer*, and *The Redskins*, were immediately provoked by the "Anti-Rent War" of 1839–1846, but they are a logical consequence of *Afloat and Ashore*, an attempt to follow a family like that of the Wallingfords in detail through four generations. The Anti-Rent War was a local issue, largely forgotten now by the historians, but important to Cooper because it struck at the heart of his ideas on property rights and therefore of his theory of democracy. The Van Rensselaer patroonship, dating from 1637 and still in the hands of the same family, was the scene of the disturbances. Originally extending for twenty-four miles along the Hudson in Albany and Rensselaer Counties, and an equal distance inland in each direction, it had suffered only minor shrinkage in the two centuries of tenure. Most of its tenants held leases in perpetuity, and the annual rent for a hundred acres varied from ten to fourteen bushels of wheat, plus, for farms of over 160 acres, four fat hens and one day's labor with horse and wagon. In addition, a sale of a lease required that a quarter of the sum received be paid to the patroon. At the death of Stephen Van Rensselaer in 1839, unpaid rents had accumulated to large amounts in many cases, and the terms of his will required their payment. The tenants, restless for many years under so anti-American a land system, used this demand as a reason for general protest. Writs were served and a local war between sheriffs' deputies and farmers resulted. Differences were arbitrated in 1840, but not before the militia had been called into action. In 1844, the tenants, disguised as Indians, once more resisted and a number of disturbances resulted. Again troops were called out and the offenders punished, but in 1846, laws were passed abolishing distress for rent and equalizing taxation. The Anti-Renters had gained their main points and the patroon system of land tenure was at an end.[107]

[107] J. B. McMaster, *A History of the People of the United States* (New York, 1886–1913), VI, 522–523, and VII, 186–189.

Cooper held no particular brief for the patroon system as opposed to a more liberal theory of land tenure. To him, the difference between his father's and the patroons' methods was of little consequence. The real point at issue was the inviolability of private property, however held or administered. The Anti-Renters defied their contracts established in law, and if they were allowed to do so without restraint, the rights of property owners of all kinds would be threatened. Hence the foundations of his theory of democracy were being undermined, further evidence that the new America had lost sight of its principles and was drifting rapidly toward mediocrity and social disintegration. The only way to point out the error was to follow the stages of development of society from the days of settlement to the present, thereby securing the established order by reference to tradition. This he attempted in the Littlepage trilogy, his most detailed fictional treatment of his matured social views and the best picture of life in early New York that has come down to us.

"It is easy to foresee that this country is destined to undergo great and rapid change," writes Cooper in the person of Cornelius Littlepage, born May 3, 1737, at Satanstoe (Mamaroneck), Westchester County, New York, subject of His Majesty, King George II. "Without a stage, in a national point of view at least, with scarcely such a thing as a book of memoirs that relates to a life passed within our own limits, and totally without light literature, to give us simulated pictures of our manners and opinions of the day, I see scarcely a mode by which the next generation can preserve any memorials of the distinctive usages and thoughts of this." [108] Of combined English and Dutch heritage, and of a family that owned land, Corny is representative of the modest aristocracy of the time. Through him, Cooper depicts the experiences and discusses the thoughts and feelings of the cultured class in colonial New York. Cour-

[108] *Satanstoe* (New York, 1860), p. 9.

age in adversity, chivalric manliness in love, kindliness toward servants, Christian charity and faith, are the chief components of his character. The text of the story is expressed by Mr. Bulstrode in the form of advice to Corny: "There are two sorts of great worlds; the great vulgar world, which includes all but the very best in taste, principles, and manners, whether it be in a capital or in a country; and the great *respectable* world, which, infinitely less numerous, contains the judicious, the instructed, the intelligent, and on some questions, the good. Now the first form fashion; whereas the last produce something far better than fashion."[109] Throughout his life, Corny acts as a member of this privileged class in a society which freely recognizes its right to rule.

In *The Chainbearer*, his son, Mordaunt, carries on the tradition through a period in which this right is challenged by shifting social conditions. "It must not be forgotten," he warns, "that land was a drug in the state of New York in the year 1784, as it is to-day on the Miami, Ohio, Mississippi, and other inland streams. The proprietors thought but little of their possessions as the means of *present* support, but rather maintained their settlements than their settlements maintained them; looking forward to another age, to their posterity, for the rewards of all their trouble and investments."[110] Thus a moral bond was established between landlord and tenant, which reached beyond their own generation. Tenants who did not respect the rights of their landlords had no rights in return.[111] The story deals with the difficulties of holding land through the period of transition, in the face of depleted values and the inroads of squatters from New England, the latter factor providing most of the narrative interest.

A generation is skipped in *The Redskins* and the narrative brought down to the current issue in the person of Hugh Roger

[109] *Ibid.*, p. 498.
[110] *The Chainbearer* (New York, 1860), p. 190.
[111] *Ibid.*, p. 203.

Littlepage, great-grandson of Corny. It was time, if there was validity in the theory of three stages of civilization which Cooper had stated in *Home as Found*, that "men and things come within the control of more general and regular laws." [112] Instead, the Littlepage heir finds the state legislature at the point of passing laws to deprive landholders of their inherited rights. "An infernal feeling of selfishness is so much talked of," says Cooper with the emphasis of capital letters, "and cited, and referred to, on all occasions, in this country, that a man almost renders himself ridiculous who appears to rest on principle." [113] "In our view," he concludes, "Oregon, Mexico, and Europe, united against us, do not threaten this nation with one-half as much real danger as that which menaces it at this moment, from an enemy that is now in possession of many of its strongholds, and which is incessantly working its evil under the cry of liberty, while laying deeper the foundations of a most atrocious tyranny." [114] The moderation of Cooper's earlier attitude had deserted him. His war with the press had done its work with his disposition.

Cooper's identification with his own past was now complete; his social philosophy might almost be taken as a rationalization of his own personality and family traditions. With the growing feeling in his latter years that the world was against him, the consolation of the religious faith with which he was early associated grew upon him. From Mamaroneck he had driven his family on Sundays to Rye in order to attend the Episcopal church. A quarter of a century later, the faith of that church came back to him with a renewed vitality, and in July of the year of his death, 1851, he was confirmed by his brother-in-law, Bishop De Lancey. [115]

It would be a mistake to find in this action any material

[112] Cf. p. lviii above.
[113] *The Redskins* (New York, 1860), p. 79.
[114] *Ibid.*, p. 536.
[115] T. R. Lounsbury, *J. F. Cooper*, p. 266.

change of heart. He had concluded *The American Democrat* many years before with a note on religion, in which he said: "As reason and revelation both tell us that this state of being is but a preparation for another of a still higher and more spiritual order, all the interests of life are of comparatively little importance, when put in the balance against the future." [116] As little concerned with sects as with political parties, he had refrained from joining any particular church. The Episcopal church had not been finally established in Cooperstown until 1811, the year of his marriage and settlement far away in Westchester County, and he had been brought up under the influence of a variety of more or less itinerant clergymen. Throughout his writing career he had preferred to preach Protestant ethics in a social context rather than the theological doctrine of any sect. But when the society about him seemed by its actions to deny his social principles as such, he was forced back upon a theoretical code of ethics, the only permanent basis for which lay in traditional religious faith. Throughout its history, the Church of England has been closely associated with the manner of life of a landed gentry . Its American counterpart had not departed far from its predominant attitudes. In it, Cooper found a hospitable refuge for his thesis not to be discovered in the secular patterns of American life in 1850. Furthermore, his wife's family, with its Tory traditions, was strongly Anglican, and there was a well established Protestant Episcopal church in Cooperstown when the Cooper family returned from its European adventures. Fenimore Cooper, his wife, and his children are buried in Christ Church churchyard, Cooperstown.

---

[116] *The American Democrat* (Cooperstown, N. Y., 1838), p. 186. H. S. Canby, in *Classic Americans*, pp. 97–142, attributes Cooper's concern with ethics to the Quaker strain in his inheritance and points out the consistency of this attitude with the frontier influence. This is an important tributary, but the immediate and most pressing influences of Cooper's inheritance and environment were not Quaker.

This tendency to shift from a social to a religious basis for ethics is apparent in most of the later novels, and his tendency to defend Trinitarianism is evidence of his growing interest in the Episcopalian dogma, but in none is it more clear than in *The Crater* (1847), the most important novel of these last years. It is a complete story of a colony founded on a volcanic reef. Mark, the hero, reviews at the end its history: "He would thus recall his shipwreck, and desolate condition when suffered first to reach the rocks; the manner in which he was the instrument of causing vegitation to spring up in barren places; the earth-quake, and the upheaving of the islands from out of the waters; the arrival of his wife and other friends; the commencement and progress of the colony; its blessings, so long as it pursued the right, and its curses, when it began to pursue the wrong; his departure, leaving it still a settlement surrounded with a sort of earthly paradise; and his return, to find it buried beneath the ocean. Of such is the world and its much-coveted advantages. For a time our efforts seem to create, and to adorn, and to perfect, until we forget our origin and destination, substituting self for that divine hand which alone can unite the elements of worlds as they float in gases, equally from His mysterious laboratory, and scatter them again into thin air when the works of His hand cease to find favor in His view." [117] Mark's reverie is at once a summary of the story, an allegorical interpreta-tion of the history and destiny of both the American people and mankind in general, and a final profession of religious fatalism.

Other of Cooper's later novels, *The Oak Openings* (1848) and *The Sea Lions* (1849), are more nearly stories in their own right, but they are dominated by the same point of view. But there is no vital significance in this more nearly complete turn to religion on Cooper's part, except as the logical outcome in later years of his social philosophy as expounded in *The*

[117] *The Crater* (New York, 1861), pp. 493–494.

American Democrat and developed in the Littlepage novels. By 1846, Cooper had stated his case.

VII. THE PLEASURE AND BUSINESS OF THE NOVEL

For Cooper, the writing of novels was a pleasure, a business, a mission, and an art. His initial impulses came from his interest in reading and in a life of action. Life was always, to him, a work of art in itself; writing, a transcript of life. His personal love of action alone made him interested in the romance of adventure; at heart he was a realist. He wished to reveal and interpret rather than to escape from the world in which he lived, however much his romances may serve as an escape for his readers.

His daughter Susan, a constant companion of his later years, gives us a full account of how he became a writer at the age of thirty. In his childhood, she says, he showed a slight interest in story telling in prose and verse, but not enough to indicate genius. At the age of eleven he composed and printed, with the aid of a friend, a tale modeled on that of "Don Belianis of Greece." On another occasion, he wrote a ballad entitled "Buffalo Burnt, or the Dreadful Conflagration" in some thirty or forty stanzas of doggerel for a balladmonger who passed through the town. The result was so successful that the man came back for a second, which was obligingly composed. But as late as a few years before the writing of *Precaution*, he opened a letter with the phrase, "Much as I dislike writing in general." Emphatically, Cooper was not an author in his youth. Instead, he devoted his time to strenuous but restrained living, at home in Cooperstown as a boy, at college, where he was known for his exploits rather than for his learning, and in the Navy. In 1818, he was a gentleman farmer with popular literary tastes and no literary ambitions.[118]

Susan also tells us a great deal about his opportunities and

118 *Pages and Pictures* (New York, 1861), pp. 18–19.

tastes for reading. "At that period," she says, "there came sailing into the harbor of New York, with each returning month, one or two packet ships, from London or Liverpool, their arrival in the lower bay being duly announced to Wall street by the unwieldy arms of the wooden telegraph on Staten Island; and, among the bales of English calicos and broadcloths, there never failed to be some smaller package of far greater and more lasting value—some volume fresh from the London press, high in merit, full of interest, a work whose appearance had been already heralded, and whose arrival was eagerly expected by every reader in the country. Perhaps it was a romance of the Waverley series, still a delightful mystery as regarded their origin, or a brilliant canto of Byron, or a charming social tale by Miss Edgeworth, or a valuable religious work by Mr. Wilberforce, or Miss More. With the next day's papers the news of the arrival spread through the country-houses of Westchester. Orders were immediately sent to the bookseller in New York. At that day each village on the sound had its own sloop, plying two or three times a week to and fro, through the perils of Hell-Gate, carrying the produce of the farms to Fulton Market, and bringing back sugar and tea, and good things of all sorts, to the rustic wharf. Among other imported luxuries came the last new book. Or perchance it was the mail-coach, which, as it travelled eastward along the winding roads of Westchester, dropped the precious parcel at the quiet village post-office. Lucky was that household deemed which could first cut the pages of the new volume; and long did its contents, rich in entertainment or instruction, offer subject for social talk and clever discussion about the firesides of the whole neighborhood. The most imposing living personages of the day, moving through the great cities and over the battlefields of old Europe, scarcely filled a wider space in familiar household talk than the brilliant figures on the many-colored canvas of Sir Walter Scott. Kings and queens, of ancient abdicated dynasties and the newly-crowned alike, victorious marshals and generals, successful statesmen, cabinet ministers and court beauties, were compelled to share the honors of fireside fame with Dominie Sampson and Eddie Ochiltree, and Jennie Deans, and Meg Merrilies.

"It is quite needless to declare that Mr. Cooper took great delight in the Waverley novels; when the secret of their authorship was still a subject for discussion, he was among those who never doubted that they were written by Walter Scott, the poet. He read aloud delightfully. His voice was very fine; deep, clear and expressive. Good reading was, with him, a natural gift, the impulse of the moment, an instinct of genius. During those quiet country evenings, he often read aloud; there was one who listened with affectionate interest—one for whom, through a long life, he read with especial pleasure. Poetry was occasionally chosen: his reading of verse was particularly good, accurate, and full of deep poetic feeling. For Shakespeare he was always ready; entering with unfeigned delight into the spirit of his works, whether comedy or tragedy. Pope, Thomson, Gray, were also in favor. But he could seldom be induced to read more than a page or two of Milton, at a time; the great epic poet he considered too correctly cold and classical in spirit, for his theme; and this opinion continued unchanged through life. 'Shakespeare should have written Paradise Lost. What a poem he would have given to the world!' was a remark he repeatedly made. But the new books were, of course, in particular request; and rapidly as the great Scotch novels succeeded each other, something more was needed to fill up those quiet evening hours at Angevine. Unfortunately those English packets brought trash, as well as literary treasures, from beyond the sea." [119]

His taste obviously ran to fiction of the romantic type, particularly that depicting action. Even in poetry, he seems to have preferred the narrative, and we may safely assume that his preference for Shakespeare lay on no deeper grounds than an

[119] *Ibid.*, pp. 16–17.

admiration for his "vigorous images." [120] He quoted from Shakespeare more than from any other author in his own chapter headings, and on many of his travels carried small volumes of his favorite plays with him. In *The Pioneers*, for example, there are eleven Shakespearean quotations, as against seven from Scott and eighteen from miscellaneous authors, most of them the popular nature poets of the eighteenth century, like Thomson, Beattie, and Goldsmith. Many of the Shakespearean gleanings are from the doubtful and little-known plays, revealing a thorough knowledge of his works. In *The Bravo* and in *Satanstoe*, novels written at intervals of about a decade later, there are twelve each, indications that his interest was as sustained as it was intense, but Byron and Rogers have supplanted the earlier poets in the former, and a group of romantics, including Burns, Shelley, Wordsworth, Byron, and Longfellow, take second place in the latter. Except for his love of Shakespeare, he seems therefore to have followed the popular taste, dropping Scott early in favor of Byron, and moving from the eighteenth century to the contemporary romantics. There is clear indication in all available evidence that, when he read for pleasure, he turned to current rather than classical literature, that he preferred writing that dealt with vigorous action or strong feeling unclouded by subtlety, and that he enjoyed rather than discriminated. His taste was eclectic and was determined by his temperament and by chance, not by his critical judgment.

When he began writing novels of his own, he had the same attitude toward his work. His technique was spontaneously imitative, not because of a conscious effort to develop an art form, but because he wrote as he read. His comment when he laid down the novel by "Mrs. Opie or one of that school," was, "I could write a better book than that myself." [121] The result,

[120] *Ibid.*, p. 202.
[121] S. F. Cooper, "Small Family Memories," in *Correspondence of J. F. Cooper*, I, 38.

Precaution, was so nearly typical of the work of the English women novelists of the time that it can almost equally well be linked with Jane Austen's *Pride and Prejudice* [122] or any one of the others, of which he had obviously read many. When he turned to tales of history, the Indians, and the sea, his material was his own but his model for form was Scott, even though nothing could irritate him more than a suggestion of such indebtedness. "If there is a term that gives me more disgust than any other," he wrote to the editor of the *New Monthly* on May 21, 1831, "it is to be called, as some on the continent *advertise me*, the 'American Sir Walter Scott.' It is offensive to a gentleman to be nicknamed at all, and there is a pretension in the title, which offends me more than all the abusive reviews that ever were written." [123] But his desire to have his work clearly distinguished from that of Scott did not rest on literary grounds as such. He never raised the question as to whether or not Scott wrote good fiction, but he objected violently to his lack of knowledge of the sea and to his Tory ideals. [124]

Throughout the period before his European trip, the pleasure motive in writing was predominant, but it gradually gave way to professional and business aims, even though his spontaneous love of action and his lack of interest in technique persisted throughout his career. Susan gives us a full account of this development. "To a spirit naturally so free and active as that of the writer of 'Precaution,' imitation must soon become wearying and irksome in the extreme," she tells us. "Disguise was now thrown off—and forever." [125] *The Spy* was to be thoroughly American. "Patriotism was to be the soul of the new book."

[122] See H. H. Scudder, "What Mr. Cooper Read to His Wife," *Sewanee Review*, XXXVI, 177–194 (April, 1928). Mr. Scudder's argument is not entirely convincing.

[123] *Correspondence of J. F. Cooper*, I, 227.

[124] See his review of the *Memoirs of the Life of Sir Walter Scott, Bart.*, by J. G. Lockhart, *Knickerbocker Magazine*, XII, 349–366 (Oct., 1838).

[125] *Pages and Pictures*, p. 26.

Again the story was suggested casually, this time by an anecdote told by Judge Jay, many years before,[126] but recalled "when, as the only atonement in his power" for the adventitious character of *Precaution*, "he determined to inflict a second book, whose subject should admit of no cavil, not only on the world, but on himself." [127] Still with no real professional intentions, the novel was undertaken, but so casual was its author's attitude toward it that he allowed the first volume to remain in print for several months before he felt the impetus to continue, and then let his publishers print and page his final chapter before the intervening ones had been written.[128] In the next year, two new editions of three and five thousand copies respectively were printed. The novel met with instantaneous welcome. "The glow of success was still fresh upon him," remarks Susan, "when he again resolved to 'try one more book.'" [129]   *The Pioneers* gave him more pleasure than any other novel he ever wrote, even though, when he assembled his Leather-Stocking tales, he was inclined to be apologetic for its "rigid adhesion to truth," which "destroys the charm of fiction." [130]

The Pilot was the last novel to be undertaken in the spirit of the amateur. At a dinner at the home of Charles Wilkes, Scott's new novel, *The Pirate*, became the subject of discussion. "'I must write one more book—a sea tale,'" Susan quotes him as remarking to a friend on the way home, "'to show what can be done in this way by a sailor!'" [131] With *Lionel Lincoln*, in 1824–1825, Cooper took up the profession of writing for the first time in all seriousness [132]—too great seriousness, as it turned out, for this was also the first novel in which he revealed how greatly his art depended upon its spontaneity for its effec-

---

[126] *Ibid.*, p. 29; Introduction to *The Spy* (New York, 1859), pp. v–ix.
[127] *Ibid.*, p. x.
[128] T. McDowell, Introduction to *The Spy* (New York, 1931), p. xiv.
[129] *Pages and Pictures*, p. 51.
[130] Introduction to *The Pioneers* (New York, 1859), pp. ix, xv.
[131] *Pages and Pictures*, p. 72.
[132] *Ibid.*, p. 99.

tiveness. "At the time of writing the book," says Susan, "the author had planned a series of works of fiction, to be drawn from the early historical sources of the country—the scene of each tale to be laid in one of the thirteen different colonies which formed the Union." [133] In preparation for this ambitious project, he went to Boston where he studied historical authorities, read state papers, examined almanacs to verify dates, and searched contemporary reports on the weather. [134] This is assuredly a new Cooper, a writer with a feeling for accuracy which had barely emerged in the earlier novels. Yet we know definitely that even his miscellaneous reading of these early years was not confined to *belles-lettres*. Susan mentions "a course of reading in English biography and heraldry" [135] which he had undertaken, and works of Heckewelder, Charlevoix, Penn, Smith, Eliot, Colden, Lang, Lewis and Clarke, and Mackenzie in preparation for his descriptions of the Indians and pioneers. [136] Incidental reading of the same sort occupied him in the later years. Not only did he exhaust authorities and manuscript sources available to him for such historical and controversial works as his *History of the Navy, Letter to Gen. Lafayette*, and *The Chronicles of Cooperstown*, but we find many references in his letters and autobiographical writings to nonfiction reading, notably the travels of Captain Basil Hall and Mrs. Trollope, Paine's *Age of Reason*, [137] Tucker's *Life of Jefferson*, [138] D'Israeli's *Curiosities of Literature*, [139] and Prescott's *Ferdinand and Isabella*. [140] Similar references reveal that he read the English and French reviews with fair regularity, especially when he was abroad, and that he kept up with the work of

[133] *Ibid.*, p. 101.
[134] T. R. Lounsbury, *J. F. Cooper*, p. 49.
[135] *Pages and Pictures*, p. 122.
[136] *Ibid.*, p. 129.
[137] *France* (New York, 1928), p. 24.
[138] *England* (New York, 1930), p. 367.
[139] *Correspondence of J. F. Cooper*, II, 733.
[140] *Ibid.*, II, 399. In the preface to *Mercedes of Castile* (Philadelphia, 1840), Cooper states that he has read all of Prescott and Irving.

Scott, Dana, Dunlap, and some light fiction. For his travels in Switzerland and Italy, he read historical and geographical works as well as the more obvious guidebooks, and he prepared himself for a visit to Pompeii by a reading of Winckelmann. He was not a systematic reader unless he had a special object in his own mind and needed to prepare himself for it by acquiring information, but he apparently read rapidly and in diversified books when he read for pleasure.

The first motive that seems to have superseded sheer pleasure and uncritical patriotism in Cooper's writing was the professional objective. America needed a literature of her own, and if she was willing to reward her authors, Cooper was ready by 1825 to throw his whole energy into this pursuit. The first evidence of a change in his plans was the move to New York city in 1822, immediately after the appearance of *The Spy*. From being a gentleman farmer he became a gentleman about town. Much of his hesitancy about his work between 1822 and 1825 may be attributed to financial uncertainty. His private income seems to have been sufficient as a basis of operations; but he was not the sort of man to take up a profession which was unsound from the business point of view. When he wrote that the most powerful obstacle to the production of an American literature was the lack of "a good, wholesome, profitable, and continued pecuniary support," [141] he had reference to his own experience. His explanation of the conditions of authorship at the time provides the reasons for his European trip in 1826: "The fact that an American publisher can get an English work without money, must, for a few years longer, (unless legislative protection shall be extended to their own authors,) have a tendency to repress a national literature. . . . A capital American publisher has assured me that there are not a dozen writers in this country, whose works he should feel confidence in publishing at all, while he reprints hundreds of English books

[141] *Notions of the Americans* (Philadelphia, 1828), II, 444–445.

without the least hesitation." The American copyright law of 1790 disregarded prior publication in other countries, but required citizenship on the part of the author; the English law, based on precedent rather than on specific legislation, required first publication in England, but made no citizenship qualifications. Cooper deliberately set about the circumvention of these laws in the interest of international and mutual protection.[142]

Precaution had brought him little or no pecuniary return. It was probably printed in America at his own expense, and was pirated by the fashionable London publisher, Henry Colburn, in 1821. There were no continental editions until after those of *The Spy*. The first practical lesson to be learned was the selection of a good American publisher. Irving had tried various New York printers before, in 1824, he sent his *Tales of a Traveller* to Mathew Carey in Philadelphia. Cooper published with Charles Wiley in New York until 1826, when he followed Irving's example and entered into a long period of business connection with the Carey firm. His usual practice seems to have been the sale of rights for limited editions for fixed sums, retaining the rights to the plates himself. For example, Carey paid $1500 for the first edition of the *Notions;*[143] and in 1845, Cooper could still sell the right to print 250 copies each of his "old books" for $200.[144]

Even connection with the Carey firm was insufficient to satisfy Cooper that he was reaping maximum return for his work. Negotiations with John Murray, Irving's London publisher, through Irving and Benjamin W. Coles, and with John Miller, Carey's London agent and an occasional publisher in his own right, were unsatisfactory.[145] *The Spy* was pirated by

[142] R. E. Spiller and P. C. Blackburn, *A Descriptive Bibliography of the Writings of J. F. Cooper* (New York, 1934), pp. 4–5.

[143] *Correspondence of J. F. Cooper*, I, 153. [144] *Ibid.*, II, 536.

[145] P. M. Irving, *Life and Letters of Washington Irving* (London, 1862–1864), II, 54–55; Samuel Smiles, *A Publisher and His Friends* (London, 1891), I, 134; and R. E. Spiller and P. C. Blackburn, *A Descriptive Bibliography*, pp. 4–6, 215–220.

Whittaker, *The Pioneers* was published by Murray on a profit-sharing agreement with a total return to Cooper of £134, and Miller, then in very shaky financial condition, published *The Pilot*, *Lionel Lincoln*, and *The Last of the Mohicans*. "Perhaps," Cooper wrote him in 1826, "I may be able to secure a right in England for the next book." [146]

The result of his hurried visit to London in the summer of that year was a profit-sharing contract with Henry Colburn for *The Prairie*. This and the next three novels were printed on the continent in small editions in English, and then sent to Colburn, to Carey, and to French and German translators simultaneously in advance sheets. Their republication was timed so that the English edition might be announced first, an arrangement which netted Cooper substantial though declining income from the English rights to his books throughout the rest of his life. Financial return from foreign translations was so slight that this part of the plan was soon dropped.

On the basis of this pecuniary security, Cooper began, in 1832, to lay plans for his return to America. "I wish you to write me," he told his nephew, Richard Cooper, on August 5, "the exact condition of the Mansion House—if it is to be bought—whether it is capable of being repaired, and the state of the judgment obtained by Bridges, etc., against your grandfather's heirs. I am not rich, but your aunt and myself possess together what would be an easy property at Cooperstown, and my annual receipts are large." [147] The plan was put into effect on his return the next year.

Even though it was at this stage in his career that the business of the professional novelist was so seriously threatened by the principles of the social idealist in him, and the attendant controversies and loss of popularity, he nevertheless continued to regard his writing as his profession. His connection with the

[146] *Correspondence of J. F. Cooper*, I, 96.
[147] *Ibid.*, I, 275.

Carey firm continued until 1844, when *Afloat and Ashore* was published "by the author." The *Gleanings* series, however, was not financially successful, and Cooper had to obtain other publishers for his non-fiction work after 1837. Henry C. Carey withdrew from the firm in 1838, and his father, Mathew Carey, died in 1839. Irving broke his connection after the publication of his *Biography of Margaret Davidson* in 1841, and Cooper after *Ned Myers* in 1843. In 1842–1843, Lea and Blanchard, the Careys' successors, reprinted the twenty-two of Cooper's works on their list, in wrappers.

During this time, the connection with Colburn's successor, Richard Bentley, was maintained. Bentley paid Cooper £1300 for the English rights to a single novel in 1831. By 1833, this rate was reduced to £700; to £400 in 1840; and to £250 in 1844. Part of the reason for the decline was Bentley's difficulty in preventing pirated editions which competed with his own, but the principal reason seems to have been the decline in Cooper's popularity on both sides of the water as the numbers of his personal enemies increased. The years 1840–1844 were the most insecure of Cooper's professional career. His revival of the Leather-Stocking tales and an experiment with historical romance in 1840, followed by a series of sea and Indian romances during the next three years, has a practical as well as a literary significance. There seems to be ample evidence in his financial history alone to account for his abandonment of non-fiction prose as the chief outlet for his abilities as a writer.

As we have seen, Cooper wrote his best social novels between 1844 and 1849. During this time he maintained his flat rate of £250 from Bentley and accepted a new plan for publication at home. The American book business was apparently at a low ebb. Burgess, Stringer and Co., of New York, were undercutting the market for bound books by issuing new titles in two paper-bound volumes at twenty-five cents per volume. Cooper succumbed to them in 1844 with the second part of *Afloat and*

Ashore (*Miles Wallingford*). The first edition of *Satanstoe* was 3600 copies, and Burgess was ready to reprint at the end of three months.[148] In addition, he paid Cooper $1000 for the right to reprint certain old books. In 1848, the firm collected Cooper's works in single volumes, bound in inexpensive cloth.[149] Although not so satisfactory as the earlier arrangement with Carey, these transactions returned to Cooper a sense of professional security and freed him from experimenting with his market instead of with his ideas.

Meanwhile he discovered the magazine market in both countries, an outlet entirely unsuited to his genius, which was not for compression. In 1841, he resurrected two forgotten tales, first published in 1823 as *Tales for Fifteen*, and sold them to *Roberts' Semi-Monthly Magazine*. *Graham's*, then at the height of its success, bought the *Autobiography of a Pocket Handkerchief* and the lives of naval officers in 1843–1845. *Jack Tier* was published serially in the same magazine (1846–1848) under the title "Islets of the Gulf," and in *Bentley's Miscellany* under the title "Captain Spike" contemporaneously. Most of Cooper's contributions to periodicals were of a controversial nature and probably brought him no financial return, but these cases are obvious exceptions.

In 1849, there was another change in his business affairs, with the newly-aroused interest of Irving's publisher, George Putnam, in his work. A revised edition of his novels was projected, which ran to eleven volumes during the next three years, and *The Ways of the Hour* was accepted for publication in a single cloth-bound volume. Things would have looked much brighter than they had for some time if the new novel had proved itself a success. But Bentley offered only £100 for it, and it met with little enthusiasm at home. In 1850, he sold "The Lake Gun" to *The Parthenon*, and his writing career was at an end. The close parallel between his fortunes as a business

---

[148] *Ibid.*, II, 552.   [149] *Ibid.*, II, 550–551.

man and the kinds and amounts of writing he did during thirty years is significant.

VIII. THE PURPOSE AND ART OF THE NOVEL

"It is impossible to discuss Cooper merely as a man of letters," wrote H. S. Canby in 1931,[150] an opinion echoed by Tremaine McDowell when he remarks, "Cooper triumphed in spite of his non-literary approach and through natural, not acquired, power." [151] This is a sound judgment as far as it goes, and will probably not be substantially changed by research or criticism. But Cooper had a few very definite and persistent ideas about his art, ideas which became increasingly clear to him with experience. The factors of imitation, enthusiasm, and business judgment, important as they were, did not prevent him from developing a literary purpose and method of his own. Furthermore, his theory of fiction, as expressed incidentally in the prefaces and introductions to his novels, shows conscious development in terms of English literary currents of the period 1820–1850. *The Last of the Mohicans* and *The Red Rover* may be taken as typical examples of his technique in the earlier days; *Satanstoe* and *The Crater* as examples of his technique when it had matured in conformity to his literary theory.

Precaution was undertaken in the spirit of patriotism, and its form was determined by imitation in the sense of attempted improvement. Cooper himself objected to its "medley of characters" and its "English plot." [152] His principal object in *The Spy* was to correct these faults; so far he had discovered no literary principle to which he could point as such. In his 1849 preface, he found fault with "the structure of the tale," and blamed it on haste of composition. With *The Pioneers*, however, he became aware of a problem for which only an aesthetic judgment would

---

[150] *Classic Americans*, p. 97.
[151] T. McDowell, Introduction to *The Spy* (New York, 1931), p. xl.
[152] Preface, 1838, in *Precaution* (New York, 1861), p. xlvi.

provide a solution. He was writing of material from his own experience, and it became necessary to discover a principle by which the imagination might operate in dealing with facts. As in all the work of this period, he proceeded inductively; and in 1850, he could look back and formulate the rules for and the defects in his method. "Rigid adhesion to truth, an indispensable requisite in history and travels, destroys the charm of fiction; for all that is necessary to be conveyed to the mind by the latter had better be done by delineations of principles, and of characters in their classes, than by too fastidious attention to originals." In elaborating this principle, Cooper assures us that "the incidents of this tale are purely a fiction. The literal facts are chiefly connected with the natural and artificial objects, and customs of the inhabitants. . . . The author has elsewhere said that the character of Leather-Stocking is a creation, rendered probable by such auxiliaries as were necessary to produce that effect. . . . There was no intention to describe with particular accuracy any real character in this book." [153]

It is easy to substantiate this analysis. Cooper has himself written of the facts of his childhood surroundings in *The Chronicles of Cooperstown*, and his daughter has supplied much further detail in her prefaces and in *Pages and Pictures*. Natural scenes are described with great accuracy in the novel; buildings with only slight modifications; characters, as in the case of Monsieur Le Quoi, often retain their original names, but are more often rechristened. Judge William Cooper becomes Judge Marmaduke Temple; his daughter retains her Christian name; Richard Smith becomes Richard Jones; the Rev. Mr. Mosely, the Rev. Mr. Grant. But in the character of Natty Bumppo there is less obvious reference to an original. "It is generally believed," writes the Rev. Ralph Birdsall, "that an old hunter named Shipman, who lived in Cooperstown during Fenimore Cooper's boyhood, suggested to the novelist the picturesque character

[153] Introduction, 1850, to *The Pioneers* (New York, 1859), pp. ix–xv.

of Leather-Stocking." [154] Cooper here illustrates his theory of the function of the imagination in fiction. "The author has often been asked if he had any original in his mind, for the character of Leather-Stocking. In a physical sense, different individuals known to the writer in early life, certainly presented themselves as models, through his recollections: but in a moral sense this man of the forest is purely a creation." [155] He could not be more explicit. The writer of fiction is permitted to take or to reject such facts as he wishes from his experience, but he is bound to these facts in no respect whatever. The materials and the course of his story are determined by its "moral" requirements. Characters, however literally derived, are not bound to their originals, even in so closely related cases as the Messieurs Le Quoi of fact and of fiction. Character traits are derived from individuals, generalized in terms of ethical motivation, and reproduced in type rather than in personal synthesis. The same principle applies to his use of scenes and of events.

Cooper felt the force of this principle even before he had formulated it specifically, and he held to it firmly throughout his work. His history and travels reveal consistent faithfulness to available facts; his fiction, however much it is localized, is never more than verisimilitude. When, as in *Lionel Lincoln* and *The Spy*, he is dependent upon historical background, he distinguishes the demands of fact in dealing with the historical framework of his story, and allows his imagination free play in the treatment of fictional characters and events.

In *The Pioneers*, *Home as Found*, and *Ned Myers*, events and characters are closest to their originals; in such tales as *The Red Rover*, *The Prairie*, and other of the Leather-Stocking and sea tales, there is a close relationship between fact and fiction in certain materials, but a freer use of imagination in forming

---

[154] R. Birdsall, *The Story of Cooperstown* (Cooperstown, 1917), p. 161.
[155] Preface, 1850, to "The Leather-Stocking Tales," in *The Deerslayer* (New York, 1861), p. vii.

and developing most of them; in *The Heidenmauer*, *The Bravo*, *Mercedes of Castile*, and *The Water-Witch*, a legend or historical circumstance furnishes the key to the story and fact is still more liberally treated; and in allegories like *The Monikins* and *The Crater*, practically all materials are drawn from the imagination.

The attempt on the part of his critics to tie Cooper down to authenticity in his fiction gave him trouble from the earliest days and is still disturbing his ghost. At first, he took the challenge in a playful but satiric spirit. "In short," he concludes the preface to *Lionel Lincoln*, "he [the author] has pilfered from no black-letter book, or sixpenny pamphlet; his grandmother unnaturally refused her assistance to his labors; and, to speak affirmatively, for once, he wishes to live in peace, and hopes to die in the fear of God." [156] In *The Water-Witch* the principle has become more clearly defined. He speaks of it as "the most imaginative book ever written by the author. Its fault is in blending too much of the real with the purely ideal. Halfway measures will not do in matters of this sort; and it is always safer to preserve the identity of a book by a fixed and determinate character, than to make the effort to steer between the true and the false." [157] In defending *The Bravo* against its critics, he repeated the principle: "The nature of the work limited the writer as to time and place, both of which, with their proper accessories, were to be so far respected as to preserve a verisimilitude to received facts, in order that the illusion of the tale should not be destroyed." [158]

The failure of Cooper's critics to accept his literary method in the use of facts was the cause of the "Effingham" controversy. The novelist asserted his right to use his own character and experience as the material for fiction in *Home as Found*, and he

[156] Preface, 1824, to *Lionel Lincoln* (New York, 1859), p. 9.
[157] Preface, 1834, to *The Water-Witch* (New York, 1860), p. vi.
[158] *A Letter to His Countrymen* (New York, 1834), p. 12.

portrayed a family almost identical with his own upon their return from Europe to a town almost identical with Cooperstown. His critics, who had been silent when the same method was used in *The Pioneers*, objected now to Cooper's comparison of American society with that of Europe, and used the close similarity between fact and fiction in the later novel as grounds for a personal attack on Cooper the man. Typical of their comment is Webb's review of the novel in the New York *Courier and Enquirer* for November 22, 1838. "At page 145 we find the following: 'As my house came to me from my Father, said Mr. Effingham, across whose *mild* and HANDSOME face a smile was gradually sliding!!'—Reader, did you ever see Mr. Cooper? If not, do not delay getting a peep at him if only for the purpose of admiring the *modesty*, depicted in his 'handsome face!'" [159] Cooper's contention that revelations of personal character incidental to fiction do not furnish adequate grounds for libelous attack was sustained by the courts in a series of litigations, but was never admitted by the press. By 1844, he had despaired of ever making clear to his public his distinction between history and work of the imagination. "The writer has published so much truth which the world has insisted was fiction," he says in the preface to *Afloat and Ashore*, "and so much fiction that has been received as truth, that, in the present instance, he is resolved to say nothing on the subject." [160] In the Littlepage novels, he ignores his critics entirely, and presents, as mock history, a series of related stories which are free in their use of typical social facts.

The more significant of his literary principles, however, is his belief that literature does not exist as an end in itself. The political idealism of the English romantics developed in the course of the nineteenth century into a more or less formulated social ethics which has come to be known as Victorianism. The

---

[159] Quoted in E. R. Outland, *The "Effingham" Libels*, pp. 69–77.
[160] Preface, 1844, to *Afloat and Ashore* (New York, 1861), p. v.

Victorian novelists and poets moved from the romanticism of Scott to the realism and social criticism of Dickens, Thackeray, and Trollope. Literature became closely linked with social commentary in Carlyle, Ruskin, and Arnold; Tennyson and Browning used poetry to express their ideals for society as well as the aspirations of their souls. In America, there was already a strong tradition of political and social idealism, and Cooper's thesis that it was the mission of American literature to find its own identity in the expression of its national ideals is a logical consequence of literary currents abroad as well as at home. The imagination which he wished to free from slavery to fact was an ethical rather than an aesthetic imagination. His desire to paint types rather than individuals was evidence of his hope that literature might aid in an understanding of man, the American man rather than John Smith. His novels ask the root questions: what is the American man, what distinguishes him from men of other times and places, what must he do to develop his fullest capacities? The modern restatement of the social point of view in literature by such descendants of Taine as Parrington and Granville Hicks should make us hesitate to condemn Cooper for his theory that literature has legitimate aims ulterior to the giving of pleasure or the expression of personal experience. We may not agree with his specific social views, we may not even agree that literature may be determined by factors extraneous to the quest for beauty, but we cannot say that Cooper, in the years of his maturity, lacked a philosophy of art.

That philosophy of art may be briefly summarized in his own words: "Every chronicle of manners," he wrote in the preface to *Satanstoe* (1845), "has a certain value. When customs are connected with principles, in their origin, development, or end, such records have a double importance."[161] He had begun his literary career with a chronicle of manners in total ignorance

[161] Preface, 1845, to *Satanstoe* (New York, 1860), p. v.

of the manners he was attempting to portray. Realizing that substance was more vital than form to him and to his nation, he turned to a first-hand examination of the substance of the American scene. In doing so, he adopted a literary mode which was then current, the romance of adventure of Scott, but gave it a realistic meaning by portraying the near in time and space rather than the far-away. He then realized that an imported definition of manners would not serve for the new country. An American writer must rely upon novelty rather than upon settled institutions for interest and meaning in his stories. He must therefore be romantic, even though his instincts lead him to realism. "He must seek his renoun in the exhibition of qualities that are general." [162] Furthermore, he must understand the principles which determine these general qualities, and his work must be an illustration of the underlying as well as the manifest truth. This truth presented itself to Cooper in terms of political liberalism during his European residence. On his return, he began consciously to do what he had been doing all along in stumbling and intuitive fashion, to develop an American novel of manners which was to serve as a commentary as well as a revelation. The elements of historical representation and romantic idealization, which had determined the earlier novels, furnished, the one a realistic approach to the material, the other a moral basis of interpretation suitable to a society in a state of rapid development and of searching self-examination. In *Satanstoe* and kindred novels, the new synthesis approaches nearest to a unified expression. The result was still crude, but America, in 1845, produced in Cooper's mature work a type of social novel which may legitimately be considered as conscious and purposive art.

[162] *Notions of the Americans* (Philadelphia, 1828), II, 450.

CHRONOLOGICAL TABLE

1789. September 15, James (Fenimore) Cooper born in Burlington, New Jersey.

1790. November 10, family moves to Cooperstown, New York.

1800. Lives with Rev. Thomas Ellison, Rector of St. Peter's Church, Albany, in order to prepare for college.

1803. Enters Yale College in class of 1806.

1805. Dismissed from college for a prank, but allowed to graduate a year later.

1806. Voyage to England and Spain in the *Sterling*. Shipmate of Ned Myers.

1808. Enlists as midshipman in the U. S. Navy. Spends winter on the shore of Lake Ontario helping to build vessel.

1809. Death of William Cooper, his father.

1811. January 1, marries Susan Augusta De Lancey at Mamaroneck, New York, and lives at Heathcote Hall. Resigns from the Navy in May.

1814. Moves to Fenimore Farm, Cooperstown.

1817. Returns to Westchester County, New York, and builds new home at Angevine Farm, near Scarsdale. Death of his mother, Elizabeth Fenimore Cooper, and division of family estate, now much depleted.

1819. Member of Westchester County Agricultural Society; Quartermaster and later Paymaster of Fourth Division of Infantry of New York State; partner of Charles T. Deering in purchase and management of whaling ship *Union*. Starts writing *Precaution*.

1820. *Precaution* published.

1821. *The Spy.*

1822. Moves to New York City and becomes leading member of Bread and Cheese Club.

1823. Unfinished house at Fenimore Farm, Cooperstown, burns down. *The Pioneers. Tales for Fifteen.*

1824. *The Pilot.* Contributes account of Lafayette's welcome to *New York American*, September 15.

1825. *Lionel Lincoln.*

1826. *The Last of the Mohicans.* June 1, sails for Europe with family of four daughters and one son. Stops in London to arrange with Henry Colburn for English publication of his novels.

1827. *The Prairie. The Red Rover.* Living in Paris in an apartment on the third floor of school attended by his daughters, and in summer at St. Ouen. Meets Lafayette and Scott.

1828. *Notions of the Americans.* Spring in London, summer in Berne, fall in Florence.

1829. *The Wept of Wish-ton-Wish.* Winter and spring in Florence, summer in Sorrento on the Bay of Naples, fall in Rome.

1830. *The Water-Witch.* Winter in Rome, returns to Paris by way of the Rhine, with short residence in Dresden.

1831. *The Bravo.* Participates in work of French and American committees for the relief of the Poles and issues *Contributions for the Poles.* Writes *Letter to General Lafayette* on the French budget controversy and follows it by letters to the [Paris] *National.*

1832. *The Heidenmauer.* Spends part of summer at Vevey, Switzerland.

1833. *The Headsman.* Spends summer without his family in London and brings them back to New York City in November. Refuses to participate in a welcome dinner.

1834. *A Letter to His Countrymen*, justifying his ideas and announcing his retirement as a writer of novels. Purchases and remodels Otsego Hall, Cooperstown, at first for a summer, later for a permanent, residence.

1835. *The Monikins.*

1836. *Sketches of Switzerland*, Parts I and II. Spends much time in Philadelphia superintending publication.

1837. *Gleanings in Europe: [France]. Gleanings in Europe: England.* Three Mile Point controversy with people of

Cooperstown. Controversy with Cooperstown and Albany newspapers.

1838. *Gleanings in Europe: Italy*. *The American Democrat*, published in Cooperstown. *The Chronicles of Cooperstown*. *Homeward Bound* and *Home as Found*. War with the press taken up by New York City editors: Webb, Weed, Benjamin, Stone, and Greeley. Reviews Lockhart's *Life of Scott* unfavorably in the *Knickerbocker Magazine*, October.

1839. *The History of the Navy of the United States of America* changes attack of editors to matters of historical accuracy, mainly concerning the Battle of Lake Erie.

1840. Returns to romance of Indians with *The Pathfinder*. *Mercedes of Castile*.

1841. *The Deerslayer* completes the Leather-Stocking series.

1842. *The Two Admirals*. Wins arbitration of naval history controversy. Begins series of naval biographies in *Graham's Magazine*, November, under variant titles.

1843. "Autobiography of a Pocket Handkerchief," in *Graham's Magazine*, starting January. Conclusion of the more important libel trials, with most of the cases settled in Cooper's favor. *The Battle of Lake Erie*. *Wyandotté*. *Ned Myers*.

1844. *Afloat and Ashore*, two parts, the first published by the author, the second by Burgess, Stringer, and Co. in paper wrappers. Attacks Commander Alexander Slidell Mackenzie in *The Cruise of the Somers* and in a review of the proceedings in his court-martial.

1845. *Satanstoe* and *The Chainbearer*.

1846. *Lives of Distinguished American Naval Officers* collected. *The Redskins*. The first installment of *Jack Tier* published simultaneously in *Graham's Magazine* and *Bentley's Miscellany*, November, with variant titles.

1847. *The Crater*. First trip west, to Detroit.

1848. *Jack Tier* published as a book. *The Oak Openings*.

1849. *The Sea Lions*.

1850. "The Lake Gun," published in *The Parthenon*. *The Ways of the Hour*. *Upside Down, or Philosophy in Petticoats*, a comedy, produced at Burton's Theatre, New York City, but never published. In New York City supervising the Putnam edition of his novels and the publication of Susan Cooper's *Rural Hours*. Consults with Dr. John W. Francis about his own health, now very poor.

1851. Becomes a communicant in the Episcopal Church, July. September 15, dies at Cooperstown and is buried in Christ Church graveyard. Leaves an unfinished manuscript on the history of New York and requests the destruction of his personal papers.

SELECTED BIBLIOGRAPHY

(Starred items are of primary importance for the general student.)

I. BIBLIOGRAPHY

The Cambridge History of American Literature. New York: 1917. I, 530–534. (The best list of secondary sources.)

Cooper, James Fenimore. A Bibliography of James Fenimore Cooper. (A typed manuscript, by Cooper's grandson, in the Yale Cooper Collection, containing some entries not listed in Lounsbury and other early bibliographies.)

Johnson, Merle. *American First Editions.* New York: 1932. (A list of Cooper items of particular interest to the collector.)

Lounsbury, Thomas R. *James Fenimore Cooper.* Boston: 1882. (The bibliography, pp. 290–299, is an accurate list of Cooper's important work.)

*Spiller, Robert E., and Blackburn, Philip C. *A Descriptive Bibliography of the Writings of James Fenimore Cooper.* New York: 1934. (A bibliographical description of first and early editions of works by Cooper, including foreign publications, translations into foreign languages, contributions to periodicals and other fugitive pieces, attributions, adaptations, and an appendix containing previously unpublished correspondence between Cooper and his various publishers. The introduction discusses conditions of publication in Cooper's day and the operation of copyright laws.)

Wegelin, Oscar. *Early American Fiction, 1774–1830.* New York: 1929. (Lists first American editions up to *The Water-Witch,* 1830.)

To keep abreast of current items, the student should consult the annual bibliographies in *American Literature* and *Publications of the Modern Language Association.*

Helpful bibliographies are included in many biographical and critical studies of Cooper. Among these, see below: Barba, P. A.; Bosset, G. C.; Cairns, W. B.; Clymer, W. B. S.; Ferguson, J. De L.; Gibb, M. M.; Morris, G. D.; Outland, E. R.; Ross, J. E.; Russell, J. A.; and Spiller, R. E., *Fenimore Cooper: Critic of His Times*.

II. WRITINGS

The American Democrat. Cooperstown, N. Y.: 1838. (Reprinted, with an introduction by H. L. Mencken. New York: 1931.)

Autobiography of a Pocket Handkerchief. With notes and introduction by Walter Lee Brown. Evanston, Ill.: 1897. (Originally published as a pamphlet under the title, *Le Mouchoir; an Autobiographical Romance*, New York: 1843, and in *Graham's Magazine* for the same year.)

The Battle of Lake Erie. Cooperstown, N. Y.: 1843. (A controversial pamphlet.)

The Chronicles of Cooperstown. Cooperstown, N. Y.: 1838. (Continued by S. T. Livermore, Albany: 1862; S. M. Shaw, Cooperstown: 1886; and Walter R. Littell, Cooperstown: 1929.)

The Cruise of the Somers. New York: 1844. (A controversial pamphlet.)

Gleanings in Europe: [France]. Philadelphia: 1837. (Published in London, 1837, under the title *Recollections of Europe*. Reprinted, with an introduction by R. E. Spiller, New York: 1928.)

Gleanings in Europe: England. Philadelphia: 1837. (Published in London, 1837, under the title *England, with Sketches of Society in the Metropolis*. Reprinted, with an introduction by R. E. Spiller, New York: 1930.)

Gleanings in Europe: Italy. Philadelphia: 1838. (Published in London, 1838, under the title *Excursions in Italy*.)

The History of the Navy of the United States of America. Philadelphia: 1839. (Revised, 1840, 1847, 1853, 1864. Abridged, Philadelphia: 1841.)

The Lake Gun. With an introduction by R. E. Spiller. New York: 1932. (Printed first in *The Parthenon*, New York: 1850.)

Letter of J. Fenimore Cooper to Gen. Lafayette. Paris: 1831. (Reprinted in facsimile, with a bibliographical note by R. E. Spiller, New York: 1931.)

A Letter to His Countrymen. New York: 1834.

Lives of Distinguished American Naval Officers. Philadelphia: 1846. (Printed first in *Graham's Magazine,* 1842–1845.)

Ned Myers. Philadelphia: 1843. (Included in the earlier collected editions of Stringer and Townsend, New York: 1852–1860. Not included in collected editions thereafter until the Mohawk Edition.)

New York. With an introduction by D. R. Fox. New York: 1930. (Printed first in *The Spirit of the Fair*, New York: 1864.)

Notions of the Americans: Picked up by a Travelling Bachelor. Philadelphia: 1828. (Included in the earlier collected editions of Stringer and Townsend, New York: 1852–1860. Not included in collected editions thereafter.)

*Novels. With illustrations by F. O. C. Darley. 32 vols. New York: 1859–1861. (The first definitive collection.)

Sketches of Switzerland. Philadelphia: 1836. (Published in London, 1836, under the title *Excursions in Switzerland.*)

Sketches of Switzerland. Part Second. Philadelphia: 1836. (Published in England, 1836, under the title *A Residence in France* [etc.].)

Tales for Fifteen. New York: 1823. (The two tales, "Imagination" and "Heart" appeared later in *Roberts' Semi-Monthly Magazine,* February and April, 1841.)

Works. Household Edition, with introductions to many of the volumes by S. F. Cooper. 32 vols. New York: 1876–1884.

*The Works of James Fenimore Cooper. 33 vols. New York: 1895–1900. (The most easily procurable edition.)

For periodical contributions and other miscellaneous writings, see Spiller and Blackburn's *Descriptive Bibliography.*

III. BIOGRAPHY AND BIOGRAPHICAL SOURCES

Adkins, Nelson F. *Fitz-Greene Halleck*. New Haven: 1930. (Miscellaneous references to Cooper.)

Adkins, Nelson F. "James Fenimore Cooper and the Bread and Cheese Club," *Modern Language Notes*, XLVII, 71–79 (February, 1932).

[Anonymous.] "Living Literary Characters, No. IV: James Fenimore Cooper," *New Monthly Magazine*, XXXI, 356–362 (April, 1831). (One of the earliest English sketches, by someone who knew Cooper slightly.)

Benedict, Clare. *Voices Out of the Past*. London: 1929, pp. 38–63.

Birdsall, Ralph. *The Story of Cooperstown*. Cooperstown, N. Y.: 1917. (Many facts and anecdotes relative to Cooper.)

*Boynton, Henry Walcott. *James Fenimore Cooper*. New York: 1931. (A human portrait based on some new material and a sympathetic treatment of old material, but with little criticism of Cooper's work.)

Browning, Charlotte Prentiss. *Full Harvest*. Philadelphia: 1932. (Incidental memories of a friend of Cooper's daughters.)

Bryant, William Cullen. "Discourse on the Life and Genius of Cooper," in *Memorial of James Fenimore Cooper*. New York: 1852. (Reprinted in *Precaution*, New York: 1861. The best biographical sketch before Lounsbury's. The *Memorial* also contains many letters from distinguished contemporaries.)

Clymer, W. B. Shubrick. *James Fenimore Cooper*. Boston: 1900. (The best short biography, with a bibliography of selected secondary sources, pp. 146–149.)

*Cooper, James Fenimore, editor. *Correspondence of James Fenimore-Cooper*. 2 vols. New Haven: 1922. (Relatively few letters from and many letters to Cooper. The editor is Cooper's grandson.)

Cooper, James Fenimore. *The Legends and Traditions of a Northern County*. New York: 1921. (Notes and documents relative to Cooperstown and the Cooper family, by Cooper's grandson.)

Cooper, Susan Fenimore. "A Glance Backward," *Atlantic Monthly*, LIX, 199–206 (February, 1887). (Westchester County recollections by Cooper's eldest daughter.)

Cooper, Susan Fenimore. "A Second Glance Backward," *Atlantic Monthly*, LX, 474–486 (October, 1887). (Italian recollections.)

Cooper, Susan Fenimore, editor. *Pages and Pictures from the Writings of James Fenimore Cooper*. New York: 1861. (Personal recollections by Cooper's daughter prefatory to each selection.)

Cooper, Susan Fenimore. Prefaces to the novels. (See above, p. xci.)

Cooper, Susan Fenimore. "Small Family Memories," in *Correspondence of J. F. Cooper*. New Haven: 1922. I, 9–72. (Personal recollections covering the period up to 1832.)

Cooper, William. *A Guide in the Wilderness*. Dublin: 1810. (Reprinted Rochester, N. Y.: 1897. Notes on the settlement of Cooperstown by Cooper's father.)

Dunlap, William. *Diary*. 3 vols. New York: 1931. (Copies of letters from Cooper and references to him.)

Francis, John W. "Reminiscences of Cooper," in *Memorial*. New York: 1852, pp. 94–103. (Personal notes by Cooper's physician.)

Goodrich, Samuel G. *Recollections of a Lifetime*. New York: 1856. (Occasional references to Cooper.)

Greene, George Washington. *Biographical Studies*. New York: 1860. (Reminiscences of an artist who met Cooper abroad.)

Griggs, Earl Leslie. "James Fenimore Cooper on Coleridge," *American Literature*, IV, 389–391 (January, 1933). (A note on Cooper's meeting with Coleridge in 1828, with a previously unpublished Cooper letter.)

Griswold, Rufus W. *Passages from the Correspondence and Other Papers of Rufus W. Griswold*. Cambridge, Mass.: 1898. (Contains two letters from and two about Cooper.)

Hemstreet, Charles. "Cooper and His Friends," in *Literary New York*. New York: 1903.

Howe, M. A. DeWolfe. *American Bookmen*. New York: 1898. (Contains a sketch of Cooper.)

Irving, Pierre M. *Life and Letters of Washington Irving*. 4 vols. New York: 1862–1864. (Incidental references to Cooper.)

Keese, J. Pomeroy. "Memories of Distinguished Authors. James Fenimore Cooper," *Harper's Weekly*, supplement, pp. 707–711 (July 29, 1871).

Littell, Walter R., editor. *A History of Cooperstown*. Cooperstown, N. Y.: 1929. (Contains Cooper's *The Chronicles of Cooperstown*. The best source for local history.)

*Lounsbury, Thomas R. *James Fenimore Cooper*. Boston: 1882. (A scholarly work, in many respects not yet superseded. Bibliography, pp. 290–299.)

Morse, Edward L., editor. *Samuel F. B. Morse, His Letters and Journals*. 2 vols. Boston: 1914. (Many references to and several letters from Cooper.)

Mulford, Anna. *A Sketch of Dr. John Smith Sage*. Sag Harbor, N. Y.: 1897. (The appendix, pp. 27–60, contains data on Cooper's venture in the whaling industry.)

Mulford, William R. "James Fenimore Cooper, His Ancestry and Writings," *New York Genealogical and Biographical Record*, XV. New York: 1884.

New York Historical Association. *Proceedings*, XVI. Albany, N. Y.: 1917. (Record of the 18th annual meeting, held at Cooperstown, N. Y., containing many articles and pictures relating to Cooper, his home, and his work. Also genealogical data compiled by W. W. Cooper, 1879. The same data are contained in a chart in the Historical Society of Pennsylvania.)

Parton, J. L. *Life of Horace Greeley*. New York: 1855. (An account of Cooper's case against the *Tribune*, apparently based on Greeley's pamphlet, published in 1843.)

Phillips, Mary E. *James Fenimore Cooper*. New York: 1913. (A biography of Cooper the man, with many illustrations.)

Sawyer, Edith A. "A Year of Cooper's Youth," *New England*

Magazine, N. S. XXXVII, 498–504 (December, 1907). (The Ned Myers incident, with a Cooper letter.)

Scott, Walter. *The Journal of Sir Walter Scott*. 2 vols. Edinburgh: 1890. (Several references to Cooper.)

Smiles, Samuel. *Memoir and Correspondence of John Murray*. 2 vols. London: 1891. (II, 134–135, contains a letter from Cooper.)

Spiller, Robert E. "Fenimore Cooper and Lafayette: The Finance Controversy of 1831–1832," *American Literature*, III, 28–44 (March, 1931).

Spiller, Robert E. "Fenimore Cooper and Lafayette: Friends of Polish Freedom, 1830–1832," *American Literature*, VII, 56–75 (March, 1935).

*Spiller, Robert E. *Fenimore Cooper, Critic of His Times*. New York: 1931. (A biography with emphasis on Cooper's social thought.)

Spiller, Robert E. "Fenimore Cooper, Critic of His Times: New Letters from Rome and Paris, 1830–1831," *American Literature*, I, 131–148 (May, 1929). (Five letters containing comment on Europe, four of them previously unpublished.)

Waples, Dorothy. "A Letter from James Fenimore Cooper," *New England Quarterly*, III, 123–132 (January, 1930).

Willis, Nathaniel Parker. "Letters from Watering Places, Letter II," in *Rural Letters*. New York: 1849, pp. 314–323. (An account of a visit to Cooperstown in June, 1848.)

Wilson, James Grant. *Bryant and His Friends*. New York: 1886, pp. 230–244. (Anecdotes and notes on Cooper.)

Wilson, James Grant. "Cooper Memorials," *Independent*, LIII, 251–253 (January 31, 1901). (Notes, including several Cooper letters.)

IV. CRITICISM

[Anonymous.] "James Fenimore Cooper," *Yale Literary Magazine*, V, 249–259 (March, 1840). (Valuable only for Cooper's own marginal comments on the copy in the Yale Cooper Collection.)

Balzac, Honoré de. "Fenimore Cooper et Walter Scott,"

Revue Parisienne (July 25, 1840). (Reprinted in *Œuvres*, XXIII, 584–592. Translated in the *Knickerbocker Magazine*, XVII, 72–77, January, 1841, and in *Personal Opinions of Balzac*, by Katherine Prescott Wormeley, Boston: 1899.)

Barba, Preston A. *Cooper in Germany.* Indiana University Studies, No. 21. Bloomington, Ind.: 1914. (Cooper's influence on German literature; his travels in Germany; Cooper and German criticism; German translations of his works.)

Bosset, G. C. *Fenimore Cooper et le roman d'aventure en France vers 1830.* Paris: [1928].

*Brownell, William C. *American Prose Masters.* New York: 1909, pp. 3–60. (Perhaps the best critical estimate, although based on the older sources. Published first in *Scribner's Magazine*, XXXIX, 455–468, April, 1906.)

Cairns, William B. *British Criticisms of American Writings, 1815–1833.* University of Wisconsin Studies in Language and Literature, No. 14. Madison, Wis.: 1922. (Contains references to Cooper's works in contemporary British periodicals.)

*Canby, Henry Seidel. *Classic Americans.* New York: 1931, pp. 97–142. (A part of this chapter was published in the *Saturday Review of Literature*, III, 747–749, April 23, 1927. A well-balanced criticism which attributes Cooper's qualities as a man to his Quaker heritage and his art to the enthusiasm of the amateur.)

Canby, Henry Seidel. *Definitions: Essays in Contemporary Criticism.* New York: 1922–1924. Series II, 254–262.

Chasles, Philarète. *Études sur la littérature et les mœurs des Anglo-Américains au XIXe siècle.* Paris: 1851, pp. 50–63.

Clavel, Marcel. Reviews of recent Cooper scholarship, *Revue Anglo-Américaine*, V, 342–354 (April, 1928); VI, 532–537 (August, 1929); VIII, 538–542 (August, 1931); XII, 167–170 (December, 1934). (M. Clavel has been working for some years on a biography of Cooper.)

Clemens, Samuel L. "Fenimore Cooper's Literary Offenses," in *How to Tell a Story, and Other Essays.* New York: 1897, pp. 78–96. (A classic attack on Cooper, in a vein of serious irony, published first in the *North American Review*, CLXI, 1–12, July, 1895.)

Connolly, J. B. "Cooper and Stories of the Sea," in *Fiction and Its Makers*, edited by F. X. Talbot. New York: 1928, pp. 171–178.

Cooke, John Esten. "Cooper's Indians," *Appleton's Journal*, XII, 264–267 (August 29, 1874). (A plea for Cooper's Indians.)

Conrad, Joseph. "Tales of the Sea," in *Notes on Life and Letters*. New York: 1921, pp. 53–57. (Appreciative discussion of Cooper and Maryatt.)

Dargan, E. Preston. "Balzac and Cooper: *Les Chouans*," *Modern Philology*, XIII, 193–213 (August, 1915). (Balzac's debt to Cooper.)

Drescher, Rudolf. "My Cooper Collection," *Freeman's Journal* (Cooperstown, N. Y.), February 13, 1929. (Other articles by Herr Drescher in the *Freeman's Journal*, December 6, 1911, and November 14, 1918; and in the newspapers of Heidelberg, Frankfort, Dresden, Berne, and Hanau-am-Main.)

Erskine, John. *Leading American Novelists*. New York: 1910, pp. 51–129. (A review of Cooper's life and of his Indian and sea romances.)

Ferguson, John De Lancey. *American Literature in Spain*. New York: 1916, pp. 32–54. (A study of translations into Spanish and of reviews in Spain of Cooper's work.)

Gibb, Margaret M. *Le Roman de bas-de-cuir; étude sur Fenimore Cooper et son influence en France*. Paris: 1927. (For a review of its defects see M. Clavel in the *Revue Anglo-Américaine*, V, 342–354, April, 1928.)

Gibb, Margaret M. "Léon Gozlan et Fenimore Cooper," *Revue de la littérature comparée*, X, 485 (July-September, 1930).

Goggio, Emil. "Cooper's *Bravo* in Italy," *Romanic Review*, XX, 222–236 (July-September, 1929). (The reactions of Italian reviewers.)

Hale, Edward Everett, Jr. "American Scenery in Cooper's Novels," *Sewanee Review*, XVIII, 317–332 (July, 1910). (Emphasis on Cooper's realism in dealing with background.)

Harden, H. "James Fenimore Cooper, ein nordamerikanisches Dichterbild," *Bibliothek der Unterhaltung und der Wissens*, X, 171–182. Stuttgart: 1888. (A biographical and critical review.)

Hawthorne, Julian. "James Fenimore Cooper," in *Warner's Classics*. New York: 1899. II (Novelists), 153–173.

Hazard, Lucy L. *The Frontier in American Literature*. New York: 1927, pp. 97–116. (An essay on Cooper's Indians and pioneers as representative of an ideal not that of Rousseau.)

Higginson, Thomas W. *Carlyle's Laugh and Other Surprises*. Boston: 1909, pp. 46–54. (An unsympathetic comment.)

Hilliard, S. G. "James Fenimore Cooper," *Atlantic Monthly*, IX, 52–68 (January, 1862). (One of the earliest appraisals of Cooper's whole work; a review of the Townsend edition of the novels.)

Howells, William Dean, "Scott's Jeanie Deans and Cooper's Lack of Heroines," in *Heroines of Fiction*. New York: 1901. I, 102–112.

Ingraham, Charles A. *Washington Irving, and Other Essays*. Cambridge, N. Y.: 1922.

Keiser, Albert. *The Indian in American Literature*. New York: 1933, pp. 101–143. (Stresses Cooper's realism in dealing with Indians, particularly in the less known novels.)

Latto, Thomas C. "James Fenimore Cooper," *Harper's Magazine*, XLI, 293–294 (July, 1870). (A long laudatory poem.)

Lawrence, D. H. *Studies in Classic American Literature.* New York: 1923, pp. 50–92. (A biased but stimulating criticism in cynical vein.)

Leisy, Ernest E. *The American Historical Novel (on American Themes) before 1860*. Urbana, Ill.: 1923. (An abstract of a thesis at the University of Illinois. A study of the early novels, 1821–1831, on historical themes.)

Loshe, Lillie D. *The Early American Novel.* New York: 1907, pp. 84–90. (Criticism of Cooper's art of characterization.)

McDowell, Tremaine. "The Identity of Harvey Birch," *American Literature*, II, 111–120 (May, 1930). (A discussion of the Enoch Crosby controversy.)

McDowell, Tremaine. "James Fenimore Cooper as Self-Critic," *Studies in Philology*, XXVII, 508–516 (July, 1930). (A study of Cooper's revisions of the text of *The Spy*.)

McDowell, Tremaine. "Scott on Cooper and Brockden Brown," *Modern Language Notes*, XLV, 18–20 (January, 1830). (A note on Scott's opinion of Cooper as quoted by S. L. Goodrich in his *Recollections*.)

*McDowell, Tremaine. Introduction to *The Spy*. New York: 1931, pp. ix–xl. (One of the most able of recent criticisms.)

Macy, John. *The Spirit of American Literature*. New York: 1913, pp. 35–44. (A brief estimate, with a biographical note.)

Matlack, T. Chalkley. Manuscript dictionary of characters in the novels of Cooper, summaries of plots, excerpts from contemporary criticisms, drawings from Darley, and maps of the scenes of the novels. Historical Societies of Pennsylvania and of Burlington, N. J.

Matthews, Brander. "The Centenary of Fenimore Cooper," in *Americanisms and Briticisms, with Other Essays on Other Isms*. New York: 1892, pp. 89–102.

Matthews, Brander. *Gateways to Literature*. New York: 1912, pp. 243–276. (Published first in *Atlantic Monthly*, C, 328–341, September, 1907.)

Maulsby, D. L. "Fenimore Cooper and Mark Twain," *Dial* (Chicago), XXII, 107–109 (February 16, 1897). (A note on Mark Twain's attack on Cooper.)

Mencken, H. L. Introduction to *The American Democrat*. New York: 1931, pp. vii–xx. (A discussion of Cooper's sagacity and priggishness.)

Messac, Régis. "Fenimore Cooper et son influence en France," *Publications of the Modern Language Association*, XLIII, 1199–1201 (December, 1928). (A brief note on Miss Gibb's treatment of the Mohicans.)

Mitchell, Donald Grant. *American Lands and Letters*. New York: 1898, pp. 225–253. (Personal and somewhat apologetic in tone.)

Morris, George D. *Fenimore Cooper et Edgar Poe d'après la critique française du dix-neuvième siècle*. Paris: 1912. (A review of the more obvious French criticisms of Cooper's work.)

Müller, Willi. *The Monikins von J. F. Cooper, in ihrem Verhältnis zu Gulliver's Travels von J. Swift.* Rostock: 1900.

Muret, Maurice. "Fenimore Cooper, américain d'hier," *Journal des Débats* (ed. heb.), XXXVIII, 670–672 (October 23, 1931).

Oakley, K. R. "James Fenimore Cooper and *Oak Openings*," *Michigan Historical Magazine*, XVI, 309–320 (Summer, 1932).

Outland, Ethel R. *The "Effingham" Libels on Cooper.* University of Wisconsin Studies in Language and Literature, No. 28. Madison, Wis.: 1929. (More valuable for its documentation than for its conclusions.)

Paine, Gregory L. "James Fenimore Cooper as an Interpreter and Critic of America," in *University of Chicago Abstracts of Theses*, Humanities Series III, Chicago, Ill.: 1924–5, pp. 363–366. (The original of this thesis is deposited in the University of Chicago library.)

Paine, Gregory L. "Cooper and the *North American Review*," *Studies in Philology*, XXVIII, 799–809 (October, 1931). (The early reviews of Cooper's work were prejudiced against him.)

Paine, Gregory L. Introduction to *The Deerslayer.* New York: 1927, pp. ix–xxxvi.

Paine, Gregory L. "The Indians of the Leather-stocking Tales," *Studies in Philology*, XXIII, 16–39 (January, 1926). (Starting with secondary rather than first-hand knowledge, Cooper tended to idealize more and more.)

Palfrey, Thomas R. "Cooper and Balzac: *The Headsman*," *Modern Philology*, XXIX, 335–341 (February, 1932). (Cooper's debt to Balzac.)

Parkman, Francis. "James Fenimore Cooper," *North American Review*, CLIV, 147–161 (January, 1852). (Praises Cooper's descriptions of nature and action, but criticizes his characters.)

*Parrington, Vernon L. *The Romantic Revolution in America.* New York: 1927, pp. 222–237. (*Main Currents in American*

Thought, Vol. II. A penetrating analysis of Cooper's political and social thought.)

Pattee, Fred Lewis. "Cooper the Critic," *Saturday Review of Literature*, V, 1107–1108 (June 15, 1929). (A review of the *Gleanings*.)

Pattee, Fred Lewis. "James Fenimore Cooper," *American Mercury*, IV, 289–297 (March, 1925). (A personal interpretation in terms of "the De Lancey wife.")

Phelps, William L. *Some Makers of American Literature*. Boston: 1923, pp. 34–64. (The Dartmouth Alumni Lectureships on the Moore Foundation, 1922. An appreciation of Cooper as representative of "the spirit of romance.")

Poe, Edgar Allan. Review of *Wyandotté, Graham's Magazine*, XXIV, 261–264 (November, 1843). (An unfavorable estimate of Cooper's art.)

Pound, Louise. "The Dialect of Cooper's Leather-stocking," *American Speech*, II, 479–488 (September, 1927).

Ross, John F. *The Social Criticism of Fenimore Cooper*. Berkeley, California: 1933. (A monograph based on the critical prose.)

Routh, James. "The Model of the Leather-stocking Tales," *Modern Language Notes*, XXVIII, 77–79 (March, 1913). (A study of parallels in character and plot in the Leather-Stocking Tales.)

Russell, J. A. "Cooper: Interpreter of the Real and Historical Indian," *Journal of American History*, XXIII, 41–71 (First quarter, 1930).

Sainte-Beuve, C. A. Review of *The Red Rover* and other comment on Cooper's work, in *Premiers lundis*. Paris: 1886. I, 288–294. (Other references to Cooper in *Portraits littéraires*.)

Sand, George. *Autour de la table*. Paris: 1875, ch. V, pp. 261–283.

Schönbach, Anton E. *Gesammelte Aufsätze zur neuren Litteratur in Deutschland, Oesterreich, Amerika*. Gratz: 1900, pp. 237–250.

Segré, Carlo. "Cooper e Loti," in *Saggi critici di letteratura straniere*. Florence: 1894.

Simms, William Gilmore. *Views and Reviews*, First Series. New York: 1845. Article VI, pp. 210–238.

Spiller, Robert E. *The American in England*. New York: 1926, pp. 300–345. (The first treatment of Cooper as primarily a social critic.)

Spiller, Robert E. "Cooper's Notes on Language," *American Speech*, IV, 294–300 (April, 1929).

Spiller, Robert E. "Fenimore Cooper's Defense of Slave-owning America," *American Historical Review*, XXXV, 575–582 (April, 1930).

Spiller, Robert E. Introduction to *The Lake Gun*. New York: 1932, pp. 7–23.

Spiller, Robert E. Introductions to *Gleanings in Europe*. Volume I, *France*. New York: 1928, pp. vii–xxxi. Volume II, *England*. New York: 1930, pp. v–xix.

Stanford, Alfred. "Cooper," in *American Writers on American Literature*, edited by John Macy. New York: 1931, pp. 72–80. (A hasty criticism, appreciative of the sea tales.)

Stedman, Edmund C. "Poe, Cooper and the Hall of Fame," *North American Review*, CLXXXV, 801–812 (August, 1907). (Fame in relation to votes for inclusion in the Hall.)

Sueffer, Carl. "War Lederstrumpf ein Deutscher?" *Westermann's Monatshefte* (Braunschweig), n. vol., 245–249 (May, 1934).

Tuckerman, Henry T. "James Fenimore Cooper," *North American Review*, CLXXXV, 289–316 (October, 1859).

Van Doren, Carl. *The American Novel*. New York: 1921, pp. 24–50. (An expansion of the chapter in *The Cambridge History of American Literature*.)

Vincent, Leon H. *American Literary Masters*. Boston: 1906, pp. 65–97. (Reviews of life and of separate works. Shows firsthand knowledge and independence if not depth of judgment.)

Winter, William. *Old Shrines and New Ivy*. New York: 1892, pp. 281–284. (Note on the suggestive power of Cooper's romantic tales.)

Wukadinovic, Spiridion. *Goethe's "Novelle"; der Schauplatz Coopersche Einflüsse*. Halle-an-der-Saale: 1909.

*

Selections from
JAMES FENIMORE COOPER

*

[THE AMERICAN SCENE]

From *Notions of the Americans*[1]

LETTER XXIII [LEARNING AND LITERATURE]

To the Abbate Giromachi, &c. &c.

Washington, ——

You ask me to write freely on the subject of the literature and the arts of the United States. The subjects are so meagre as to render it a task that would require no small portion of the talents necessary to figure in either, in order to render them of interest. Still, as the request has come in so urgent a form, I shall endeavour to oblige you.

The Americans have been placed, as respects moral and intellectual advancement, different from all other infant nations. They have never been without the wants of civilization, nor have they ever been entirely without the means of a supply. Thus pictures, and books, and statuary, and every thing else which appertains to elegant life, have always been known to them in an abundance, and of a quality exactly proportioned to their cost. Books, being the cheapest, and the nation having great leisure and prodigious zest for information, are not only the most common, as you will readily suppose, but they are probably more common than among any other people. I scarcely remember ever to have entered an American dwelling, however humble, without finding fewer or more books. As they form the most essential division of the subject, not only on account of their greater frequency, but on account of their far greater importance, I shall give them the first notice in this letter.

Unlike the progress of the two professions in the countries of our hemisphere, in America the printer came into existence

[1] Superior figures throughout the text refer to correspondingly numbered notes at the end of the volume, pp. 327 ff.

before the author.[2] Reprints of English works gave the first
employment to the press. Then came almanacs, psalm-books,
religious tracts, sermons, journals, political essays, and even
rude attempts at poetry. All these preceded the revolution. The
first journal was established in Boston at the commencement
of the last century. There are several original polemical works
of great originality and power that belong to the same period.
I do not know that more learning and talents existed at that
early day in the States of New-England than in Virginia, Maryland and the Carolinas, but there was certainly a stronger desire
to exhibit them.

The colleges or universities, as they were somewhat prematurely called, date very far back in the brief history of the
country.[3] There is no stronger evidence of the intellectual
character, or of the judicious ambition of these people, than
what this simple fact furnishes. Harvard College, now the
university of Cambridge—(it better deserves the title at this
day)—was founded in 1638; within less than *twenty years* after
the landing of the first settlers in New-England! Yale (in Connecticut) was founded in 1701. Columbia (in the city of New-
York) was founded in 1754. Nassau Hall (in New-Jersey) in
1738; and William and Mary (in Virginia) as far back as 1691.
These are the oldest literary institutions in the United States,
and all but the last are in flourishing conditions to the present
hour. The first has given degrees to about five thousand graduates, and rarely has less than three hundred and fifty or four
hundred students. Yale is about as well attended. The others
contain from a hundred and fifty to two hundred under-gradu-
ates. But these are not a moiety of the present colleges, or universities, (as they all aspire to be called,) existing in the country.
There is no State, except a few of the newest, without at least
one, and several have two or three.

Less attention is paid to classical learning here than in Europe;
and, as the term of residence rarely exceeds four years, profound
scholars are by no means common. This country possesses
neither the population nor the endowments to maintain a large
class of learned idlers, in order that one man in a hundred may

contribute a mite to the growing stock of general knowledge. There is a luxury in this expenditure of animal force, to which the Americans have not yet attained. The good is far too problematical and remote, and the expense of man too certain, to be prematurely sought. I have heard, I will confess, an American legislator quote Horace and Cicero; but it is far from being the humour of the country. I thought the taste of the orator questionable. A learned quotation is rarely of any use in an argument, since few men are fools enough not to see that the application of any maxim to politics is liable to a thousand practical objections, and, nine times in ten, they are evidences of the want of a direct, natural, and vigorous train of thought. They are the affectations, but rarely the ebullitions of true talent. When a man feels strongly, or thinks strongly, or speaks strongly, he is just as apt to do it in his native tongue as he is to laugh when he is tickled, or to weep when in sorrow. The Americans are strong speakers and acute thinkers, but no great quoters of the morals and axioms of a heathen age, because they happen to be recorded in Latin.

The higher branches of learning are certainly on the advance in this country. The gentlemen of the middle and southern States, before the revolution, were very generally educated in Europe, and they were consequently, in this particular, like our own people.[4] Those who came into life during the struggle, and shortly after, fared worse. Even the next generation had little to boast of in the way of instruction. I find that boys entered the colleges so late as the commencement of the present century, who had read a part of the Greek Testament, and a few books of Cicero and Virgil, with perhaps a little of Horace. But great changes have been made, and are still making, in the degree of previous qualification.

Still, it would be premature to say that there is any one of the American universities where classical knowledge, or even science, is profoundly attained, even at the present day. Some of the professors push their studies, for a life, certainly; and you well know, after all, that little short of a life, and a long one too, will make any man a good general scholar. In 1820, near eight thousand graduates of the twelve oldest colleges of this country (according to their catalogues) were then living. Of this number, 1,406 were clergymen. As some of the catalogues consulted were several years old, this number was of necessity greatly within the truth. Between the years 1800 and 1810, it is found that of 2,792 graduates, four hundred and fifty-three became clergymen. Here is pretty good evidence that religion is not neglected in America, and that its ministers are not, as a matter of course, absolutely ignorant.

But the effects of the literary institutions of the United States are somewhat peculiar. Few men devote their lives to scholarship. The knowledge that is actually acquired, is perhaps quite sufficient for the more practical and useful pursuits. Thousands of young men, who have read the more familiar classics, who have gone through enough of mathematics to obtain a sense of their own tastes, and of the value of precision, who have cultivated *belles lettres* to a reasonable extent, and who have been moderately instructed in the arts of composition, and in the rules of taste, are given forth to the country to mingle in its active employments. I am inclined to believe that a class of American graduates carries away with it quite as much general and diversified knowledge, as a class from one of our own universities. The excellence in particular branches is commonly wanting; but the deficiency is more than supplied by variety of information. The youth who has passed four years within the walls of a college, goes into the office of a lawyer for a few more. The profession of the law is not subdivided in America. The same man is counsellor, attorney, and conveyancer. Here the student gets a general insight into the principles, and a familiarity with the practice of the law, rather than an acquaintance with the study as a science. With this instruction he enters the world as a practitioner. Instead of existing in a state of dreaming retrospection, lost in a maze of theories, he is at once turned loose into the jostlings of the world. If perchance he encounters an antagonist a little more erudite than himself, he seizes the natural truth for his sheet-anchor, and leaves precedent and quaint follies to him who has made them his study and delight. No doubt he often blunders, and is frequently, of necessity, defeated. But in the course of this irreverent treatment, usages and opinions, which are bottomed in no better foundation than antiquity, and which are as inapplicable to the present state of the world, as the present state of the world is, or ought to be, unfavourable to all feudal absurdities, come to receive their death-warrants. In the mean time, by dint of sheer experience, and by the collision of intellects, the practitioner gets a stock of learning, that is acquired in the best possible school; and, what is of far more importance, the laws themselves get a dress which brings them within the fashions of the day. This same man becomes a legislator perhaps, and, if particularly clever, he is made to take an active part in the framing of laws that are not to harmonize with the other parts of an elaborate theory, but which are intended to make men comfortable and happy. Now, taken with more or less qualification, this is the history of thousands in this country, and it is also an important part of the history of the country itself.

In considering the course of instruction in the United States, you are always to commence at the foundation. The common schools, which so generally exist, have certainly elevated the population above that of any other country, and are still elevating it higher, as they improve and increase in numbers. Law is getting every day to be more of a science, but it is a science that is forming rules better adapted to the spirit of the age. Medicine is improving, and in the cities it is, perhaps now, in point of practice, quite on a level with that of Europe.[5] Indeed, the well-educated American physician very commonly enjoys an advantage that is little known in Europe. After obtaining a degree in his own country, he passes a few years in London, Edinburgh, Paris, and frequently in Germany, and returns with his gleanings from their several schools. This is not the case with one individual, but with many, annually. Indeed, there is so much of a fashion in it, and the custom is attended by so many positive advantages, that its neglect would be a serious obstacle to any very eminent success. Good operators are by no means scarce, and as surgery and medicine are united in the same person, there is great judgment in their practice. Human life is something more valuable in America than in Europe, and I think a critical attention to patients more common here than with us, especially when the sufferer belongs to an inferior condition in life. The profession is highly respectable; and in all parts of the country the better sort of its practitioners mingle, on terms of perfect equality, with the highest classes of society. There are several physicians in Congress, and a great many in the different State legislatures.

Of the ministry it is unnecessary to speak. The clergy are of all denominations, and they are educated, or not, precisely as they belong to sects which consider the gift of human knowledge of any importance. You have already seen how large a proportion of the graduates of some of the colleges enter the desk.

As respects authorship, there is not much to be said. Compared to the books that are printed and read, those of native origin are few indeed. The principal reason of this poverty of original writers, is owing to the circumstance that men are not yet driven to their wits for bread. The United States are the first nation that possessed institutions, and, of course, distinctive opinions of its own, that was ever dependent on a foreign people for its literature. Speaking the same language as the English, and long in the habit of importing their books from the mother country, the revolution effected no immediate change in the nature of their studies, or mental amusements. The works were re-printed, it is true, for the purposes of economy, but they still continued English. Had the latter nation used this powerful engine with tolerable address, I think they would have secured such an ally in this country as would have rendered their own decline not only more secure, but as illustrious as had been their rise. There are many theories entertained as to the effect produced in this country by the falsehoods and jealous calumnies which have been undeniably uttered in the mother country, by means of the press, concerning her republican descendant. It is my opinion that, like all other ridiculous absurdities, they have defeated themselves, and that they are now more laughed at and derided, even here, than resented. By all that I can learn, twenty years ago, the Americans were, perhaps, far too much disposed to receive the opinions and to adopt the prejudices of their relatives; whereas, I think it is very apparent that they are now beginning to receive them with singular distrust. It is not worth our while to enter further into this subject, except as it has had, or is likely to have, an influence on the national literature.*

It is quite obvious, that, so far as taste and forms alone are concerned, the literature of England and that of America must be fashioned after the same models. The authors, previously to the revolution, are common property, and it is quite idle to say that the American has not just as good a right to claim Milton, and Shakspeare, and all the old masters of the language, for his countrymen, as an Englishman. The Americans having continued to cultivate, and to cultivate extensively, an acquaintance with the writers of the mother country, since the separation, it is evident they must have kept pace with the trifling changes of the day. The only peculiarity that can, or ought to be expected in their literature, is that which is connected with the promulgation of their distinctive political opinions.[6] They have not been remiss in this duty, as any one may see, who chooses to examine their books. But we will devote a few minutes to a more minute account of the actual condition of American literature.

The first, and the most important, though certainly the most familiar branch of this subject, is connected with the public journals. It is not easy to say how many newspapers are printed in the United States. The estimated number varies from six hundred to a thousand. In the State of New-York there are more than fifty counties. Now, it is rare that a county, in a

* The writer might give, in proof of this opinion, one fact. He is led to believe that, so lately as within ten years, several English periodical works were re-printed, and much read in the United States, and that now they patronize their own, while the former are far less sought, though the demand, by means of the increased population, should have been nearly doubled. Some of the works are no longer even re-printed. [*Cooper's note.*]

State as old as that of New-York, (especially in the more northern parts of the country), does not possess one paper at least. The cities have many. The smaller towns sometimes have three or four, and very many of the counties four or five. There cannot be many less than one hundred and fifty journals in the State of New-York alone. Pennsylvania is said to possess eighty. But we will suppose that these two States publish two hundred journals. They contain about 3,000,000 of inhabitants. As the former is an enlightened State, and the latter rather below the scale of the general intelligence of the nation, it may not be a very bad average of the whole population. This rate would give eight hundred journals for the United States, which is probably something within the truth.[7] I confess, however, this manner of equalizing estimates in America, is very uncertain in general, since a great deal, in such a question, must depend on the progress of society in each particular section of the country.

As might be expected, there is nearly every degree of merit to be found in these journals. No one of them has the benefit of that collected talent which is so often enlisted in the support of the more important journals of Europe. There is not often more than one editor to the best; but he is usually some man who has seen, in his own person, enough of men and things to enable him to speak with tolerable discretion on passing events. The usefulness of the American journals, however, does not consist in their giving the tone to the public mind, in politics and morals, but in imparting facts. It is certain that, could the journals agree, they might, by their united efforts, give a powerful inclination to the common will. But, in point of fact, they do not agree on any one subject, or set of subjects, except, perhaps, on those which directly affect their own interests. They, consequently, counteract, instead of aiding each other, on all points of disputed policy; and it is in the bold and sturdy discussions that follow, that men arrive at the truth. The occasional union in their own favour, is a thing too easily seen through to do either good or harm. So far, then, from the journals succeeding in leading the public opinion astray, they are invariably obliged to submit to it. They serve to keep it alive, by furnishing the means for its expression, but they rarely do more. Of course, the influence of each particular press is in proportion to the constancy and the ability with which it is found to support what is thought to be sound principles; but those principles must be in accordance with the private opinions of men, or most of their labour is lost.

The public press in America is rather more decent than that of England, and less decorous than that of France. The tone of the nation, and the respect for private feelings, which are, perhaps, in some measure, the consequence of a less artificial state of society, produce the former; and the liberty, which is a necessary attendant of fearless discussion, is, I think, the cause of the latter. The affairs of an individual are rarely touched upon in the journals of this country; never, unless it is thought they have a direct connexion with the public interests, or from a wish to do him good. Still there is a habit, getting into use in America, no less than in France, that is borrowed from the English, which proves that the more unworthy feelings of our nature are common to men under all systems, and only need opportunity to find encouragement. I allude to the practice of repeating the proceedings of the courts of justice, in order to cater to a vicious appetite for amusement in the public.

It is pretended that, as a court of justice is open to the world, there can be no harm in giving the utmost publicity to its proceedings. It is strange the courts should act so rigidly on the principle, that it is better a dozen guilty men should go free, than that one innocent man should suffer, and yet permit the gross injustice that is daily done by means of this practice. One would think, that if a court of justice is so open to the world, that it should be the business of the people of the world to enter it, in order that they might be certain that the information they crave should be without colouring or exaggeration. It is idle to say that the reports are accurate, and that he who reads is enabled to do justice to the accused, by comparing the facts that are laid before him. A reporter may give the expression of the tongue; but can he convey that of the eye, of the countenance, or of the form?—without regarding all of which, no man is perfectly master of the degree of credibility that is due to any witness of whose character he is necessarily ignorant. But every man has an infallible means of assuring himself of the value of these reports. Who has ever read a dozen of them without meeting with one (or perhaps more,) in which the decision of the court and jury is to him a matter of surprise? It is true he assumes, that those who were present knew best, and as he has no great interest in the matter, he is commonly satisfied. But how is it with the unfortunate man who is wrongfully brought out of his retirement to repel an unjust attack against his person, his property, or his character? If he be a man of virtue, he is a man of sensibility; and not only he, but, what is far worse, those tender beings, whose existence is wrapped up in his own, are to be wounded daily and hourly, for weeks at a time, in order that a depraved appetite should be glutted. It is enough for justice that her proceedings should be so public as to prevent the danger of corruption; but we pervert a blessing to a curse, in making that which was intended for our protection, the means of so much individual misery. It is an unavoidable evil of the law that it necessarily works some wrong, in order to do much good; but it is cruel that even the acquittal of a man should be unnecessarily circulated, in a manner to make all men remember that he had been accused. We have proof of the consequences of this practice in England. Men daily shrink from resistance to base frauds, rather than expose themselves to the observations and comments of those who enliven their breakfasts by sporting with these exhibitions of their fellow-creatures. There are, undoubtedly, cases of that magnitude which require some sacrifice of private feelings, in order that the community should reap the advantage; but the regular books are sufficient for authorities— the decisions of the courts are sufficient for justice—and the utmost possible oblivion should prove as nearly sufficient as may be to serve the ends of a prudent and righteous humanity.

Nothing can be more free than the press of this country, on all subjects connected with politics.[8] Treason cannot be written, unless by communicating with an open enemy. There is no other protection to a public man than that which is given by an independent jury, which punishes, of course, in proportion to the dignity and importance of the injured party. But the utmost lenity is always used in construing the right of the press to canvass the public acts of public men. Mere commonplace charges defeat themselves, and get into discredit so soon as to be lost, while graver accusations are met by grave replies. There is no doubt that the complacency of individuals is sometimes disturbed by these liberties; but they serve to keep the officers of the government to their work, while they rarely do any lasting, or even temporary injury. Serious and criminal accusations against a public man, if groundless, are, by the law of reason, a crime against the community, and, as such, they are punished. The general principle observed in these matters is very simple. If A. accuse B. of an act that is an offence against law, he may be called on for his proof, and if he fail he must take the consequences. But an editor of a paper, or any one else, who should bring a criminal charge, no matter how grave, against the President, and who could prove it, is just as certain of doing it with impunity, as if he held the whole power in his own hands. He would be protected by the invincible shield of public opinion, which is not only in consonance with the law, but which, in this country, makes law.

Actions for injuries done by the press, considering the number of journals, are astonishingly rare in America. When one remembers the usual difficulty of obtaining legal proof, which is a constant temptation, even to the guilty, to appeal to the courts; and, on the other hand, the great freedom of the press, which is a constant temptation to abuse the trust, this fact, in itself, furnishes irresistible evidence of the general tone of decency which predominates in this nation. The truth is, that public opinion, among its other laws, has imperiously prescribed that, amidst the utmost latitude of discussion, certain limits shall not be passed; and public opinion, which is so completely the offspring of a free press, must be obeyed in this, as well as in other matters.

Leaving the journals, we come to those publications which

make their appearance periodically. Of these there are a good many, some few of which are well supported. There are several scientific works, that are printed monthly, or quarterly, of respectable merit, and four or five reviews. Magazines of a more general character are not much encouraged. England, which is teeming with educated men, who are glad to make their bread by writing for these works, still affords too strong a competition for the success of any American attempts, in this species of literature. Though few, perhaps no English magazine is actually republished in America, a vast number are imported and read in the towns, where the support for any similar original production must first be found.

The literature of the United States, has indeed, too [two] powerful obstacles to conquer before (to use a mercantile expression) it can ever enter the markets of its own country on terms of perfect equality with that of England. Solitary and individual works of genius may, indeed, be occasionally brought to light, under the impulses of the high feeling which has conceived them; but, I fear, a good, wholesome, profitable and continued pecuniary support, is the applause that talent most craves.[9] The fact, that an American publisher can get an English work without money, must, for a few years longer, (unless legislative protection shall be extended to their own authors,) have a tendency to repress a national literature. No man will pay a writer for an epic, a tragedy, a sonnet, a history, or a romance, when he can get a work of equal merit for nothing. I have conversed with those who are conversant on the subject, and, I confess, I have been astonished at the information they imparted.

A capital American publisher has assured me that there are not a dozen writers in this country, whose works he should feel confidence in publishing at all, while he reprints hundreds of English books without the least hesitation. This preference is by no means so much owing to any difference in merit, as to the fact that, when the price of the original author is to be added to the uniform hazard which accompanies all literary speculations, the risk becomes too great. The general taste of the reading world in this country is better than that of England.* The fact is both proved and explained by the circumstance that thousands of works that are printed and read in the mother country, are not printed and read here. The publisher on this side of the Atlantic has the advantage of seeing the reviews of every book he wishes to print, and, what is of far more importance, he knows, with the exception of books that he is sure of selling, by means of a name, the decision of the English critics before he makes his choice. Nine times in ten, popularity, which is all he looks for, is a sufficient test of general merit. Thus, while you find every English work of character, or notoriety, on the shelves of an American book-store, you may ask in vain for most of the trash that is so greedily devoured in the circulating libraries of the mother country, and which would be just as eagerly devoured here, had not a better taste been created by a compelled abstinence. That taste must now be overcome before such works could be sold at all.

When I say that books are not rejected here, from any want of talent in the writers, perhaps I ought to explain. I wish to express something a little different. Talent is sure of too many avenues to wealth and honours, in America, to seek, unnecessarily, an unknown and hazardous path. It is better paid in the ordinary pursuits of life, than it would be likely to be paid by an adventure in which an extraordinary and skilful, because practised, foreign competition is certain. Perhaps high talent does not often make the trial with the American bookseller; but it is precisely for the reason I have named.

The second obstacle against which American literature has to contend, is in the poverty of materials.[10] There is scarcely an ore which contributes to the wealth of the author, that is found, here, in veins as rich as in Europe. There are no annals for the historian; no follies (beyond the most vulgar and commonplace) for the satirist; no manners for the dramatist; no

---

* The writer does not mean that the best taste of America is better than that of England; perhaps it is not quite so good; but, as a whole, the American reading world requires better books than the whole of the English reading world. [*Cooper's note.*]

obscure fictions for the writer of romance; no gross and hardy offences against decorum for the moralist; nor any of the rich artificial auxiliaries of poetry. The weakest hand can extract a spark from the flint, but it would baffle the strength of a giant to attempt kindling a flame with a pudding-stone. I very well know there are theorists who assume that the society and institutions of this country are, or ought to be, particularly favourable to novelties and variety. But the experience of one month, in these States, is sufficient to show any observant man the falsity of their position. The effect of a promiscuous assemblage any where, is to create a standard of deportment; and great liberty permits every one to aim at its attainment. I have never seen a nation so much alike in my life, as the people of the United States, and what is more, they are not only like each other, but they are remarkably like that which common sense tells them they ought to resemble. No doubt, traits of character that are a little peculiar, without, however, being either very poetical, or very rich, are to be found in remote districts; but they are rare, and not always happy exceptions. In short, it is not possible to conceive a state of society in which more of the attributes of plain good sense, or fewer of the artificial absurdities of life, are to be found, than here. There is no costume for the peasant, (there is scarcely a peasant at all,) no wig for the judge, no baton for the general, no diadem for the chief magistrate. The darkest ages of their history are illuminated by the light of truth; the utmost efforts of their chivalry are limited by the laws of God; and even the deeds of their sages and heroes are to be sung in a language that would differ but little from a version of the ten commandments. However useful and respectable all this may be in actual life, it indicates but one direction to the man of genius.

It is very true there are a few young poets now living in this country, who have known how to extract sweets from even these wholesome, but scentless native plants. They have, however, been compelled to seek their inspiration in the universal laws of nature, and they have succeeded, precisely in proportion as they have been most general in their application. Among these gifted young men, there is one (Halleck)[11] who is remarkable for an exquisite vein of ironical wit, mingled with a fine, poetical, and, frequently, a lofty expression. This gentleman commenced his career as a satirist in one of the journals of New-York. Heaven knows, his materials were none of the richest; and yet the melody of his verse, the quaintness and force of his comparisons, and the exceeding humour of his strong points, brought him instantly into notice. He then attempted a general satire, by giving the history of the early days of a *belle*. He was again successful, though every body, at least every body of any talent, felt that he wrote in leading-strings. But he happened, shortly after the appearance of the little volume just named, (Fanny,) to visit England. Here his spirit was properly excited, and, probably on a rainy day, he was induced to try his hand at a *jeu d'esprit*, in the mother country. The result was one of the finest semi-heroic ironical descriptions to be found in the English language.* This simple fact, in itself, proves the truth of a great deal of what I have just been writing, since it shows the effect a superiority of material can produce on the efforts of a man of true genius.

Notwithstanding the difficulties of the subject, talent has even done more than in the instance of Mr. Halleck. I could mention several other young poets of this country of rare merit. By mentioning Bryant, Percival, and Sprague, I shall direct your attention to the names of those whose works would be most likely to give you pleasure. Unfortunately they are not yet known in Italian, but I think even you would not turn in distaste from the task of translation which the best of their effusions will invite.

The next, though certainly an inferior branch of imaginative writing, is fictitious composition. From the facts just named, you cannot expect that the novelists, or romance writers of the United States, should be very successful. The same reason will be likely, for a long time to come, to repress the ardour of dramatic genius. Still, tales and plays are no novelties in the

---

* This little *morceau* of pleasant irony is called Alnwick Castle. [*Cooper's note.*]

literature of this country. Of the former, there are many as old
as soon after the revolution; and a vast number have been published within the last five years. One of their authors of romance, who curbed his talents by as few allusions as possible to
actual society, is distinguished for power and comprehensive-
ness of thought.[12] I remember to have read one of his books
(Wieland) when a boy, and I take it to be a never-failing evidence of genius, that, amid a thousand similar pictures which
have succeeded, the images it has left, still stand distinct and
prominent in my recollection. This author (Mr. Brockden
Brown) enjoys a high reputation among his countrymen, whose
opinions are sufficiently impartial, since he flattered no particular prejudice of the nation in any of his works.

The reputation of Irving is well known to you. He is an
author distinguished for a quality (humour) that has been
denied his countrymen; and his merit is the more rare, that it
has been shown in a state of society so cold and so restrained.
Besides these writers, there are many others of a similar character, who enjoy a greater or less degree of favour in their own
country.[13] The works of two or three have even been translated (into French) in Europe, and a great many are reprinted in
England. Though every writer of fiction in America has to contend against the difficulties I have named, there is a certain
interest in the novelty of the subject, which is not without its
charm. I think, however, it will be found that they have all
been successful, or the reverse, just as they have drawn warily,
or freely, on the distinctive habits of their own country. I now
speak of their success purely as writers of romance. It certainly would be possible for an American to give a description
of the manners of his own country, in a book that he might
choose to call a romance, which should be read, because the
world is curious on the subject, but which would certainly
never be read for that nearly indefinable poetical interest which
attaches itself to a description of manners less bald and uniform.
All the attempts to blend history with romance in America,
have been comparatively failures, (and perhaps fortunately,)
since the subjects are too familiar to be treated with the freedom

that the imagination absolutely requires. Some of the descriptions of the progress of society on the borders, have had a rather better success, since there is a positive, though no very poetical, novelty in the subject; but, on the whole, the books which have been best received, are those in which the authors have trusted most to their own conceptions of character, and to qualities that are common to the rest of the world and to human nature. This fact, if its truth be admitted, will serve to prove that the American writer must seek his renown in the exhibition of qualities that are general, while he is confessedly compelled to limit his observations to a state of society that has a wonderful tendency not only to repress passion, but to equalize humours.

The Americans have always been prolific writers on polemics and politics. Their sermons and fourth of July orations are numberless. Their historians, without being very classical or very profound, are remarkable for truth and good sense.[14] There is not, perhaps, in the language a closer reasoner in metaphysics than Edwards; and their theological writers find great favour among the sectarians of their respective schools.

The stage of the United States is decidedly English.[15] Both plays and players, with few exceptions, are imported. Theatres are numerous, and they are to be found in places where a traveller would little expect to meet them. Of course they are of all sizes, and of every degree of decoration and architectural beauty known in Europe, below the very highest. The façade of the principal theatre in Philadelphia, is a chaste specimen in marble, of the Ionic, if my memory is correct. In New-York, there are two theatres about as large as the Théâtre Français (in the interior), and not much inferior in embellishments. Besides these, there is a very pretty little theatre, where lighter pieces are performed, and another with a vast stage for melo-dramas. There are also one or two other places of dramatic representation in this city, in which horses and men contend for the bays.

The Americans pay well for dramatic talent. Cooke, the greatest English tragedian of our age, died on this side of the Atlantic; and there are few players of eminence in the mother

country who are not tempted, at some time or other, to cross
the ocean. Shakspeare is, of course, the great author of America,
as he is of England, and I think he is quite as well relished here
as there. In point of taste, if all the rest of the world be any
thing against England, that of America is the best, since it unquestionably approaches nearest to that of the continent of
Europe. Nearly one-half of the theatrical taste of the English is
condemned by their own judgments, since the stage is not much
supported by those who have had an opportunity of seeing any
other. You will be apt to ask me how it happens, then, that the
American taste is better? Because the people, being less exaggerated in their habits, are less disposed to tolerate caricatures,
and because the theatres are not yet sufficiently numerous
(though that hour is near) to admit of a representation that shall
not be subject to the control of a certain degree of intelligence.
I have heard an English player complain that he never saw such
a dull audience as the one before which he had just been exhibiting; and I heard the same audience complain that they
never listened to such dull jokes. Now, there was talent enough
in both parties; but the one had formed his taste in a coarse
school, and the others had formed theirs under the dominion of
common sense. Independently of this peculiarity, there is a vast
deal of acquired, travelled taste in this country. English
tragedy, and high English comedy, both of which, you know,
are excellent, never fail here, if well played; that is, they never
fail under the usual limits of all amusement. One will cloy of
sweets. But the fact of the taste and judgment of these people,
in theatrical exhibitions, is proved by the number of their good
theatres, compared to their population.

Of dramatic writers there are none, or next to none. The
remarks I have made in respect to novels apply with double
force to this species of composition. A witty and successful
American comedy could only proceed from extraordinary
talent. There would be less difficulty, certainly, with a tragedy;
but still, there is rather too much foreign competition, and too
much domestic employment in other pursuits, to invite genius
to so doubtful an enterprise. The very baldness of ordinary

American life is in deadly hostility to scenic representation. The character must be supported solely by its intrinsic power. The judge, the footman, the clown, the lawyer, the belle, or the beau, can receive no great assistance from dress. Melo-dramas, except the scene should be laid in the woods, are out of the question. It would be necessary to seek the great clock, which is to strike the portentous twelve blows, in the nearest church; a vaulted passage would degenerate into a cellar; and, as for ghosts, the country was discovered, since their visitations have ceased. The smallest departure from the incidents of ordinary life would do violence to every man's experience; and, as already mentioned, the passions which belong to human nature must be delineated, in America, subject to the influence of that despot—common sense.

Notwithstanding the overwhelming influence of British publications, and all the difficulties I have named, original books are getting to be numerous in the United States. The impulses of talent and intelligence are bearing down a thousand obstacles. I think the new works will increase rapidly, and that they are destined to produce a powerful influence on the world. We will pursue this subject another time.—Adieu.

LETTER XXIV [SCIENCE AND THE ARTS]

To the Abbate Giromachi, &c. &c. Florence.

Washington, ——

—You will be satisfied with these reasons for the abrupt conclusion of my last. I shall now tax your patience for a short continuation of the subject.

Although there are so many reasons why an imaginative literature should not be speedily created in this country, there is none, but that general activity of employment which is not favourable to study, why science and all the useful arts should not be cultivated here, perhaps, more than any where else. Great attention is already paid to the latter. Though there is scarce such a thing as a capital picture in this whole country, I have seen more beautiful, graceful, and convenient ploughs in posi-

tive use here, than are probably to be found in the whole of
Europe united. In this single fact may be traced the history
of the character of the people, and the germ of their future
greatness. Their axe is admirable for form, for neatness, and
precision of weight, and it is wielded with a skill that is next to
incredible. Reapers are nearly unknown; but I have seen single
individuals enter a field of grain in the morning, and clear acres
of its golden burthen, by means of the *cradle*,* with a rapidity
that has amazed me. The vast multitude of their inventions, as
they are exhibited in the Patent Office in this city, ought to
furnish food for grave reflection to every stranger. Several large
rooms are filled with the models, many of which give evidence
of the most acute ingenuity. When one recollects the average
proportion of adults to which the population must have been
confined during the last thirty-five years,† the number of their
inventions is marvellous. A great many of these models contain no new principle, nor any new application of an old principle; but, as in such cases money has been paid by those who
deposit them there without an object, it is fair to presume that
they were inventions so far as the claimants were concerned.
There are so few means by which men, in remote districts of
this country, can profit by the ideas of other people in these
matters, that it is probable there are not a dozen machines
lodged in the office, of which the parties concerned did not
honestly believe themselves the inventors. You may estimate
the activity of thought, which distinguishes the mass of this
nation from all other people, by this fact. It is in itself a prodigious triumph to a young people to have given form and useful existence to the greatest improvement of our age; but the
steam-boats are not the only gift of this nature, by many, that
Europe has already received from the western hemisphere.

The general accumulation of science in this country is exceedingly great, though it is quite likely that few men have yet
attained to a very eminent degree of knowledge in any one

* The writer does not know whether this implement is an American
invention or not.

†The whole period that the Patent Office has been in existence. [*Cooper's* notes.]

particular branch. Still it is probable, that the amount of science in the United States, at this day, compared to what it was even fifteen years ago, and without reference to the increase of population, is as five to one, or even in still much greater proportion. Like all other learning, it is greatly on the advance.

In architecture the Americans have certainly no great reason to exult. They appear to have inherited the peculiarity of their ancestors, in all matters of mere taste. Their houses are mostly built of wood in the country and in the villages, and of bricks in the towns. There are, however, exceptions, in all cases, which reverse the rule. There are many farm-houses, seats, churches, court-houses, &c. in the country and smaller towns, which are of stone. Marble and granite are getting a good deal into use, too, in the more northern cities. The principal motive which controls their taste is economy. It is commonly cheapest to build of wood in the country, but where stone is at hand, and of a good quality, it begins to be preferred, in what may be called the second and third stages of the settlements. As the materials are cheap, the buildings are in common much larger than would be occupied by men of the same wealth in Europe. A house of forty or of forty-five feet front, and of thirty or thirty-five feet in depth, of two stories, with cellars, and garret, and with offices attached, is a usual dwelling for the owner of one or of two hundred acres of land, in a part of the country that has been under cultivation thirty or forty years. Such a man may be worth from five to ten thousand dollars. He has his growing orchard; fifty sheep; some eight or ten cows; a stock of young cattle; three or four horses; one or two yoke of oxen; hogs, poultry, and all the other provisions of a small farm. He grows his own maize; fattens his own pork; makes his own cider; kills his own beef; raises his own wheat, rye, and flax; and, in short, lives as much as possible on the articles of his own production. There are thousands and tens of thousands of these sturdy, independent yeomen in the eastern, middle and north-western States.

The villas and country-seats are commonly pretty, without

ever attaining much elegance of size. A better sort of American
country-house will cover perhaps sixty or seventy feet of
ground in length, and from fifty to sixty in depth. There are
some of twice this size; but I should say the first was a fair
average. There are a great many a size smaller. The expense
of building is, of course, in proportion to the general cost of
every article in the particular place where the house is erected.
I am told the best buildings in New-York cost from thirty to
forty thousand dollars. A few are even much more expensive.
But the town-houses, occupied by a majority of their gentlemen (those who own their own dwellings), cost probably
something under twenty thousand.* These are the habitations
of the rich, exclusively. They are every where exceedingly
neat, prettily furnished, frequently with great elegance, and are
always comfortable.

As some general idea of the state of the useful arts must have
been obtained, in the course of my previous letters to the
fraternity, I shall now pass to those which are intended exclusively to embellish life.

The United States, considered with reference to their means
and opportunities, have been exceedingly prolific in painters.[16]
It is rather remarkable, that, in a country where active and less
hazardous employments are so open to talent, men should take
an inclination to a pursuit that is rarely profitable, and in which
mediocrity is as annoying as success is triumphant. I cannot
say that the majority of these gentlemen acknowledge that the
fine arts are greatly encouraged in America, nor has it yet been
my happy lot to enter a country in which artists and authors
were very generally of opinion that the pen and the pencil received the rewards and honours which no one will deny they

---

* The writer afterwards saw a row of buildings in New-York of the following cost and dimensions; twenty-five feet front, (in marble) fifty-five
feet deep, and of three stories, besides the basement. The lots were two
hundred feet in depth. The buildings were about as well finished as a
third-rate London town-house. The cost of the whole was ten thousand
dollars, and the rent six hundred dollars a-year. These houses were in the
dearest city of America, but not in the dearest part of the town. [*Cooper's
note.*]

merit. A very great majority of the American artists are portrait painters. Some of them are highly esteemed by their own
countrymen, and certainly there are a few of a good deal of
merit. They are generally more distinguished for spirit and
character, than for finish or grace; but it is quite evident that, as
a class, they are rapidly improving. Drawing is the point in
which they chiefly fail; and this, too, is probably an inherited
defect, since most of them are disciples of the English school.

There are some highly respectable professional landscape
painters. One of them (a Mr. Cole) possesses the rare faculty
of giving to his pictures the impression of nature, to a degree so
extraordinary, that he promises to become eminent. You know
my eye is only for nature. I have heard both high eulogiums
and sneering critiques on the powers of this young man, as an
artist; some declaring that he has reached a point far beyond
that attained by any of his competitors, and others denying
that he knows how to make a sky look blue, *secundum artem.*
To me his scenery is like the scenery from which he drew; and
as he has taste and skill enough to reject what is disagreeable,
and to arrange the attractive parts of his pictures, I only hope
he will continue to study the great master from whom he has
drawn his first inspirations. America has produced several
historical painters. West, though a native of this country, and,
perhaps with a pardonable vanity, claimed as such by these
people, was, to all intents and purposes an English artist. There
are one or two of his pupils who practise their skill here, and a
few others have aspired to the highest branch of their art. One
of them (Mr. Alston) is said to be employed on a great and
elaborate picture (the handwriting on the wall;) and as his
taste and merit are universally admitted, a good deal is expected
from his pencil. It may serve to give you a better idea of the
taste for pictures in this country, or rather of the desire which
exists to encourage talent, if I mention the price he is to receive
for this work. A company of gentlemen are said to have
bought the picture, in advance, by agreeing to pay ten thousand
dollars. I believe it is their intention to remunerate themselves
by exhibiting it, and then to deposit the work in some public

place. Cabinet pieces, by this artist, are readily sold for prices of between three hundred and a thousand dollars, and the pencil of Cole is employed as much as he pleases. There are many other artists that paint portraits and landscapes, who seldom want orders. The government of the United States has paid Trumbull thirty-two thousand dollars for the four historical paintings that are destined to fill as many compartments in the rotunda, or the great hall of the Capitol.

It is plain that the system of elementary education pursued by this country, must bring an extraordinary quantity of talent, within the influence of those causes which lead to renown. If we suppose one hundred men in America to possess the same amount of native talent as one hundred men in any other part of the world, more of it will, of necessity, be excited to action, since more individuals are placed in situations to feel and to improve their infant powers. Although a certain degree of excellence in the higher branches of learning and art, may yet be necessary to create a standard, and even for the establishments of higher schools or real universities, still the truth of this position is proved by the fact, that there already exists, among this people, a far more advanced state of improvement in all that relates to the familiar interests of life than among any other. It is true that a division of labour, and vast competition, may create a degree of minute perfection in many articles of European manufacture, that is not known in the same articles manufactured here; but I think it will be commonly found, in all such cases, that these wary people have counted the profit and cost with sufficient accuracy. As circumstances vary, they instantly improve; and, once induced to persevere, they soon fearlessly challenge competition.

The purely intellectual day of America is yet in its dawn. But its sun will not arise from darkness, like those of nations with whose experience we are familiar; nor is the approach of its meridian to be calculated by the known progress of any other people. The learned professions are now full to overflowing, not so much with learning as with incumbents, certainly, but so much so, as to begin to give a new direction to education and talents. Writers are already getting to be numerous, for literature is beginning to be profitable. Those authors who are successful, receive prices for their labours, which exceed those paid to the authors of any country, England alone excepted; and which exceed even the prices paid to the most distinguished authors of the mother country, if the difference in the relative value of money in the two countries, and in the luxury of the press, be computed. The same work which is sold in England for six dollars, is sold in the United States for two. The profit to the publisher is obtained out of a common rate of per centage. Now, as thirty-three and a third per cent. on six thousand dollars, is two thousand,* and on two thousand dollars, only six hundred and sixty-six, it is quite evident, that if both parties sell one thousand copies of a work, the English publisher pockets three times the most profit. And yet, with one or two exceptions, and notwithstanding the great difference in the population of the two countries, the English bookseller rarely sells more, if he does as many, copies of a book, than the American. It is the extraordinary demand which enables the American publisher to pay so well, and which, provided there was no English competition, would enable him to pay still better, or rather still more generally, than he does at present.

The literature of the United States is a subject of the highest interest to the civilized world; for when it does begin to be felt, it will be felt with a force, a directness, and a common sense in its application, that has never yet been known. If there were no other points of difference between this country and other nations, those of its political and religious freedom, alone, would give a colour of the highest importance to the writings of a people so thoroughly imbued with their distinctive principles, and so keenly alive to their advantages. The example of America has been silently operating on Europe for half a century; but its doctrines and its experience, exhibited with the understanding of those familiar with both, have never yet been

* This calculation supposes one-third of the price to go to the trade in discount, one-third to the expenses, and the other third to constitute the joint profit of the author and publisher. [*Cooper's note.*]

pressed on our attention. I think the time for the experiment is getting near.

A curious inquiry might be raised as to the probable fate of the English language, among so many people having equal claims to its possession. I put this question to my friend, who has kindly permitted me to give you the substance of his reply. You will at once understand that this is a subject which requires a greater knowledge of the matter in dispute, than what I, as a foreigner, can claim:—

"In order to decide which nation speaks the English language best, it becomes necessary to refer to some standard. If it be assumed that the higher classes in London are always to set the fashion in pronunciation, and the best living writers in England are to fix the meaning of words, the point is clearly decided in their favour, since one cannot see on what principle they are to be put in the wrong. That the better company of London must set the fashion for the pronunciation of words in England, and indeed for the whole English empire, is quite plain; for, as this very company comprises all those whose manners, birth, fortune, and political distinction, make them the objects of admiration, it becomes necessary to imitate their affectations, whether of speech or air, in order to create the impression that one belongs to their society. It is absurd to think that either parliament, or the stage, or the universities, or the church, can produce any very serious effect on the slighter forms of utterance adopted by this powerful caste. The player may hint at the laws of prosody for ever, unless his rule happens to suit the public ear, it becomes no more than the pronunciation of the stage. The fellow, when he gets beyond his cloisters, is glad to conceal the habits of retirement in the language of the world; and as for the member of Parliament, if he happen to be of the caste, he speaks like the rest of them; and if not, he is no better than a vulgar fellow, who is very glad to conceal his provincialisms by having as little said about them as possible. In short, the bishop might just as well expect to induce the exquisite to wear a copy of his wig, or the representative of Othello, to set the fashion of smooty faces, as either of them to think of giving the tone to pronunciation, or even to the meaning of words. A secret and lasting influence is no doubt produced by education; but fashion is far more imperious than even the laws of the schools. It is, I think, a capital mistake, to believe that either of the professions named, produce any great impression on the spoken language of England. They receive more from fashion than they give to it; and they each have their particular phrases, but they rarely go any farther than their own limits. This is more or less the case in all other European nations. The rule is more absolute, however, in England than in France, for instance, because the former has no academy, and because men of letters have far less circulation, and, of course, far less influence in society there, than in the neighbouring kingdom. The tendency of every thing in England is to aristocracy. I can conceive that the King of England might very well set a fashion in the pronunciation of a word, because, being the greatest aristocrat of the nation, the smaller ones might be ambitious of showing that they kept enough of his company to catch his imperfections of speech; but, as for the King of France, he sits too much on a pinnacle for men to presume to imitate his blunders. A powerful, wealthy, hereditary, but subsidizing aristocracy, rules all things in England; but, while wit gives up to the King and *la charte*,[17] the control of politics in France, it asserts its own prerogative over every other interest of the empire, religion, perhaps, a little excepted.

"There exists a very different state of things in America. If we had a great capital, like London, where men of leisure, and fortune, and education, periodically assembled to amuse themselves, I think we should establish a fashionable aristocracy, too, which should give the mode to the forms of speech, as well as to that of dress and deportment. Perhaps the influence of talent and wit would be as much felt in such a town as in Paris; for it is the great peculiarity of our institutions to give more influence to talents than to any one other thing. But we have no such capital, nor are we likely, for a long time to come, to have one of sufficient magnitude to produce any great effect on the language. In those States where many men of leisure and education are to be found, there are large towns, in which they pass their winters, and where, of course, they observe all those forms which are more or less peculiar to themselves. The habits of polite life, and even the pronunciation of Boston, of New-York, of Baltimore, and of Philadelphia, vary in many things, and a practised ear may tell a native of either of these places, from a native of any one of the others, by some little peculiarity of speech. There is yet no predominating influence to induce the fashionables of these towns to wish to imitate the fashionables of any other. If any place is to possess this influence, it will certainly be New-York; but I think, on an examination of the subject, that it can be made to appear that an entirely different standard for the language must be established in the United States, from that which governs so absolutely in England.

"If the people of this country were like the people of any other country on earth, we should be speaking at this moment a great variety of nearly unintelligible patois; but, in point of fact, the people of the United States, with the exception of a few of German and French descent, speak, as a body, an incomparably better English than the people of the mother country. There is not, probably, a man (of English descent) born in this country, who would not be perfectly intelligible to all whom he should meet in the streets of London, though a vast number of those he met in the streets of London would be nearly unintelligible to him. In fine, we speak our language, as a nation, better than any other people speak their language.* When one reflects on the immense surface of country that we occupy, the general accuracy, in pronunciation and in the use of words, is quite astonishing. This resemblance in speech can only be ascribed to the great diffusion of intelligence, and to the inexhaustible activity of the population, which, in a manner, destroys space.

"It is another peculiarity of our institutions, that the language of the country, instead of becoming more divided into provin-

* Of course the writer calls Italy one nation, and all Germany one nation, so far as language is concerned. [*Cooper's note.*]

cial dialects, is becoming, not only more assimilated to itself as a whole, but more assimilated to a standard which sound general principles, and the best authorities among our old writers, would justify. The distinctions in speech between New-England and New-York, or Pennsylvania, or any other State, were far greater twenty years ago than they are now. Emigration alone would produce a large portion of this change; but emigration would often introduce provincialisms without correcting them, did it not also, by bringing acute men together, sharpen wits, provoke comparisons, challenge investigations, and, finally, fix a standard.

"It has been a matter of hot dispute, for the last twenty years, in which of our large towns the best English is spoken. The result of this discussion has been to convince most people who know any thing of the matter, that perfectly pure English is spoken nowhere, and to establish the superiority, on one point in favour of Boston, on another in favour of New-York, and so on to the end of the chapter. The effect of all this controversy is, to make men think seriously on the subject, and thinking seriously is the first step in amendment. We do amend, and each year introduces a better and purer English into our country. We are obliged, as you may suppose, to have recourse to some standard to settle these contentions. What shall this standard be? It is not society, for that itself is divided on the disputed points; it cannot be the church, for there is none that will be acknowledged by all parties; it cannot be the stage, for that is composed of foreigners, and possesses little influence on morals, politics, or any thing else; nor the universities, for they are provincial, and parties to the dispute; nor Congress, for that does not represent the fashion and education of the nation; nor the court, for there is none but the President, and he is often a hot partisan; nor the fashions of speech of England, for we often find as much fault with them as we do with our own. Thus, you see, we are reduced to the necessity of consulting reason, and authority, and analogy, and all the known laws of language, in order to arrive at our object. This we are daily doing, and I think the consequence will be, that, in another generation or two, far more *reasonable* English will be used in this country than exists here now. How far this melioration or purification of our language will affect the mother country, is another question.

"It is, perhaps, twenty years too soon to expect that England will very complacently submit to receive opinions or fashions very directly from America." [What she will do twenty years later, is a question that little concerns us, dear Abbate, since I have not, and you ought not to have, any very direct interests in the fortunes of posterity.][18] "But the time has already arrived, when America is beginning to receive with great distrust fashions and opinions from England. Until within the last fifteen years, the influence of the mother country, in all things connected with mere usages, was predominant to an incredible extent; but every day is making a greater change.

"On a thousand subjects we have been rudely provoked into comparisons,—an experiment that the most faultless generally find to be attended with hazard. We are a bold though a quiet people, and names and fashions go for but little when set in opposition to the unaccommodating and downright good sense of this nation. It may be enough for an Englishman that an innovation on language is supported by the pretty lips of such or such a belle of quality and high degree; but the American sees too many pretty lips at home, to be very submissive to any foreign dictation of this sort. I think it plain, therefore, that the language must be reduced to known general rules, and rules, too, that shall be respected as such rules should be, or else we shall have a dialect distinct from that of the mother country.[19] I have not, however, the slightest apprehensions of any thing of the kind arriving, since any one who understands the use of figures can estimate the probable influence of the two nations half a century hence. I think it will be just as much the desire of England then to be in our fashion, as it was our desire twenty years ago to be in hers, and for precisely the same reason. The influence of fifty millions of people, living under one government, backed by enormous wealth, extended intelligence, a powerful literature, and unrivalled freedom, cannot be very problematical, in the eyes of any man who is capable of regarding the subject free from prejudice or passion. I very well know there is a fashion of predicting the separation of our States, and a consequent disorganization of society, which would certainly weaken that influence. These predictions were made fifty years ago with rather more confidence than they are made now, and those who know most in the matter, treat them with very little deference. But, admitting that they should be realized, in what particular will the result materially affect the question before us? A division of this republic into two or three republics, is the utmost that can be expected. There would still exist those intimate relations between the parts of our present empire which find their support in a conformity of principles, and our intercourse and literature would necessarily be essentially the same. I cannot see that the impression on the language would in any degree be weakened, except that, by dividing our power, we might retard a little the period when the weight of that power should obtain its natural and necessary preponderance. You may be assured, that, in thinking on this subject, I have not forgotten that history supplies sufficient evidence that small communities may exercise a vast influence over larger; but I do not know where to find a precedent for a large community, possessing equal activity and intelligence, submitting to be controlled, either morally or politically, by one physically much weaker. Our own history already furnishes a striking example of the very reverse; and as we are bent on perpetuating all the means of our present independence, it is fair to presume that we shall gain a moral ascendancy in the world, in proportion as we gain physical force. If a pretty duchess can now set a fashion in speech, what will not a combination of two hundred millions of persons do, (the number is not at all exaggerated if we carry the time forward a century and a half,)[20] more especially if all of them shall happen to possess a reasonable knowledge of the use of letters.

"You may have a curiosity to know something of the present state of the language in America. I have already said that there is no patois throughout the whole of this country. There is

broken English among the Germans, French, and other foreigners, but nothing that is very widely distinct from the language of London. Still there are words of perfectly provincial
use, most of which were brought from certain parts of the
mother country, and which have been preserved here, and a
few which have been introduced from wantonness or necessity.
There is much more difference in intonation, and in the pronunciation of particular words, than in the use of terms unknown
to England. The best English is spoken by the natives of the
middle States, who are purely the descendants of English parents, without being the descendants of emigrants from New-
England. The educated men of all the southern Atlantic States,
especially the members of those families which have long been
accustomed to the better society of their towns, also speak an
English but little to be distinguished from that of the best circles of the mother country. Still there are shades of difference
between these very persons, that a nice and practised ear can
detect, and which, as they denote the parts of the Union to
which they belong, must be called provincialisms. These little
irregularities of language solely arise from the want of a capital.

"Throughout all New-England, and among most of the descendants of the people of New-England, the English language
is spoken with more or less of an intonation derived, I believe,
from the western counties of England, and with a pronunciation
that is often peculiar to themselves.[21] They form so large a
proportion of the entire population of the country, that some
of their provincialisms are getting to form a part of our ordinary
language. The peculiarity of the New-England dialect (the
term is almost too strong) is most discernible in the manner in
which they dwell on the last word of a sentence, or the last
syllable of a word. It is not properly drawling, for they speak
very quick in common, much quicker than the English; so
quick, indeed, as to render syllables frequently indistinct: but,
in consequence of the peculiar pause they make on the last word,
I question if they utter a sentence in less time than those who
dwell more equally on its separate parts.* Among men of the

* The phrase of "I wonder if he did," is very common in New-England.

world and of education, this peculiarity is, of course, often lost; but education is so common, and the state of society so simple in New-England, as to produce less apparent distinction in speech and manners than it is usual to find elsewhere.

"Another marked peculiarity of New-England is the pronunciation of a great many words. The fact that a vast improvement has occurred in this respect within the last thirty years, however, goes to prove the truth of what I have just told you, no less than of the increasing intelligence of the nation.

"When I was a boy, I was sent from a middle State, for my education, to Connecticut.[22] I took with me, of course, the language of my father's house. In the first year I was laughed out of a great many correct sounds, and into a great many vulgar and disagreeable substitutes. At my return home to pass a vacation, I almost threw my sister into fits by calling one of her female friends a 'virtuous *an*-gel,' pronouncing the first syllable of the last word like the article. It was in vain that I supported my new reading by the authorities of *the university*. The whole six weeks were passed in hot discussions between my sister and myself, amidst the laughter and merriment of a facetious father, who had the habit of trotting me through my Connecticut prosody by inducing me to recite Pope's Temple of Fame, to the infinite delight of two or three waggish elder brothers, who had got their English longs and shorts in a more southern school. It was at a time of life when shaving was a delight instead of a torment. I remember they were always sure of drawing me out by introducing the subject of my beard, which I pedantically called *berd;* or, for which, if pushed a little harder than common, I gave them a choice between *berd* and *baird*. Even to this hour, it is rare to find a native of New-England who does not possess some of these marked provincialisms of speech. By a singular corruption, the word *stone* is often pronounced *stun*, while *none* is pronounced *noane*, or nearly like

---

It is usually uttered "I wonder if he de-e-e-ed," with a falling of the voice at the last word, to nearly an octave below the rest of the sentence. Sometimes there is more than one resting point, in a sentence of any length. [*Cooper's note.*]

known. The latter is almost a shibboleth, as is *nothing*, pronounced according to the natural power of the letters, instead of *nuthing*. I think, however, a great deal of the peculiarity of New-England pronunciation is to be ascribed to the intelligence of its inhabitants. This may appear a paradox; but it can easily be explained. They all read and write; but the New-England-man, at home, is a man of exceedingly domestic habits. He has a theoretical knowledge of the language, without its practice. Those who migrate lose many of their peculiarities in the mixed multitudes they encounter; but *into* New-England the current of emigration, with the exception of that which originally came from the mother country, has never set. It is vain to tell a man who has his book before him, that *cham* spells *chame*, as in *chamber;* or *an*, *ane*, as in *angel;* or *dan*, *dane*, as in *danger*. He replies by asking what sound is produced by *an*, *dan*, and *cham*. I believe it would be found, on pursuing the inquiry, that a great number of their peculiar sounds are introduced through their spelling-books, and yet there are some, certainly, that cannot be thus explained. It is not too much to say that nine people in ten, in New-England, pronounce *does*, *dooʒe*, when the mere power of the letters would make it nearer *doʒe*. There is one more singular corruption, which I shall mention before I go farther south, and which often comes from the mouths of men, even in Boston, who, in other respects, would not be much criticised for their language: the verb *to show* was formerly, and is even now, spelt *shew*, and *shewed* in its participle; I have heard men of education and manners, in Boston, say, "he *shew* me that," for, he *showed* me that.

"With these exceptions, which are sufficiently numerous, and the hard sound they almost always give the letter *u*, the people of New-England speak the language more like the people of Old-England than any other parts of our country. They speak with a closer mouth, both physically and morally, than those who live further south and west. There is also a little of a nasal sound among some of them, but it is far from being as general as the other peculiarities I have named.

"The middle States certainly speak a softer English than their brethren of the east. I should say, that when you get as far south as Maryland, the softest, and perhaps as pure an English is spoken as is any where heard. No rule on such a subject, however, is without many exceptions in the United States. The emigration alone would, as yet, prevent perfect uniformity. The voices of the American females are particularly soft and silvery; and I think the language, a harsh one at the best, is made softer by our women, especially of the middle and southern States, than you often hear it in Europe.

"New-York, Philadelphia, and Baltimore, have each their peculiar phrases. Some of the women have a habit of dwelling a little too long on the final syllables, but I think it is rare among the higher classes of society. I don't know that it exists at all, as far south as Baltimore. As you go further south, it is true, you get a slower utterance, and other slight varieties of provincialism. In Georgia, you find a positive drawl, among what are called the "crackers."[23] More or less of this drawl, and of all the peculiar sounds, are found in the south-western and western States; but they are all too new to have any fixed habits of speech of their own.

"The usual vulgar phrases which are put into the mouths of Americans, are commonly caricatured, though always founded in truth. 'I guess,' is a phrase of New-England. It is used a great deal, though not as often, as 'you know,' by a cockney. It proceeds, I think, from the cautious and subdued habit of speaking which is characteristic of these people. The gentlemen rarely use it, though I confess I have heard it, interlarding the conversation of pretty lips that derived none of their beauty from the Puritans. You see, therefore, that it has been partially introduced by the emigrants into the middle States. Criticism is here so active, just now, that it is rapidly getting into disuse. The New-Yorker frequently says, 'I suspect,' and the Virginian, 'I reckon.' But the two last are often used in the best society in the mother country.*

* The negroes have a habit of saying, "you sabber dat," for, you know that; can this be one of their African terms, or is it a corruption of "saber," or of "savoir," that has found its way to the continent from the neighbouring islands? [*Cooper's note.*]

"The difference in pronunciation and in the use of words, between the really good society of this country and that of England, is not very great. In America, we can always tell an Englishman by what we are pleased to call his provincialisms (and, quite half the time, the term is correct). I was struck at the close resemblance between the language of the higher classes in the mother country, and the higher classes of my own, especially if the latter belong to the middle States. There are certainly points of difference, but they as often proceed from affectation in individuals, as from the general habits of the two countries. Cockneyisms are quite as frequent in the language of an English gentleman, as provincialisms in the mouth of an American gentleman of the middle States. I now use the word gentleman in its strict meaning. I have heard many people of high rank in England, for instance, pronounce 'yours' as if it were spelt 'yers.' If affectations are to become laws, because they are conceived in the smoke of London, then they are right; but, if old usage, the rules of the language, and the voices of even educated men are to prevail, then are they wrong. This is but one among a hundred similar affectations that are detected every day by an attentive and critical ear. But mere rank, after all, is not always a criterion of correct pronunciation in an Englishman or an Englishwoman. I have met with people of rank who have spoken in very perceptible provincial dialects. Parliament is very far from being faultless in its English, putting the Irish, Scotch, and aldermen out of the question. I have heard a minister of state speak of the '*o*-casion,' with a heavy emphasis; and just before we sailed, I remember to have burst into involuntary laughter at hearing a distinguished orator denounce a man for having been the 'recipient of a bribe of ten guineas.' The language of Parliament is undeniably far more correct than that of Congress; but when it is recollected that the one body is a representation of the aristocracy of a condensed community, and the other a representation of the various classes of a widely-spread people, the rational odds is immensely in our favour. I am not sure that one, who took pleasure in finding fault, might not detect quite as many corruptions of the English language in the good society of the mother country, as in the good society of our own. The latter, strictly considered, bears a less proportion to our numbers, however, than the same class bears to the population of England. The amount of the whole subject I take to be simply this: allowing for all the difference in numbers, there is vastly more bad English, and a thousand times more bad grammar spoken in England than in America; and there is much more good English (also allowing for the difference in numbers) spoken there than here. Among the higher and better educated classes, there are purists in both countries, who may write and talk to the end of time; innovations have been made, are made, and will be made in both countries; but as two nations now sit in judgment on them, I think when words once get fairly into use, their triumph affords a sufficient evidence of merit to entitle them to patronage."

LETTER XXXVII [ECONOMIC RESOURCES]

To the Comte Jules de Béthizy &c. &c.

Washington, ——

My pen grows weary, for I have seen so much, and written so little to the purpose, that I feel disposed to throw it away altogether. After making the tour of the coast of New-England, and seeing all its large towns, I have returned here to prepare for my departure. I cannot quit the country, however, without giving you a summary of the information I have gained, or without indulging a little in speculations to which that information must naturally give rise.

The first reflection that is excited in the mind of an intelligent foreigner, after visiting these States, is an inquiry into the causes that have affected so much with means so limited, and in a time so short. A century ago, the whole of the 1,000,000 of square miles that are now more or less occupied by these people, did not contain a million of souls. So late as the year 1776, the population was materially under 3,000,000; nor at the time did they actually cover more than 200,000 square miles, if indeed they covered as much. But since the peace of 1783, activity, enterprise, intelligence, and skill, appear to have been contending with each other, and they have certainly produced a result that the world has never before witnessed. I have heard Europeans say, that when they have heard that the Americans, of whom they had been accustomed to think as dwellers in remote and dark forests, possessed a million of tons of shipping, they believed their neutral character had made their flag a cloak for the enterprise and wealth of other nations. No doubt their commerce was a little unnaturally forced, and many frauds did exist; but the motives for deception have ceased these dozen years, and still America has a million and a half of tonnage. Perhaps no one demonstration of the energy of this population has excited in Europe the surprise that has been created by the boldness and dexterity with which they have constructed canals, that put to shame all similar works any where else. We understand the nature and the expense of this description of public works, and we know how to make a proper estimate of the enterprise necessary to effect them. But although the system of canals, which has broke [*sic*] so suddenly into existence in the United States, within the last ten years, argues an advanced and advancing state of society, it manifests no new principle of energy. It may be a higher exhibition of the quality, since the stage of improvement demands a superior manifestation of skill; but, believe me, the spirit which has produced it has not been dormant an hour since the British colonies have achieved their independence.

Although circumstances have lessened the interest which Europe has felt in America, it may be well questioned, whether the United States do not, at this hour, enjoy a higher consideration, on our side of the Atlantic, than the political doctrines, formerly in fashion, would have given to a people so dispersed, so few in numbers, and so remote.[24] Their vast and growing commerce, alone, makes them an object of the greatest attention; and the sure conviction that the child of that commerce, a marine, is likely soon to play its part in the great game of nations, gives additional interest to this republic. Still our anticipations are vague, founded on data but imperfectly understood, and, at all times, fettered by the prejudices and distinctive opinions of our own hemisphere.

In the first place, the influence of emigration on the growth of the United States has been usually overrated by Europeans. I have had occasion to say, already, that for thirty years it did not add many more than five thousand souls, annually, to the population. The fact is sufficiently known by the returns of the custom-houses, where all masters of vessels are obliged to report the number of their passengers. It is true, that thousands, who leave the mother country for the British provinces, find their way into the republic by land; but, perhaps, an equal number of natives have removed into the Canadas, the upper province of which is nearly, or quite half, peopled by emigrants from the States, or their descendants.

The first, the most important and the least understood, cause of the exceeding advance of the American States, is to be found in the character of their population. The general diffusion of a respectable degree of intelligence, would, of itself, produce an effect that it might be difficult to estimate precisely, but which may be always traced in its strongest point of view, in the respective conditions of the savage and of the civilized man. In addition to this general and mighty cause, the actual necessities of society supply an incentive to ingenuity and talent, that are wanted elsewhere. Were the American an indolent and contented being, nurtured in dulness, and kept in ignorance of the incentives which prompt men to exertion, this very state of necessity might serve to depress him still lower in the scale of being. But there is nothing more surprising in the country, than the universal knowledge which exists of the condition of Europe. Their wants, therefore, feed their desires, and, together, they give birth to all the thousand auxiliaries of exceeding ingenuity. A proof of this fact is to be found in the manner in which the first canal of any importance was constructed.[25] As it speaks volumes on the subject, I shall relate it.

Five-and-twenty years ago, engineers from Europe began to make their appearance in America. They brought with them the rules of science, and a competent knowledge of the estimates of force, and the adaptation of principles to results; but they brought them, all calculated to meet the contingencies of the European man. Experience showed that they neither knew how to allow for the difficulties of a novel situation, nor for the excess of intellect they were enabled to use. Their estimates were always wild, uncertain, and fatal, in a country that was still experimenting. But five-and-twenty years ago was too soon for canals in America. It was wise to wait for a political symptom in a country where a natural impulse will always indicate the hour for action. Though five-and-twenty, or twenty, or even fifteen years, were too soon, still ten were not. Ten years ago, demonstrations had been made which enabled keen observers to detect that the time for extraordinary exertion had come. The great western canal of New-York was conceived and planned. But instead of seeking for European engineers, a few of the common surveyors of the country were called to the aid of those who were intrusted with the duty of making the estimates; and men of practical knowledge, who understood the people with whom they had to deal, and who had tutored their faculties in the thousand collisions of active life, were brought to the task as counsellors. The result is worthy of grave attention. The work, in its fruits and in its positive extent, exceeded any thing of a similar nature ever attempted in Christendom. The authority to whom responsibility was due, was more exacting than any of our hemisphere. Economy was inculcated to a degree little known in other nations; and, in short, greater accuracy than usual was required under circumstances apparently the least favourable to attain it. Now, this canal was made (with such means) at a materially less cost, in infinitely less time, and with a boldness in the estimates, and an accuracy in the results, that were next to marvellous. There was not a man of any reputation for science employed in the work. But the utmost practical knowledge of men and of things was manifested in the whole of the affair. The beginning of each year brought its estimate of the expense, and of the profits, and the close its returns, in wonderful conformity. The labour is completed, and the benefit is exceeding the hopes of the most sanguine.

In this sketch of the circumstances under which the New-York canal has been made, we may trace the cause of the prodigious advance of this nation. Some such work as this was necessary to demonstrate to the world, that the qualities which are so exclusively the fruits of liberty and of a diffused intelligence, have an existence elsewhere than in the desires of the good. Without it, it might have been said, the advance of America is deceptive; she is doing no more than our own population could do under circumstances that admitted of so much display; but she will find the difference between felling trees, and burning forests, and giving the finish which denotes the material progress of society. The mouths of such critics are now silenced. The American can point to his ploughs, to his ships, to his canals, to his bridges, and, in short, to every thing that is useful in his particular state of society, and demand, where a better or a cheaper has been produced, under any thing like circumstances of equality?

It is vain to deny the causes or the effects of the American system, dear Béthizy; nor should a man as philanthropic as yourself wish to deny them, since they rest on principles that favour the happiness and prosperity of the human race. We should not cavil about names, nor minor distinctions, in governments, if the great and moving principles are such as contemplate the improvement of the species in the mass, and not in exclusive and selfish exceptions.

The second great cause of the advancement of the United States is the abundance which is the consequence of room and of intelligence[26] united, and which admits of so rapid an increase of its positive physical force. It is known that the population has doubled in about twenty-three years, though it is supposed that this rate of increase is gradually diminishing. It is probable that in the next fifty-five years, there will be two more duplications of the amount. Of this number, supposing that slavery continues in its present form, and under its present influences, (two things that cannot be rationally supposed,) seven millions will be slaves, and forty-three millions freemen. But slavery, though on the increase, as a whole, is known not to be on the increase in a ratio equal to that of the whites.[27]

The third cause of the great progress of this country, and it is one intimately blended with all the other moral causes, is the perfect freedom of its civil and religious institutions, which give the utmost possible play to the energies, and the strongest possible inducements to the laudable ambition of man.

There is unquestionably a powerful action and reaction between all these influences, which produce a vast combined result. A rapid review of what has been done in the way of general improvement, in the nation, may serve to give some idea of their effects.

I shall not write here of the condition of the army, and navy, and militia, since enough has been already said to furnish a sufficiently accurate knowledge of those branches of the subject.

The finances of the United States, you know to be prosperous. The public debt, at the close of the last war, (1815,) amounted to about 120,000,000 [dollars]. On the first of October, 1827, it was 68,913,541 dollars. But as seven millions of this debt was created for the purchase of the bank stock so often named, the true debt should not be estimated at more than 61,913,541 dollars.* This debt pays an interest of 6, 5, 4½, and 3 per cent. On 13,296,247 dollars, an interest of 3 per cent. is paid; on 28,831,128, an interest of 6 per cent. is paid; on 15,993,-972, an interest of 4½ per cent. is paid; on 5,792,000, an interest of 5 per cent. is paid. These sums make the amount named.[28] The gradual diminution of the debt is taking place as fast as the terms of the loans will admit, and on those portions which pay the highest rate of interest. The last *may* be redeemed in 1835, and probably *will* be redeemed, at the present rate of diminution, before the end of the next dozen years, unless some new causes for loans should occur. In addition to these facts, it must

* On the first of January 1828, it was estimated to be 67,413,377 dollars; or, deducting the seven millions for bank stock, at 60,413,377. The writer has since seen it announced, that 5,000,000 of principal will be paid on the 1st of July, 1828, so that the debt of the United States, on that day, will be about 55,413,377 dollars, if the cost of the bank stock shall be deducted. [*Cooper's note.*]

be remembered that a stock which pays but three per cent. is never worth par. Thus, if the 13,296,247 of the 3 per cents. can be bought for 80 dollars in the 100, this portion of the debt is also reduced in point of fact to 10,596,963 dollars. So that, all things considered, the whole actual debt of the United States cannot be considered as being more (on the 1st of July, 1828) than 52,714,098 dollars, or something less than 12,000,000 of pounds sterling.

In a country so united in interests, but so separated by distance, a system of extended and easy internal communications is of vital importance. Without it, neither commerce, nor political harmony, nor intelligence, could exist to the degree that is necessary to the objects of the confederation. It has therefore been effected at some cost, but in a manner that is already returning its reward in pecuniary profit, as well as in the other great essentials named. The subject naturally divides itself into three branches, viz. that of information, that of internal trade, and that of personal communication.

For the first, the general post-office, with its numberless dependencies, has been established. The diffusion of intelligence is justly considered by the American statesmen to be no less important to the preservation of their institutions, than to the general advancement of the character and power of the nation. There are in the country about 7000 post-offices, (1828,) and a nearly incalculable distance of post route. The chief of this department says, that there is now scarcely an inhabited district of any size in all these vast regions, to which the ramifications of these routes do not extend. The same admirable economy exists in the management of this department, as in all the others of the government. Although it is quite plain that comparatively little correspondence can exist to defray the expenses of routes so extended, yet the department not only pays for itself, but it is beginning to yield a small revenue to the country. One would think that, under such circumstances, the cost of letters and journals was greater here than elsewhere. You shall judge for yourself. A letter for less than thirty miles pays six cents; for less than eighty, and over thirty, ten cents; for less than one hundred and fifty miles, and over eighty, twelve and a half cents; for all distances over four hundred miles, twenty-five cents. A cent is one hundredth part of a dollar, or about an English half-penny: thus a letter will be transferred fifteen hundred miles, for a shilling sterling. Double letters pay double, until they attain a certain weight, when they begin to pay by the ounce. Printed sheets, journals, or any thing else, pay one cent, for less than one hundred miles, per sheet, and one cent and a half for all distances over. The editors of public journals receive all their printed sheets gratis. The mail is carried in coaches a great proportion of the distance, in sulkies in other portions, and on horseback the rest.

The personal communication is effected by means of stage-coaches and steam-boats. The vast rivers, and the prodigious facilities that are offered by means of the bays, enable passengers to travel with astonishing ease, rapidity and cheapness. The traveller may leave Boston by land; a ride of forty-five miles brings him to Providence; here he embarks for New-York, 200 miles further, by way of the sound of Long Island; the Raritan carries him to Brunswick; a few miles more of land carriage takes him to the Delaware; the river and bay of that name bring him to Newcastle; three hours by land, and he is on the waters of the Chesapeake; from the bay he may ascend half a dozen rivers, or proceed along the coast. At Norfolk, he enters a canal, and by means of sounds, bays, and trifling land carriage, it is quite possible to reach the southern limits of Georgia. Most of this route is travelled in the manner I have described, and the rest of it is daily getting to be more so.

The internal commerce of America exists with the least possible encumbrance. It is conducted chiefly by water, and an immense deal of it is done coastwise, by means of the rivers, that are so many arteries penetrating the country in every direction. A license costs a few dollars, (two I believe,) and when a vessel is provided with such a document, there is no impediment to its passage into any of the public waters of the country. The whole confederation is unqualifiedly one nation in respect to commerce.

The government of the United States is also making certain military roads that are intended to intersect the country in those directions in which water does not flow. In addition to these improvements, States and chartered companies are effecting a vast deal more in the same way, that I have neither the room nor the knowledge necessary to communicate. As the debt is discharged, and larger sums come into the disposal of Congress, it is to be presumed that they will increase the expenditures, by advancing the improvement of the country in all things that properly belong to their power.

In manufactures, the Americans have made immense progress, since their separation from the mother country. The great Lord Chatham declared it should be the policy of England to prevent her colonies from manufacturing even a hobnail; and this plan of monopolizing wealth was tolerably successful, so long as the Americans were dependent on England, and even for many years afterwards. But, although the importations of this country, for home consumption, are greater now than they ever have been, its own manufactures have increased fifty-fold.

The question of protecting manufactures by legislative enactments, is the one which involves more political warmth, at the present time, than any other question of mere policy.[29] Indeed, it may be said to be the only one. The disputants are chiefly men that are immediately interested in the result, though it is certain, that a few leading politicians adopt the opposite sides on policy or on principle. The only real point in dispute is, whether America has reached the period when it has become her interest to encourage her manufactures, at some little expense to her commerce, or rather at some little expense and loss to those who are engaged in particular branches of commerce, since it is obvious that nothing can have a greater tendency to increase the trade between different sections of a country like this, than increasing its objects. A vast deal is said, pro and con, on this subject. One party contends that it will destroy the shipping, and prove fatal to the revenue. If this reasoning be true, then the time is inevitable when the shipping and revenue of the United States must disappear, for nothing is more certain than that the time will come, when a vast proportion of their population will find that no great community can exist in prosperity, without a division of employment. But it is plain that these partisans utter absurdities, since it is a matter of perfect indifference to the citizen to whom or by what process he pays the dollar of duty that he is now obliged to pay for his coat. If the collector of some port does not receive it, some other collector can and will. But this dollar will be paid on an increased price, since the American manufacturer cannot put his goods in the market as cheap as the foreign manufacturer, or he would not ask for protection. This may be true at the moment, and I am of opinion, that, with the exception of articles that are deemed important to defence, and perhaps to certain articles that require some little time to give them the perfection necessary to competition, no laws will be passed immediately on the subject. The question of manufactures is, however, clearly one of interest. Of their usefulness, and of their being one of the most active agents of wealth, as well as of the comfort of society, there can be no doubt. It is therefore like so many other questions in America, purely one of time. Although it may not accord with her policy this year, to encourage them, or for her citizens to embark in them, the result is inevitable. A nation that lives as fast as this, does not compute time by ordinary calculations. Fifty years ago, they manufactured next to nothing. They now manufacture almost every article of familiar use, and very many of them, much better than the articles that are imported. They even begin to export. The coarse cotton goods of this country are already sent to South America, and I am told that they are preferred to the British. Importations of coarse cottons from India have entirely ceased; and indeed I was assured that their coarse cottons were greatly preferred in their own markets to any other.

The American manufacturer has to contend with one difficulty, that is not known to the manufacturers of other countries. The unobstructed commerce of the United States admits of importations from all quarters, and of course the consumer is accustomed to gratify his taste with the best articles. A French duke might be content to use a French knife or a French lock;

but an American merchant would reject both: he knows that the English are better. On the other hand, an English duchess (unless she could smuggle a little) might be content with an English silk; but an American lady would openly dress herself in silk manufactured at Lyons. The same is true of hundreds of other articles. The American manufacturer is therefore compelled to start into existence full grown, or nearly so, in order to command success. I think this peculiarity will have, and has had, the effect to retard the appearance of articles manufactured in the country, though it will make their final success as sure as their appearance will be sudden.

It is impossible to speak with certainty on the details of a question so complicated. A thousand articles are manufactured already, and may be considered as established. Twenty years ago, the Americans imported all their good hats; fifteen years ago, they imported most of their coarse cottons; and ten years ago, they imported most, if not all, of their fine glass and ornamental hardware, such as fire-grates, &c. A vast deal of these importations have ceased, and I am told that, considering the increase of the consumers, they are diminishing daily.

Though the particular matter that is now in dispute may be one of deep interest to certain merchants and manufacturers, it is clearly not the main question. Manufacturing is a pursuit so natural, and one so evidently necessary to all extended communities, that its adoption is inevitable at some day or other. The policy of the Americans wisely leaves them, in all cases except those of extraordinary necessity, (which become exceptions of course,) to the operation of natural influences. Policy will, nineteen times in twenty, indicate its own wants. If it be admitted that a people, who possess the raw materials in abundance, who enjoy the fruits of the earth to an excess that renders their cultivation little profitable, must have recourse to their ingenuity, and to their industry, to find new employments and different sources of wealth, then the Americans must become manufacturers. When the true hour shall arrive, it will be vain to utter speculative reasons, for the wants of the nation will work out their own cure. If restrictive laws shall be necessary to effect it, the people will allow of a lesser evil to get rid of a greater. When the manufacturers of America have once got fairly established, so that practice has given them skill, and capital has accumulated a little, there will be no fear of foreign competition. The exceeding ingenuity and wonderful aptitude of these people will give them the same superiority in the fabrication of a button or of a yard of cloth, as they now possess in the construction of a ship, or as they have manifested that they possess in the construction of a canal. A sufficient motive is all that is necessary to induce exertion. They have taken the infallible measure to insure success, in bringing the greatest possible number of competitors into action, by diffusing intelligence so widely, and to an extent so creditable. I think that most questions of manufacturing will be settled practically in the next five-and-twenty years.

The vast extent of the United States affords all the means of wealth and comfort that climate, mines, and other natural facilities, can supply. They are known to possess lead, copper, gold, iron, salt, and coal. The lead mines of Missouri are very extensive, and, with little or no skill, are already productive. The gold of Carolina is probably quite as abundant as is desirable. Copper is found in many places, but it is not yet much wrought. Iron is abundant, much worked, and some of it is more esteemed than any imported. Salt abounds, and could easily supply the whole country, or even furnish the article for exportation. It is not mined for yet, since the springs are found so saturated with the mineral as to render the process of boiling and evaporation more profitable. Coal exists in various parts of the country. It is procured, however, chiefly in Virginia, Pennsylvania, and Rhode Island. It is of various kinds, and of different degrees of excellence. That most in use is of the class *anthracite*. Of this species there are several gradations of quality. That of Pennsylvania is said to be the best. Mountains of coal exist in that State, and the people of the growing manufacturing town of Pittsburgh cut it out of the hills with as much facility as they would bring away an equal weight of dirt. Canals and railways are made to several of the coal mines, or rather coal *mountains*, and domestic coal is getting into very general use. The coal of eastern Pennsylvania is most fortunately placed. It lies within sixty or seventy miles of Philadelphia, to which place it is already conveyed by water. Philadelphia has a large capital, is now a great manufacturing town, and will probably be one of the largest in the world in the course of half a century. When at Philadelphia, coal, or any thing else, can be carried by water to any part of the country which has a water communication with the ocean.

The cultivation of the vine has commenced. Wine is already made; though, as time is absolutely necessary to produce excellence in the quality of the grape, and as capital is still easily convertible to so many lucrative uses, it is possible that half a century may elapse before the United States shall export their liquors. That they will sooner or later do so, is, I think, beyond a doubt. The silk-worm is also beginning to attract attention, and plantations of the olive are coming daily more into fashion. In short, there are no means of comfort, indulgence, or wealth, that the Americans, in some one part of their country, cannot command; and it would be as weak, as it will unquestionably be false, to suppose that a people so sagacious and so active will neglect them beyond the moment when circumstances shall render their adoption profitable or convenient.

The construction of canals, on a practical scale, the mining for coal, the exportation of cotton goods, and numberless other improvements, which argue an advancing state of society, have all sprung into existence within the last dozen years.* It is a knowledge of these facts, with a clear and sagacious understanding of their immense results, coupled with the exciting moral causes, that render the American sanguine, aspiring, and confident in his anticipations. He sees that his nation lives centuries in an age, and he feels no disposition to consider himself a child, because other people, in their dotage, choose to remember the hour of his birth.

How pitiful do the paltry criticisms of an inn, or the idle, and,

* Forty years ago, no cotton was raised in the United States. [*Cooper's note.*]

half the time, vulgar comments on the vulgarity of a *parvenu*, become, when objects and facts like these are pressing themselves on the mind! I have heard it said, that there are European authors who feel a diffidence of contracting acquaintances with American gentlemen, because they feel a consciousness of having turned the United States into ridicule! I can tell these unfortunate subjects of a precipitate opinion, that they may lay aside their scruples. No American of any character, or knowledge of his own country, can feel any thing but commiseration for the man who has attempted to throw ridicule on a nation like this. The contest is too unequal to admit of any doubt as to the result, and the wiser way will be for these Quixotes in literature to say and think as little as possible about their American tilting match, in order that the world may not liken their lances to that used by the hero of La Mancha, and their helmets to barbers' basins.

LETTER XXXVIII [POLITICAL IDEALS]

To Sir Edward Wallter, Bart. &c. &c.

Washington, ——

Having given so much of our attention to the subject of the sources of the national importance possessed by the Americans, it may not be without its use to devote an hour to the consideration of the manner in which they will probably be used. The points of main interest are, whether the present republican institutions of the country will endure, and whether the States will long continue to act as one people, or will submit to be divided into two or more confederacies.

The first fact that strikes an intelligent man, in considering the structure of this government, and the state of society that exists under it, is its perfectly natural formation. It is scarcely possible, I am not sure that it is possible, to conceive of a community which has attained the advantages of high civilization, that is less artificial.

In order that individual efforts should be excited (without which nations must inevitably become sluggish, and finally barbarous, though dwelling in any abundance,) the rights of property are respected. Beyond this the law leaves every man (the slaves in the southern States excepted) on grounds of perfect equality. This equality is, however, an equality of rights only; since talents, money, and enterprise, being left to their natural influences, produce their natural effects, and no more.

In respect to the continuation of the present republican institutions of this country, every fact, every symptom, and all reasoning, is, I think, in their favour. In the first place, they have, in substance, continued for nearly, and in some instances for quite, two centuries. The habits of the people, their education, their feelings, and their interests, unite to preserve them. It is true, there are not many instances in the world, of governments on an extended scale, existing for any great length of time, in forms nearly resembling those of the United States; but there are examples enough to prove that governments have endured for centuries on *principles* that will make this endure, though policy were less active than it is in contributing to its preservation. We will endeavour to find some of them. The government of England is representative, and to a great degree it is free; that is to say, it is a government of laws, instead of being a government of will, which I take it constitutes the essential difference between liberty and despotism. Now, the main point of difference between the government of England, and that of the United States, is in the bodies that are the respective repositories of power. In the former country, the power is in the aristocracy; in the latter country, it is in the people. That the latter is more natural, is sufficiently evident, from the fact that England itself has been quietly tending towards the same result, during two centuries, under circumstances that have been calculated to bring natural influences into play.[30] It is true, that the power still rests in the aristocracy, but it is not an aristocracy that is exclusive. To speak of the *governing* aristocracy of England, as a class of nobles, is absurd; it is the aristocracy of wealth, of talents, and of enterprise, that rules Great Britain. Were the avenues to political power closed against the approach of new aspirants, the government of Great Britain would be overturned in a dozen years. It is not in the power of art to repress the energy of natural influences, when they have once gathered head. The effect of vast commerce, of intelligence diffused to a certain degree, and of individual enterprise, has been to wrest the power from the crown, to curtail its influence in the lords, and to repose most of its exercise in the commons. Now, all that democracy can do without recourse to violence in England, is here done, because it is obeying a natural law. But the very difficulty which is found in effecting a final triumph, (as by compelling the lords to acquiesce at all times in the wishes of the commons,) proves the difficulty of completely wresting power from those who hold it, though they may happen to be the few. So far it is an argument in favour of the perpetuity of the American democracies, for they, too, are used to the authority of the people. Still, public opinion, which is no more than popular law, is so triumphant, that it is difficult to conceive a question on which a clear majority of the people of England should be decidedly united, that the three estates would incur the risk of opposing. Let us turn the picture to the side of America.

Here we have a government in which the people are the sources of power. The state of society is precisely that (though in a still higher degree) which in England has wrought a change from absolute monarchy to a species of qualified aristocracy. Instead of waiting for the march of natural events, circumstances permitted that they should be anticipated. They have been anticipated, and so far from a reaction being the result, greater harmony is daily occurring between causes and effects, as the government gets more adapted to practical objects.

I see but one possible manner in which the people of the United States can ever lose any of their liberty. They may enact laws of a more rigid character as the advancement or corruption of society shall require them, and they may possibly be driven to some slight curtailments of the franchise for the same reason: but this will, in no degree, change the principle of their government. By losing their intelligence, the people of the United States may lose the consciousness of their rights, and with it their enjoyment. But all experience goes to show how difficult it is to wrest vested rights from communities.

But the vulgar argument against the perpetuity of the American government, is the impossiblity that the rich should not govern the poor, and the intellectual the weak of mind. The continuation of property in families, and its consequent accumulation in individuals, by entails, is a provision of aristocracy in order to secure its power. The very provision itself argues a consciousness of natural weakness. It is evident, that it is as unjust, as it is opposed to our common affections, to make one child affluent at the expense of half a dozen others. No man, left to the operation of natural feeling, would do so cruel an act. This fact is sufficiently proved by the example of the Americans themselves, who have a perfect right to do this injustice if they please, by simply making those in existence, and who have a natural hold on their affections, the subjects of the wrong. Still no man does it. It is true that the father of an only son might create a sort of short entail, that should work injustice to descendants he could not know; or a father who was educated under an artificial system, where advantages are actually established from the practice, might do the same thing; but we have proof in the United States, that the father will not do it, under the operation of natural causes. Now, the Americans have taken care that this artificial state of things shall not occur, for strict entails cannot be made; and if one father should be so obdurate and unnatural as to do a wrong, in order to rob parties who were strangers to him, of their natural rights to his estate, he has no pledge that his son will be as absurd as himself. There is no truth more certain, than that property will regulate itself when left to itself. It will change hands often, and become the reward of industry, talent, and enterprise. But we have no need of speculating in order to know what effect money will produce on the institutions of America. There are thousands of rich men here, and of very rich men too, and there is not a class of the community that has less political power. There are many reasons why it should be so.

Wealth gives no direct influence in politics.[31] Seats in Con-

gress are not bought and sold. Then the owners of great
wealth are two-thirds of the time more agreeably employed in
its increase, than in courting popularity, without which, nothing political can be done; and there is also a reluctance to give
men, who have much money, places of much profit at all. But
it is plain, that wealth, even supposing it could be brought to act
in concert throughout a country like this, can never work a
change in its institutions, until it can be accumulated for generations; and that is a result the institutions themselves forbid.
Indeed, so little do I think a danger that is so often named is to
be dreaded, that I think there would be vastly more danger,
that the people of a nation like this would find means to strip
any given set of men of exorbitant wealth, than the set of men
themselves would find means to strip the nation of its liberties.
Neither case is likely to occur, however, since the danger is
scarcely within the bounds of a reasonable probability.

Talents may unite to destroy the rights of the people. I take
it, that talents are just as likely to regulate themselves, and to
produce an equality, as money. It is not in nature, that any
great number of talented men should conspire to overturn the
government, since, in the first place, it would require an improbable unanimity of talent, and, in the second place, a majority
of the conspirators would be literally selling their birthrights
for messes of pottage. If there be a country in the world where
talent has already a certain and manly road to preferment, it is in
this. Under the present system, each man can work for himself, whereas, by changing it to a monarchy, the many would
have to toil for the advantage of the few. As to those inducements which are known to influence men in Europe, such as
titles, and decorations, they are entirely artificial; and I know,
from observation, that it would be a difficult matter to get, even
now, a vast proportion of the Americans to consent to use them.
We are completely the creatures of habit in all these matters,
and it is the habit of the American to look on distinctions of this
nature with a cold eye. This peculiarity of opinion is gaining
ground daily, for there was, for a time, on precisely the same
principle of habit, a lingering of the ancient prejudices. We

should never forget that the moral influence of this nation is beginning to manifest itself in stronger colours every hour. The time, I think, is near, when the American gentleman will pride himself as much on his peculiar simplicity, as gentlemen of our nations take pride in their quarterings and titles. The strength of this feeling will keep even pace with the power of the nation, until it will become difficult indeed, to persuade a man that glories in having no worldly superior, to submit to a division of society, that, by an artificial arrangement, shall place him beneath so many others. You will remember, that the great difference between this government and most others, is the important fact, that the Americans began at the bottom to raise their superstructure, whereas we have, in nearly every instance, begun at the top to work downwards. Men have been elevated towards the throne in our systems; but in what manner are you to elevate a man who finds himself already at the summit? It is true, that if a hundred, or a thousand Americans could monopolize the honours and emoluments of a change of government, that number might conspire to keep their present elevation, and force the rest of the nation below them. But a thousand, nor ten thousand men of the highest talent, could not persuade a million to give up rights that they are educated to believe inherent, even if these ten thousand could agree among themselves as to the gradations of their own rewards. A nobleman of France, or of England, cannot understand the sort of veneration that a vizier feels for the Grand Turk; and any attempt on the part of the sovereigns of these two countries, to bring the peers into the abject submission that is practised in the seraglio, would induce a singular commotion. Now, to the American it is just as inconceivable how one man can yield precedency, or respect, or submission to another, merely because he happens to be born an eldest son. You see all this is artificial, and the fact of its long existence in the world establishes nothing, but the opinions of the world. Opinions that are the nearest to nature, are the least liable to change. The world thought that the sun moved round the earth until quite lately, and yet the fact, I believe, is not so. We will sum up this

argument in a very few words. Ten centuries ago, one century
since, nay, twenty years since, very different opinions existed in
Europe on the subject of governments from those that are now
getting into fashion. The tendency is to natural rights, at the
expense of artificial institutions. In some few instances, change
has been attempted by revolution; but revolution is a dangerous
remedy. The Americans had no revolution, strictly speaking;
they have only preceded the rest of Christendom in their reforms, because circumstances permitted it. If they have gone
farther than it may be wise for other nations to follow, it is no
reason that they are not safe themselves. So has England gone
farther than France, and France farther than Sweden, and
Sweden farther than Russia. There is no danger of reaction in
America, for there has been no blow to produce the rebound.
The progress has been steady and natural; and there must be a
gradual return to the ignorance of the thirteenth and four-
teenth centuries, to effect any material change. It is odd enough,
that in an age when even despotism is fettered by public opinion,
men should affect to believe that a people who feel its influence
more than any other, who have fortified their institutions by
law, by habit, and by common sense, are liable to be affected by
causes that are hourly losing their ascendancy in every other
country.

I shall state one more simple fact, leaving you to reason on it
for yourself. So far from increasing familiarity and intercourse
with the system of Europe producing any desire for imitation
on the part of those Americans who are brought in contact
with our privileged orders, it is notorious, that it produces
quite a contrary effect.

But the question of infinitely the most interest is that which
touches the durability of the confederation. It is the only one
of the two that is worthy of grave comment.

If we fix the habitable territory of the United States, east of
the Rocky Mountains, at 1,000,000 of square miles, we shall not
exceed the truth. By giving a population of 150 to the square
mile, we get a gross amount of 150,000,000 for the population
of this republic. In 1850, the population will probably be

24,000,000; in 1880, 48,000,000; and in 1920, near, or quite, 100,000,000. I do not think there are sufficient reasons to distrust the increase so far as the period named. If any thing, I believe I am materially within bounds.

Now the first impression that strikes the mind, is the impossibility that 100,000,000 of people should consent to live quietly under the same government. It is quite certain that such vast masses of intelligent men could not be controlled by force; but it remains to be proved that they cannot be kept together by interest. Let us examine how far the latter agent will be active.

The people of the United States can, under no other arrangement, enjoy protection against foreign wars at so cheap a rate. Aggression on their rights will be out of the question, should they remain united. Should they separate, they would make rivals, and of course enemies, at their own doors. Nature has adapted these vast regions to profit by internal trade. This species of commerce can never be conducted on terms so favourable as those offered by the Union. Should they separate, a thousand irritating and embarrassing questions about the right to navigate the rivers and bays, would unavoidably occur, which now are unknown. They are a people of peculiar institutions, and vast political weight is necessary to secure the proud and manly population of this country, the respect they claim in foreign countries. They have felt the degradation of being contemned; they are beginning to know the privileges of being respected; and they will shortly enjoy the advantages of being feared. It is not in nature to suppose that men will wilfully and blindly throw away their superiority. I think there will also be an outward pressure that will tend to unite them still closer.

The confederated government of the United States has not power enough to make itself dangerous to the rights of the States. In the first place, it is no more than a representation of the people in another form; and there is little probability that any decidedly unpopular policy can long continue, if, indeed, it could be adopted at all. Each hour lessens the danger of particular States receding from the Union, by lessening their relative importance.[32] Even New-York, with ten millions of inhabitants, would be embarrassed, surrounded by a powerful rival of fifty or sixty millions. The great communities would be safer, and more important, by exercising their natural influence in the confederation, and the smaller could not exist separately. But it may be thought that the separation will take place in such a manner as to divide the present Union into two great nations. That these expectations are vague, and founded on a general reasoning that may be false when applied to a particular case, is evident by the fact that men are divided on the grounds of this separation. Some say that the slave-holders will separate from their northern brethren; and some think that the line will be drawn north and south. Now, in point of fact, there is no solid reason in either of these opinions, except as they have a general reference to the difficulty of keeping such masses of men together. My own opinion is, that the United States are now passing, or, in fact, have in a great measure passed, the ordeal of the durability of the Union.

As to grave shakings of the head, and general assertions, they prove nothing, unless, as they often do, they prove ignorance. Forty years ago, unbelievers would have shaken their heads, had they been told that a constitutional government would now exist in France. We must look at plain, direct, and natural causes, for the influences that are to support, or to destroy, this confederation. We can easily see the advantages of the connexion, now let us endeavour to seek the disadvantages.

The first objection that presents itself is distance. But distance is an object that has more force now, when roads and communication by water are in their infancy, than it can ever have hereafter. Existing facts, therefore, not only show that the United States are sufficiently near to each other for all practical and desirable purposes of general government, but that in truth the empire might still be extended without material inconvenience.

The next objection is the question of slaves and of freedom. The control of the slaves is a matter left entirely to the States who hold them; and, so far as they have any direct influence on the durability of the Union, it is, I think, in its favour, by adding an additional motive for its continuance to the southern States. One might acknowledge a danger of a difference of habits arising under the slave policy, that would induce a dangerous difference in character, were it not for the fact, that this state of things has existed so long, and that the people of the north and the people of the south are rather assimilating than becoming more widely distinct in their habits and opinions.

Next comes local interest. This, after all, is the only point worthy of much consideration. It is a branch of the subject that presents two or three different aspects. That of employment, that of geographical inducements to divide, and that of minute separate interests. It is plain that the people of a country in which there is so great a diversity of soil and of climate, must pursue different employments. But is not this fact rather a motive of harmony than of dissension? They can supply each other's wants, without incurring the danger of rivalry. The northern man will exercise his ingenuity, and will be the mariner; the man of the middle States will grow the primary necessaries of life; and the southern man will supply both with luxuries. The manufacturer will buy wheat, and tobacco, and wine, and fifty other necessaries, of the Virginian, Marylander, &c. and cotton, and sugar, and olives, and fruits, of the southern man. They are necessary to each other; and it is therefore plain their interests are united.

As to the geographical inducements to separate, it is impossible (when distance is admitted to be conquered) to discover more than one. There might, under certain circumstances, be a reason why countries that lie on the tributaries of the Mississippi, for instance, should wish to be under one government. But they *are* under one government already, and by what process can they be more so than they are at this moment? The Kentuckian, and the Tennessean, and Ohiese, and Indianian, might lose some advantages, in the way of geographical inducements, by separating from New-York to cling to Louisiana, or *vice versa;* but what could he possibly gain? There might have been a danger of such a separation, when the outlet of the Mississippi was the property of another nation; but the outlet of the Mississippi is now the property of the republicans themselves. The citizen of New-Orleans has just as much influence in the general government as the citizen of New-York or Boston. Independently of these facts, which, I think, contain an unanswerable argument, each day is so ramifying and connecting interests throughout the whole of this Union, as to render it difficult to the States, which might be thought to be the most exposed to what I have called geographical inducements, to make a selection, even in circumstances that should compel a choice.

The control of minute interests might easily lead to dissensions, in a free country. But the natural and exceedingly happy constitution of American society leaves the States the control of all matters that do not require concentrated action; it leaves even the counties and towns, also, the right of controlling their more minute interests.

Now, where are we to seek a rational argument for believing that this confederation will dissolve? Its plan of government leaves as few matters of contention as possible; while the interests, the habits, the feelings, and the history, of the people, are the same. Moral and physical causes unite to keep them together, while nothing indicates that they must divide, but sage and incredulous shakings of the head! I make no doubt, that if Cœur de Lion had been told his brother would be forced to grant a charter to his barons, his head would have been shaken too; and that Queen Elizabeth would not have believed that the royal *veto* could ever slumber for a century; or that Isabel might have entertained rational doubts of her American provinces becoming more important dominions than her own Aragon—and yet all these things have come to pass! Are we to believe for ever only what we wish? We are told that China contains a hundred and fifty millions of people, in one empire; and why are we to believe that semi-barbarians have more wisdom than a nation that has shown itself as shrewd, as firm, and as constant as the Americans?

Let us give one moment's attention to the political history of the republic since its establishment.

Between the years 1775 and 1789, a confederation existed, which, though it imperfectly answered the objects of the war, partook of that flimsiness of texture which has proved the bane and weakness of so many previous political unions. The Americans, instead of becoming impatient and restive under acknowledged difficulties, deliberately went to work to remedy the evil. The present constitution was formed. Its chief merit consists in its yielding to unavoidable evils, its consulting natural objects, and its profiting by those advantages which had endured the test of time. This is a broad foundation on which to repose the fabric of government.

Until near the end of Washington's administration, the Americans were scarcely treated with the courtesy that was due to a nation. The character of that illustrious man lent a dignity to his government, which adventitious circumstances would have refused. England boldly held military posts within the undeniable limits of the country;[33] and a thousand indignities, and numberless acts of injustice, disgraced the history of that period. Commanders of vessels of war exercised a lawless authority on the coasts of the republic; and there is an instance on record of a captain of a sloop of war, openly and insolently refusing to obey the civil authorities of the country, because he knew that he commanded a greater nautical force than that of the whole republic united. At that day, Europeans generally believed these people black and barbarous; and they listened to accounts of their proceedings, as we listen to the events of farther India.

Then followed the general war, with its abuses. The vast commerce of America grew, but it became a prey to all the belligerents. Acts, that would disgrace any man of the smallest pretension to character, were committed by boastful nations, under the pitiful plea of power; and the complaints of a remote people, were despised and ridiculed, for no other reason than that they were a nation weak and dispersed. But a mighty spirit was in the land. The statesmen were wary, firm in their principles, yielding to events while they protested against injustice, and watchful to let no opportunity of regaining their rights pass without improvement. At this period, an immense region, which possessed countless positive advantages, which offered a foothold to rivals, and which was a constant temptation to division among themselves, was peaceably acquired.[34] The purchase of Louisiana was the greatest masterstroke of policy that has been done in our times. All the wars, and conquests, and cessions of Europe, for the last hundred years, sink into insignificance, compared with the political consequences that are dependent on this increase of territory. Spain had been accessory to the wrongs, and Spain too was quietly made to contribute to the peace and security of the republic, by a cession of the Floridas.[35]

A new era is now about to dawn on this nation. It has ceased to creep; it begins to walk erect among the powers of the earth. All these things have occurred within the life of man. Europeans may be reluctant to admit the claims of a competitor, that they knew so lately a pillaged, a wronged, and a feeble people; but Nature will have her laws obeyed, and the fulfilment of things must come. The spirit of greatness is in this nation: its means are within their grasp; and it is as vain as it is weak to attempt to deny results that every year is rendering more plain, more important, and more irresistible.

[PARIS UNDER THE BOURBONS]

From *France* (Vol. II, Letter VII)[36]

I have said very little, in my previous letters, on the subject of our personal intercourse with the society of Paris.[37] It is not always easy for one to be particular in these matters, and maintain the reserve that is due to others. Violating the confidence he may have received through his hospitality, is but an indifferent return from the guest to the host. Still there are men, if I may so express it, so public in their very essence, certainly in their lives, that propriety is less concerned with a repetition of their sentiments, and with delineations of their characters, than in ordinary cases; for the practice of the world has put them so much on their guard against the representations of travellers, that there is more danger of rendering a false account, by becoming their dupes, than of betraying them in their unguarded moments. I have scarcely ever been admitted to the presence of a real notoriety, that I did not find the man, or woman—sex making little difference—an actor; and this, too, much beyond the every day and perhaps justifiable little practices of conventional life. Inherent simplicity of character, is one of the rarest, as, tempered by the tone imparted by refinement, it is the loveliest of all our traits, though it is quite common to meet with those who affect it, with an address that is very apt to deceive the ordinary, and most especially the flattered, observer.

Opportunity, rather than talents, is the great requisite for circulating gossip; a very moderate degree of ability, sufficing for the observation which shall render private anecdotes, more especially when they relate to persons of celebrity, of interest to the general reader. But there is another objection to being merely the medium of information of this low quality, that I should think would have great influence with every one who has the common self-respect of a gentleman. *There is a tacit admission of inferiority* in the occupation, that ought to prove too humiliating to a man accustomed to those associations, which imply equality. It is permitted to touch upon the habits and appearance of a truly great man; but to dwell upon the peculiarities of a duke, merely because he is a duke, is as much as to say he is your superior; a concession I do not feel disposed to make in favour of any *mere duke* in Christendom.

I shall not, however, be wholly silent on the general impressions left by the little I have seen of the society of Paris; and, occasionally, when it is characteristic, an anecdote may be introduced, for such things sometimes give distinctness, as well as piquancy, to a description.

During our first winter in Paris, our circle, never very large, was principally confined to foreign families, intermingled with a few French; but since our return to town, from St. Ouen, we have seen more of the people of the country. I should greatly mislead you, however, were I to leave the impression that our currency in the French capital has been at all general, for it certainly has not. Neither my health, leisure, fortune, nor opportunities, have permitted this. I believe few, perhaps no Americans, have very general access to the best society of any large European town; at all events, I have met with no one who, I have had any reason to think was much better off than myself in this respect; and, I repeat, my own familiarity with the circles of the capital, is nothing to boast of. It is in Paris, as it is every where else, as respects those who are easy of access. In all large towns there is to be found a troublesome and pushing set, who, requiring notoriety, obtrude themselves on strangers, sometimes with sounding names, and always with offensive pretensions of some sort or other; but the truly respectable and estimable class, in every country, except in cases that cannot properly be included in the rule, are to be sought. Now, one must feel that he has peculiar claims, or be better furnished with letters than happened to be my case, to get a ready admission into this set, or, having obtained it, to feel that his position enabled him to maintain the intercourse, with the ease and freedom that could alone render it agreeable.[38] To be shown about as a lion, when circumstances offer the means; to be stuck up at a dinner table, as a piece of luxury, like strawberries in February, or peaches in April, can hardly be called association: the terms being much on a par with that which forms the *liaison*, between him who gives the entertainment, and the hired plate with which his table is garnished. With this explanation, then, you are welcome to an outline of the little I know on the subject.

One of the errors respecting the French, which has been imported into America, through England, is the impression that they are not hospitable. Since my residence here, I have often been at a loss to imagine how such a notion could have arisen, for I am acquainted with no town, in which it has struck me there is more true hospitality, than in Paris. Not only are dinners, balls, and all the minor entertainments frequent, but there is scarcely a man, or a woman, of any note in society, who does not cause his or her doors to be opened, once a fortnight at least, and, in half the cases, once a week. At these *soirées* invitations are sometimes given, it is true, but then they are general, and for the whole season; and it is not unusual, even, to consider them free to all who are on visiting terms with the family. The utmost simplicity and good taste prevail at these places, the refreshments being light and appropriate, and the forms exacting no more than what belongs to good breeding. You will, at once, conceive the great advantages that a stranger possesses in having access to such social resources. One, with a tolerable visiting list, may choose his circle for any particular evening, and, if by chance, the company should not happen to be to his mind, he has still before him the alternative of several other houses, which are certain to be open. It is not easy to say what can be more truly hospitable than this.

. . . .

I have had an odd pleasure in driving from one house to another, on particular evenings, in order to produce as strong contrasts as my limited visiting list will procure. Having a fair opportunity a few nights since, in consequence of two or three invitations coming in, for the evening on which several houses where I occasionally called were opened, I determined to make a night of it, in order to note the effect. As A——[39] did not know several of the people, I went alone, and you may possibly be amused with an account of my adventures: they shall be told.

In the first place I had to dress, in order to go to dinner at a house that I had never entered, and with a family of which I had never seen a soul. These are incidents which frequently come over a stranger, and, at first, were not a little awkward, but use hardens us to much greater misfortunes. At six, then, I stepped punctually into my *coupé*, and gave Charles the necessary number and street. I ought to tell you that the invitation had come a few days before, and, in a fit of curiosity, I had accepted it, and sent a card, without having the least idea who my host and hostess were, beyond their names. There was something *piquant* in this ignorance, and I had almost made up my mind to go in the same mysterious manner, leaving all to events, when happening, in an idle moment, to ask a lady of my acquaintance, and for whom I have a great respect, if she knew a *Madame de* ——, to my surprise, her answer was—"Most certainly—she is my cousin, and you are to dine there to-morrow." I said no more, though this satisfied me that my hosts were people of some standing. While driving to their hotel, it struck me, under all the circumstances, it might be well to know more of them, and I stopped at the gate of a female friend, who knows every body, and who, I was certain, would receive me even at that unseasonable hour. I was admitted, explained my errand, and inquired if she knew *a M. de* ——. "*Quelle question!*" she exclaimed—"*M. de* —— *est Chancelier de la France!*" Absurd, and even awkward, as it might have proved, but for this lucky thought, I should have gone and dined with the French Lord High Chancellor, without having the smallest suspicion of who he was!

The hotel was a fine one, though the apartment was merely good, and the reception, service and general style of the house were so simple that neither would have awakened the least suspicion of the importance of my hosts. The party was small and the dinner modest. I found the *chancelier* a grave dignified man, a little curious on the subject of America, and his wife, apparently a woman of great good sense, and, I should think, of a good deal of attainment. Every thing went off in the quietest manner possible, and I was sorry when it was time to go.

From this dinner, I drove to the hotel of the *Marquis de Marbois*, to pay a visit of digestion. M. de Marbois retires so early, on account of his great age, that one is obliged to be punctual, or he will find the gate locked at nine. The company had got back into the drawing-room, and as the last week's guests were mostly there, as well as those who had just left the table, there might have been thirty people present, all of whom were men but two. One of the ladies was Madame de Souza, known in French literature as the writer of several clever novels of society. In the drawing-room, were grouped, in clusters, the Grand Referendary, M. Cuvier, M. Daru, M. Villemain, M. de Plaisance, Mr. Brown, and many others of note. There seemed to be something in the wind, as the conversation was in low confidential whispers, attended by divers ominous shrugs. This could only be politics, and watching an opportunity, I questioned an acquaintance. The fact was really so. The appointed hour had come, and the ministry of M. de Villèle was in agony.[40] The elections had not been favourable, and it was expedient to make an attempt to reach the *old* end, by what is called a *new* combination. It is necessary to understand the general influence of political intrigues on certain *côteries* of Paris, to appreciate the effect of this intelligence, on a drawing-room filled, like this, with men who had been actors in the principal events of France, for forty years. The name of M. Cuvier was even mentioned as one of the new ministers. Comte Roy was also named, as likely to be the new premier. I was told that this gentleman was one of the greatest landed proprietors of France, his estates being valued at four millions of dollars. The fact is curious, as showing, not on vulgar rumour, but from a respectable source, what is deemed a first rate landed property in this country. It is certainly no merit, nor do I believe it is any very great advantage; but, I think we might materially beat this, even in America. The company soon separated, and I retired.

From the *Place de la Madeleine*, I drove to a house near the *Carrousel*, where I had been invited to step in, in the course of the evening. All the buildings that remain within the intended parallelogram, which will some day make this spot one of the finest squares in the world, have been bought by the government, or nearly so, with the intent to have them pulled down, at a proper time; and the court bestows lodgings, *ad interim*, among them, on its favourites. Madame de —— was one of these favoured persons, and she occupies a small apartment in the third story of one of these houses. The rooms were neat and well arranged, but small. Probably the largest does not exceed fifteen feet square. The approach to a Paris lodging is usually either very good, or very bad. In the new buildings may be found some of the mediocrity of the new order of things; but in all those which were erected previously to the revolution, there is nothing but extremes in this, as in most other things. Great luxury and elegance, or great meanness and discomfort. The house of Madame de —— happens to be of the latter class, and although all the disagreeables have disappeared from her own rooms, one is compelled to climb up to them, through a dark well of a staircase, by flights of steps not much better than those we use in our stables. You have no notion of such staircases as those I had just descended in the hotels of the *Chancelier* and the *Premier President;** nor have we any just idea, as connected with respectable dwellings, of these I had now to clamber up. M. de —— is a man of talents and great respectability, and his wife is exceedingly clever, but they are not rich. He is a professor, and she is an artist. After having passed so much of my youth, on top-gallant-yards, and in becketting royals, you are not to suppose, however, I had any great difficulty in getting up these stairs, narrow, steep, and winding as they were.

* M. de Marbois was the first president of the Court of Accounts. [*Cooper's note.*]

We are now at the door, and I have rung. On whom do you imagine the curtain will rise? On a *réunion* of philosophers come to discuss questions in botany, with M. de ——, or on artists, assembled to talk over the troubles of their profession, with his wife? The door opens, and I enter.

The little drawing-room is crowded; chiefly with men. Two card tables are set, and at one I recognize a party, in which are three dukes of the *veille cour*, with M. de Duras at their head! The rest of the company was a little more mixed, but, on the whole, it savoured strongly of Coblentz and the *emigration*. This was more truly French than any thing I had yet stumbled on. One or two of the grandees looked at me as if, better informed than Scott, they knew that General La Fayette had not gone to America to live. Some of these gentlemen certainly do not love us; but I had cut out too much work for the night to stay and return the big looks of even dukes, and, watching an opportunity, when the eyes of Madame de —— were another way, I stole out of the room.

Charles now took his orders, and we drove down into the heart of the town, somewhere near the general post-office, or into those mazes of streets that, near two years of practice, have not yet taught me to thread. We entered the court of a large hotel, that was brilliantly lighted, and I ascended, by a noble flight of steps, to the first floor. Ante-chambers communicated with a magnificent saloon, which appeared to be near forty feet square. The ceilings were lofty, and the walls were ornamented with military trophies, beautifully designed, and which had the air of being embossed and gilded. I had got into the hotel of one of Napoleon's marshals, you will say, or at least into one of a marshal of the old *régime*. The latter conjecture may be true, but the house is now inhabited by a great woollen manufacturer, whom the events of the day has thrown into the presence of all these military emblems. I found the worthy *industriel* surrounded by a group, composed of men of his own stamp, eagerly discussing the recent changes in the government. The women, of whom there might have been a dozen, were ranged, like a neglected parterre, along the opposite side of the room. I paid my compliments, staid a few minutes, and stole away to the next engagement.

We had now to go to a little, retired, house on the *Champs Elysées*. There were only three or four carriages before the door, and on ascending to a small, but very neat apartment, I found some twenty people collected. The mistress of the house was an English lady, single, of a certain age, and a daughter of the Earl of ——, who was once governor of New York. Here was a very different set. One or two ladies of the old court, women of elegant manners, and seemingly of good information, several English women, pretty, quiet and clever, besides a dozen men of different nations. This was one of those little *réunions* that are so common in Paris, among the foreigners, in which a small infusion of French serves to leaven a considerable batch of human beings from other parts of the world. As it is always a relief to me to speak my own language, after being a good while among foreigners, I staid an hour at this house. In the course of the evening an Irishman of great wit and of exquisite humour, one of the paragons of the age in his way, came in. In the course of conversation, this gentleman, who is the proprietor of an Irish estate, and a Catholic, told me of an atrocity in the laws of his country, of which until then I was ignorant. It seems that any younger brother, or next heir, might claim the estate by turning Protestant, or drive the incumbent to the same act. I was rejoiced to hear that there was hardly an instance of such profligacy known.* To what baseness will not the struggle for political ascendancy urge us!

In the course of the evening, Mr. ——, the Irish gentleman, gravely introduced me to a Sir James ——, adding, with perfect gravity, "a gentleman whose father humbugged the Pope— humbugged infallibility." One could not but be amused with such an introduction, urged in a way so infinitely droll, and I ventured, at a proper moment, to ask an explanation, which, unless I was also humbugged, was as follows.

Among the *détenus* in 1804, was Sir William ——, the

* I believe this infamous law, however, has been repealed. [*Cooper's note.*]

father of Sir James ———, the person in question. Taking advantage of the presence of the Pope at Paris, he is said to have called on the good-hearted Pius, with great concern of manner, to state his case. He had left his sons in England, and through his absence they had fallen under the care of two Presbyterian aunts; as a father he was naturally anxious to rescue them from this perilous situation. "Now Pius," continued my merry informant, "quite naturally supposed that all this solicitude was in behalf of two orthodox Catholic souls, and he got permission from Napoleon for the return of so good a father, to his own country, never dreaming that the conversion of the boys, if it ever took place, would only be from the Protestant Episcopal Church of England, to that of Calvin; or a rescue from one of the devil's furnaces, to pop them into another." I laughed at this story, I suppose with a little incredulity, but my Irish friend insisted on its truth, ending the conversation with a significant nod, Catholic as he was, and saying—"humbugged infallibility!"

By this time it was eleven o'clock, and as I am obliged to keep reasonable hours, it was time to go to *the* party of the evening. Count ———, of the ——— Legation, gave a great ball. My carriage entered the line at the distance of near a quarter of a mile from the *hôtel; gensdarmes* being actively employed in keeping us all in our places. It was half an hour before I was set down, and the *quadrilles* were in full motion when I entered. It was a brilliant affair, much the most so I have ever yet witnessed in a private house. Some said there were fifteen hundred people present. The number seems incredible, and yet, when one comes to calculate, it may be so. As I got into my carriage to go away, Charles informed me that the people at the gates affirm that more than six hundred carriages had entered the court that evening. By allowing an average of little more than two to each vehicle, we get the number mentioned.

I do not know exactly how many rooms were opened on this occasion, but I should think there were fully a dozen. Two or three were very large *salons*, and the one in the centre, which was almost at fever heat, had crimson hangings, by way of cooling one. I have never witnessed dancing at all comparable to that of the quadrilles of this evening. Usually there is either too much or too little of the dancing master, but on this occasion every one seemed inspired with a love of the art. It was a beautiful sight to see a hundred charming young women, of the first families of Europe, for they were there of all nations, dressed with the simple elegance that is so becoming to the young of the sex, and which is never departed from here until after marriage, moving in perfect time to delightful music, as if animated by a common soul. The men, too, did better than usual, being less lugubrious and mournful than our sex is apt to be in dancing. I do not know how it is in private, but in the world, at Paris, every young woman seems to have a good mother; or, at least, one capable of giving her both a good tone, and good taste.

At this party I met the ———, an intimate friend of the ambassador, and one who also honours me with a portion of her friendship. In talking over the appearance of things, she told me that some hundreds of *applications for invitations* to this ball had been made. "Applications! I cannot conceive of such meanness. In what manner?" "Directly; by note, by personal intercession—almost by tears. Be certain of it, many hundreds have been refused." In America we hear of refusals to go to balls, but we have not yet reached the pass of sending refusals to invite! "Do you see Mademoiselle ———, dancing in the set before you?" She pointed to a beautiful French girl, whom I had often seen at her house, but whose family was in a much lower station in society than herself. "Certainly—pray how came *she* here?" "I brought her. Her mother was dying to come, too, and she begged me to get an invitation for her and her daughter; but it would not do to bring the mother to such a place, and I was obliged to say no more tickets could be issued. I wished, however, to bring the daughter, she is so pretty, and we compromised the affair in that way." "And to this the mother assented!" "Assented! How can you doubt it —what funny American notions you have brought with you to France!"

I got some droll anecdotes from my companion, concerning

the ingredients of the company on this occasion, for she could be as sarcastic as she was elegant. A young woman near us attracted attention by a loud and vulgar manner of laughing. "Do you know that lady?" demanded my neighbour. "I have seen her before, but scarcely know her name." "She is the daughter of your acquaintance, the *Marquise de* ———." "Then she is, or was, a *Mademoiselle de* ———." "She is not, nor properly ever was, a *Mademoiselle de* ———. In the revolution the *Marquis* was imprisoned by you wicked republicans, and the *Marquise* fled to England, whence she returned, after an absence of three years, bringing with her this young lady, then an infant a few months old." "And *Monsieur le Marquis?*" "He never saw his daughter, having been beheaded in Paris, about a year before her birth." "*Quelle contre tems!*" "*Ne c' est-ce pas?*"[41]

It is a melancholy admission, but it is no less true, that good breeding is sometimes quite as active a virtue, as good principles. How many more of the company present were born about a year after their fathers were beheaded, I have no means of knowing; but had it been the case with all of them, the company would have been of as elegant demeanor, and of much more *retenue* of deportment, than we are accustomed to see, I will not say in *good*, but certainly in *general* society, at home. One of the consequences of good breeding is also a disinclination, positively a distaste, to pry into the private affairs of others. The little specimen to the contrary, just named, was rather an exception, owing to the character of the individual, and to the indiscretion of the young lady in laughing too loud, and then the affair of a birth so *very* posthumous was rather too *patent* to escape all criticism.

My friend was in a gossiping mood this evening, and as she was well turned of fifty, I ventured to continue the conversation. As some of the *liaisons* which exist here must be novel to you, I shall mention one or two more.

A *Madame de J*——— passed us, leaning on the arm of *M. de C*———. I knew the former, who was a widow; had frequently visited her, and had been surprised at the intimacy which existed between her and *M. de C*——, who always appeared quite at home, in her house. I ventured to ask my neighbour if the gentleman were the brother of the lady. "Her brother! It is to be hoped not, as he is her husband." "Why does she not bear his name, if that be the case?" "Because her first husband is of a more illustrious family than her second; and then there are some difficulties on the score of fortune. No, no. These people are *bonâ fide* married. *Tenez*—do you see that gentleman who is standing so assiduously near the chair of *Madame de S*——? He who is all attention and smiles to the lady?" "Certainly—his politeness is even affectionate." "Well it ought to be, for it is *M. de S*——, her husband." "They are a happy couple, then." "*Hors de doute*—he meets her at *soirées* and balls; is the pink of politeness; puts on her shawl; sees her safe into her carriage, and—" "Then they drive home together, as loving as Darby and Joan." "And then he jumps into his *cabriolet*, and drives to the lodgings of ——. *Bon soir, monsieur* ——, you are making me fall into the vulgar crime of scandal."

Now, as much as all this may sound like invention, it is quite true, that I repeat no more to you than was said to me, and no more than what I believe to be exact. As respects the latter couple, I have been elsewhere told that they literally never see each other, except in public, where they constantly meet, as the best friends in the world.

I was lately in some English society, when Lady G—— bet a pair of gloves with Lord R—— that he had not seen Lady R—— in a fortnight. The bet was won by the gentleman, who proved satisfactorily that he had met his wife at a dinner party, only ten days before.

After all I have told you, and all that you may have heard from others, I am nevertheless inclined to believe, that the high society of Paris is quite as exemplary as that of any other large European town. If we are any better ourselves, is it not more owing to the absence of temptation, than to any other cause? Put large garrisons into our towns, fill the streets with idlers, who have nothing to do but to render themselves agreeable, and with women with whom dress and pleasure are the principal occupations, and then let us see what protestantism and liberty will avail us, in this particular. The intelligent French say that their society is improving in morals. I can believe this, of which I think there is sufficient proof by comparing the present with the past, as the latter has been described to us. By the past, I do not mean the period of the revolution, when vulgarity assisted to render vice still more odious—a happy union, perhaps, for those who were to follow—but the days of the old *régime*. Chance has thrown me in the way of three or four old dowagers of that period, women of high rank, and still in the first circles, who, amid all their *finesse* of breeding, and ease of manner, have had a desperate *rouée* air about them. Their very laugh, at times, has seemed replete with a bold levity, that was as disgusting as it was unfeminine. I have never, in any other part of the world, seen loose sentiments *affichés*, with more effrontery. These women are the complete antipodes of the quiet, elegant *Princesse de ——*,[42] who was at Lady —— ——'s, this evening; though some of them write *Princesses* on their cards, too.

The influence of a court must be great on the morals of those who live in its purlieus. Conversing with the Duc de ——, a man who has had general currency in the best society of Europe, on this subject, he said,— "England has long decried our manners. Previously to the revolution, I admit they were bad; perhaps worse than her own; but I know nothing in our history as bad as what I lately witnessed in England. You know I was there, quite recently. The king invited me to dine at Windsor. I found every one in the drawing-room, but His Majesty and Lady ——. She entered but a minute before him, like a queen. Her reception was that of a queen; young, unmarried females kissed her hand. Now, all this might happen in France, even now; but Louis XV., the most dissolute of our monarchs, went no farther. At Windsor, I saw the husband, sons, and daughters of the favourite, in the circle! *Le parc des Cerfs* was not as bad as this."

"And yet, M. de ——, since we are conversing frankly,

listen to what I witnessed, but the other day, in France. You know the situation of things at St. Ouen, and the rumours that are so rife. We had the *fête Dieu*, during my residence there. You, who are a Catholic, need not be told that your sect believe in the doctrine of the 'real presence.' There was a *reposior* erected in the garden of the *château*, and God, in person, was carried, with religious pomp, to rest in the bowers of the ex-favourite. It is true, the husband was not present: he was only in the provinces!"

"The influence of a throne makes sad parasites and hypo-crites," said M. de ——, shrugging his shoulders.

"And the influence of the people, too, though in a different way. A courtier is merely a well-dressed demagogue."

"It follows, then, that man is just a poor devil."

But I am gossiping away with you, when my Asmodean career[43] is ended, and it is time I went to bed. Good night.

From *France* (Vol. I, Letter VIII)

Since our arrival there have been several great military displays, and I have made it a point to be present at them all. The first was a *petite guerre*,* on the plains of Issy, or within a mile of the walls of the town. There may have been 15,000 men assembled for the occasion, including troops of all arms.

One of the first things that struck me at Paris, was the care-less militia-like manner in which the French troops marched about the streets. The disorder, irregularity, careless and in-different style of moving, were all exactly such as I have heard laughed at, a thousand times, in our own great body of national defenders. But this is only one of many similar instances, in which I have discovered that what has been deemed a peculiarity in ourselves, arising from the institutions perhaps, is a very general quality belonging rather to man than to any particular set of men. Our notions, you will excuse the freedom of the remark, are apt to be a little provincial, and every one knows that fashions, opinions and tastes, only become the more exag-

* Sham-fight. [*Cooper's note.*]

gerated, the farther we remove from the centre of light. In this way, we come to think of things in an exaggerated sense, until, like the boy who is disappointed at finding a king a man, we form notions of life that are any thing but natural and true.

I was still so new to all this, however, that I confess I went to the plain of Issy, expecting to see a new style of manœuvring, or, at least, one very different from that which I had so often witnessed at home, nor, can I say that, in this instance, there was so much disappointment. The plan of the day did not embrace two parties, but was merely an attack on an imaginary position, against which the assailants were regularly and scientifically brought up, the victory being a matter of convention. The movements were very beautiful, and were made with astonishing spirit and accuracy. All idea of disorder, or the want of regularity, was lost, here, for entire battalions advanced to the charges without the slightest apparent deviation from perfectly mathematical lines.

When we reached the acclivity that overlooked the field, a new line was forming directly beneath us, it being supposed that the advance of the enemy had already been driven in upon his main body, and the great attack was just on the point of commencing.

A long line of infantry of the French guards, formed the centre of the assailants. Several batteries of artillery were at hand, and divers strong columns of horse and foot were held in reserve. A regiment of lancers was on the nearest flank, and another of cuirassiers was stationed at the opposite. All the men of the royal family were in the field, surrounded by a brilliant staff. A gun was fired near them, by way of signal, I suppose, when two brigades of artillery galloped through the intervals of the line, unlimbered, and went to work as if they were in downright earnest. The cannonade continued a short time, when the infantry advanced in line, and delivered its fire by companies, or battalions, I could not discern which, in the smoke. This lasted some ten minutes, when I observed a strong column of troops dressed in scarlet, moving up, with great steadiness and regularity, from the rear. These were the Swiss guards, and there might have been fifteen hundred, or two thousand of them. The column divided into two, as it approached the rear of the line, which broke into column, in turn, and for a minute there was a confused crowd of red and blue coats, in the smoke, that quite set my nautical instinct at defiance. The cuirassiers chose this moment to make a rapid and menacing movement in advance, but without opening their column, and some of the artillery reappeared and commenced firing, at the unoccupied intervals. This lasted a very little while, for the Swiss displayed[44] into line like clock-work, and then made a quick charge, with beautiful precision. Halting, they threw in a heavy fire, by battalions; the French guard rallied and formed upon their flanks; the whole reserve came up; the cuirassiers and lancers charged, by turning the position assailed, and for ten or fifteen minutes there was a succession of quick evolutions, which, like the *finale* of a grand piece of music, appeared confused even while it was the most scientific, and then there was a sudden pause. The position, whose centre was a copse, had been carried, and we soon saw the guards formed on the ground that was supposed to have been held by the enemy. The artillery still fired, occasionally, as on a retreating foe, and the lancers and cuirassiers were charging and manœuvring, half a mile farther in advance, as if following up their advantage.

Altogether, this was much the prettiest field exercise I ever witnessed. There was a unity of plan, a perfection of evolution, and a division of *matériel* about it, that rendered it to my eyes, as nearly perfect as might be. The troops were the best of France, and the management of the whole had been confided to some one accustomed to the field. It contained all the poetry, without any of the horrors of a battle. It could not possess the heart-stirring interest of a real conflict, and yet it was not without great excitement.

Some time after the *petite guerre* of Issy, the capital celebrated the *fête* of the Trocadero. The Trocadero, you may remember, was the fortress of Cadiz, carried by assault, under the order of the *Dauphin*, in the war of the late Spanish revolution. This government, which has destroyed all the statues of the Emperor, proscribed his family, and obliterated every visible mark of his reign in their power, has had the unaccountable folly of endeavouring to supplant the military glory acquired under Napoleon, by that of Louis Antoine, Dauphin of France![45] A necessary consequence of the attempt, is a concentration of all the military *souvenirs* of the day, in this affair of the Trocadero. Bold as all this will appear to one who has not the advantage of taking a near view of what is going on here, it has even been exceeded, through the abject-spirit of subserviency in those who have the care of public instruction, by an attempt to exclude even the name of the Bonaparte from French history. My girls have shown me an abridgment of the history of France, that has been officially prepared for the ordinary schools, in which there is no sort of allusion to him. The wags here, say that a work has been especially prepared for the heir presumptive, however, in which the emperor is a little better treated; being spoken of as "a certain *Marquis de Bonaparte*, who commanded the armies of the king."

The mimic attack on the Trocadero, like its great original, was at night. The troops assembled in the *Champs de Mars*, and the assault was made, across the beautiful bridge of Jena, on a sharp acclivity near Passy, which was the imaginary fortress. The result was a pretty good effect of night-firing, some smoke, not a little noise, with a very pretty movement of masses. I could make nothing of it, of much interest, for the obscurity prevented the eyes from helping the imagination.

Not long since, the king held a great review of regular troops and of the entire body of the National Guards of Paris and its environs. This review also took place in the *Champs de Mars*, and it was said that nearly a hundred thousand men were under arms, for the occasion. I think there might have been quite seventy thousand. These mere reviews have little interest, the evolutions being limited to marching by regiments on and off the ground. In doing the latter, the troops defile before the king. Previously to this, the royal cortége passed along the several lines, receiving the usual honours.

On this occasion, the *Dauphine* and the *Duchesse de Berri*,[46] followed the king in open carriages, accompanied by the little *Duc de Bordeaux* and his sister. I happened to be at an angle of the field, as the royal party, surrounded by a showy group of marshals and generals, passed, and when there seemed to be a little confusion. As a matter of course, the cry of *vive le roi* had passed along with the procession, for, popular or not, it is always easy for a sovereign to procure this sign of affection, or, for others to procure it for him. You will readily understand that *employés* of the government, are especially directed to betray the proper enthusiasm on such occasions. There was, however, a cry at this corner of the area, that did not seem so unequivocally loyal, and, on inquiry, I was told that some of the National Guards had cried *à bas les ministres*. The affair passed off without much notice, however, and I believe it was generally forgotten by the population, within an hour. The desire to get rid of *M. de Villèle*, and his set, was so general in Paris, that most people considered the interruption quite as a matter of course.

The next day the capital was electrified by a royal ordinance disbanding all the National Guards of Paris! A more infatuated, or if it were intended to punish the disaffected, a more unjust decree, could not easily have been issued. It was telling the great majority of the very class which forms the true force of every government, that their rulers could not confide in them. As confidence, by awakening pride, begets a spirit in favour of those who depend on it, so does obvious distrust engender disaffection. But the certainty that Louis XVIth, lost his throne and his life for the want of decision, has created one of those sweeping opinions, here, of the virtue of energy, that constantly leads the rulers into false measures. An act that might have restrained the France of 1792, would be certain to throw the France of 1827, into open revolt. The present generation of Frenchmen, in a political sense, have little in common with even the French of 1814, and measures must be suited to the times in which we live. As well might one think of using the birch on the man, that had been found profitable with the boy, as to suppose these people can be treated like their ancestors.

As might have been expected, a deep, and what is likely to

prove a lasting discontent, has been the consequence of the blunder. It is pretended that the shop-keepers of Paris are glad to be rid of the trouble of occasionally mounting guard, and that the affair will be forgotten in a short time. All this may be true enough, in part, and it would also be true in the whole, were there not a press to keep disaffection alive, and to inflame the feelings of those who have been treated so cavalierly, for he knows little of human nature who does not understand that, while bodies of men commit flagrant wrongs without the responsibility being kept in view by their individual members, an affront to the whole is pretty certain to be received as an affront to each of those who make an integral part.

.   .   .   .

The army of France is understood to be very generally disaffected. The restoration has introduced into it, in the capacity of general officers, many who followed the fortunes of the Bourbons into exile, and some, I believe, who actually fought against this country, in the ranks of her enemies. This may be, in some measure, necessary, but it is singularly unfortunate.

I have been told, on good authority, that, since the restoration of 1815, several occasions have occurred, when the court thought itself menaced with a revolution. On all these occasions, the army, as a matter of course, has been looked to, with hope, or with distrust. Investigation is said to have always discovered so bad a spirit, that little reliance is placed on its support.

The traditions of the service are all against the Bourbons. It is true, that very few of the men who fought at Marengo and Austerlitz still remain, but then the recollection of their deeds forms the great delight of most Frenchmen. There is but one power that can counteract this feeling, and it is the power of money. By throwing itself into the arms of the industrious[47] classes, the court might possibly obtain an ally, sufficiently strong to quell the martial spirit of the nation; but, so far from pursuing such a policy, it has all the commercial and manufacturing interests marshalled against it, because it wishes to return to the *bon vieux temps* of the old system.

After all, I much question if any government in France, will have the army cordially with it, that does not find it better employment than mock-fights on the plain of Issy, and night attacks on the mimic Trocadero.

From *France* (Vol. II, Letter X)

We all went to bed, a night or two since, as usual, and awoke to learn that there had been a fight in the capital. One of the countless underplots had got so near the surface, that it threw up smoke. It is said, that about fifty were killed and wounded, chiefly on the part of the populace.

The insecurity of the Bourbons is little understood in America. It is little understood even by those Americans, who pass a few months in the country, and in virtue of frequenting the *cafés*, and visiting the theatres, fancy they know the people. Louis XVIII. was more than once on the point of flying, again, between the year 1815 and his death; for since the removal of the allied troops, there is really no force for a monarch to depend on, more especially in and around the capital, the army being quite as likely to take sides against them, as for them.

The government has determined on exhibiting vigour, and there was a great show of troops the night succeeding the combat. Curious to see the effect of all this, two or three of us got into a carriage and drove through the streets, about nine o'clock. We found some two or three thousand men on the *boulevards*, and the *rue St. Denis*, in particular, which had been the scene of the late disorder, was watched with jealous caution. In all, there might have been four or five thousand men under arms. They were merely in readiness, leaving a free passage for carriages, though in some of the narrow streets, we found the bayonets pretty near our faces.

An American being supposed *ex officio*, as it were, to be a well-wisher to the popular cause, there is, perhaps, a slight disposition to look at us with distrust. The opinion of our *travellers'* generally favouring liberty is, in my judgment, singularly erroneous, the feelings of a majority being, on the whole, just the other way, for, at least, the first year or two of their European experience;[48] though, I think, it is to be noticed, by the end of that time, that they begin to lose sight of the personal interests which, at home, have made them any thing but philosophers on such subjects, and to see and appreciate the immense advantages of freedom over exclusion, although the predominance of the former may not always favour their own particular views. Such, at least, has been the result of my own observations, and so far from considering a fresh arrival from home, as being likely to be an accession to our little circle of liberal principles, I have generally deemed all such individuals as being more likely to join the side of the aristocrats, or the exclusionists in politics. This is not the moment to enter into an examination of the causes that have led to so singular a contradiction between opinions and facts, though I think the circumstance is not to be denied, for it is now my intention to give you an account of the manner in which matters are managed here, rather than enter into long investigations of the state of society at home.

Not long after my arrival in France, a visit was announced, from a person who was entirely unknown to me, but who called himself a *littérateur*. The first interview passed off, as such interviews usually do, and circumstances not requiring any return on my part, it was soon forgotten. Within a fortnight, however, I received visit the second, when the conversation took a political turn, my guest freely abusing the Bourbons, the aristocrats, and the present state of things in France. I did little more than listen. When the way was thus opened, I was asked if I admired Sir Walter Scott, and particularly what I thought of Ivanhoe, or rather, if I did not think it an indifferent book. A little surprised at such a question, I told my *littérateur*, that Ivanhoe appeared to me to be very unequal, the first half being incomparably the best, but that, as a whole, I thought it stood quite at the head of the particular sort of romances to which it belonged. The Antiquary, and Guy Mannering, for instance, were both much nearer perfection, and, on the whole, I thought both better books; but Ivanhoe, especially its commencement, was a noble poem. But did I not condemn the want of historical truth in its pictures? I did not consider Ivanhoe as intended to be history; it was a work of the imagination, in which all the fidelity that was requisite, was enough to be probable and natural, and that requisite I thought it possessed in an eminent degree. It is true, antiquarians accused the author of having committed some anachronisms, by confounding the usages of different centuries, which was perhaps a greater fault, in such a work, than to confound mere individual characters; but of this I did not pretend to judge, not being the least of an antiquarian myself. Did I not think he had done gross injustice to the noble and useful order of the Templars?[49] On this point I could say no more than on the preceding, having but a very superficial knowledge of the Templars, though I thought the probabilities seemed to be perfectly well respected. Nothing could *seem* to be more true, than Scott's pictures. My guest then went into a long vindication of the Templars, stating that Scott had done them gross injustice, and concluding with an exaggerated compliment, in which it was attempted to persuade me that I was the man to vindicate the truth, and to do justice to a subject that was so peculiarly connected with liberal principles. I disclaimed the ability to undertake such a task, at all; confessed that I did not wish to disturb the images which Sir Walter Scott had left, had I the ability; and declared I did not see the connection between his accusation, admitting it to be true, and liberal principles. My visitor soon after went away, and I saw no more of him for a week, when he came again. On this occasion, he commenced by relating several *piquant* anecdotes of the *Bourbons* and their friends, gradually and ingeniously leading the conversation, again, round to his favourite Templars. After pushing me, for half an hour, on this point, always insisting on my being the man to vindicate the order, and harping on its connection with liberty, he took advantage of one of my often-repeated protestations of ignorance of the whole matter, suddenly to say—"well, then, *Monsieur, go and see for yourself*, and you will soon be satisfied that my account of the order is true." "Go and see what?" "The Templars." "There are no longer any." "They exist still." "Where?" "Here, in Paris." "This is new to me; I do not understand it." "The Templars exist; they possess documents to prove how much Scott has misrepresented them, and—but, you will remember that the actual government has so much jealousy, of every thing it does not control, that secrecy is necessary—and, to be frank with you, M. ——, I am commissioned by the Grand Master, to invite you to be present, at a secret meeting, this very week."

Of course, I immediately conjectured that some of the political agitators of the day had assumed this taking guise, in order to combine their means, and carry out their plans.* The proposition was gotten rid of, by my stating, in terms that could not be misunderstood, that I was a traveller, and did not wish to meddle with any thing that required secrecy, in a foreign government; that I certainly had my own political notions, and if pushed, should not hesitate to avow them anywhere; that the proper place for a writer to declare his sentiments, was in his books, unless under circumstances which authorized him to act; that I did not conceive foreigners were justifiable in going beyond this; that I never had meddled with the affairs of foreign countries, and that I never would; and that the fact of this society's being secret, was sufficient to deter me from visiting it. With this answer, my guest departed, and he never came again.

Now, the first impression was, as I have told you, and I supposed my visitor, although a man of fifty, was one of those who innocently lent himself to these silly exaggerations; either as a dupe, or to dupe others. I saw reason, however, to change this opinion.

At the time these visits occurred, I scarcely knew any one in Paris, and was living in absolute retirement—being, as you know already, quite without letters. About ten days after I saw the last of my *littérateur*, I got a letter from a high functionary of the government, sending me a set of valuable medals. The following day, these were succeeded by his card, and an invitation to dinner. Soon after, another person, notoriously con-

---

* Since the revolution of 1830, these Templars have made public, but abortive efforts, to bring themselves into notice, by instituting some ceremonies, in which they appeared openly in their robes. [*Cooper's note.*]

nected with court intrigues, sought me out, and overwhelmed me with civilities. In a conversation that shortly after occurred between us, this person gave a pretty direct intimation, that by pushing a little, a certain decoration that is usually conferred on literary men, was to be had, if it were desired. I got rid of all these things, in the straight-forward manner, that is the best for upsetting intrigues; and having really nothing to conceal, I was shortly permitted to take my own course.

I have now little doubt that the *littérateur* was a *spy*, sent either to sound me on some point connected with La Fayette and the republicans, or possibly to lead me into some difficulty, though I admit that this is no more than conjecture. I give you the facts, which, at the time, struck me as, at least, odd, and you may draw your own conclusions. This, however, is but one of a dozen adventures, more or less similar, that have occurred, and I think it well to mention it, by way of giving you an insight into what sometimes happens here.*

My rule has been, whenever I am pushed on the subject of politics, to deal honestly and sincerely with all with whom I am brought in contact, and in no manner to leave the impression, that I think the popular form of government an unavoidable evil, to which America is obliged to submit. I do not shut my eyes to the defects of our own system, or to the bad consequences that flow from it, and from it alone; but, the more I see of other countries, the more I am persuaded, that, under circumstances which admit but of a choice of evils, we are greatly the gainers by having adopted it. Although I do not believe every other nation is precisely fitted to imitate us, I think it is their misfortune they are not so. If the inhabitants of other countries do not like to hear such opinions, they should avoid the subject with Americans.

* A conversation, which took place *after* the revolution of 1830, with one of the parties named, leaves little doubt as to the truth of the original conjecture. [*Cooper's note.*]

[LONDON ON THE EVE OF THE REFORM BILL]

From *England* (Vol. I, Letter XI)[50]

Among the acquaintances for whom I am indebted to the letters of Mr. Spencer, is Mr. Sotheby the poet. This gentleman, now no longer young, lives in a good style here, being apparently a man of fortune and condition. He is a good specimen of the country, simple, quiet, and, unless his countenance and manners are sad hypocrites, benevolent and honest. Indeed I have seldom seen any one who has left a more favourable impression, as respects the two latter qualities, on a short acquaintance.

Mr. Sotheby invited me to dinner, pretty much as a matter of course, for all social intercourse in England, as in America, and in France, is a good deal dependent on the table. I found him living in a house, that, so far as I could see, was American, as American houses used to be before the taste became corrupted by an uninstructed pretension. I was one of the first; but Mr. Coleridge was already in the drawing-room. He was a picture of green old age; ruddy, solid, and with a head as white as snow. His smile was benevolent, but I had scarcely time to reconnoitre him, before Sir Walter Scott appeared, accompanied by Mr. Lockhart. The latter is a genteel person, of a good carriage, with the air of a man of the world, and with a sort of Scotch-Spanish face. His smile is significant, and not a bad one for a reviewer. The wife of the Bishop of London, and two or three more formed our party.

At table I sat directly opposite to Sir Walter Scott, with Mr. Coleridge on my left. Nothing passed during dinner, worth mentioning, except a remark or two from the latter. He said that he had been employed, when secretary to Sir Alexander Ball, the Governor of Malta, to conduct a correspondence between the commander of our squadron and the government of Tripoli. I presume this must have been while Commodore Morris was in command, that officer being on very familiar terms with Admiral Ball, as the following anecdote will show.

The late Captain Bainbridge had a duel with an English officer
at Malta, and under circumstances that enlisted the public feeling
of [on?] his side, in which the latter was killed. The same day
Commodore Morris breakfasted with the Governor. After
breakfast, Sir Alexander Ball mentioned the affair to his guest,
with proper expressions of regret, adding it would be his duty
to demand[51] Mr. Bainbridge. Of course, nothing was to be said
to the contrary, and the Commodore took his leave. While
pulling off to his ship he casually observed that Mr. Bainbridge
would be demanded. The midshipman of the boat reported it
to the lieutenant of the deck, who sent notice to Mr. Bainbridge,
forthwith. In due time the official demand appeared. The Commodore sent orders to the different ships to deliver the delin-
quent, and received answers that he was no longer in the squadron. He had, in truth, hurried off to Sicily in a hired felucca.
This showed a good feeling on the part of Sir Alexander Ball,
who always manifested a seaman's desire that we should flog the
barbarians. Mr. Coleridge did not tell this anecdote, but I had
it, many years since, from my old friend Commodore Morris,
himself.

.   .   .   .

When the ladies had retired, the conversation turned on
Homer, whom, it is understood Mr. Sotheby is now engaged
in translating. Some one remarked that Mr. Coleridge did not
believe in his unity, or rather that there was any such man. This
called him out, and certainly I never witnessed an exhibition as
extraordinary as that which followed. It was not a discourse,
but a dissertation. Scarcely any one spoke besides Mr. Coleridge, with the exception of a brief occasional remark from Mr.
Sotheby, who held the contrary opinion, and I might say no
one *could* speak. At moments he was surprisingly eloquent,
though a little discursive, and the whole time he appeared to be
perfectly the master of his subject and of his language. As near
as I could judge, he was rather more than an hour in *possession
of the floor*, almost without interruption. His utterance was
slow, every sentence being distinctly given, and his pronunciation accurate. There seemed to be a constant struggling between

an affluence of words and an affluence of ideas, without either hesitation or repetition. His voice was strong and clear, but not pitched above the usual key of conversation. The only peculiarity about it, was a slightly observable burring of *r. r. rs.*, but scarcely more than what the language properly requires.

Once or twice, when Mr. Sotheby would attempt to say a word on his side of the question, he was permitted to utter just enough to give a leading idea, but no argument, when the reasoning was taken out of his mouth by the essayist, and continued, pro and con, with the same redundant and eloquent fluency. I was less struck by the logic than by the beauty of the language, and the poetry of the images. Of the theme, in a learned sense, I knew too little to pretend to any verbal or critical knowledge, but he naturally endeavoured to fortify his argument by the application of his principles to familiar things; and here, I think, he often failed. In fact, the exhibition was much more wonderful than convincing.

At first I was so much struck with the affluent diction of the poet, as scarcely to think of any thing else; but when I did look about me, I found every eye fastened on him. Scott sat, immoveable as a statue, with his little grey eyes looking inward and outward, and evidently considering the whole as an exhibition, rather than as an argument; though he occasionally muttered, "eloquent!" "wonderful!" "very extraordinary!" Mr. Lockhart caught my eye once, and he gave a very hearty laugh, without making the slightest noise, as if he enjoyed my astonishment. When we rose, however, he expressed his admiration of the speaker's eloquence.

The dissertations of Mr. Coleridge cannot properly be brought in comparison with the conversation of Sir James M'Intosh. One lectures, and the other converses. There is a vein of unpretending philosophy, and a habit of familiar analysis in the conversation of the latter, that causes you to remember the substance of what he has said, while the former, though synthetick and philosophical as a verbal critic, rather enlists the imagination than any other property of the mind. M'Intosh is willing enough to listen, while Coleridge reminded me of a barrel to which every other man's tongue acted as a spigot; for no sooner did the latter move, than it set his own contents in a flow.

We were still at table, when the constant raps at the door gave notice that the drawing-room was filling above. Mr. Coleridge lectured on, through it all, for half an hour longer, when Mr. Sotheby rose. The house was full of company assembled to see Scott. He walked deliberately into a maze of petticoats, and, as he had told me at Paris, let them play with his mane as much as they pleased. I had an engagement, and went to look for my hat, which, to escape the fangs of the servants, who have an inconvenient practice, here, of taking your hat out of the drawing-room while you are at dinner, I had snugly hid under a sofa. The Bishop of London was seated directly above it, and completely covered it with his petticoat. Mr. Sotheby observing that I was aiming at something there, kindly inquired what I wanted. I told him I was praying for the translation[52] of the Bishop of London, that I might get my hat, and, marvellous as it may seem, he has already been made Archbishop of Canterbury!

From *England* (Vol. I, Letter XIV)

Were the people of England, free from the prejudices of their actual situation and absolutely without a political organization, assembled to select a polity for their future government, it is probable that the man who should propose the present system, would at once be set down as a visionary, or a fool. Could things be reversed, however, and the nation collected for the same purpose, under the influence of the opinions that now prevail, the proposer of the system that would be very likely to be adopted in the former case, would be lucky if he escaped with his ears. It is safer that facts should precede opinions in the progress of political meliorations, than that opinions should precede facts; though it would be better still, could the two march *pari passu*. All essential changes in the control of human things, must be attended by one of two species of contests, the struggles of those who would hasten, or the struggles of those who would retard events. The active portion of the former are usually so small a minority, that it is pretty accurate to affirm they are more useful as pioneers than as pilots, while it is in the nature of things that the latter should gradually lose their power by desertions, until compelled by circumstances to yield.

The considerations connected with these truths teach us that reform is generally a wiser remedy than revolution. Still it must be recollected that the progress of things is not always in the right direction. Artificial and selfish combinations frequently supplant the natural tendency to improvement, and a people, by waiting the course of events, might sometimes be the supine observers of the process of forging their own chains. In all such cases, unless the current can be turned, it must be made to lose its influence by being thrown backward.

In continuing the subject of the last letter, I am of opinion that the present system of England is to undergo radical alterations, by the safest of the two remedies, that of reform; a denial of which will certainly produce convulsions.[53] The hereditary principle, as extended beyond the isolated abstraction of a monarch, is offensive to human pride, not to say natural justice, and I believe the world contains no instance of an enlightened people's long submitting to it, unless it has been relieved by some extraordinary, mitigating, circumstances of national prosperity. The latter has been the fact with England; but, as is usually the case with all exceptions to general rules, it has brought with it a countervailing principle that, sooner or later, will react on the system.

Hitherto, England has had a monopoly of available knowledge. Protected by her insular situation, industry has taken refuge in the island; and, fostered by franchises, it has prospered beyond all former example. The peculiar construction of the empire, in which national character and conquest have been mutually cause and effect, has turned a flood of wealth into that small portion of it, which, being the seat of power, regulates the tone of the whole, as the heart controls the pulsations of the body. This is the favourable side of the question, and on it are to be found the temporal advantages that have induced men to submit to an ascendancy that they might otherwise resist.

The unfavourable is peculiarly connected with the events of the last thirty years. In order to counteract the effects of the French revolution, the aristocracy carried on a war, that has cost the country a sum of money which, still hanging over the nation in the shape of debt, is likely to produce a radical change in the elements of its prosperity. In the competition of industry which is now spreading itself throughout Christendom, it is absolutely necessary to keep down the price of labour in England, to prevent being undersold in foreign markets, and to keep up the prices of food, in order to pay taxes. These two causes united have created an excess of pauperism, that hangs like a dead weight on the nation, and which helps to aid the rivalry of foreign competition. Taking the two together, about one hundred and thirty millions of dollars annually are paid by the nation, and much the greater part as a fine proceeding from the peculiar form of the government; for the sacrifices that were made, were only to be expected from those who were contending especially for their own privileges. As the territories of England were impregnable, no mere monarch could have carried on the system of Mr. Pitt, since the rich would not have submitted to it, and as for the people, or the mass, there would have been no sufficient motive. In order to appreciate these efforts, and their consequences, it will be necessary to consider the vast annual sums expended by Great Britain during the late wars, and then look around for the benefits. One undeniable result is, I take it, that industry is quitting the kingdom, under the influence of precisely the same causes as those by which it was introduced. I do not mean so much that capitalists depart, as they left Flanders, for the scale on which things are now graduated, renders more regular changes necessary, but that the skill emigrates, to avoid the exactions of the state. I may, however, go further, and add that capital also quits the country. It takes longer to subvert the sources of national than of individual prosperity, and we are not to look for results in a day. Still these results, I think, are already apparent. They appear in the moderated tone of this government, in its strong disinclination to war, and, in fact, on an entire change in its foreign policy.

It is quite obvious that the English aristocracy is existing in a state of constant alarm. The desperate expedient of Mr. Pitt, that of undertaking a crusade against popular rights, is already producing its reaction.[54] It is seldom that the human mind can be brought to an unnatural tension on one side, without recoiling to the other extreme, as soon as liberated. Men are constantly vibrating around truth, the passions and temporary interests acting as the weights to keep the pendulum in motion. The result of the present condition of the English aristocracy, is to put them, in a political as well as a social sense, on their good behaviour. Although so great a proportion of the peculiar embarrassments of Great Britain may be traced, with sufficient clearness, to the exclusive features of the government, there probably never has been a period in the history of the nation, when the power of the few has been so undisputed in practice, or its exercise more under the sense of correction.

. . . .

Still the aristocracy of this country is very powerful. It has enlisted in its favour a strong national feeling, a portion of which is well founded, a part of which is fraudulent, and even wicked, and some of which is dependent on one of the most abject conditions of the mind to which man is liable. By aristocracy I do not now mean merely the peers and their heirs, but that class which is identified by blood, intermarriages, possessions, and authority in the government, for you are never to forget, though the House of Commons does contain a few members who are exceptions, that the controlling majority of that body is, to all intents and purposes, no more than another section of the interests represented by the peers. The two bodies may occasionally disagree, but it is as partners discuss their common concerns, and as the lords frequently disagree among themselves.

The English gentlemen have the merits of courage, manliness, intelligence, and manners.—Their morals are overrated, except as to the vices which are connected with meanness. Perhaps there is less of the latter than is commonly found in countries where the upper classes are more directly under the influence of courts, but even of this there is much, very much, more than it is common to believe in America. As between the English and ourselves, I honestly think we have the advantage of them on this point. They are our superiors in manners and in intelligence; they are our superiors in all that manliness which is dependent on opinion, but certainly I have known things practised, and that pretty openly, in connexion with interest, by men of condition here, which could not well be done by a gentleman with us, without losing *caste*. In the northern states we have very few families whose sons would now hesitate about embarking in commerce, at need, and this, of itself, is a great outlet (as well as inlet) for the vices of a pecuniary nature. The prejudices connected with this one subject are the cause of half the meannesses of Europe. The man who would hesitate about suffering his name to appear in a commercial firm would pass his life in a commission of meannesses, not to say crimes, that should put him to the ban of society. This feeling is daily becoming weaker in England, but it is still strong. Men of family scarcely ever engage *openly* in commerce, though they often do things *covertly*, which, besides possessing the taint of trade, have not the redeeming merit of even its equivocal ethics. To them the army, navy, church and government patronage are almost the only resources. The latter facts have given rise to two of the most odious of the practical abuses of the present system. A few occasionally appear at the bar, but more as criminals than as advocates. The profession is admitted within the pale of society, as it opens the way to the peerage and to parliament, but it requires too much labour and talents to be in favour. A physician in England ranks higher, professionally, than almost any where else, but he is scarcely considered an equal in the higher set. The younger sons of peers enter all the professions but that of medicine, I never heard of one who chose to be a doctor. A curate may become Archbishop of Canterbury, but a physician can merely hope to reach a baronetcy, a dignity little coveted. Like our "Honourables," and "Colonels," it is not in vogue with the higher classes. I cannot better illustrate the state of feeling here, in relation to these minor titles, than by our own relation to the appellations named, which are of much account in certain sets, but which it is thought bad taste to bandy among gentlemen.

From *England* (Vol. II, Letter XXVIII)

In England, the disaffected to the government, are among precisely those who most sustain government in America; and the disaffected in America, (if so strong a word can properly be used, as applied to natives,) are of a class whose interests it is to sustain government in England.* These facts give very different aspects to the general features of society. Walking in Regent street, lately, I witnessed an attempt of the police, to compel some hackney coachmen to quit their boxes, and go with them before the magistrate.[55] A crowd of a thousand people collected immediately, and its feeling was decidedly against the ministers of the law; so much so, indeed, as to render it doubtful, whether the coachmen, whose conduct had been flagrantly criminal, would not be rescued. Now, in America, I think, the feeling of such a crowd, would have been just the other way. It would have taken an interest in supporting the authorities of the country, instead of an interest in opposing them. This was not the case of a mob, you will remember, in which passion puts down reason, but an ordinary occurrence of the exercise of the power of the police. Instances of this nature, might be multiplied, to

* When the writer went to Europe, it was so unusual to hear any thing against the system of America, that disaffection may be said to have become extinct. On his return, however, after an absence of less than eight years, he was astonished to hear monarchical sentiments openly declared, and he believes that it will be generally admitted by all candid observers, that their avowal is now more open and more frequent, than they have been at any time, within the present century. This is not the place to discuss the reasons, but this explanation is due from the writer, on his own account, as, without it, a change that has actually taken place among others, may be ascribed to himself. No one need be ashamed of having honestly altered his opinions, for good cause, and after mature examination; but since the publication of these letters has commenced, the writer has been openly accused of changes that, in point of fact, have occurred among other people. Another occasion may offer to examine this point. [*Cooper's note.*]

show that the mass of the two people, act under the influence of feelings diametrically opposed to each other.

On the other hand, Englishmen of the higher classes are, with very few exceptions, and these exceptions are usually instances of mere party opposition, attached to their system, sensitive on the subject of its merits or defects, and ever ready to defend it when assailed. The American of the same class is accustomed to sneer at democracy, to cavil at its fruits, and to colour and exaggerate its faults. Though this latter disposition may be, to a degree, accounted for by the facts, that all merit is comparative, and most of our people have not had the opportunities to compare; and that it is natural to resist most that which most annoys, although the substitution of any other for the actual system would produce even greater discontent; still, I think, the general tendency of aristocratical institutions on the one hand, and of democratical on the other, is to produce this broad difference in feeling, as between classes.

Both the Americans and the English are charged with being offensively boastful and arrogant, as nations, and too much disposed to compare themselves advantageously with their neighbours. I have visited no country in which a similar disposition does not exist, and as communities are merely aggregations of men, I fancy that the disposition of a people to take this view of their own merits, is no more than carrying out the well known principle of individual vanity. The English and ourselves, however, well may, and probably do differ from other nations, in one circumstance connected with such a failing. The mass in both nations, are better instructed, and are of more account than the mass in other countries, and their sentiments form more of a public opinion than elsewhere. When the bulk of a people are in a condition to make themselves heard, one is not to expect much refinement or delicacy, in the sentiments they utter. The English do not strike me as being a vainer nation than the French, although, in the way of ordinary intercourse, I believe that both they and we are more boastful.

The English are to be particularly distinguished from the Americans, in the circumstance of their being proud people.

This is a useful and even ennobling quality, when it is sustained by facts, though apt to render a people both uncomfortable and unpleasant, when the glory on which they pique themselves is passed away. We are almost entirely wanting in national pride, though abundantly supplied with an irritable vanity, that might rise to pride, had we greater confidence in our facts. Most intelligent Englishmen are ready enough to admit the obvious faults of their climate, and even of their social condition, but it is an uncommon American that will concede any thing material, on such points, unless it can be made to bear on democracy. We have the sensitiveness of provincials, increased by the consciousness of having our spurs to earn, on all matters of glory and renown, and our jealousy extends even to the reputations of the cats and dogs. It is but an indifferent compliment to human nature to add, that the man who will join, complacently, and I may say ignorantly, in the abuse of foreigners against the institutions of the country, and even against its people, always reserving a saving clause in favour of his own particular class, will take fire if an innuendo is hazarded against its beef, or a suggestion made that the four thousand feet of the Round Peak, are not equal to the thirteen thousand of the *Jung Frau*. The English are tolerably free from this weakness, and travelling is daily increasing this species of liberality, at least. I presume that the insular situation of England, and our own distance from Europe, are equally the causes of these traits, though there may be said to be a "property qualification" in the very nature of man, that disposes him to view his own things with complacency, and those of his neighbors with distrust. Bishop Heber, in one of his letters to Lord Grenville, in speaking of the highest peaks of the Himalayas, throws into a parenthesis, "which I feel some exultation in saying, is completely within the limits of the British empire," a sort of sentiment, of which, I dare say, neither St. Chrysostom nor Polycarp was entirely free.[56]

On the subject of sensibility to comments on their national habits and national characters, neither France nor England is by any means as philosophical or indifferent as one might suppose. As a rule, I believe all men are more easily enraged when their real faults are censured, than when their virtues are called in question; and, if the defect happen to be unavoidable, or one for which they are not fairly responsible, the resentment is two-fold that which would attend a comment on a vice. The only difference I can discover between the English and ourselves, in this particular, is easily to be traced to our greater provincialism, youth, and the consciousness that we are obliged to anticipate some of our renown. I should say that the English are *thin-skinned*, and the Americans *raw*. Both resent fair, frank, and manly comments with the same bad taste, resorting to calumny, blackguardism, and abuse, when wit and pleasantry would prove both more effective and wiser, and, perhaps, reformation, wisest of all. I can only account for this peculiarity, by supposing that the institutions and political facts of the two countries have rendered vulgar-minded men of more account, than is usually the case, and that their influence has created a species of public opinion which is less under the correction of taste, principles, and manners, than is the case in nations where the mass is more depressed. Of the fact, itself, there can be no question.

In order to appreciate the effect of refinement on this nation, it will be necessary to recur to some of its statistical facts. England, including Wales, contains rather less than fifty-eight thousand square miles of territory; the state of New York, about forty-three thousand. On the former surface, there is a population of something like fifteen millions; on the latter, a population of less than two. One gives a proportion of about two hundred and sixty to the square mile, and the other a proportion of less than fifty. These premises, alone, would show us the immense advantage that any given portion of surface in England, must possess over the same extent of surface in America, in all those arts and improvements, that depend on physical force. If there were ten men of education, and refinement, and fortune, in a county of New York, of one thousand square miles in extent, there ought to be more than fifty men of the same character and means, in an English county of equal territory. This is supposing that the real premises offer nothing more against us, than the disproportion between numbers and surface; whereas, in fact, time, wealth, and an older civilization, more than quadruple the odds. Even these do not make up the sum of the adverse elements. Though England has but fifteen millions of souls, the empire she controls has nearly ten times that population, and a very undue proportion of the results of so great a physical force, centre in this small spot.

The consideration of these truths suggest several useful heads of reflection. In the first place, they show us, if not the absolute impossibility, the great improbability, that the civilization, refinement, knowledge, wealth, and tastes of even the best portions of America, can equal those of this country, and suggest the expediency of looking to other points for our sources of pride. I have said, that the two countries act under the influence of moral agencies that are almost the converse of each other. The condensation of improvement and cultivation is so great here, that even the base of society is affected by it, even to deportment; whereas, with us, these properties are so dispersed, as to render it difficult for those who are lucky enough to possess them, to keep what they have got, in face of the overshadowing influence of a lower school, instead of being able to impart them to society. Our standard, in nearly all things, as it is popular, is necessarily one of mediocrity; a highly respectable, and, circumstances considered, a singularly creditable one, but still a mediocrity; whereas, the condition of these people has enabled them to raise a standard, which, however much it may be and is wanting in the better elements of a pure taste, has immensely the advantage of our own, in most of the obvious blandishments of life. More than half of the peculiarities of America, peculiarities for which it is usual to seek a cause in the institutions, simply because they are so peculiar themselves, are to be traced to facts like these; or, in other words, to the disproportion between surface and numbers, the want of any other than commercial towns, and our distance from the rest of the world.

Every condition of society has its own advantages, and its own disadvantages. To claim perfection for any one, in particular, would be to deny the nature of man. Their comparative merits are to be decided, only, by the comparative gross results, and it is in this sense, that I contend for the superiority of our own. The utilitarian school,[57] as it has been popularly construed, is not to my taste, either, for I believe there is great utility in the grace and elegance of life, and no one would feel more disposed to resist a system, in which these essential properties are proscribed. That we are wanting in both, I am ready to allow; but I think the reason is to be found in facts entirely independent of the institutions, and that the time will come, when the civilization of America will look down that of any other section of the world, if the country can pass that state of probation, during which it is and will be exposed to the assaults of secret combinations to destroy it; and during which, moreover, it is, and in an especial degree, liable to be affected by inherited opinions, and opinions that have been obtained under a system that has so many of the forms, while it has so few of the principles of our own, as easily to be confounded with it, by the ignorant and the unreflecting.

We over-estimate the effects of intelligence, as between ourselves and the English. The mass of information, here, probably exceeds that of America, though it is less equally distributed. In *general* knowledge of a practical nature, too, I think no people can compete with our own. But there is a species of information, that is both useful and refining, in which there are few European nations that do not surpass us. I allude, in particular, to most things that serve to embellish life. In addition to this superiority, the Europeans of the better classes very obviously possess over us an important advantage, in their intimate associations with each other, by which means they insensibly imbibe a great deal of current knowledge, of which the similar classes in America are nearly ignorant; or, which, if known at all, is only known through the medium of books. In the exhibition of this knowledge, which embraces all that belongs to what is commonly termed a knowledge of the world, the difference between the European and the American is the difference to be seen between the man who has passed all his days in good society, and the man who has got his knowledge of it from novels and plays.

In a correct estimate of their government, and in an acquaintance with its general action, the English are much our superiors, though we know most of details. This arises from the circumstances that the rights of an Englishman are little more than franchises, which require no very profound examination to be understood, while those of the American depend on principles that demand study, and which are constantly exposed to the antagonist influence of opinions that have been formed under another system. It is true the English monarchy, as a monarchy and as it now exists, is a pure mystification, but the supremacy of parliament being admitted, there can arise no great difficulty on the score of interpretation. The American system, moreover, is complicated and double, and the only true Whig and Tory parties that can exist must have their origin in this circumstance. To these reasons may be added the general fact, that the educated Englishman reasons on his institutions like an Englishman only, while his American counterpart oftener reasons on the institutions of the republic like an Englishman too, than like an American. A single fact will show you what I mean, although a hundred might be quoted. In England the government is composed, in theory, of three bases and one summit; in America, it is composed of one base and three summits. In one, there is supposed to be a balance in the powers of the state; and as this is impossible in practice, it has resulted in a consolidated authority in its action; in the other, there is but one power, that of the entire people, and the balance is in the action of their agents.[58] A very little reflection will show that the maxims of two such systems ought to be as different as the systems themselves.

The English are to be distinguished from the Americans, by greater independence of personal habits. Not only the institutions, but the physical condition of our own country has a tendency to reduce us all to the same level of usages. The steamboats, the over-grown taverns, the speculative character of the enterprises, and the consequent disposition to do all things in common, aid the tendency of the system in bringing about such a result. In England a man dines by himself, in a room filled with other hermits; he eats at his leisure; drinks his wine in silence;

reads the paper by the hour, and, in all things, encourages his individuality and insists on his particular humours. The American is compelled to submit to a common rule; he eats when others eat; sleeps when others sleep; and he is lucky, indeed, if he can read a paper in a tavern without having a stranger looking over each shoulder.* The Englishman would stare at a proposal that should invade his habits under the pretence of a common wish, while the American would be very apt to yield tacitly, though this common wish should be no more than an impudent assertion of some one who had contrived to affect his own purposes, under the popular plea. The Englishman is so much attached to his independence that he instinctively resists every effort to invade it, and nothing would be more likely to arouse him than to say the mass thinks differently from himself; whereas the American ever seems ready to resign his own opinion to that which is made to seem to be the opinion of the public. I say *seems* to be, for so manifest is the power of public opinion, that one of the commonest expedients of all American managers, is to create an impression that the public thinks in a particular way, in order to bring the common mind in subjection. One often renders himself ridiculous by a foolish obstinacy, and the other is as often contemptible by a weak compliance. A portion of what may be called the *community* of character and habits in America, is doubtless owing to the rustic nature of its society, for one more easily maintains his independence in a capital than in a village, but I think the chief reasons are to be found in the practice of referring every thing to the common mind.

It is usual to ascribe the solitary and unsocial habits of English life, to the natural dispositions of the people, but I think unjustly. The climate is made to bear the blame of no small portion of this peculiarity. Climate, probably, has an influence on us all, for we know that we are more elastic, and more ready to be pleased in a clear bracing air, than in one that is close and *sciroccoish*,[59] but, on the whole I am led to think, the English

* Exaggerated as this may appear, the writer has actually been driven away, by strangers leaning over him, in this manner, no less than eleven times, at the Astor House, within the last twelvemonths. [*Cooper's note.*]

owe their habits to their institutions, more than to any natural causes.

I know no subject, no feeling, nothing, on which an Englishman, as a rule, so completely loses sight of all the better points of his character, on which he is so uniformly bigotted and unjust, so ready to listen to misrepresentation and caricature, and so unwilling to receive truth, on which, in short, he is so little like himself in general, as on those connected with America.

As the result of this hasty and imperfect comparison, I am led to believe, that a national character somewhere between the two, would be preferable to either, as it is actually found. This may be saying no more than that man does not exist in a condition of perfection; but were the inequalities named, pared off from both people, an ingenious critic might still find faults of sufficient magnitude, to preserve the identity with the human race, and qualities of sufficient elevation, to entitle both to be considered among the greatest and best nations of modern, if not of any other, times.

In most things that pertain to taste, the English have greatly the advantage of us, though *taste* is certainly not the strong side of English character. On this point, alone, one might write a book, but a very few remarks must now satisfy you. In nothing, however, is this superiority more apparent, than in their simplicity, and, particularly, in their simplicity of language. They call a spade, a spade. I very well know, that neither men nor women, in America, who are properly educated, and who are accustomed to its really better tone, differ much, if any, from the English in this particular, but, in this case, as in most others, in which *national* peculiarities are sought, the better tone of America is overshadowed by its mediocrity.* Although I deem the government of this country the very quintessence of hocus pocus, having scarcely a single practice that does not violate its theory, I believe that there is more honesty of public sentiment in England than in America. The defect at home, I ascribe, in common with the majority of our national failings, to the greater activity, and greater *unresisted* force of ignorance and cupidity,

* [Cooper's note on Fanny Kemble's journal omitted.]

there, than here. High qualities are nowhere collected in a sufficient phalanx to present a front to the enemy, in America.

The besetting, the degrading vice of America, is the moral
cowardice by which men are led to truckle to what is called
public opinion; though this opinion is as inconstant as the winds,
though, in all cases, that enlist the feelings of factions there are
two, and sometimes twenty, each differing from all the others,
and though, nine times in ten, these opinions are mere engines
set in motion by the most corrupt and the least respectable portion of the community, for unworthy purposes. The English
are a more respectable and constant nation than the Americans,
as relates to this peculiarity; probably, because the condensed
masses of intelligence and character enable the superior portion
of the community to produce a greater impression on the inferior, by their collective force. In standing prejudices, they
strike me as being worse than ourselves; but in passing impressions greatly our superiors.

For the last I have endeavoured to account, and I think the
first may be ascribed to a system that is sustained by errors that
it is not the interest of the more enlightened to remove, but
which, instead of weakening in the ignorant, they rather encourage in themselves.

[THE ALPS]

From *Switzerland, Part I* (Vol II, Letter XVI)[60]

DEAR ——,

I took a room at the Ox, the best inn, and hastened towards
the abbey.[61] As I can scarcely recall a day of stronger or more
varied sensations than this, it may be well to give you a brief
history of the causes which have brought the shrine of Einsiedeln into so much repute.

A hermit* of great sanctity lived near the spot many cen-

---

* He is said to have been a contemporary of Charlemagne, and a member
of the house of Hohenzollern, which is now seated on the throne of
Prussia. [*Cooper's note.*]

turies since. This man was murdered, and respect for his memory induced a religious community to establish themselves around his cell. On the occasion of a consecration of a chapel, the bishop, it is affirmed, was anticipated by angels, who performed the rite to heavenly music, at midnight. This event at once brought our Lady of the Hermits, as she is called, into high request, and from that day to this, or for nine centuries, Mary of Einsiedeln has been a favourite with pilgrims of all the surrounding nations. Other traditions are also connected with the principal miracle. The Saviour is stated to have visited the shrine dedicated to his mother, in the human form. There is a copious fountain before the church, which has fourteen spouts, and at one of these (which is not known) he is believed to have drunk. He also left a complete impression of his hand on a silver plate; but the French removed both impression and plate at the time of their invasion; for it would have been the greater miracle of the two had they left any thing formed of the precious metals behind them.

Einsiedeln, unlike Loretto, has never been much frequented by the great. There is an unction about Italy, in such matters, with which it is nearly vain to hope to compete; and the difficulty of access and the proximity of heresy may have aided in diverting the current of pilgrimage. But, at the present time, Einsiedeln has probably more votaries than the shrine of the Roman States, though they certainly are of a greatly inferior quality. It has struck me that this particular species of devotion, or, indeed, most of those ancient observances of the church of Rome, which depend more on tradition than on doctrine and revelation, are fast falling into disrepute with all classes of society but its two extremes; the princes and the peasants; superstition, it would seem, being as much the companion of very high as of very low fortunes. In the latter case, it is the result of ignorance, and of a misery that seeks all modes of relief: and, in the former, of that innate sense of unworthiness, which renders every man conscious of his own inability to control high events, and secretly disposes him to lean on a supernatural power. That they do not place their reliance on more rational aids, is, probably, in both cases, the fault of education, little more being taught to princes than the accomplishments which are useful in maintaining the representation of their rank. Thus they are all linguists, but very rarely logicians. Napoleon himself is said to have believed in his fortune, and to have been much under the influence of superstition; a fact, which, with his education and previous disposition, must be attributed solely to the consciousness of being required to decide on events that belong rather to destiny than to any human will. Thus, you perceive, as "hypocrisy is the homage that vice pays to virtue," I am ready to maintain that superstition is no other than an involuntary admission of our want of the higher attributes of intelligence. Perhaps no man is entirely without it.

At all events, princes and peasants are the two classes who now appear to retain the greatest respect for the ancient superstitions of the Catholic Church. Policy, no doubt, in some measure, influences the first; but I think the world does not give them credit always for a sincerity which, for the reasons named, I believe they oftener feel than is supposed.

Pilgrims were arriving throughout the day, in parties varying from a dozen to a hundred. Their approach was always announced by the untiring repetitions of the prayers, the effect of which, in the distance, especially when male and female voices alternated, was poetical and plaintive. All drank at the fountain, and nearly all its several spouts, in order to make sure of pressing their lips to the one which is supposed to have been consecrated by the lips of the Saviour. They then invariably entered the building, serious, earnest, and devout, and knelt before the shrine.

The church is large, and almost worthy of being ranked with the cathedrals of Italy. It is a good deal ornamented, having many marble altars, painted ceilings, and much gilding. The shrine is of marble, and it stands quite near the great doors. Iron gratings in front, and on parts of the two sides, permit views of the interior, where the bronzed images of the mother and child are so placed as to receive the rays of a single but strong lamp. Their habiliments resembled pure gold.

When I entered, hundreds of pilgrims were kneeling on the pavement around the grates, keeping their eyes riveted, without an exception, on the dark, mysterious faces within. Many maintained this position for hours, and all appeared to be absorbed in subdued devotion. The light of the church was growing dim with the decline of day, and I walked stealthily around the groups, and through the vaulted aisles, with feelings of reverence, pity, admiration and awe, so blended, that I find it difficult to describe them. I knew that the temple was God's, and that his Spirit was present; I felt persuaded that much devout reliance on his mercy was blended with the superstition I witnessed; and, while my reason showed how fearfully near idolatry these poor people had approached, the mystery of the incarnation never appeared so sublime, and, if I may so express it, so palpable, as at that moment. I believe few men are less under the influence of superstition, or a dread of any sort connected with spiritual agencies than myself, and yet I found it necessary to draw largely on my Protestant insensibilities, in order to gaze at the bronzed countenance of Mary with indifference. Sympathy with the earnest and well-meaning crowd who knelt before her, a belief which, while it rejected so much of the embellishment of their own faith, admitted so much of its substance, and a sense of common inability to penetrate the great secret of the system of the universe, disposed me to be charitable. It was impossible to witness the pain and labour with which these poor people had traversed plains and mountains to reach the shrine, the subdued and imploring air with which they approached the image, and the fixed attitudes of reverence and deprecation, mingled with a strange sentiment of affectionate reliance, that all assumed, without feeling how insignificant shades in creed become, when devotion really occupies the soul. In short, I was in no humour to be critical, and felt strongly disposed to receive every thing as it was offered, and as it wished to appear.

Most of the pilgrims were Germans. A large portion were from the Black Forest, though there were also a good many Alsaciens, and a few Italians in the different groups. Some of the men had noble classical faces; and I can recall one or two, who, bending on the stones with naked knees, heads inclined, and eyes humbly but steadily riveted on the bronzed image, were perfect models of manly submission to an omnipotent and incomprehensible Power. I did not see a comely female among them. Beauty, real and of a high character, is everywhere rare; but that near approach to it, which we receive as its substitute, and which we should be willing to admit is beauty itself, but for the occasional exceptions that serve to raise the standard, and which is so very common in America, is of very unfrequent occurrence in this portion of Europe. A pretty peasant is hardly ever seen, and the costumes which appear so well in prints, are actually neutralized by the want of personal attractions in those who wear them. Nothing could be more wretched in externals than most of the female pilgrims on this occasion, though even they seemed respectable and more human than usual, while grouped around the shrine, in quiet, enduring, earnest devotion.

The twilight was still in the aisles, when a procession of monks entered by a lateral door, and approached the shrine. I had seen one or two of the fraternity gliding among the pillars of the narrow galleries that connect the upper portions of the church, apparently looking down, in watchfulness, at the devotees; but, though picturesque to the eye, their flitting about in this manner had recalled me from more pleasing thoughts, to recollections of monkish craft, and I fancied their presence unseasonable. Now, however, they came in a body, the princely abbot at their head, and began to chant the offices. The delusion was disturbed by this idle parade; for there is usually a want of reverence in the manner of the officials in Catholic worship, that does not at all comport with Protestant humility. They soon withdrew in the same order; and then commenced a scene that was still less in unison with our opinions. The pilgrims pressed forward, offering boxes of beads, images, and other similar articles, to a monk who remained in the shrine, and who, after touching the image with the different objects, returned them to their several owners to be preserved as relics. Nothing could be more business-like than the whole process, which, unfortunately for previous impressions, I mentally compared at the moment to the rapid evolutions of a notorious vender of *galettes* on the *Boulevard St. Martin,* at Paris. Such ludicrous associations make sad inroads on the touching and the beautiful; and I turned away, to stroll up the body of the church, devoured by skepticism. Every altar was crowded, and by this time the light was so dim as to give a shadowy appearance to the images of the edifice, its rich ornaments, its columns, galleries, aisles, and even to the kneeling pilgrims. I took this opportunity, while the last impressions were agreeable, to quit the place, and to return to the inn.

Several bodies of pilgrims had arrived since myself; and at the inn I still heard them repeating their prayers in the streets. As soon as I had dined, I sent for the guide, in order to measure the *étape* for the next day's march. He had hardly entered before the sound of voices in the street drew us to the window, which a party of seventy-four pilgrims was passing. The men walked bareheaded on one side of the road, and the women on the other. The guide shook his head, as if he looked on all this as very wicked. He is an inveterate Protestant, and got himself in difficulty not long since by speaking his sentiments on the subject, a little too freely. According to his account of the matter, it would have been very easy for either of us to gain the honours of martyrdom, by just stepping into the square, and proclaiming our private opinions concerning the divine consecration of the chapel of our Lady of the Hermits. I earnestly advised him to try the experiment; but this he adroitly evaded, by saying he owed it to his character and conscience to see me safe back to Thun. Of course, after this considerate explanation, I did not press the matter. While we were discussing the point, another party passed, barefoot as well as bareheaded.

As we concluded it was the most expedient not to attack the angelic consecration, I settled the affair of the next day's march as fast as possible, and hurried back to the church. The building was now dimly lighted, and the pilgrims still knelt in its gloomy shadows, resembling statues of stone. Many of them had their packs on their backs, like types of their sins. Two females of better appearance than usual were praying at a side altar; but no one else of either sex, of a station above that of a peasant, was in the church, the officials and myself excepted. The books certainly say that men of condition do make this pilgrimage; but if any such were here to-day, they were thoroughly disguised; so completely so, I should think, as to baffle the penetration of even our Lady of the Hermits.

I could not lose three days, at this late season, (Friday 12th September, 1828,) in order to witness the ceremonies of the succeeding Sunday, and we departed, therefore, on foot, early on the following morning. The road was lined for some distance with "stations," as they are called, or little chapels that usually represent the passions of the Redeemer, in which the pious go through a succession of prayers suited to their own weaknesses,—a common observance in Catholic countries. Pilgrims were still met, every half mile, some coming from the cantons, some from Germany, and some from the Tyrol. One party were carrying their packs on their heads, another were barefooted, and each apparently had some peculiar form of penance.

We also met many boys and girls bearing fruit to the village. As the day proved very warm, it was grateful to cool the palate with plums and pears, while toiling up the sharp and frequent ascents. I had got completely out of my reckoning, though the fact that we were on the broken surface of a mountain was sufficiently evident, not only by its productions, but by the air which bounded the view towards the south; in Switzerland, the landscape being usually in a grand setting of rocks, unless the spectator is on an elevation.

After more than an hour of hard walking, we came to an ascent that was steeper than common. As we drew near the top, I observed the eyes of the guide were getting to be restless, and began to think he was disposed to try a little Kirschwasser, for he had just told me there was an inn at the summit, where very good liquor was to be had. I did the old man injustice. He was thinking, altogether in the way of his vocation, of the glory of Switzerland, and of an agreeable surprise that lay before me. The ascent brought us suddenly to the summit of that mountain which bounds the southern shore of the lake of Zurich, and the region to the north and west of that sheet of water being what may be called a champaign country for the Alps, we were on the threshold of "a view." A few steps brought us to the verge of the declivity, where the eye ranged over a vast reach of country into Germany. We were about two thousand feet above the lake of Zurich, a portion of which lay at our feet, cut by the bridge of Rapperschwyl. The island of Ufnau was also in sight; and the mountain that we had descended on our way from the Tockenberg, lay a little on the left. In short, it was completely the reverse of the picture we had seen on the occasion of passing up the other shore of the lake, as already mentioned in our late excursion.

The road was quite good; but it was a dogged pull directly up the side of the mountain. In the sharpness and length of the ascent, it resembled that of the Am Stoss, though I think the last still entitled to precedence. Luckily, instead of climbing, it was now our agreeable duty to descend, and, after delaying a few minutes to enjoy the scene, we plunged towards the valleys.

The view increased, both in beauty and breadth, as we descended. Nearly all of the lake of Zurich became visible, both shores of which, lined with villages, churches, and cottages, in white, like so many brides, and beautifully relieved by verdure, forming parts of the landscape. Ufnau was so distinct as to permit me to distinguish the chapel, barn, meadow, and crosses. Here and there, a line of deep blue appeared among the undulating swells on the remoter side of the picture, looking like patches of the purest sky. These were lakes, whose names you would not recognise, were you to hear them. Switzerland has three classes of these fresh waters: the lakes that have a reputation for their varying but extraordinary beauties, such as those of Geneva, Lucerne, Zurich, and Constance; the lakes that are smaller in size, though still of very respectable dimensions, and which are known more for their accidental positions in frequented parts of the country, or for battles that have been fought on their banks; and the lakes that, enjoying neither of these advantages, are seldom visited by the traveller, or even named. I write with the map open, and a dozen of these nameless waters lie before me, not one of which have I seen, except in bird's eye glimpses, obtained in the manner just mentioned, from the tops of the mountains.

A fountain, in stone, surmounted by an image of Mary, crowned with a gilded glory, stood by the way-side. Delicious water spouted from it, and a boy was in attendance to earn a *batz* by offering a cup. His object, probably, was to lie in wait for the pilgrims, of whom, however, we had seen none for the last hour.

When halfway down the mountain, the guide took a path that diverged from the highway towards the east. It led us through meadows and orchards, and by a most delightful descent to the valley, which we reached near Lacken. I breakfasted in a room that overhung the lake, and the view across the placid water was, as usual, a picture to admire. Looking down from lofty heights astonishes, and, for a time, excites the feelings; but I cling to the opinion, that we most love the views, at which we are accustomed to gaze from the margin of quiet waters, or from the depths of valleys. That picturesque and quaint-looking place, Rapperschwyl, had more of the air of a small walled city, seen from this side, than viewed from the other.

I ordered a *char*, which made its appearance, here, in the shape of a small one-horse phæton, with an apron *à cabriolet*. Though in the very heart of Switzerland, I have not seen a single real *char à banc* since leaving Berne. In our former tour we met very few, from all which I conclude they are not in as general use as is commonly thought.

The road now lay on the margin of a wide marshy district, that was once under water, the lake probably extending, in former ages, thus far. We got pretty views of the convent above Uznach, mentioned in a former letter, of Uznach itself, and of all the long mountain side, by which we had descended. It was pleasant to reverse the picture in this manner, and, to say the truth, Switzerland generally "gives as good as it receives."

After journeying for a league or two we stopped to feed the horse, at an inn so near the mountain as to be in the shadow at two o'clock! I asked the waiter, who spoke French, for some pears. "*Pois! des petits pois!*" he roared; "why, *monsir*, the *peas* have been gone these six weeks." "I do not ask for '*pois*,' but for '*poires*,' '*des poir-r-es*,' which are just in season." One would think this explanation sufficient, and that I might have been quietly answered, yes or no;—not at all. My sturdy Swiss very coolly turned upon me, and gave me to understand that the reason he had not comprehended me at first was my very bad pronunciation. "*Fous n'abez bas un bon bronunciashun, Monsir; voilà, pourquoi je ne fous ai bas combris.*" Certes, my French is any thing but faultless, though I have no reason to suppose it worse than that of my castigator, who made a most ludicrous appearance as he reproved me for calling a pear, peas; an offence, by-the-way, of which I was not at all guilty. Now, what would have been thought, if such a thing had occurred in an American inn! As we drove from this school of quantities, the guide, who had been much shocked by his countryman's dogmatism and want of politeness, by way of atonement remarked, that "*ce gasson là n'est bas, pien boli.*"

In another hour we entered the canton of Glaris. These central states are soon traversed, for they are among the smallest of Switzerland, Schwytz being the seventeenth canton in size, and Glaris the sixteenth. The first has also the same rank in population, while the latter ranks even one degree lower. Schwytz contains rather more than thirty thousand souls; but Glaris has less than twenty-five thousand. The entire population of Lucerne, Zug, Schwytz, Unterwalden, Glaris, and Uri, or, of the six cantons that form the territorial nucleus of the Confederation, according to the official enumeration of the Federal Diet, is only 184,300 souls. If we deduct Lucerne, (86,700,) the five remaining cantons do not much surpass, in population, the smallest American state, proverbially minute as we deem our own little sister to be.[62]

Not long after I had escaped from my purist, we met a highly respectable-looking divine in the road. He was walking, though evidently a traveller, accompanied by an ecclesiastic of inferior station. Soon after, an old-fashioned, heavy coach, drawn by four sleek, well-fed clerical-looking horses, with servants, in quaint, old-fashioned, liveries, followed. On inquiry, this personage proved to be the Bishop of Coire, (the successor of the princely abbots of St. Gall, in a clerical sense at least,) who was proceeding to Einsiedeln, to take part in the approaching ceremonies. I presume most of the Catholics of this portion of the country are under his ecclesiastical jurisdiction; though those on the other side of the lake of Lucerne are generally connected with German dioceses.

The houses along the road side, and even in Schwytz itself, are less Swissish than they are in Berne. After travelling a league, we turned into an enormous ravine, or valley, and drove to the town of Glaris. I was now in the glen which had lain opposite to us when descending from Herisau, the day we reached Rapperschwyl. The surface of this vast gorge is smooth, and its width is rather more than a mile; but the height and perpendicularity of the mountains give it a straitened appearance. The battle of Naefels[63] was fought near its entrance, under a sublime precipice, worthy to overlook so gallant a struggle. The whole canton, in effect, lies in this valley, and in one or two others of less size, which open into it. There is a good deal of mountain, it is true, but the rocks lie nearer the surface here, than in other parts of Switzerland, and the beautiful Alpine pastures are neither so rich nor so abundant as in the Oberland. The rocky pinnacles that enclose this country vary in height, from seven thousand to more than eleven thousand feet above the level of the Mediterranean. The Linth flows through the principal valley, and washes the skirts of the town. Nowhere is the contrast between the mild verdure of the valleys, and the savage aspect of the mountains, more marked than in Glaris: still the latter nourish vast herds of cattle, which constitute a principal part of the wealth of the canton.

The town, which contains some five or six thousand souls, lies along the Linth, principally in one extended street. This is the place where the cheese so well known in America, the

Schrabzieger, is made.* The peculiar smell of the cheese was quite strong on approaching the town. It was like meeting with an old acquaintance, and, as I had but an hour to stay, I hastened to one of the places where it is made.

The curds are formed on the mountains, the milk of goats and cows being used indifferently. Indeed, so far as I could hear or see, the cheese, in this respect, differs from no other, except that it is made of the whey left after churning. When formed, the curds are brought down to the valley in bags. I met a wagon loaded with them, as we entered the place. In this state, there is nothing peculiar in the taste, nor does the material seem at all rich, as you can very well imagine. It is pressed as dry as possible, and then put into a mill, resembling a small cider-mill; the one I examined being turned by water. There might have been a hundred weight of curds in this mill, and the wheel was passing over it constantly, with no one to superintend the operation. I presume the consistency of the cheese is owing to this thorough kneading, and the subsequent pressure, though those I questioned pretended that there is a virtue in the particular pastures. The peculiar colour, scent, and flavour are imparted by the herb,† which is grown in the valley, dried, pulverized, and incorporated with the mass in the mill. The odour of the powder was strong, and its taste vegetable, but I liked it less, pure, than in the cheese. The latter is thought to attain perfection in a twelvemonth, though it will keep a long time. I bought a small cheese, and took my leave of the establishment. Out of Glaris, I know no place where the Schrabzieger is so often met with as in Broadway. The name, so far as my knowledge extends, is compounded of *zieger*, (goats,) and some local word that means either plant, or the name of a plant. The latter, however, is purely conjecture. *Busch* is shrub, in German, but *schrab* sounds so near it, that I dare say it is some obsolete word of the same signification, although it is no more than fair to repeat to you that this is sheer conjecture.

* I never met with one of these cheeses in any part of Europe, Glaris itself excepted; nor did I ever hear an Englishman, German, or Frenchman say that he knew the cheese at all.

† Trifolium melilot. cærul., or, a blue pansy. [*Cooper's notes.*]

Glaris has some manufactures, that are conducted in a pastoral and pleasing manner, and in a way greatly to obviate the vices and broken constitutions of a crowded population. I saw an orchard this afternoon, completely covered with pocket handkerchiefs, bleaching on the grass, the sight creating an irresistible desire to blow one's nose!

The town is principally built of stone, rough-cast. The houses have projecting roofs, but, in other respects, are more like the buildings near the Rhine, than those we are accustomed to consider Swiss. Many are painted externally, in designs, one of which was as follows. The basement was quite plain, having two doors, and a single grated window. All this is above ground, you will understand, no people burrowing, I believe, but the Manhattanese, and their humble imitators. The first floor had one large window, also protected by a grate, that had once been gilded; then comes a bit of wall, that was painted to resemble a window, a lion rampant being visible within. The rest of this floor had the common small Swiss windows, or, in other words, was nearly all window. The second floor had two small windows, with a coat of arms between them, bearing the coronet of a count, by which you will perceive the house I am describing was patrician. On the space of wall on one side of the window is a mounted knight, armed *cap-à-pié*, with his lance in the rest, in the act of tilting. On the opposite space, another mounted warrior, without armour, is drawing an arrow to the head. They appear to be opposed to each other, though separated by the windows and the armorial bearings. All the windows have painted ornaments, and a little boy, who forms part of the one nearest the armed knight, is stretching out a hand, as if to seize the head of his lance. The third floor has three windows, well garnished with boys. The fourth has but one real window, but near it is one painted, at which a lady is seated, looking down complacently, and pointing with a finger at the armed knight. The figures are all as large as life. The whole is in colours, and the paintings are far from being as bad as the conceits would give reason to suppose. These are queer ornaments, certainly, for the exterior of a nobleman's dwelling, though it is probable they have some allusion to a material passage in the history of the family. They may possibly refer to the battle of Naefels, in which a few mountaineers defeated the heavily armed troops of Austria.

Opposite this patrician dwelling is an inn, bearing the date of 1609, with a wild man, some twelve or fifteen feet high, painted on the plaster. The colours are quite fresh, and look as if they had been recently retouched.

There is certainly some hazard in a traveller's entering a country and quitting it within six hours, and then pretending to give an account of its habits. I believe my whole visit to the canton of Glaris did not occupy more time than this, and yet I cannot quit the place without protesting against one of its practices. Cattle are slaughtered in the public streets. I saw three sheep and a calf, under the hands of as many butchers, in the very heart of the place. I have seen something like this in French villages, but never before in a capital!

In the evening we returned, by the road we had come, to a point near the battle ground of Naefels, where we crossed the valley; and, following the banks of the foaming Linth, proceeded to Wesen, on the shore of the lake of Wallenstadt, in the canton of St. Gall. The boundary is a canal, which connects the Wallenstadt with the lake of Zurich.

This little inroad into Glaris already seems like a dream. The place is so retired, the mountains are so wild and abrupt, and there is so great an admixture of the savage with the civilized, that it stands distinct and isolated, amid the multitude of images that this fruitful region has supplied.

[LIBERAL FLORENCE]

From *Italy* (Vol. I, Letter III) [64]

As it was our intention to pass the winter here, old Caspar was discharged, and we took lodgings.[65] Florence is full of noble hotels, which are termed palaces in the language of the country, and, few families still retaining a sufficient portion of the ancient wealth to occupy the whole of such huge edifices, apartments are let in them, furnished, or not, as it may happen, on the French plan. Hunting for lodgings gives one a good idea of the domestic economy of a place, for we entered some twenty or thirty of these palaces with this object. Rooms are unusually cheap, notwithstanding the number of strangers who resort to the place, for the town has shrunk to less than half its ancient population, and probably to a tithe of its ancient magnificence.

We become fully impressed with the changes that time produces, not only in things, but in the moral aspect of the world, by seeing a town like Florence. In our age, the man who should dream of making an inland place, in the heart of the Apennines, the focus of trade, would be set down as a simpleton; nor could any powers of combination or of wealth now overcome the efforts of those who would naturally resort to more favourable positions.

These old merchants, however, men who truly ennobled commerce, and not commerce them, have left behind them more durable remains of their ascendency than can be seen in almost any other place. As they were not particularly pacific, the constant struggles of factions in the streets induced a style of architecture that is almost peculiar to Florence, for every palace is a sort of fortress. We took an apartment in one that belongs to an ancient family who still inhabit a portion of the building, and as our rooms are on the street, we may be said to occupy the fortress. The great gate is of iron, and the great stairs, of course, massive and solid. The lower floor is occupied only for the offices and stables. Then comes what is called a *mezzinino*, or a low story, with small windows, but which has some very good rooms. Above this is our apartment, with ceilings nearly twenty feet high, large rooms all *en suite*, and windows to look out of which we ascend two steps. The walls would bear considerable battering, though the position of the house protected it from any danger of such a nature. Forty or fifty stout-hearted retainers, and the number would not be great for the old Florentines, must have been able to stand a respectable seige in such an abode.

You will ask me what are my impressions, on finding myself entrenched behind such works, with a thousand recollections of the Medici and the Strozzi, and the Capponi, to awaken the love of the romantic and interesting? Alas! I am filled with the consciousness of the impotency of man, who, after rearing these piles, and guarding against the violence and ungovernable passions of his fellows, is obliged to allow that all his resources cannot keep out the musquitoes [*sic*].

We have two noble bed-rooms, besides several smaller; a large drawing-room, and a larger dining-room; a good cabinet for myself; an ante-chamber, and baths, offices, &c., &c., all furnished, for the moderate sum of sixty dollars a month. We have ten good rooms in all, besides the offices.

Our hotel has a small court, and, I believe, a garden; though I have not had access to the latter. By the side of the great gate is a small hole in the wall, closed in general by a shutter. At eleven o'clock every day, people come to this shutter and rap, and it is opened by a steward of the family. The applicant puts in an empty flask and a paul (ten cents), receiving in return a flask filled with wine. In this manner, I understand, most of the great families of Florence now dispose of the products of their vines! It would be curious to learn if the Medici carried on this trade. The wine of our palace is among the best of Tuscany, and I drink it with great satisfaction; the more so because its cost is about four cents the bottle. It is positively much better wine than half the claret that is drunk in Paris. Twice a week, a donkey appears in the court, dragging a little cart filled with flasks from the estate, and carrying away the "dead soldiers." We are, however, a little above the market, as our wine commands fully a cent a flask, or about four mills a bottle, more than most of the Tuscan liquor.

We burn in our lamps oil that you would be happy to get on your lobsters and salads. In other respects the market is good, and cloths are both fine and cheap, finer and cheaper than I remember to have seen them any where else, and yet they are imported! The shop-keepers are moderate in their wishes, preferring the *dolce far niente* to the more terrible *energies* of trade.

There is a sleepy indolence in these Italians, that singularly suits my humour. They seem too gentlemanlike to work, or to be fussy, but appear disposed to make a *siesta* of life, and to enjoy the passing moment. The Tuscans seem full of sentiment, and though the poor, as is the case all over the continent of Europe, are very poor, the class immediately above them have as much satisfaction, I fancy, as they who dream dollars and talk dollars from "the rising of the sun unto the going down of the same." If you ask me if I would exchange populations and habits, I shall answer, we cannot afford it. It would check our career short of perfect civilisation. We have arts to acquire, and tastes to form, before we could enter at all into the enjoyments of these people; one half of their pleasures depending on recollections that possibly may have had their origin in the *energies* of the first of the Medici; and there are things that must be created, but which give more satisfaction in after ages than during the period of their formation. For myself, I begin to feel I could be well content to vegetate here for one half my life, to say nothing of the remainder. All who travel know that the greatest pleasure is in the recollections; and I fancy that nations in their decline enjoy more true happiness than nations in their advance.[66]

Of course, I have visited the Venus, and the Pitti, and all the other marvels of art that Florence contains. These things have been so often described, that my remarks shall be limited to such gleanings as others appear to have left, or as are suggested by my own passing feelings. The tribune of the gallery contains the most precious collection of ancient art, perhaps, in the world. Every thing in it is a *chef-d'œuvre* in its way; though I am far from seeing the necessity of believing that every old statue that is exhumed is an original. When I was introduced into this place, I felt as if approaching the presence of illustrious personages, and stood, hat in hand, involuntarily bowing to the circle of marble figures that surrounded me, as if they were endowed with sensibilities to appreciate my homage. You are not, however, to suppose that a love of art was so much at the bottom of this reverence, as association. There was a set of engravings in my father's house that represented most of the antique statues, and for these I had imbibed the respect of a child. The forms had become familiar by years of observation, and the Venus, the wrestlers, the dancing faun, and the knife grinder, four of my oldest acquaintances on paper, now stood before my eyes, looking like living beings.

Florence is walled, but it is in the style of three or four centuries ago, and the defences may be set down as of no account in the warfare of our own times. There is a citadel, however, of a more warlike character, reserved, I suspect, for state purposes. The walls are picturesque, but, failing of the great military object, they are next to useless, as they are not provided with promenades. *Au reste*, they are a little *Jerichoish*, or as I have already described those of Morat to be.[67]

Economy, the galleries, the facility with which one obtains lodgings, caprice and the court, unite to make Florence a favourite residence with strangers. The court has a little more of air and pretension than it might otherwise possess, from the circumstance of the sovereign being an archduke. Tuscany, however, is a respectable state, having nearly a million and a half of subjects, with Lucca in reversion.[68]

Among the strangers the English and Russians predominate; especially the former, who are found in swarms, on the continent, in all the most agreeable places of residence. The policy of the Tuscan government encourages diplomatic appointments, and I believe all the great courts of Europe have ministers here, the French, Russians, English, Austrians, and Prussians have ministers plenipotentiaries, and many others *chargés d'affaires*. All these things contribute to render the place gay; nor is it without brilliancy at times, the little court appearing at the festivals and other ceremonies with sufficient pomp. I shall not philosophise on these things, but I fancy they do more good and less harm than is commonly thought by us democrats. I have often compared the *agrémens* of this little town with those of one of our own larger cities. New York, which is four times as large as Florence, and ten times as rich, does not possess a tithe—nay, not a hundredth part of its attractions. To say nothing of taste, or of the stores of ancient art, or of the noble palaces and

churches, and the other historical monuments the circle of living
creatures here affords greater sources of amusement and instruction than are to be found in all the five great American
towns [69] put together. Every one appears to be at leisure, and
the demon money seems to be forgotten, unless, indeed, he
occasionally shows his talons at the gaming-table. An evening
party offers the oddest collection of human beings imaginable;
for the natives of half the civilised countries of the world appear
to have met on neutral ground in this little capital, the government having the liberality to tolerate even men of political
opinions that are elsewhere proscribed. I met at a *soirée*, lately,
besides a proper sprinkling of Tuscans, and Italians from the
other parts of Italy, French, Swiss, Germans from half a dozen
states, English, Russians, Greeks, Americans from several different countries, Dutch, an Algerine, an Egyptian, and a Turk.
There were, in addition, sundry adventurers from the islands of
the Mediterranean.

This is the age of cosmopolitism, real or pretended; and
Florence, just at this moment, is an epitome, both of its spirit
and of its representatives. So many people travel, that one is
apt to ask who can be left at home; and some aim at distinction
in this era of migration by making it a point to see every thing.
Of this number is a certain Count di V———, whom I met in
America just before leaving home. This gentleman went
through the United States, tablets in hand, seeming to be dis-
satisfied with himself if he quitted one of our common-place
towns with a hospital unexamined, a mineral unregistered, or
a church unentered. It struck me at the time that he was making
a toil of a pleasure, especially in a country that has so little worth
examining. But a short time since, I dined with my banker here.
At table, I was seated between the Marchese G———, a Sar-
dinian, and the Baron P———, a Neapolitan. Alluding to the
locomotive propensities of our times, I mentioned the ardour
for travelling, and the industry I had witnessed in the aforesaid
Count di V———. Signor G——— told me that he knew him
intimately, having himself visited all the North of Europe in his
company, previously to which his friend had explored Greece,

Egypt, Northern Africa, and the West of Asia, by himself. "When he left the United States," continued Signor G———, "it was to go—where?" "To the West Indies and Mexico." "True; and from the latter he came through Columbia [*sic*] to Brazil, where I was at the time. He left me there to cross the Andes, and I cannot tell you what has become of him." "Why do you not come to the East Indies?" said an English woman to me the same evening, and to whom I had been introduced as to a lady who lived in that part of the world, but who had taken run from Calcutta to pass the summer in Switzerland, and the winter in Italy. "I fancy few mere travellers get as far as Hindostan?" "Oh, we have them occasionally. Now, the winter before I left home, we had one for several weeks in our own house; he only left us to go to the Himalayah mountains and return a few months before I sailed."—"An Englishman, of course?"—"No, indeed; an Italian."—"Pray, ma'am, was it Count Carlo di V———!"—"Yes it was."—"And may I ask what has become of him?"—"He left Calcutta to go to Ceylon and Manilla, on his way to China." So much for our own times!*

The strangers are at the head of the gaiety of this place, few of the Florentines *receiving* much. In this number may be included Prince Borghese, the brother-in-law of Napoleon, an amiable, well-intentioned, and modest man, who has abandoned Rome, his proper country, to reside here, where he maintains a good style, opening his palace periodically for the reception of all who choose to come. Then we have besides the regular exhibitions of the town, rival houses in two English theatres, with amateur-performers; at the head of one of which is Lord B———, and at the head of the other Lord N———. At the latter only, however, can one be said to see the legitimate drama;

* This unhappy gentleman subsequently lost his life by falling into a boiling spring in the island of Batavia! He was probably the greatest traveller that ever lived; having, so far as the writer can learn, visited every country in Europe, Persia, Palestine, Egypt, and all northern Africa; nearly, if not every country in America, and most of the East! By adding New Holland and the islands, he would have seen the world. Would he have been any happier for all his toils and dangers? It may be doubted. [*Cooper's note.*]

the other running rather into music,—an experiment not to be idly attempted in Italy.

We have seen Shakspeare in the hands of these noble actors once or twice, and found the representation neither quite good enough to please, nor yet bad enough to laugh at. Occasionally, a character was pretty well represented; but the natural facility of the other sex in acting was sufficiently apparent, the women making out much better than the men. It was like all private theatricals, well enough for a country house, but hardly in its place in the capital of Tuscany. We had a specimen of the feeling of the English towards America, as well as of national manners, the other evening, that is worth a passing notice. One of the players sang, with a good deal of humour, a comic song, that attempted to delineate national traits. There was a verse or two appropriated to the English, the French, the Germans, &c. &c. and the *finale* was an American. The delineations of all the first were common-place enough; the humour consisting chiefly in the mimicry, the ideas themselves having no particular merit. But the verse for the American seemed to be prepared with singular care, and was given with great unction. It represented a quasi Western man, who is made to boast that he is the lad to eat his father, whip his mother, and to achieve other similar notable exploits. I do not know that I am absolutely destitute of an appreciation of wit or humour, but certainly, it struck me this attempt was utterly without either. It was purely an exaggerated and coarse caricature, positively suited only to the tastes of a gallery in a sea-port town. The other verses had been laughed at, as silly drollery, perhaps; but this was received with—how shall I express it?—a *yell of delight* would not be a term too strong!

No one is more ready to give proper credit to the just-mindedness and liberality of a portion of the English than myself: but the truth would not be told, were I to leave you under the impression that their tone prevails even among the better classes of their society, in relation to ourselves. You will remember that this song was not given to the pit or galleries of an ordinary theatre, but to a society in which there were none beneath the

station of gentlemen, and that I should deem this caricature altogether beneath the intelligence and breeding of the company,
were it not for the singular rapture with which it was greeted.
It is a much more laughable commentary on this extraordinary
scene, that, just as it was finished, the Count di ——— leaned
over and whispered to me that the dislike and *"jealousy"* (I use
his own words) of the English for the Americans seemed in-
appeasable! I observed that the side of the room that was chiefly
occupied by the people of rank was mute, the nobles maintaining a cold and polished indifference; but in the other end of the
sala, which was filled with half-pay officers and the *oi polloi* of
the travellers, the *yell* was quite suited to the theme. One might
have fancied it the murdered father shrieking under the knife of
the parricidal son.

At the *receptions* of Don Camillo Borghese, as the Romans
style him, one sees most of the strangers. These entertainments
are *dansantes*, and, as the rooms are large and the music noble,
they are imposing; though the company is far from being of the
purest water. As a proof of this, a noisy party preceded us, the
other evening, the young men calling out to each other, "Where
is the fat man?"—"Now for the fat man," &c. the prince being
almost unwieldy from his size. Waltzes are the favourite
dances; though no people know how to waltz but the Germans—
or, indeed, to play the necessary airs, but their musicians. It
has struck me that I have seen no people who had the organ of
time, but the Germans and the negroes of America: and a waltz
without the utmost accuracy in the movement is a ridiculous
dance. I have observed that the young women of condition in
France and Italy were not often permitted to join in this dance,
by their mothers, with men as partners, unless the latter were
near connexions; and as the latter arrangement cannot well be
made in a public ball, none joined in the waltzes here.

As a specimen of the sort of *omnium gatherum* that Florence
has become, I will give you a list of some of the notables that
were seen, recently, in the first row of the Pergola, the principal
opera-house, here. First, there was the Count St. Leu, as he is
styled, or the ex-king of Holland. Near him was the Prince de

Monfort, his brother, or the ex-king of Westphalia. In the same row was Mrs. Patterson, once the wife of the last-named personage. At no great distance was Prince Henry of Prussia, a brother of the reigning king. In the same line, and at no great distance, sat Madame Christophe, ex-empress of Hayti, with a daughter or two. In addition to these, there was a pretty sprinkling of chiefs of revolutions, *littérateurs* of all nations, ex-ambassadors, and politicians *en retraite*, to say nothing of mere people of fashion.

The winter has come upon us sharply, ice forming freely in the ditches around the town, and skates being brought into requisition. I have seen snow impending over us, in falling clouds even, but it vanishes before it reaches the ground: though the Apennines are occasionally powdered. Once, and once only, a little has lain in the street, but not long enough, or in sufficient quantities to enable one to say it has covered the stones. Still it is snapping cold, and we find our good wood fires as comfortable as in New York.

[THE RHINE]

Introduction to *The Heidenmauer*[70]

I shall crave your forbearance a little; may be, I will call upon you anon, for some advantage to yourself.—Measure for Measure.

Contrary to a long-established usage, a summer had been passed within the walls of a large town; but, the moment of liberation arrived, the bird does not quit its cage with greater pleasure, than that with which post-horses were commanded. We were four in a light travelling calêche, which strong Norman cattle transported merrily toward their native province. For a time we quitted Paris, the queen of modern cities, with its tumults and its order; its palaces and its lanes; its elegance and its filth; its restless inhabitants and its stationary politicians; its theories and its practices; its riches and its poverty; its gay and its sorrowful; its rentiers and its patriots; its young liberals and its old illiberals; its three estates and its equality; its delicacy of speech and its strength of conduct; its government of the people, and its people of no government; its bayonets and its moral force; its science and its ignorance; its amusements and its revolutions; its resistance that goes backward, and its movement that stands still; its milliners, its philosophers, its opera-dancers, its poets, its fiddlers, its bankers, and its cooks. Although so long enthralled within the barriers, it was not easy to quit Paris entirely without regret—Paris, which every stranger censures and every stranger seeks; which moralists abhor and imitate; which causes the heads of the old to shake, and the hearts of the young to beat—Paris, the centre of so much that is excellent, and of so much that cannot be named.

That night we laid our heads on rustic pillows, far from the French capital. The succeeding day we snuffed the air of the sea. Passing through Artois and French Flanders, on the fifth morning we entered the new kingdom of Belgium, by the historical and respectable towns of Douaï, and Tournaï, and Ath. At every step we met the flag which flutters over the pavilion of the Tuileries, and recognized the confident air and swinging gait of French soldiers. They had just been employed in propping the crumbling throne of the house of Saxe.[71] To us they seemed as much at home as when they lounged on the Quai d'Orsay.

There was still abundant evidence visible at Brussels of the fierce nature of the struggle that had expelled the Dutch.[72] Forty-six shells were sticking in the side of a single building of no great size, while ninety-three grape-shot were buried in one of its pilasters! In our own rooms, too, there were fearful signs of war. The mirrors were in fragments, the walls broken by langrage, the wood-work of the beds was pierced by shot, and the furniture was marked by rude encounters. The trees of the park were mutilated in a thousand places, and one of the little Cupids, that we had left laughing above the principal gate three years before, was now maimed and melancholy, whilst its companion had altogether taken flight on the wings of a cannon-ball. Though dwelling in the very centre of so many hostile vestiges, we happily escaped the sight of human blood; for we understood from the obliging Swiss who presides over the hotel, that his cellars, at all times in repute, were in more than usual request during the siege. From so much proof we were left to infer that the Belgians had made stout battle for their emancipation, one sign at least that they merited to be free.

Our road lay by Louvain, Thirlemont, Liège, Aix-la-Chapelle, and Juliers, to the Rhine. The former of these towns had been the scene of a contest between the hostile armies, the preceding week. As the Dutch had been accused of unusual excesses in their advance, we looked out for the signs. How many of these marks had been already obliterated we could not well ascertain; but those which were still visible gave us reason to think that the invaders did not merit all the opprobrium they had received. Each hour, as life advances, am I made to see how capricious and vulgar is the immortality conferred by a newspaper!

It would be injustice to the ancient Bishopric of Liège to pass its beautiful scenery without a comment. The country possesses nearly every requisite for the milder and more rural sort of landscape—isolated and innumerable farm-houses, herds in the fields, living hedges, a waving surface, and a verdure to rival the emerald. By a happy accident, the road runs for miles on an elevated ridge, enabling the traveller to enjoy these beauties at his ease.

At Aix-la-Chapelle [73] we bathed, visited the relics, saw the scene of so many coronations of emperors of more or less renown, sat in the chair of Charlemagne, and went our way.

The Rhine was an old acquaintance. A few years earlier I had stood upon the sands, at Katwyck, and watched its periodical flow into the North Sea, by means of sluices made in the short reign of the good King Louis, and the same summer I had bestrode it, a brawling brook, on the icy side of St. Gothard. We had come now to look at its beauties in its most beautiful part, and to compare them, so far as native partiality might permit, with the well-established claims of our own Hudson.

Quitting Cologne, its exquisite but incomplete cathedral, with the crane that has been poised on its unfinished towers towards five hundred years, its recollections of Rubens and its royal patroness, we travelled up the stream so leisurely as to examine all that offered, and yet so fast as to avoid the hazard of satiety. Here we met Prussian soldiers, preparing, by mimic service, for the more serious duties of their calling. Lancers were galloping in bodies across the open fields; videttes were posted, the cocked pistol in hand, at every hay-stack; while couriers rode, under the spur, from point to point, as if the great strife, which is so menacingly preparing, and which sooner or later must come, had actually commenced. As Europe is now a camp, these hackneyed sights scarce drew a look aside. We were in quest of the interest which nature, in her happier humors, bestows.

There were ruined castles, by scores; gray fortresses; abbeys, some deserted and others yet tenanted; villages and towns; the seven mountains; cliffs and vineyards. At every step we felt how intimate is the association between the poetry of nature and that of art; between the hill-side with its falling turret, and the moral feeling that lends them interest. Here was an island, of no particular excellence, but the walls of a convent of the Middle Ages crumbled on the surface. There was a naked rock, destitute of grandeur, and wanting in those tints which milder climates bestow, but a baronial hold tottered on its apex. Here Cæsar led his legions to the stream, and there Napoleon threw his *corps-d'armée* on the hostile bank; this monument was to Hoche, and from that terrace the great Adolphus directed his battalions. Time is wanting to mellow the view of our own historical sites; for the sympathy that can be accumulated only by the general consent of mankind, has not yet clothed them with the indefinable colors of distance and convention.

In the mood likely to be created by a flood of such recollections, we pursued our way along the southern margin of this great artery of central Europe. We wondered at the vastness of the Rheinfels, admired the rare jewel of the ruined church at Baccarach, and marveled at the giddy precipice on which a prince of Prussia even now dwells, in the eagle-like grandeur and security of the olden time. On reaching Mayence [Mainz] the evening of the second day, we deliberately and, as we hoped, impartially compared what had just been seen, with that which is so well and so affectionately remembered.

I had been familiar with the Hudson from childhood. The great thoroughfare of all who journey from the interior of the State toward the sea, necessity had early made me acquainted with its windings, its promontories, its islands, its cities, and its villages. Even its hidden channels had been professionally examined, and time was when there did not stand an unknown seat on its banks, or a hamlet that had not been visited. Here, then, was the force of deep impressions to oppose to the influence of the objects still visible.

To me it is quite apparent that the Rhine, while it frequently possesses more of any particular species of scenery within a given number of miles than the Hudson, has none of so great excellence. It wants the variety, the noble beauty, and the broad grandeur of the American stream. The latter, within the distance universally admitted to contain the finest parts of the Rhine, is both a large and a small river; it has its bays, its narrow passages among the meadows, its frowning gorges, and its reaches resembling Italian lakes; whereas the most that can be said of its European competitor is, that all these wonderful peculiarities are feebly imitated. Ten degrees of a lower latitude supply richer tints, brighter transitions of light and shadow, and more glorious changes of the atmosphere, to embellish the beauties of our western clime. In islands, too, the advantage is with the Hudson, for, while those of the Rhine are the most numerous, those of the former stream are bolder, better placed, and, in every natural feature, of more account.[74]

When the comparison between these celebrated rivers is extended to their artificial accessories, the result becomes more doubtful. The buildings of the older towns and villages of Europe seem grouped especially for effect, as seen in the distant view, though security was in truth the cause, while the spacious, cleanly, and cheerful villages of America must commonly be entered to be appreciated. In the other hemisphere, the maze of roofs, the church-towers, the irregular faces of wall, and frequently the castle rising to a pinnacle in the rear, give a town the appearance of some vast and antiquated pile devoted to a single object. Perhaps the boroughs of the Rhine have less of this picturesque, or landscape effect than the villages of France and Italy, for the Germans regard space more than their neighbors, but still are they less commonplace than the smiling and thriving little marts that crowd the borders of the Hudson. To this advantage must be added that which is derived from the countless ruins, and a crowd of recollections. Here, the superiority of the artificial auxiliaries of the Rhine ceases, and those of her rival come into the ascendant. In modern abodes, in villas, and even in seats, those of princes alone excepted, the banks of the Hudson have scarcely an equal in any region. There are finer and nobler edifices on the Brenta, and in other favored spots, certainly, but I know no stream that has so many that please and attract the eye. As applied to moving objects, an important feature in this comparison, the Hudson has perhaps no rival in any river that can pretend to a picturesque character. In numbers, in variety of rig, in beauty of form, in swiftness and dexterity of handling, and in general grace and movement, this extraordinary passage ranks among the first of the world. The yards of tall ships swing among the rocks and forests of the highlands, while sloop, schooner, and bright canopied steamboat, yacht, periagua, and canoe are seen in countless numbers, decking its waters. There is one more eloquent point of difference that should not be neglected. Drawings and engravings of the Rhine lend their usual advantages, softening, and frequently rendering beautiful, objects of no striking attractions when seen as they exist; while every similar attempt to represent the Hudson at once strikes the eye as unworthy of its original.[75]

Nature is fruitful of fine effects in every region, and it is a mistake not to enjoy her gifts, as we move through life, on account of some fancied superiority in this or that quarter of the world. We left the Rhine, therefore, with regret, for, in its way, a lovelier stream can scarce be found.

At Mayence we crossed to the right bank of the river, and passing by the Duchies of Nassau and Darmstadt, entered that of Baden, at Heidelberg. Here we sat upon the Tun, examined the castle, and strolled in the alleys of the remarkable garden. Then we proceeded to Manheim, turning our faces once more toward the French capital. The illness of one of the party[76] compelled us to remain a few hours in the latter city, which presented little for reflection, unless it were that this, like one or two other towns we had lately seen, served to convince us that the symmetry and regularity which render large cities magnificent, cause those that are small to appear mean.

It was a bright autumnal day when we returned to the left bank of the Rhine, on the way to Paris. The wishes of the invalid had taken the appearance of strength, and we hoped to penetrate the mountains which bound the Palatinate on its southwestern side, and to reach Kaiserslautern, on the great Napoleon road, before the hour of rest. The main object had been accomplished, and, as with all who have effected their purpose, the principal desire was to be at home. A few posts convinced us that repose was still necessary to the invalid. This conviction, unhappily as I then believed, came too late, for we had already crossed the plain of the Palatinate, and were drawing near to the chain of mountains just mentioned, which are a branch of the Vosges, and are known in the country as the Haart. We had made no calculations for such an event, and former experience had caused us to distrust the inns of this isolated portion of the kingdom of Bavaria. I was just bitterly regretting our precipitation, when the church-tower of Deurck-heim peered above the vineyards; for, on getting nearer to the base of the hills, the land became slightly undulating, and the vine abundant. As we approached, the village or borough promised little, but we had the word of the postilion that the post-house was an inn fit for a king; and as to the wine, he could give no higher eulogium than a flourish of the whip, an eloquent expression of pleasure for a German of his class. We debated the question of proceeding, or of stopping, in a good deal of doubt, to the moment when the carriage drew up before the sign of the Ox. A substantial looking burgher came forth to receive us. There was the pledge of good cheer in the ample development of his person, which was not badly typified by the sign, and the hale, hearty character of his hospitality removed all suspicion of the hour of reckoning. If he who travels much is a gainer in knowledge of mankind, he is sure to be a loser in the charities that sweeten life. Constant intercourse with men who are in the habit of seeing strange faces, who only dispose of their services to those that are likely never to need them again, and who, of necessity, are removed from most of the responsibilities and affinities of a more permanent intercourse, exhibits the selfishness of our nature in its least attractive form. Policy may suggest a specious blandishment of air, to conceal the ordinary design on the pocket of the stranger; but it is in the nature of things that the design should exist. The passion of gain, like all other passions, increases with indulgence; and thus do we find those who dwell on beaten roads more rapacious than those in whom the desire is latent, for want of use.

Our host of Deurckheim offered a pledge, in his honest countenance, independent air, and frank manner, of his also being above the usual mercenary schemes of another portion of the craft, who, dwelling in places of little resort, endeavor to take their revenge of fortune, by showing that they look upon every post-carriage as an especial godsend. He had a garden, too, into which he invited us to enter, while the horses were changing, in a way that showed he was simply desirous of being benevolent, and that he cared little whether we stayed an hour or a week. In short, his manner was of an artless, kind, natural, and winning character, that strongly reminded us of home, and which at once established an agreeable confidence that is of an invaluable moral effect. Though too experienced blindly to confide in national characteristics, we liked, too, his appearance of German faith, and more than all were we pleased with the German neatness and comfort, of which there was abundance, unalloyed by the swaggering pretension that neutralizes the same qualities among people more artificial. The house was not a beer-drinking, smoking caravanserai, like many hotels in that quarter of the world, but it had detached pavilions in the gardens, in which the weary traveller might, in sooth, take his rest. With such inducements before our eyes, we determined to remain, and we were not long in instructing the honest burgher to that effect. The decision was received with great civility, and, unlike the immortal Falstaff, I began to see the prospects of taking "mine ease in mine inn," without having a pocket picked.[77]

The carriage was soon housed, and the baggage in the chambers. Notwithstanding the people of the house spoke confidently, but with sufficient modesty, of the state of the larder, it wanted several hours, agreeable to our habits, to the time of dinner, though we had enjoyed frequent opportunities of remarking that in Germany a meal is never unseasonable. Disregarding hints, which appeared more suggested by humanity than the love of gain, our usual hour for eating was named, and, by way of changing the subject, I asked—

"Did I not see some ruins, on the adjoining mountains, as we entered the village?"

"We call Deurckheim a city, mein Herr," rejoined our host of the Ox; "though none of the largest, the time has been when it was a capital!"

Here the worthy burgher munched his pipe and chuckled, for he was a man that had heard of such places as London, and Paris, and Pekin, and Naples, and St. Petersburg, or, haply, of the Federal City itself.

"A capital! It was the abode of one of the smaller princes, I suppose; of what family was your sovereign, pray?"

"You are right, mein Herr. Deurckheim, before the French revolution, was a residence (for so the political capitals are called in Germany), and it belonged to the princes of Leiningen, who had a palace on the other side of the city (the place may be about half as large as Hudson, or Schenectady), which was burnt in the war. After the late wars, the sovereign was *médiatisé*, receiving an indemnity in estates on the other side of the Rhine."

As this term of *médiatisé* has no direct synonym in English, it may be well to explain its signification. Germany, as well as most of Europe, was formerly divided into a countless number of petty sovereignties, based on the principle of feudal power.

As accident, or talent, or alliances, or treachery advanced the interests of the stronger of these princes, their weaker neighbors began to disappear altogether, or to take new and subordinate stations in the social scale. In this manner has France been gradually composed of its original, but comparatively insignificant kingdom, buttressed, as it now is, by Brittany, and Burgundy, and Navarre, and Dauphiny, and Provence, and Normandy, with many other states; and in like manner has England been formed of the Heptarchy. The confederate system of Germany has continued more or less of this feudal organization to our own times. The formation of the empires of Austria and Prussia has, however, swallowed up many of these principalities, and the changes produced by the policy of Napoleon gave the death-blow, without distinction, to all in the immediate vicinity of the Rhine. Of the latter number were princes of Leiningen, whose possessions were originally included in the French republic, then in the empire, and have since passed under the sway of the King of Bavaria, who, as the legitimate heir of the neighboring duchy of Deux Ponts, had a nucleus of sufficient magnitude in this portion of Germany to induce the congress of Vienna to add to his dominions; their object being to erect a barrier against the future aggrandizement of France. As the dispossessed sovereigns are permitted to retain their conventional rank, supplying wives and husbands, at need, to the reigning branches of the different princely families, the term *médiatisé* has been aptly enough applied to their situation.

"The young prince was here no later than last week," continued our host of the Ox; "he lodged in that pavilion, where he passed several days. You know that he is a son of the Duchess of Kent, and half-brother to the young princess who is likely, one day, to be Queen of England."

"Has he estates here, or is he still, in any way, connected with your government?"

"All they have given him is in money, or on the other side of the Rhine. He went to see the ruins of the old castle; for he had a natural curiosity to look at a place which his ancestors had built."

"It was the ruins of the castle of Leiningen, then, that I saw on the mountain, as we entered the town?"

"No, mein Herr. You saw the ruins of the Abbey of Limburg; those of Hartenburg, for so the castle was called, lie farther back among the hills."

"What! a ruined abbey, and a ruined castle, too! Here is sufficient occupation for the rest of the day. An abbey and a castle!"

"And the Heidenmauer, and the Teufelstein."

"How! a Pagan's Wall, and a Devil's Stone! You are rich in curiosities!"

The host continued to smoke on philosophically.

"Have you a guide who can take me by the shortest way to these places?"

"Any child can do that."

"But one who can speak French is desirable—for my German is far from being classical."

The worthy innkeeper nodded his head.

"Here is one Christian Kinzel," he rejoined, after a moment of thought, "a tailor who has not much custom, and who has lived a little in France; he may serve your turn."

I suggested that a tailor might find it healthful to stretch his knee-joints.

The host of the Ox was amused with the conceit, and he fairly removed the pipe, in order to laugh at his ease. His mirth was hearty, like that of a man without guile.

The affair was soon arranged. A messenger was sent for Christian Kinzel, and taking my little male travelling companion by the hand,[78] I went leisurely ahead, expecting the appearance of the guide. But, as the reader will have much to do with the place about to be described, it may be desirable that he should possess an accurate knowledge of its locality.

Deurckheim lies in that part of Bavaria which is commonly called the circle of the Rhine. The king of the country named may have less than half a million of subjects in this detached part of his territories, which extends in one course from the river to Rhenish Prussia, and in the other from Darmstadt to France.

It requires a day of hard posting to traverse this province in any direction, from which it would appear that its surface is about equal to two thirds of that of Connecticut. A line of mountains, resembling the smaller spurs of the Alleghanies, and which are known by different local names, but which are a branch of the Vosges, passes nearly through the centre of the district, in a north and south course. These mountains cease abruptly on their eastern side, leaving between them and the river a vast level surface, of that description which is called "flats," or "bottom land," in America. This plain, part of the ancient Palatinate, extends equally on the other side of the Rhine, terminating as abruptly on the eastern as on the western border. In an air line, the distance between Heidelberg and Deurckheim, which lie opposite to each other on the two lateral extremities of the plain, may a little exceed twenty miles, the Rhine running equi-distant from both. There is a plausible theory which says that the plain of the Palatinate was formerly a lake, receiving the waters of the Rhine, and of course discharging them by some inferior outlet, until time, or a convulsion of the earth, broke through the barrier of the mountains at Bingen, draining off the waters, and leaving the fertile bottom described. Irregular sand-hills were visible, as we approached Deurckheim, which may go to confirm this supposition, for the prevalence of northerly winds might easily have cast more of these light particles on the southwestern than on the opposite shore. By adding that the eastern face of the mountains, or that next to the plain, is sufficiently broken and irregular to be beautiful, while it is always distinctly marked and definite, enough has been said to enable us to proceed with intelligence.

It would appear that one of the passes that has communicated, from time immemorial, between the Rhine and the country west of the Vosges, issues on the plain through the gorge near Deurckheim. By following the windings of the valleys, the post-road penetrates, by an easy ascent, to the highest ridge, and following the water-courses that run into the Moselle, descends nearly as gradually into the duchy of Deux Ponts, on the other side of the chain. The possession of this pass, therefore, in the ages of lawlessness and violence, was, in itself, a title to distinction and power; since all who journeyed by it, lay in person and effects more or less at the mercy of the occupant.

On quitting the town, my little companion and myself immediately entered the gorge. The pass itself was narrow, but a valley soon opened to the width of a mile, out of which issued two or three passages, besides that by which we had entered, though only one of them preserved its character for any distance. The capacity of this valley or basin, as it must have been when the Palatinate was a lake, is much curtailed by an insulated mountain, whose base, covering a fourth of the area, stands in its very centre, and which doubtless was an island when the valley was a secluded bay. The summit of this mountain or island-hill is level, of an irregularly oval form, and contains six or eight acres of land. Here stand the ruins of Limburg, the immediate object of our visit.[79]

The ascent was exceedingly rapid, and of several hundred feet; reddish freestone appeared everywhere through the scanty soil; the sun beat powerfully on the rocks; and I was beginning to weigh the advantages and disadvantages of proceeding, when the tailor approached, with the zeal of new-born courage.

"Voici Christian Kinzel!" exclaimed ———, to whom novelty was always an incentive, and who, in his young life, had eagerly mounted Alp and Apennine, Jura and Calabrian hill, tower, monument, and home, or whatever else served to raise him in the air; "Allons,—grimpons!"

We scrambled up the hill-side, and, winding among terraces on which the vine and vegetables were growing, soon reached the natural platform. There was a noble view from the summit, but it would be premature to describe it here. The whole surface of the hill furnished evidence of the former extent of the abbey, a wall having encircled the entire place; but the principal edifices had been built, and still remained, near the longitudinal centre, on the very margin of the eastern precipice. Enough was standing to prove the ancient magnificence of the structure. Unlike most of the ruins which border the Rhine, the masonry was of a workmanlike kind, the walls being not only massive, but composed of the sandstone just mentioned, neatly hewn, for immense strata of the material exist in all this region. I traced the chapel, still in tolerable preservation; the refectory, that never-failing solacer of monastic seclusion; several edifices apparently appropriated to the dormitories, and some vestiges of the cloisters. There is also a giddy tower, of an ecclesiastical form, that sufficiently serves to give a character to the ruins. It was closed, to prevent idlers from incurring foolish risks by mounting the crazy steps; but its having formerly been appropriated to the consecrated bells was not at all doubtful. There is also a noble arch near, with several of its disjointed stones menacing the head of him who ventures beneath.

Turning from the ruin, I cast a look at the surrounding valley. Nothing could have been softer or more lovely than the near view. That sort of necessity which induces us to cherish any stinted gift, had led the inhabitants to turn every foot of the bottom land to the best account. No Swiss Alp could have been more closely shaved than the meadows at my feet, and a good deal had been made of two or three rivulets that meandered among them. The dam of a rustic mill threw back the water into a miniature lake, and some zealous admirer of Neptune had established a beer-house on its banks, which was dignified with the sign of the "Anchor!" But the principal object in the interior or upland view was the ruins of a castle, that occupied a natural terrace, or rather the projection of a rock against the side of one of the nearest mountains. The road passed immediately beneath its walls, a short arrow-flight from the battlements, the position having evidently been chosen as the one best adapted to command the ordinary route of the traveller. I wanted no explanation from the guide to know that this was the castle of Hartenburg. It was still more massive than the remains of the abbey, built of the same material, and seemingly in different centuries; for while one part was irregular and rude, like most of the structures of the Middle Ages, there were salient towers filled with embrasures, for the use of artillery. One of their guns, well-elevated, might possibly have thrown its shot on the platform of the abbey-hill, but with little danger even to the ruined walls.

After studying the different objects in this novel and charming scene for an hour, I demanded of the guide some account of the Pagan's Wall and of the Devil's Stone. Both were on the mountain that lay on the other side of the ambitious little lake, a long musket-shot from the abbey. It was even possible to see a portion of the former, from our present stand; and the confused account of the tailor only excited a desire to see more. We had not come on this excursion without a fit supply of road-books and maps. One of the former was accidentally in my pocket, though so little had we expected anything extraordinary on this unfrequented road, that as yet it had not been opened. On consulting its pages now, I was agreeably disappointed in finding that Deurckheim and its antiquities had not been thought unworthy of the traveller's especial attention. The Pagan's Wall was there stated to be the spot in which Attila passed the winter before crossing the Rhine, in his celebrated inroad against the capital of the civilized world, though its origin was referred to his enemies themselves. In short, it was believed to be the remains of a Roman camp, one of those advanced works of the empire by which the barbarians were held in check, and of which the Hun had casually and prudently availed himself, in his progress south. The Devil's Stone was described as a natural rock, in the vicinity of the encampment, on which the Pagans had offered sacrifices. Of course the liberated limbs of the guide were put in requisition, to conduct us to a spot that contained curiosities so worthy of even his exertions.

As we descended the mountain of Limburg, Christian Kinzel lighted the way by relating the opinions of the country concerning the places we had seen and were about to see. It would appear by this legend that when the pious monks were planning their monastery, a compact was made with the devil to quarry the stones necessary for so extensive a work, and to transport them up the steep acclivity. The inducement held forth to the evil spirit, for undertaking a work of this nature, was the pretense of erecting a tavern, in which, doubtless, undue quantities of Rhenish wine were to be quaffed, cheating human reason, and leaving the undefended soul more exposed to the usual assaults of temptation. It would seem, by the legends of the Rhine, that the monks often succeeded in outwitting the arch foe in this sort of compact, though perhaps never with more signal success than in the bargain in question. Completely deceived by the artifices of the men of God, the father of sin lent himself to the project with so much zeal, that the abbey and its appendages were completed in a time incredibly short; a circumstance that his employers took good care to turn to account, after their own fashion, by ascribing it to a miracle of purer emanation. By all accounts the deception was so well-managed, that notwithstanding his proverbial cunning, the devil never knew the true destination of the edifice until the abbey bell actually rang for prayers. Then, indeed, his indignation knew no bounds, and he proceeded forthwith to the rock in question, with the fell intent of bringing it into the air above the chapel, and, by its fall, of immolating the monks and their altar together, to his vengeance. But the stone was too firmly rooted to be displaced even by the devil; and he was finally compelled, by the prayers of the devotees, who were now, after their own fashion of fighting, fairly in the field, to abandon this portion of the country in shame and disgrace. The curious are shown certain marks on the rock, which go to prove the violent efforts of Satan, on this occasion, and among others the prints of his form, left by seating himself on the stone, fatigued by useless exertions. The more ingenious even trace, in a sort of groove, evidence of the position of his tail, during the time the baffled spirit was chewing the cud of chagrin on his hard stool.

We were at the foot of the second mountain when Christian Kinzel ended this explanation.

"And such is your Deurckheim tradition concerning the Devil's Stone?" I remarked, measuring the ascent with the sight.

"Such is what is said in the country, mein Herr," returned the tailor; "but there are people hereabouts who do not believe it."

My little travelling companion laughed, and his eyes danced with expectation.

"Allons, grimpons!" he cried again; "allons voir ce Teufel-stein!"

In a suitable time we were in the camp. It lay on an advanced spur of the mountain, a sort of salient bastion made by nature, and was completely protected on every side, but that at which it was joined to the mass, by declivities so steep as to be even descended with some pain. There was the ruin of a circular wall, half a league in extent, the stones lying in a confused pile around the whole exterior, and many vestiges of foundations and intersecting walls within. The whole area was covered with a young growth of dark and melancholy cedars. On the face exposed to the adjoining mountain there had evidently been the additional protection of a ditch.

The Teufelstein was a thousand feet from the camp. It is a weather-worn rock, that shows its bare head from a high point in the more advanced ranges of the hills. I took a seat on its most elevated pinnacle, and for a moment the pain of the ascent was forgotten.

The plain of the Palatinate, far as the eye could reach, lay in the view. Here and there the Rhine and the Neckar glittered like sheets of silver among the verdure of the fields, and towers of city and of town, of Manheim, Spires, and Worms, of name-less villages, and of German residences, were as plenty in the scene as tombs upon the Appian Way. A dozen gray ruins clung against the sides of the mountains of Baden and Darm-stadt, while the castle of Heidelberg was visible, in its romantic glen, sombre, courtly, and magnificent. The landscape was German, and in its artificial parts slightly Gothic; it wanted the warm glow, the capricious outlines, and seductive beauty of Italy, and the grandeur of the Swiss valleys and glaciers; but it was the perfection of fertility and industry embellished by a crowd of useful objects.

It was easy for one thus placed to fancy himself surrounded by so many eloquent memorials of the progress of civilization, of the infirmities and constitution, of the growth and ambition of the human mind. The rock recalled the age of furious superstition and debased ignorance—the time when the country lay in forest, over which the hunter ranged at will, contending with the beast for the mastery of his savage domain. Still the noble creature bore the image of God, and occasionally some master mind pierced the shades, catching glimpses of that eternal truth which pervades nature. Then followed the Roman, with his gods of plausible attributes, his ingenious and specious philosophy, his accumulated and borrowed art, his concerted and overwhelming action, his love of magnificence, so grand in its effects, but so sordid and unjust in its means, and last, the most impressive of all, that beacon-like ambition which wrecked his hopes on the sea of its vastness, with the evidence of the falsity of his system as furnished in his fall. The memorial before me showed the means by which he gained and lost his power. The barbarian had been taught, in the bitter school of experience, to regain his rights, and in the excitement of the moment it was not difficult to imagine the Huns pouring into the camp, and calculating their chances of success by the vestiges they found of the ingenuity and resources of their foes.

The confusion of misty images that succeeded was an apt emblem of the next age. Out of this obscurity, after the long and glorious reign of Charlemagne, arose the baronial castle, with feudal violence and its progeny of wrongs. Then came the abbey, an excrescence of that mild and suffering religion, which had appeared on earth, like a ray of the sun, eclipsing the factitious brilliancy of a scene from which natural light had been excluded for a substitute of a meretricious and deceptive quality. Here arose the long and selfish strife between the antagonist principles, that has not yet ceased. The struggle was between the power of knowledge and that of physical force. The former, neither pure nor perfect, descended to subterfuge and deceit; while the latter vacillated between the dread of unknown causes and the love of domination. Monk and baron came in collision; this secretly distrusting the faith he professed, and that trembling at the consequences of the blow which his own sword had given; the fruits of too much knowledge in one, and of too little in the other, while both were the prey of those incessant and unwearied enemies of the race, the greedy passions.

A laugh from the child drew my attention to the foot of the rock. He and Christian Kinzel had just settled, to their mutual satisfaction, the precise position that had been occupied by the devil's tail. A more suitable emblem of his country than that boy, could not have been found on the whole of its wide sur-face. As secondary to the predominant English or Saxon stock, the blood of France, Sweden, and Holland ran, in nearly equal currents, in his veins. He had not far to seek, to find among his ancestors the peaceful companion of Penn, the Huguenot, the Cavalier, the Presbyterian, the follower of Luther and of Calvin. Chance had even deepened the resemblance; for, a wanderer from infancy, he now blended languages in merry comments on his recent discovery. The train of thought that his appearance suggested was natural. It embraced the long and mysterious concealment of so vast a portion of the earth as America, from the acquaintance of civilized man; its discovery and settlement; the manner in which violence and persecution, civil wars, oppression, and injustice, had thrown men of all nations upon its shores; the effects of this collision of customs and opinions, unenthralled by habits and laws of selfish origin; the religious and civil liberty that followed; the novel but irref-utable principle on which its government was based; the silent working of its example in the two hemispheres, one of which had already imitated the institutions that the other was strug-gling to approach, and all the immense results that were de-pendent on this inscrutable and grand movement of Providence. I know not indeed but my thoughts might have approached the sublime, had not Christian Kinzel interrupted them, by point-ing out the spot where the devil had kicked the stone, in his anger.

Descending from the perch, we took the path to Deurck-heim. As we came down the mountain, the tailor had many philosophical remarks to make, that were chiefly elicited by the forlorn condition of one who had much toil and little food.

In his view of things, labor was too cheap, and wine and potatoes were too dear. To what depth he might have pushed reflections bottomed on principles so natural, it is impossible to say, had not the boy started some doubts concerning the reputed length of the devil's tail. He had visited the Jardin des Plantes at Paris, seen the kangaroos in the Zoölogical Garden in London, and was familiar with the inhabitants of a variety of caravans encountered at Rome, Naples, Dresden, and other capitals; with the bears of Berne he had actually been on the familiar terms of a friendly visiting acquaintance. Having also some vague ideas of the analogies of things, he could not recall any beast so amply provided with such an elongation of the dorsal bone, as was to be inferred from Christian Kinzel's gutter in the Teufelstein. During the discussion of this knotty point we reached the inn.

The host of the Ox had deceived us in nothing. The viands were excellent, and abundant to prodigality. The bottle of old Deurckheimer might well have passed for Johannisberger, or for that still more delicious liquor, Steinberger, at London or New York; and the simple and sincere civility with which everything was served, gave a zest to all.

It would have been selfish to recruit nature without thought of the tailor, and after so many hours of violent exercise in the keen air of the mountains. He too had his cup and his viands, and when both were invigorated by these natural means, we held a conference, to which the worthy postmaster was admitted.

The following pages are the offspring of the convocation held in the parlor of the Ox. Should any musty German antiquary discover some immaterial anachronism, a name misplaced in the order of events, or a monk called prematurely from purgatory, he is invited to wreak his just indignation on Christian Kinzel, whose body and soul may St. Benedict of Limburg protect, for evermore, against all critics.[80]

[PARIS AFTER THE JULY REVOLUTION]
From *Switzerland*, Part II (Vol. I, Letter I)[81]

Paris, February, 1832.

Dear ————,

Your speculations concerning the influence of the late revolution,[82] on the social habits of the French, are more ingenious than true. While the mass of this nation has obtained less than they had a right to expect by the severe political convulsions they have endured, during the last forty years, they have, notwithstanding, gained something in their rights; and, what is of far more importance, they have gained in a better appreciation of those rights, as well as in the knowledge of the means to turn them to a profitable and practical account. The end will show essential improvements in their condition, or rather the present time shows it already. The change in polite society has been less favourable, although even this is slowly gaining in morals, and in a healthier tone of thought. No error can be greater, than that of believing France has endured so much, without a beneficial return.

In making up my opinions of the old *régime*, I have had constant recourse to General La Fayette[83] for information. The conversations and anecdotes already sent you, will have prepared you for the fine tone, and perfect candour, with which he speaks even of his bitterest enemies; nor can I remember, in the many confidential and frank communications with which I have been favoured, a single instance where there has been the smallest reason to suspect he has viewed men through the medium of personal antipathies and prejudices. The candour and simplicity of his opinions, form beautiful features in his character; and the *bienséance* of his mind (if one may use such an expression) throws a polish over his harshest strictures, that is singularly adapted to obtain credit for his judgment.

Your desire to know more of the private life of this extraordinary man, is quite natural; but he has been so long before the public, that it is not easy to say any thing new. I may, however, give you a trait or two, to amuse you.

I have seen more of him this winter than the last, owing to the circumstance of a committee of Americans, that have been appointed to administer succour to the exiled Poles, meeting weekly at my house, and it is rare, indeed, that he is not present on these benevolent occasions. He has discontinued his own *soirées*, too; and, having fewer demands on his time, through official avocations, I gain admittance to him during his simple and quiet dinners, whenever it is asked.

These dinners, indeed, are our usual hours of meeting, for the occupations of the General, in the chambers, usually keep him engaged in the morning; nor am I commonly at leisure, myself, until about this hour of the day. In Paris, every one dines, nominally, at six; but the deputies being often detained a little later, whenever I wish to see him, I hurry from my own table, and generally reach the *rue d'Anjou* in sufficient season to find him still at his.

On quitting the *Hôtel de l'Etat Major*, after being dismissed so unceremoniously from the command of the National Guard, La Fayette returned to his own neat but simple lodgings in the *rue d'Anjou*. The *hôtel*, itself, is one of some pretensions, but his apartments, though quite sufficient for a single person, are not among the best it contains, lying on the street, which is rarely or never the case with the principal rooms. The passage to them communicates with the great staircase, and the door is one of those simple, retired entrances that, in Paris, so frequently open on the abodes of some of the most illustrious men of the age. Here have I seen princes, marshals, and dignitaries of all degrees ringing for admission, no one appearing to think of aught but the great man within. These things are permitted here, where the mind gets accustomed to weigh in the balance, all the different claims to distinction, but it would scarcely do in a country, in which the pursuit of money is the sole and engrossing concern of life; a show of expenditure becoming necessary to maintain it.

The apartments of La Fayette consist of a large ante-chamber, two *salons*, and an inner room, where he usually sits and writes, and in which, of late, he has had his bed. These rooms are *en suite*, and communicate, laterally, with one or two more, and the offices. His sole attendants in town are the German valet, named *Bastien*, who accompanied him in his last visit to America, the footman who attends him with the carriage, and the coachman; (there may be a cook, but I never saw a female in the apartments.) Neither wears a livery, although all his appointments, carriages, horses, and furniture, are those of a gentleman. One thing has struck me as a little singular. Notwithstanding his strong attachment to America and to her usages, La Fayette, while the practice is getting to be common in Paris, has not adopted the use of carpets. I do not remember to have seen one, at *la Grange*, or in town.

When I show myself at the door, *Bastien*, who usually acts as porter, and has got to be quite a diplomatist in these matters, makes a sign of asser.t, and intimates that the general is at dinner Of late, he commonly dispenses with the ceremony of letting it be known who has come, but I am at once ushered into the bedroom. Here I find La Fayette seated at a table, just large enough to contain one cover and a single dish; or a table, in other words, so small as to be covered with a napkin. His little white lap dog is his only companion. As it is always understood that I have dined, no ceremony is used, but I take a seat at the chimney corner, while he goes on with his dinner. His meals are quite frugal, though good; a *poulet roti* invariably making one dish. There are two or three removes, a dish at a time, and the dinner usually concludes with some preserves or dried fruits, especially dates, of which he is extremely fond. I generally come in for one or two of the latter.

All this time, the conversation is on what has transpired in the *chambers* during the day, the politics of Europe, nullification in America,[34] or the gossip of the *château*,[35] of which he is singularly well informed, though he has ceased to go there.

The last of these informal interviews with General La Fayette, was one of peculiar interest. I generally sit but half an hour, leaving him to go to his evening engagements, which, by the way, are not frequent; but, on this occasion, he told me to remain, and I passed nearly two hours with him.

We chatted a good deal of the state of society under the old *régime*. Curious to know his opinions of their private characters, I asked a good many questions concerning the royal family. Louis XVI. he described as a well meaning man, addicted a little too much to the pleasures of the table, but who would have done well enough had he not been surrounded by bad advisers. I was greatly surprised by one of his remarks. "Louis XVI.," observed La Fayette, "owed his death as much to the bad advice of Gouverneur Morris,[86] as to any one other thing." You may be certain I did not let this opinion go unquestioned; for, on all other occasions, in speaking of Mr. Morris, his language had been kind and even grateful. He explained himself, by adding, that Mr. Morris, coming from a country like America, was listened to with great respect, and that on all occasions he gave his opinions against democracy, advising resistance, when resistance was not only too late, but dangerous. He did not call in question the motives of Mr. Morris, to which he did full justice, but merely affirmed that he was a bad adviser. He gave me to understand that the representatives of America had not always been faithful to the popular principle, and even went into details that it would be improper for me to repeat. I have mentioned this opinion of Mr. Morris, because his aristocratical sentiments were no secret, because they were mingled with no expressions of personal severity, and because I have heard them from other quarters. He pronounced a strong eulogium on the conduct of Mr. Crawford,[87] which he said was uniformly such as became an American minister.

There is nothing, however, novel in these instances, of our representatives proving untrue to the prominent feeling of the country, on the subject of popular rights. It is the subject of very frequent comment in Europe, and sometimes of complaint on the part of those who are struggling for what they conceive to be their just privileges; many of them having told me, personally, that our agents frequently stand materially in their way.

Louis XVIIIth La Fayette pronounced to be the *falsest* man he had ever met with; to use his own expression, "*l'homme le plus faux.*" He gave him credit for a great deal of talent, but added that his duplicity was innate, and not the result of his position, for it was known to his young associates, in early youth, and that they used to say among themselves, as young men, and in their ordinary gaieties, that it would be unsafe to confide in the *Comte de Provence*.

Of Charles Xth, he spoke kindly, giving him exactly a different character. He thought him the most honest of the three brothers, though quite unequal to the crisis in which he had been called to reign. He believed him sincere in his religious professions, and thought the charge of his being a professed Jesuit by no means improbable.

Marie Antoinette he thought an injured woman. On the subject of her reputed gallantries, he spoke cautiously, premising that, as an American, I ought to make many allowances for a state of society that was altogether unknown in our country. Treating this matter with the discrimination of a man of the world, and the delicacy of a gentleman, he added that he entirely exonerated her from all the coarse charges that had proceeded from vulgar clamor, while he admitted that she had betrayed a partiality for a young Swede* that was, at least, indiscreet for one in her situation, though he had no reason to believe her attachment had led her to the length of criminality.

I asked his opinion concerning the legitimacy of the Duc de Bordeaux, but he treated the rumour to the contrary, as one of those miserable devices to which men resort to effect the ends of party, and as altogether unworthy of serious attention.

I was amused with the simplicity with which he spoke of his own efforts to produce a change of government, during the last reign. On this subject he had been equally frank even before the recent revolution, though there would have been a manifest impropriety in my repeating what had then passed between us. This objection is now removed in part, and I may recount one of his anecdotes, though I can never impart to it the manner of cool and quiet humour with which it was related. We were speaking of the attempt of 1822, or the plot which existed in the army. In reply to a question of mine, he said—"Well, I was to

* A Count Koningsmarke. [*Cooper's note.*]

have commanded in that revolution, and when the time came, I got into my carriage, without a passport, and drove across the country to ——, where I obtained post-horses, and proceeded as fast as possible towards ——. At ——, a courier met me, with the unhappy intelligence that our plan was discovered, and that several of our principal agents were arrested. I was advised to push for the frontier, as fast as I could. But we turned round in the road, and I went to Paris, and took my seat in the Chamber of Deputies. They looked very queer, and a good deal surprised when they saw me, and I believe they were in great hopes that I had run away. The party of the ministers were loud in their accusations against the opposition for encouraging treason, and Perier and Constant, and the rest of them, made indignant appeals against such unjust accusations. I took a different course. I went into the tribune, and invited the ministers to come and give a history of my political life; of my changes and treasons as they called them; and said that when they had got through, I would give the character and history of theirs. This settled the matter, for I heard no more from them." I inquired if he had not felt afraid of being arrested and tried. "Not much," was his answer. "They knew I denied the right of foreigners to impose a government on France, and they also knew they had not kept faith with France under the charter. I made no secret of my principles, and frequently put letters unsealed into the post office, in which I had used the plainest language about the government. On the whole, I believe they were more afraid of me, than I was of them."

It is impossible to give an idea, in writing, of the pleasant manner he has of relating these things—a manner that receives additional piquancy from his English, which, though good, is necessarily broken. He usually prefers the English in such conversations.

"By the way," he suddenly asked me, "where was the idea of Harvey Birch, in the Spy, found?"[88] I told him that the thought had been obtained from an anecdote of the revolution, related to me by Governor Jay, some years before the book was written. He laughingly remarked that he could have supplied the hero of a romance, in the person of a negro named Harry (I believe, though the name has escaped me,) who acted as a spy, both for him and Lord Cornwallis, during the time he commanded against that officer in Virginia. This negro he represented as being true to the American cause, and as properly belonging to his service, though permitted occasionally to act for Lord Cornwallis, for the sake of gaining intelligence. After the surrender of the latter, he called on General La Fayette, to return a visit. Harry was in an ante-room cleaning his master's boots, as Lord Cornwallis entered. "Ha! Master Harry," exclaimed the latter, "you are here, are you?" "Oh, yes, masser Corwallis—muss try to do little for de country," was the answer. This negro he said was singularly clever and bold, and of sterling patriotism!

He made me laugh with a story, that he said the English officers had told him of General Knyphausen, who commanded the Hessian mercenaries, in 1776. This officer, a rigid martinet, knew nothing of the sea, and not much more of geography. On the voyage between England and America, he was in the ship of Lord Howe, where he passed several uncomfortable weeks, the fleet having an unusually long passage, on account of the bad sailing of some of the transports. At length Knyphausen could contain himself no longer, but marching stiffly up to the admiral one day, he commenced with—"My lord, I know it is the duty of a soldier to be submissive at sea, but, being intrusted with the care of the troops of His Serene Highness, my master, I feel it my duty, just to inquire, if it be not possible, that during some of the dark nights we have lately had, *we may have sailed past America?*"

I asked him if he had been at the *château* lately. His reply was very brief and expressive. "The king denies my account of the *programme* of the *hotel de ville*, and we stand in the position of two gentlemen, who, in substance, have given each other the lie. Circumstances prevent our going to the *Bois de Boulogne*, to exchange shots," he added smiling, "but they also prevent our exchanging visits." I then ventured to say that I had long foreseen what would be the result of the friendship of Louis Philippe and, for the first time, in the course of our conversations, I adverted to my own visit to the palace in his company,[89] an account of which I will extract, for your benefit, from my note book.*

"In the morning I received a note from General La Fayette, in which he informed me that Mr. McLane,[90] who is here on a visit from London, was desirous of being presented; that there was a reception in the evening, at which he intended to introduce the minister to England, Mr. Rives[91] not having yet received his new credentials, and, of course, not appearing in matters of ceremony. Gen. La Fayette pressed me so strongly to be of the party, in compliment to Mr. McLane, that, though but an indifferent courtier and it was so contrary to my quiet habits, I could do nothing but comply.

"At the proper hour, Gen. La Fayette had the good nature to call and take me up, and we proceeded, at once, for Mr. McLane. With this gentleman we drove to the *Palais Royal*, my old brother officer, Mr. T——, who was included in the arrangement, following in his own carriage.

"We found the inner court crowded, and a throng about the entrance to the great stair-case, but the appearance of La Fayette, cleared the way, and there was a movement in the populace which denoted his great personal popularity. I heard the words '*des Américains*' passing from one to another, showing how completely he was identified with us and our principles, in the popular mind. One or two of the younger officers of the court were at the foot of the stairs to receive him, though whether their presence was accidental, or designed, I cannot say; but I suspect the latter. At all events the General was received with the profoundest respect, and the most smiling assiduity.

"The ante-chamber was already crowded, but following our leader, his presence cleared the way for us, until he got up quite near to the doors, where some of the most distinguished men of France were collected. I saw many in the throng whom I knew, and the first minute or two were passed in nods of recognition.

* The period referred to was in 1830. [*Cooper's note.*]

My attention was, however, soon attracted to a dialogue between Marshal Soult and La Fayette, that was carried on with the most perfect *bonhomie* and simplicity. I did not hear the commencement, but found they were speaking of their legs, which both seemed to think the worse for wear. 'But you have been wounded in the leg, Monsieur?' observed La Fayette. 'This limb was a little *mal traitée* at Genoa,' returned the Marshal, looking down at a leg that had a very game look, 'but you, General, you too, were hurt in America?' 'Oh! that was nothing; it happened more than fifty years ago, and *then it was in a good cause*—it was the fall and the fracture that made me limp.' Just at this moment, the great doors flew open, and this *quasi* republican court standing arrayed before us, the two old soldiers limped forward.

"The King stood near the door, dressed as a General of the National Guards, entirely without decorations, and pretty well *tri-colored*. The Queen, Madame Adelaide, the Princesses, and several of the children, were a little farther removed, the two former standing in front, and the latter being grouped behind them. But one or two ladies were present, nor did I see any thing at the commencement of the evening, of the *Ducs d'Orleans* and *de Nemours*.

"La Fayette was one of the first that entered, and of course we kept near him. The King advanced to meet him with an expression of pleasure—I thought it studied—but they shook hands quite cordially. We were then presented by name, and each of us had the honour of shaking hands, if that can be considered an honour, which fell to the share of quite half of those who entered. The press was so great there was no opportunity to say any thing. I believe we all met with the usual expressions of welcome, and there the matter ended.

"Soon after we approached the Queen, with whom our reception had a more measured manner. Most of those who entered did little more than make a distant bow to this group, but the Queen manifesting a desire to say something to our party, Mr. McLane and myself approached them. She first addressed my companion in French, a language he did not speak, and I was obliged to act as interpreter. But the Queen instantly said she understood English, though she spoke it badly, and begged he would address her in his own tongue. Madame Adelaide made out better. But the conversation was necessarily short, and not worth repeating.

"Queen Amélie is a woman of a kind, and, I think, intelligent countenance. She has the Bourbon rather than the Austrian outline of face. She seemed anxious to please, and in her general air and carriage, has some resemblance to the Duchess of St. Leu.* She has the reputation of being an excellent wife and mother, and really, not to fall too precipitately into the vice of a courtier, she appears as if she may well deserve it. She is thin, but graceful, and I can well imagine that she has been more than pretty in her youth.

"I do not remember a more frank, intelligent, and winning countenance than that of *Madame Adelaide*, who is the King's sister. She has little beauty left, except that of expression, but this must have made her handsome once, as it renders her singularly attractive now. Her manner was less nervous than that of the Queen, and I should think her mind had more influence over her exterior.

"The Princess *Louise* (the Queen of Belgium) and the Princess *Marie* are pretty, with the quiet subdued manner of well-bred young persons. The first is pale, has a strikingly Bourbon face, resembling the profiles on the French coins, while the latter has an Italian and classical outline of features, with a fine colour.

"They were all dressed with great simplicity; scarcely in high dinner dress; the Queen and *Madame Adelaide* wearing evening hats. The Princesses, as is uniformly the case with unmarried French girls of rank, were without any ornaments, wearing their hair in the usual manner.

"After the ceremonies of being presented were through, I amused myself with examining the company. This was a levee, not a drawing room, and there were no women among the visiters. The men, who did not appear in uniform, were in

* Hortense. [*Cooper's note.*]

common evening dress, which has degenerated of late into black stocks, and trousers.

"Accident brought me next to an old man, who had exactly that revolutionary air which has become so familiar to us by the engravings of Bonaparte and his generals that were made shortly after the Italian campaign. The face was nearly buried in neckcloth, the hair was long and wild, and the coat was glittering, but ill-fitting and stiff. It was, however, the coat of a *Maréchal;* and, what rendered it still more singular, it was entirely without orders. I was curious to know who this relic of 1797 might be; for, apart from his rank, which was betrayed by his coat, he was so singularly ugly as scarcely to appear human. On inquiry it proved to be Marshal Jourdan.

"There was some amusement in watching the different individuals who came to pay their court to the new dynasty. Many were personally and familiarly known to me as very loyal subjects of the last reign; soldiers who would not have hesitated to put Louis Philippe *au fil de l'épée,* three months before, at the command of Charles X. But times were changed. They now came to show themselves to the new sovereign; most of them to manifest their disposition to be put in the way of preferment, some to reconnoitre, others to conceal their disaffection, and all to subserve their own interests. It was laughably easy to discern who were confident of their reception by being of the ruling party, who distrusted, and who were indifferent. The last class was small. A general officer, whom I personally knew, looked like one who had found his way into a wrong house by mistake. He was a Bonapartist by his antecedents, and in his true way of thinking; but accident had thrown him into the hands of the Bourbons, and he had now come to see what might be gleaned from the House of Orleans. His reception was not flattering, and I could only compare the indecision and wavering of his manner to that of a regiment that falters before an unexpected volley.

"After amusing ourselves some time in the great throng, which was densest near the King, we went towards a secondary circle that had formed in another part of the room, where the Duke of Orleans had appeared. He was conversing with La Fayette, who immediately presented us all, in succession. The Prince is a genteel, handsome young man, with a face much more Austrian than that of any of his family, so far as one can judge of what his younger brothers are likely to be hereafter. In form, stature, and movements, he singularly resembles W——, and there is also a good deal of likeness in the face, though in this particular the latter has the advantage. He was often taken for the *Duc de Chartres* during our former residence at Paris. Our reception was gracious, the heir to the throne appearing anxious to please every one.

"The amusing part of the scene is to follow. Fatigued with standing, we had got chairs in a corner of the room, behind the throng, where the discourtesy of being seated might escape notice. The king soon after withdrew, and the company immediately began to go away. Three-fourths, perhaps, were gone, when an *aide de camp* came up to us and inquired if we were not the three Americans who had been presented by General La Fayette? Being answered in the affirmative, he begged us to accompany him. He led us near a door at the other end of the *salle*, a room of great dimensions, where we found General La Fayette in waiting. The *Aide*, or officer of the court, whichever might be his station, passed through the door, out of which the king immediately came. It appeared to me as if the General was not satisfied with our first reception, and wished to have it done over again. The king looked grave, not to say discontented, and I saw, at a glance, that he could have dispensed with this extra attention. Mr. M'Lane standing next the door, he addressed a few words to him, in English, which he speaks quite readily, and without much accent. Indeed he said little to any one else, and the few words that he did utter were exceedingly general and unmeaning. Once he got as far as T——, whom he asked if he came from New York, and he looked hard at me, who stood farther from the door, mumbled something, bowed to us all, and withdrew. I was struck with his manner, which seemed vexed and unwilling, and the whole thing struck me as awkward and uncomfortable. I thought it a bad omen for the influence of the general.

"By this time the great *salle* was nearly empty, and we moved off together to find our carriages. General La Fayette preceded us, of course, and as he walked slow, and occasionally stopped to converse, we were among the last in the ante-chamber. In passing into the last or outer ante-chamber, the General stopped nearly in the door to speak to some one. Mr. M'Lane and Mr. T—— being at his side, they so nearly stopped the way that I remained some distance in the rear, in order not to close it entirely. My position would give an ordinary observer reason to suppose that I did not belong to the party. A young officer of the court (I call them *aides*, though, I believe, they were merely substitutes for chamberlains, dignitaries to which this republican reign has not yet given birth,) was waiting in the outer room to pass, but appeared unwilling to press too closely on a group of which General La Fayette formed the principal person. He fidgetted and chafed evidently, but still kept politely at a distance. After two or three minutes the party moved on, but I remained stationary, watching the result. Room was no sooner made than the officer brushed past, and gave vent to his feelings by saying, quite loudly and distinctly, '*Adieu l'Amérique!*'

"It is a pretty safe rule to believe that in the tone of courtiers is reflected the feeling of the monarch. The attention to General La Fayette had appeared to me as singularly affected and forced, and the manner of the king any thing but natural; and several little occurrences during the evening had tended to produce the impression that the real influence of the former, at the palace, might be set down as next to nothing. I never had any faith in a republican king from the commencement, but this near view of the personal intercourse between the parties served to persuade me that General La Fayette had been the dupe of his own good faith and kind feelings.

"In descending the great stairs I mentioned the occurrence just related to Mr. M'Lane, adding, that I thought the days of our friend were numbered, and that a few months would produce a schism between him and Louis Philippe. Every thing, at the moment, however, looked so smiling, and so much outward respect was lavished on General La Fayette, that this opinion did not find favour with my listener, though I believe, he saw reason to think differently, after another visit to court. We all got invitations to dine at the palace in a day or two, and my next letter will most probably contain the gossip of a royal entertainment."

I did not, however, touch upon the *"adieu, l'Amérique,"* which I have always deemed a subject too delicate to be mentioned. He was silent, and by way of changing the conversation, I alluded to the queer scene of the reception of the American ladies,[92] but this he also appeared to think went off better than, from my letter on the subject, you will have seen was my own notion of the matter.

He startled me by suddenly putting the question, whether I thought an executive, in which there should be but one agent, as in the United States, or an executive in which there should be three, or five, would best suit the condition of France? Though so well acquainted with the boldness and steadiness of his views, I was not prepared to find his mind dwelling on such a subject, at the present moment. The state of France, however, is certainly extremely critical, and we ought not to be surprised at the rising of the people at any moment.

I told General La Fayette that, in my poor judgment, the question admitted of a good deal of controversy. Names did not signify much, but every administration should receive its main impulses, subject to the common wishes and interests, from a close conformity of views, whether there were one incumbent or a dozen. The English system certainly made a near approach to a divided executive, but the power was so distributed as to prevent much clashing; and when things went wrong, the ministers resigned; parliament, in effect, holding the control of the executive as well as of the legislative branches of the government. Now I did not think France was prepared for such a polity, the French being accustomed to see a real as well as a nominal monarch, and the disposition to intrigue would, for a long time to come, render their administrations fluctuating and insecure. A directory would either control the chambers or be controlled by them. In the former case it would be apt to be divided in itself; in the latter, to agitate the chambers by factions that would not have the ordinary outlet of majorities to restore the equilibrium.

He was of opinion himself that the expedient of a directory had not suited the state of France. He asked me what I thought of universal suffrage for this country. I told him, I thought it altogether unsuited to the present condition of France. I did not attach much faith to the old theory of the necessary connexion between virtue and democracy, as a cause; though it might, with the necessary limitations, follow as an effect. A certain degree of knowledge of its uses, *action*, and objects was indispensable to a due exercise of the suffrage; not that it was required every elector should be learned in the theory of governments, but that he should know enough to understand the general connexion between his vote and his interests, and especially his rights. This knowledge was not at all difficult of attainment, in ordinary cases, when one had the means of coming at facts. In cases that admit of argument, as in all the questions on political economy, I did not see that any reasonable degree of knowledge made the matter much better, the cleverest men usually ranging themselves on the two extremes of all mooted questions. Concerning the right of every man, who was qualified to use the power, to have his interests directly represented in a government, it was unnecessary to speak, the only question being who had and who had not the means to make a safe use of the right, in practice. It followed from these views, that the great *desiderata* were to ascertain what these means were.

In the present state of the world, I thought it absolutely necessary that a man should be able to read, in order to exercise the right to vote with a prudent discretion. In countries where every body reads, other qualifications might be trusted to, provided they were low and within reasonable reach of the mass; but, in a country like France, I would allow no man to vote until he knew how to read, if he were as rich as Crœsus.

I felt convinced the present system could not continue long in France. It might do for a few years, as a reaction, but when things were restored to their natural course, it would be found that there is an unnatural union between facts that are peculiar to despotism, and facts that are peculiarly the adjuncts of liberty; as in the provisions of the *Code Napoleon*, and in the liberty of the press, without naming a multitude of other discrepancies. The *juste milieu* that he had so admirably described* could not last long, but the government would soon find itself driven into strong measures, or into liberal measures, in order to sustain itself. Men could no more serve "God and Mammon" in politics than in religion. I then related to him an anecdote that had occurred to myself the evening of the first anniversary of the present reign.

On the night in question, I was in the *Thuileries*, with a view to see the fire-works. Taking a station a little apart from the crowd, I found myself under a tree alone with a Frenchman of some sixty years of age. After a short parley, my companion, as usual, mistook me for an Englishman. On being told his error, he immediately opened a conversation on the state of things in France. He asked me if I thought they would continue. I told him, no; that I thought two or three years would suffice to bring the present system to a close. "*Monsieur*," said my companion, "you are mistaken. It will require ten years

* When the term *juste milieu* was first used by the king, and adopted by his followers, La Fayette said in the Chamber, that "he very well understood what a *juste milieu* meant, in any particular case; it meant neither more nor less than the truth, in that particular case: but as to a political party's always taking a middle course, under the pretence of being in a *juste milieu*, he should liken it to a discreet man's laying down the proposition that four and four make eight, and a fool's crying out, 'Sir, you are wrong, for four and four make ten,' whereupon the advocate for the *juste milieu* on system, would be obliged to say, 'Gentlemen, you are equally in extremes, *four and four make nine*.'" It is the fashion to say La Fayette wanted *esprit*. This was much the cleverest thing the writer ever heard in the French Chambers, and, generally, he knew few men who said more witty things in a neat and unpretending manner than General La Fayette. Indeed this was the bias of his mind, which was little given to profound reflections, though distinguished for a *fort bon sens*. [*Cooper's note.*]

to dispossess those who have seized upon the government, since the last revolution. All the young men are growing up with the new notions, and in ten years they will be strong enough to overturn the present order of things. Remember that I prophesy the year 1840,[93] will see a change of government in France."

La Fayette laughed at this prediction, which, he said, did not quite equal his impatience. He then alluded to the ridicule which had been thrown upon his own idea of "A monarchy with republican institutions," and asked me what I thought of the system. As my answer to this, as well as to his other questions, will serve to lay before you my own opinions, which you have a right to expect from me, as a traveller rendering an account of what he has seen, I shall give you its substance, at length.

So far from finding any thing as absurd as is commonly pretended in the plan of a "throne surrounded by republican institutions," it appears to me to be exactly the system best suited to the actual condition of France. By a monarchy, however, a real monarchical government, or one in which the power of the sovereign is to predominate, is not to be understood, in this instance, but such a semblance of a monarchy as exists to-day, in England, and formerly existed in Venice and Genoa under their Doges. In England the aristocracy notoriously rules, through the king, and I see no reason why in France, a constituency with a base sufficiently broad to entitle it to assume the name of a republic, might not rule, in its turn, in the same manner. In both cases the sovereign would merely represent an abstraction; the sovereign power would be wielded in his name, but at the will of the constituency; he would be a parliamentary echo, to pronounce the sentiment of the legislative bodies, whenever a change of men, or a change of measures became necessary. It is very true that, under such a system, there would be no real separation, in principle, between the legislative and the executive branches of government; but such is, to-day, and such has long been the actual condition of England, and her statesmen are fond of saying the plan "works well." Now, although the plan does not work half as well in

England, as is pretended, except for those who more especially reap its benefits, simply because the legislature is not
established on a sufficiently popular basis, still it works better,
on the whole, for the public, than if the system were reversed,
as was formerly the case, and the king ruled through the parliament, instead of the parliament ruling through the king. In
France the facts are ripe for an extension of this principle, in its
safest and most salutary manner. The French of the present
generation are prepared to dispense with a hereditary and political aristocracy, in the first place, nothing being more odious to
them than privileged orders, and no nation, not even America,
having more healthful practices or wiser notions on this point
than themselves. The experience of the last fifteen years has
shown the difficulty of creating an independent peerage in
France, notwithstanding the efforts of the government sustained by the example and wishes of England, have been steadily
directed to that object. Still they have the traditions and *prestige*
of a monarchy. Under such circumstances, I see no difficulty
in carrying out the idea of La Fayette. Indeed, some such polity
is indispensable, unless liberty is to be wholly sacrificed. All
experience has shown that a king, who is a king in fact as well
as name, is too strong for law, and the idea of restraining such a
power by *principles*, is purely chimerical. He may be curtailed
in his authority, by the force of opinion and by extreme constructions of these principles; but if this be desirable, it would
be better to avoid the struggle, and begin, at once, by laying the
foundation of the system in such a way, as will prevent the
necessity of any change.

As respects France, a peerage, in my opinion, is neither desirable nor practicable. It is certainly possible for the king to
maintain a chosen political corps, as long as he can maintain
himself, which shall act in his interests and do his bidding; but
it is folly to ascribe the attributes that belong to a peerage to such
a body of mercenaries. They resemble the famous *mandamus*
counsellors, who had so great an agency in precipitating our
own revolution, and are more likely to achieve a similar dis-
service to their master than any thing else. Could they be-

come really independent, to a point to render them a masculine feature in the state, they would soon, by their combinations, become too strong for the other branches of the government, as has been the case in England, and France would have a "throne surrounded by aristocratic institutions." The popular notion that an aristocracy is necessary to a monarchy, I take it, is a gross error. A titular aristocracy, in some shape or other, is always the *consequence* of a monarchy, merely because it is the reflection of the sovereign's favour, policy or caprice; but *political* aristocracies like the peerage, have, nine times in ten, proved too strong for the monarch. France would form no exception to the rule, but, as men are apt to run into the delusion of believing it liberty to strip one of power, although his mantle is to fall on the few, I think it more than probable the popular error would be quite likely to aid the aristocrats in effecting their object; after habit had a little accustomed the nation to the presence of such a body. This is said, however, under the supposition that the elements of an independent peerage could be found in France, a fact that I doubt, as has just been mentioned.

If England can have a throne, then, surrounded by aristocratical institutions, what is there to prevent France from having a throne "surrounded by republican institutions?" The word "Republic," though it does not exclude, does not necessarily include the idea of a democracy. It merely means a polity, in which the predominant idea is the "public things," or common weal, instead of the hereditary and inalienable rights of one. It would be quite practicable, therefore, to establish in France such an efficient constituency as would meet the latter conditions, and yet to maintain the throne, as the machinery necessary, in certain cases, to promulgate the will of this very constituency. This is all that the throne does in England, and why need it do more in France? By substituting then a more enlarged constituency, for the borough system of England, the idea of La Fayette would be completely fulfilled. The reform in England, itself, is quite likely to demonstrate that his scheme was not as monstrous as has been affirmed. The throne of France should be occupied as Corsica is occupied, not for the affirmative good it does the nation, so much as to prevent harm from its being occasionally vacant.

In the course of the conversation I gave to General La Fayette the following outline of the form of government I could wish to give to France, were I a Frenchman, and had I a voice in the matter. I give it to you on the principle already avowed, or as a traveller furnishing his notions of the things he has seen, and because it may aid in giving you a better insight into my views of the state of this country.

I would establish a monarchy, and Henry V. should be the monarch. I would select him on account of his youth, which will admit of his being educated in the notions necessary to his duty; and on account of his birth, which would strengthen his nominal government, and, by necessary connexion, the actual government; for, I believe, that, in their hearts, and notwithstanding the professions to the contrary, nearly half of France would greatly prefer the legitimate line of their ancient kings to the actual dynasty. This point settled, I would extend the suffrage as much as facts would justify; certainly so as to include a million or a million and a half of electors. All idea of the *representation* of property should be relinquished, as the most corrupt, narrow and vicious form of polity that has ever been devised, invariably tending to array one portion of the community against another, and endangering the very property it is supposed to protect. A moderate property *qualification* might be adopted, in connexion with that of intelligence. The present scheme in France unites, in my view of the case, precisely the two worst features of admission to the suffrage that could be devised. The qualification of an elector is a given amount of direct contribution. This *qualification* is so high as to amount to *representation*, and France is already so taxed as to make a diminution of the burdens one of the first objects at which a good government would aim; it follows that as the ends of liberty are attained, its foundations would be narrowed, and the *representation* of property would be more and more assured. A simple property qualification would, therefore, I think, be a better scheme than the present.

Each department should send an allotted number of deputies, the polls being distributed on the American plan. Respecting the term of service, there might arise various considerations, but it should not exceed five years, and I would prefer three. The present house of peers should be converted into a senate, its members to sit as long as the deputies. I see no use in making the term of one body longer than the other, and I think it very easy to show that great injury has arisen from the practice among ourselves. Neither do I see the advantage of having a part go out periodically; but, on the contrary, a disadvantage, as it leaves a representation of old, and, perhaps, rejected opinions, to struggle with the opinions of the day. Such collisions have invariably impeded the action and disturbed the harmony of our own government. I would have every French elector vote for each senator; thus the local interests would be protected by the deputies, while the senate would strictly represent France. This united action would control all things, and the ministry would be an emanation of their will, of which the king should merely be the organ.

I have no doubt the action of our own system would be better, could we devise some plan by which a ministry should supersede the present executive. The project of Mr. Hillhouse, that of making the senators draw lots annually for the office of President, is, in my opinion, better than the elective system; but it would be, in a manner, liable to the old objection, of a want of harmony between the different branches of the government. France has all the machinery of royalty, in her palaces, her parks, and the other appliances of the condition; and she has, moreover, the necessary habits and opinions, while we have neither. There is, therefore, just as much reason why France should not reject this simple expedient for naming a ministry, as there is for our not adopting it. Here, then, would be, at once, a "throne surrounded by republican institutions," and, although it would not be a throne as powerful as that which France has at present, it would, I think, be more permanent than one surrounded by bayonets, and leave France, herself, more powerful, in the end.

The capital mistake made in 1830, was that of establishing the *throne* before establishing the *republic;* in trusting to *men,* instead of trusting to *institutions*.

I do not tell you that La Fayette assented to all that I said. He had reason for the impracticability of setting aside the personal interests which would be active in defeating such a reform, that involved details and a knowledge of character to which I had nothing to say; and, as respects the *Duc de Bordeaux*, he affirmed that the reign of the *Bourbons* was over, in France. The country was tired of them. It may appear presumptuous in a foreigner to give an opinion against such high authority; but, "what can we reason but from what we know?" and truth compels me to say, I cannot subscribe to this opinion. My own observation, imperfect though it be, has led to a different conclusion. I believe there are thousands, even among those who throng the *Tuileries*, who would hasten to throw off the mask at the first serious misfortune that should befall the present dynasty, and who would range themselves on the side of what is called legitimacy. In respect to parties, I think the republicans the boldest, in possession of the most talents compared to numbers, and the least numerous. The friends of the King (active and passive) the least decided, and the least connected by principle, though strongly connected by a desire to prosecute their temporal interests, and more numerous than the republicans; the Carlists or *Henriquinquists* the most numerous, the most generally, but secretly, sustained by the rural population, particularly in the west and south.

La Fayette frankly admitted, what all now seem disposed to admit, that it was a fault not to have made sure of the institutions before the King was put upon the throne. He affirmed, however, it was much easier to assert the wisdom of taking this precaution, than to have adopted it in fact. The world, I believe, is in error, about most of the political events that succeeded the three days.

[TOWARD MENTAL INDEPENDENCE]

From *A Letter to His Countrymen* [94]

The private citizen who comes before the world with matter relating to himself, is bound to show a better reason for the measure than the voluntary impulses of self-love. In my own case, it might, perhaps, appear a sufficient excuse for the step now taken, that I am acting chiefly on the defensive; that the editors of several of the public journals have greatly exceeded their legitimate functions, by animadverting on my motives and private affairs; and that assertions, opinions, and acts, have been openly attributed to me, that I have never uttered, entertained, or done. When an individual is thus dragged into notice, the right of self-vindication would seem to depend on a principle of natural justice; and yet, if I know the springs of my own conduct, I am less influenced by any personal considerations in what I am now doing, than by a wish to check a practice that has already existed too long among us; which appears to me to be on the increase; and which, while it is degrading to the character, if persisted in, may become dangerous to the institutions of this country.

The practice of quoting the opinions of foreign nations, by way of helping to make up its own estimate of the degree of merit that belongs to its public men, is, I believe, a custom peculiar to America. That our colonial origin, and provincial habits, should have given rise to such a usage, is sufficiently natural; that journals which have a poverty of original matter, should have recourse to that which can be obtained not only gratuitously, but by an extraordinary convention, without loss of reputation, and without even the necessity of a translation, need be no mystery; but the readiness with which the practice can be accounted for, will not, I think, prove its justification, if it can be shown that it is destructive of those sentiments of self-respect, and of that manliness and independence of thought, that are necessary to render a people great, or a nation respectable. Questions have now arisen between a portion of the press and myself, which give me more authority to speak in the matter than might belong to one whose name had not been so freely used, and it is my intention, while I endeavor to do myself justice, to make an effort to arrest the custom to which there is allusion; and which, should it continue to prevail, must render every American more or less subject to the views of those who are hostile to the prosperity, the character, and the power of his native land.

. . . .

The habit of fostering this deference to foreign opinion is dangerous to the very institutions under which we live. This is the point at which I have aimed from the commencement; for, while I feel that every defender of the action of our own system is entitled to fair-play, I have never had the weakness to believe that any personal interests of my own are a matter of sufficient importance to others, to require a publication like the present.

The practice of deferring to foreign opinion is dangerous to the institutions of the country.

In order to render the case that I wish to present clear, it will be necessary to take a short review of the institutions themselves.

The government of the United States is a peculiar confederation of many different bodies politic, for specified objects embracing certain of the higher functions of sovereignty, and to which we have given the appropriate name of a Union. The action of this government is obtained by a system of representation which, while it is compound and complicated in its elements, possesses, in fact, the redeeming and essential quality of simplicity, by providing that none but common interests shall be subject to its control. And, yet, while we actually possess, under the provisions of the Constitution, the essential requisite of an *ensemble* in the legal operation and spirit of the institutions, nothing is easier than to create an antagonist action, by overstepping the limits of the compact. A single glance at the instrument itself will explain my meaning.

A Union, from its very nature, must be a representative form of government; but the mere circumstance that a government is representative by no means establishes its character, which depends on the fact of whom the parties are that are represented. Under our system, each State is the arbiter of its own constituency, subject to the single condition that its form of polity shall be that of a Republic. A republic is a government in which the executive power is not hereditary, or in which the laws are administered in the name of a Commonwealth instead of that of a Prince. Venice, Poland, Frankfort, Unterwalden, Berne and Connecticut, are or were all republics. New-York, in virtue of its reserved rights, has decided that its constituency shall be represented on the principle of universal suffrage.[95] Virginia has a freehold qualification. Either of these States has a right to modify its representation as it shall think best for its own interests. In point of fact, it is true the states of this Union are nearly all democracies, but they have attained this near approach to harmony by their own acts; for, under the limitations of the Federal Constitution, it is quite within the legal competency of the several bodies corporate which compose the Union, to make that Union a representation of democracies, or of aristocracies, or of a mixture of both, by altering the characters of the respective constituencies. Did the government of the United States possess more minute powers, therefore, and were the States to exercise the privilege just mentioned, making their representations a mixture of aristocracies and democracies, disunion or revolution would inevitably follow. Although there are instances in which monarchies and aristocracies coalesce in confederations for defined objects, as in Germany,[96] and in which aristocracies and democracies unite for the same purposes, there is no instance in history in which these antagonist principles have long existed, in the full exercise of equal powers, in the form of a consolidated community. The struggle between them has always produced revolution in fact, whatever may have been done in form. By studying, then, the danger of a union of great antagonist principles in a consolidated form of government, we are admonished to respect the conditions on which the possibility of their co-existence is admitted into our own system. Although Virginia, and certain other States, may possibly be termed representative democracies, when considered solely in reference to their white population, they are in truth, even now, mild aristocracies, when considered in reference to their whole population. Immaterial as the difference is in most cases between the polity of Virginia and that of New-York, there are some points of disagreement that sufficiently show how easy it is, by transcending the conditions of the Union, to awaken a spirit of hostility, and to endanger the existence of the compact that now binds them together. To these points of difference in principle may be added, as temporary causes of disunion, those interests which arise from difference of climate and productions.

Every government has two great classes of obstacles to contend with:—the propensities of human nature, and the difficulties that arise from its particular manner of controling its own affairs. As the first is an evil that we share in common with all men, it may be dismissed without comment; but in the case of the second, it will be useful to allude here to one or two of these particular causes of embarrassment as they exist under our own system.

The first great difficulty with which this government has to contend, is, for reasons that are obvious, the accurate discrimination between the powers that are granted to the Union and those that are reserved by the states. The contests which may arise on these vital questions can give birth to the only true whigs and tories of America. The object of this Union was not simply government—this was possessed in the several states— but it was to extend a uniform system over so large a space, as to reap the greatest benefit from its action.

It has been said by others that the advantages of the Union, while they are admitted to be of the last importance, are of a purely negative character. This, I apprehend, is little more than clothing a truism in pretending language. The object of society in general is to enjoy the advantages of association and protection; to say, therefore, that we should be worse off without the Union, is but another method of saying that we are better off with it. In Europe, when the enemies of this system (and they are the friends of all others) are driven from position to position in the arguments that frequently occur between them and Americans, concerning the merits and probable duration of our polity, they uniformly raise the objection, "that your government is only a compromise." [97] Every government is a compromise, or something worse. Every community that is not founded on such a principle must sacrifice some of its interests to others; and, in our own case, so far from believing that the mutual concessions that have been made in the compact of the Union are opposed to the true spirit of government, I shall contend that they are proofs that its real objects and just limitations were properly understood. Disputes have certainly occurred, originating in a diversity of employments; but we have not yet reached the period when all the ordinary interests of civilized society are properly balanced. When that period shall arrive, and it cannot be distant, I think it will be found that this diversity of employments is an additional ligament to the Union. But, while no great weight is to be given to a mere diversity of employments, every attention is due to those feelings that enter into the daily habits and prejudices of men. In this country, facts greatly outrun opinion. This is one of the reasons that we see men looking behind them to Europe for precedents, instead of being willing to conduct their own affairs on their own principles. Had congress the right to control those minute interests of society that touch the rooted practices of different sections of the Union, as they are now controlled by the state legislatures, the revenue of the Union would not be worth a year's purchase; for nothing but force would compel the Virginian and the Vermontese to submit to the same detail of social organization. In such a case we should quickly see the vicious influence of the adverse principles of democracy and aristocracy. Still, the constitution of the United States contemplates the co-existence of these antagonist forces in our system, through the several states, and it fully admits of their representation, for it leaves to each community the power to decide on the character of its constituency. It follows as a corollary from the proposition, that either the framers of the constitution were guilty of the gross neglect of admitting into the government of the Union the seeds of its own destruction, or that they devised means to obviate the natural conflict between principles so irreconcileably hostile. They did the latter, by limiting the powers of the new government to the control of those interests that take the same general aspects under every form of civilized society, let the authority emanate from what sources it may. This provision, then, is our only safeguard, and while it is respected there is little serious ground to apprehend the downfall of the system; but as soon as innovation shall make any serious inroads on these sacred limits, the bond which unites us will be severed. From all this is to be inferred the immense importance of keeping the action of the general government most rigidly within its defined sphere, to the utter exclusion of all construction but that which is clearly and distinctly to be inferred by honest deductions of powers that are conceded in terms.

To the danger which awaits any departure from a severe interpretation of the constitution, as it is to be apprehended from the possibility, and indeed it might be added the actual existence of different elements in the federal constituency, may be added that which arises from the facility of action through the organized forms of the state governments.[98] The latter, however, when considered as distinct from the difference in these elements themselves, is a danger that arises solely from the inherent vices and weaknesses of man. They may or they may not lead to evil, as circumstances shall direct; but the existence of antagonist principles, or of conflicting elements, in the construction of any government, *must lead to dissension*, unless some unusual preventive is devised. As has been seen, in our own case, the expedient is a limitation of powers.

The second embarrassment dependant on its own details, with which the federal government has to contend, is the possibility of an occasional want of concurrence in views and action between the different branches of the constituted authorities. This evil is peculiar to our own form of polity. It does not exist in England, and is almost the only solid advantage which that country, in a political point of view, possesses over our own.

As I am aware there will be a disposition to cavil at many of these positions, I may be permitted a word in the way of explanation. It has been said that in no other form of government is there the same danger from temporary collisions between the different branches of power, as in our own. To this would probably be objected the examples of England, at certain periods of her history, of France, since the restoration, and of divers of what are called the constitutional states of Germany; such as Bavaria, Saxony, Wurtemberg, the Hessen and Nassau. As respects the latter, while they are included in the reasons about to be given in relation to the two others, the instances they afford are entitled to no respect, for they are all under the control of an external and a superior force. Austria, Prussia and Russia would interfere to coerce the people,* and the knowledge of this fact only has probably prevented revolution in them all.

England, so far from being an exception to the ground just taken, affords the strongest proof of its justice. The revolution of 1668 [1688?] was owing to a struggle between the powers of the state. Previously to that period the prerogative was in the ascendant, and since that period it has been constantly on the wane, until it is completely annihilated as to all practical political authority. The laws are still administered in the name of the king it is true, his signature is necessary to certain acts, and he is yet called the head of the church and state; but aristocracy has cast its web about him with so much ingenuity, that the premier conducts his hand, the chancellor wields his conscience, and parliament feeds him, until he is reduced to the condition of a well dressed lay-figure. There undeniably was a contest between parliament and the prerogative during the four reigns that preceded the last, and the result goes to prove the very position I have taken.[99] This contest has wrought the effects of revolu-

* France also might now be added to the list of those states that would directly, or indirectly, lend its influence to effect the same object. [*Cooper's note.*]

tion, perverting the government from a monarchy to an oligarchy. The entire authority of the state, even to that of dictating his ministers to the king, is virtually in the hands of parliament. Open, palpable revolution has been carefully avoided, simply because the tendency of such convulsions is to elevate the low and to depress the great, and it was the wish of the aristocracy to effect its purpose by indirect means, and by the fictions of legality. The ascendancy of the thousand families who control the British empire has been obtained under the cry of liberty.

As the situation of France has not admitted of as much legal fraud as that of England, her example, since the restoration, is still more plainly in favor of the truth of our position. The contest between the crown and the chambers led Louis XVIII. to alter the charter; and a few years later, when opinion had gathered force, and legislation began to assume most of its ordinary attributes, his successor lost his crown, in making a similar attempt.

Thus far, in quoting the examples of the European states, it has been the intention to show merely the inevitable tendency of struggles between the executive and the legislature, considered in connexion with leading principles, and under the supposition that the constituency and the representation are of the same mind. In the cases of what are called in Europe representative governments, the eventual* danger has been somewhat lessened, and the temporary inconvenience removed, by a very simple expedient. The crown has power to prorogue or dissolve the legislature. The reasons, therefore, why the embarrassment that arises from temporary collisions between the executive and the legislature is greater in America than in England or France, are to be found in the fact that the chambers can be dissolved, and the fact that should the new elections be

* In England the danger has been averted by virtually reducing all the powers of the government to one body. The constituency of England is, as to political effect, the property of the representation. In cases where the landlord does not control, the open vote gives the richest man nearly the certainty of being elected. The exceptions do not affect the rule. [*Cooper's note.*]

adverse to those who wield the power of the crown, the chambers, in their turn, compel a change of ministers. The alternative, as was the case in France in 1830, is revolution. It is unnecessary to say that the executive of this country has no power to dissolve congress, or congress any power to dissolve a ministry. The inevitable consequences of the continuance of such collisions, viz. revolution, or changes equal in effect to revolution, is obviated only by the frequency of the elections.

We will return to our own polity.

It will be admitted that the government of the United States is one of the powers delegated for limited and defined purposes. Its authority is to be found only in the constitution. Precedent, as it is derived from our own practice, is valuable merely as it has been established on sound principles, and as it is derived from the practices of others, is to be received with a cautious examination into its fitness for our peculiar condition.

The highest authority known to the constitution, in its spirit, is the constituency. It sits in judgment over all, and approves or condemns at pleasure. All the branches of the deputed government, executive, legislative and judicial, are equally amenable to its decisions. It has retained the power of even changing the characters of its several servants; of placing the authority of the president in the hands of a committee of congress, or in any other depository it shall select; of dispensing with the judiciary altogether, or of modifying its duties at pleasure; of re-modelling the legislature and of issuing to it new commissions, as it shall see fit. The only restraint it has laid on its own acts, is a provision pointing out the form in which its will is to be expressed, and a solitary condition touching that delicate point of the rights of the several states, which secures to each an equal representation in the senate. When the constituency and the people are identical, this becomes political liberty.

The highest attributes of the constituency are delegated to the legislature, whose powers are as carefully and as distinctly defined, as the nature of things would well permit. The judiciary and the executive are, in a great degree, subordinate to the will of the latter, on which there is no restraint but the provisions of the compact, and from which, when legitimately exercised, there is no appeal but to the constituency. Its members act with no other responsibility than that which they owe to their own body, and to the judgments that may be passed upon their measures by those who issued their commissions. Unlike the executive and the judiciary, they are liable to no impeachment.* When the irresponsible nature of such a power, divided as it is among many, is taken in connexion with its extent, it is very obvious that far more danger is to be apprehended from the legislature, through innovations on the principles of the constitution under the forms of law, than from either of the two other branches of the government. They all exercise delegated powers, it is true, and powers that can be perverted from their legitimate uses; but congress is the least restrained, while it possesses the highest authority. It follows of necessity that it is the branch of this government most likely to abuse its trust.

Obvious as are these facts, what has just been said is not the popular manner of viewing the subject. The English aristocracy has so long been innovating on the prerogative of the crown, under the cry of liberty, and the *theory* of the English constitution [100] has so artfully favored such a mystification, that we have caught the feeling of another country, and are apt to consider those to whom we have confided the greatest authority under the least responsibility, the exclusive guardians of our liberties! Such an opinion can only be entertained by a sacrifice of both fact and reason. The constituency is its own protector, or our pretension to real liberty would be idle. The executive is a creature of our own forming, and for our own good, and it is manifestly a weakness to confound him or his authority, with a prince and his prerogative, the latter being based on the divine right.

In a monarchy power is supposed to be the prerogative of the

---

* This is an instance in which imitation has led us astray from the commencement. What sufficient reason can be given why the representative, in a system like ours, should not be tried and punished for an abuse of trust, as well as a judge, or the president? In countries in which the representative is either an advocate or a master, there is good cause for his impunity, but in ours, where he is only a servant, there is none. [*Cooper's note.*]

crown, and what is called liberty is no more than concessions
obtained from the sovereign in behalf of the subject. Under
really free institutions, government itself is no more than a concession of powers for the benefit of protection and association.
It is very possible that these mutual concessions should produce
an exactly similar set of subordinate ordinances or laws, and yet
one government shall enjoy real freedom, and the other possess
no more than its shadow. The essence of liberty is in the ultimate power to control, as residing in the body of the nation.
Its form is exhibited through the responsibility of the public
agents.

The inference that I could wish to draw from this brief statement is the absolute necessity of construing the Constitution of
the United States on its own principles; of rigidly respecting the
spirit as well as the letter of its provisions; and of never attempting to avert any evil which may arise under the practice of the
government, in any other manner than that which is pointed out
by the instrument itself. On no other terms can this Union be
perpetuated, and on these terms, there is reason to believe that
our prospect of national happiness and power exceeds that of
any other people on the globe.

.   .   .   .

I came before you, as a writer, when the habit of looking to
others for mental aliment most disqualified the public to receive
a native author with favor. It has been said lately that I owe the
little success I met with at home, to foreign approbation. This
assertion is unjust to you. Accident first made me a writer, and
the same accident gave a direction to the subject of my pen.
Ashamed to have fallen into the track of imitation, I endeavored
to repair the wrong done to my own views, by producing a work
that should be purely American, and of which love of country
should be the theme. This work most of you received with a
generous welcome that might have satisfied any one that the
heart of this great community is sound. It was only at a later
day, when I was willing more obviously to substitute American
principles for American *things*, that I was first made to feel how
far opinion, according to my poor judgment, still lags in the rear

of facts. The American who wishes to illustrate and enforce the peculiar principles of his own country, by the agency of polite literature, will, for a long time to come, I fear, find that *his* constituency, as to all purposes of distinctive thought, is still too much under the influence of foreign theories, to receive him with favor. It is under this conviction that I lay aside the pen. I am told that this step will be attributed to the language of the journals, and some of my friends are disposed to flatter me with the belief that the journals misrepresent the public sentiment. On this head, I can only say that, like others similarly situated, I must submit to any false inferences of this nature to which accident shall give birth. I am quite unconscious of giving any undue weight to the crudities of the daily press, and as to the press of this country in particular, a good portion of the hostility it has manifested to myself, is so plainly stamped with its origin, that it never gave me any other uneasiness, than that which belongs to the certainty that it must be backed by a strong public opinion, or men of this description would never have presumed to utter what they have. The information on which I act is derived from sources entitled to more respect than the declamations of the press.

I confess I have come to this decision with reluctance, for I had hoped to be useful in my generation, and to have yet done something which might have identified my name with those who are to come after me. But it has been ordered differently. I have never been very sanguine as to the immortality of what I have written, a very short period having always sufficed for my ambition; but I am not ashamed to avow, that I have felt a severe mortification that I am to break down on the question of distinctive American thought. Were it a matter of more than feeling, I trust I should be among the last to desert my post. But the democracy of this country is in every sense strong enough to protect itself. Here, the democrat is the conservative, and, thank God, he has something worth preserving. I believe he knows it, and that he will prove true to himself. I confess I have no great fears of our modern aristocracy, which is wanting in more of chivalry than the *accolade*.

ON DISTINCTIVE AMERICAN PRINCIPLES

Distinctive American principles as properly refer to the institutions of the states as to those of the Union. A correct notion of the first cannot be formed without keeping the latter constantly in view.

The leading distinctive principle of this country, is connected with the fact that all political power is strictly a trust, granted by the constituent to the representative. These representatives possess different duties, and as the greatest check that is imposed on them, while in the exercise of their offices, exists in the manner in which the functions are balanced by each other, it is of the last importance that neither class trespass on the trusts that are not especially committed to its keeping.

The machinery of the state being the same in appearance, in this country and in that from which we are derived, inconsiderate commentators are apt to confound their principles. In England, the institutions have been the result of those circumstances to which time has accidentally given birth. The power of the king was derived from violence, the monarch, before the act of succession, in the reign of Queen Anne, claiming the throne in virtue of the conquest by William, in 1060 [1066?]. In America, the institutions are the result of deliberate consultation, mutual concessions, and design. In England, the people may have gained by diminishing the power of the king, who first obtained it by force; but, in America, to assail the rightful authority of the executive, is attacking a system framed by the constituencies of the states, who are virtually the people, for their own benefit. No assault can be made on any branch of this government, while in the exercise of its constitutional duties, without assaulting the right of the body of the nation, which is the foundation of the whole polity.

In countries, in which executive power is hereditary, and

clothed with high prerogatives, it may be struggling for liberty to strive to diminish its influence; but, in this republick, in which the executive is elective, has no absolute authority in framing the laws, serves for a short period, is responsible, and has been created by the people, through the states, for their own purposes, it is assailing the rights of that people, to attempt in any manner to impede its legal and just action.

It is a general law in politics, that the power most to be distrusted, is that which, possessing the greatest force, is the least responsible. Under the constitutional monarchies of Europe, (as they exist in theory, at least,) the king, besides uniting in his single person all the authority of the executive, which includes a power to make war, create peers, and unconditionally to name to all employments, has an equal influence in enacting laws, his veto being absolute; but, in America, the executive, besides being elective, is stripped of most of these high sources of influence, and is obliged to keep constantly in view the justice and legality of his acts, both on account of his direct responsibilities, and on account of the force of public opinion.[102]

In this country, there is far more to apprehend from congress, than from the executive, as is seen in the following reasons:—Congress is composed of many, while the executive is one, bodies of men notoriously acting with less personal responsibilities than individuals; congress has power to enact laws, which it becomes the duty of the executive to see enforced, and the really legislative authority of a country is always its greatest authority; from the decisions and constructions of the executive, the citizen can always appeal to the courts for protection, but no appeal can lie from the acts of congress, except on the ground of unconstitutionality; the executive has direct personal responsibilities under the laws of the land, for any abuses of his authority, but the member of congress, unless guilty of open corruption, is almost beyond personal liabilities.

It follows that the legislature of this country, by the intention of the constitution, wields the highest authority under the least responsibility, and that it is the power most to be distrusted. Still, all who possess trusts, are to be diligently watched, for there is no protection against abuses without responsibility, nor any real responsibility, without vigilance.

Political partisans, who are too apt to mistake the impulses of their own hostilities and friendships for truths, have laid down many false principles on the subject of the duties of the executive. When a law is passed, it goes to the executive for execution, through the executive agents, and, at need, to the courts for interpretation. It would seem that there is no discretion vested in the executive concerning the constitutionality of a law. If he distrust the constitutionality of any law, he can set forth his objections by resorting to the veto; but it is clearly the intention of the system that the whole legislative power, in the last resort, shall abide in congress, while it is necessary to the regular action of the government, that none of its agents, but those who are especially appointed for that purpose, shall pretend to interpret the constitution, in practice. The citizen is differently situated. If he conceive himself oppressed by an unconstitutional law, it is his inalienable privilege to raise the question before the courts, where a final interpretation can be had. By this interpretation the executive and all his agents are equally bound to abide. This obligation arises from the necessity of things, as well as from the nature of the institutions. There must be somewhere a power to decide on the constitutionality of laws, and this power is vested in the supreme court of the United States, on final appeal.

When called on to approve a law, even though its principle should have been already pronounced on by the courts, the executive is independent. He is now a legislator, and can disregard all other constructions of the constitution, but those dictated by his own sense of right. In this character, to the extent of his veto-power, he is superior to the courts, which have cognizance of no more than each case as it is presented for their consideration. The president may approve of a law that the court has decided to be unconstitutional in principle, or he may veto a law that the court has decided to be constitutional in principle. The legislator himself, is compelled to submit to the interpretation of the court, however different his own views of the law may have been in passing it, but as soon as he comes to act again as a legislator, he becomes invested with all his own high duties and rights. The court cannot make the constitution, in any case; it only interprets the law. One court may decide differently from another, and instances often occur in which the same judges see reason to change their own decisions, and it would be, to the last degree, inexpedient, to give the court an authority beyond the necessity of the circumstances.

Although the court can render a law null, its power does not extend beyond the law already passed. Congress may re-enact it, as often as it please, and the court will still exercise its reason in rejecting it. This is the balance of the constitution, which invites inquiry, the constituencies of the states holding a legal authority to render that constitutional which the courts have declared to be unconstitutional, or vice versa, by amendments to the instrument itself; the supremacy of the court being merely temporary, conditional, and growing out of expediency and necessity.

It has been said that it is a vital principle of this government, that each of its branches should confine itself to the particular duties assigned it by the constitution, and in no manner exceed them. Many grave abuses have already arisen from losing sight of this truth, and there is danger that the whole system will be perverted from its intention, if not destroyed, unless they are seasonably corrected. Of these, the most prevalent, the one most injurious to the public service, that which has been introduced the most on foreign and the least on American principles, is the practice of using the time and influence of the legislatures, for the purpose of acting on the public mind, with a view to affect the elections. The usage has already gained so much footing, as seriously to impede the course of legislation.

This is one of the cases, in which it is necessary to discriminate between the distinctive principles of our own government, and those of the government of the country from which we are derived. In England, by the mode in which the power of the executive has been curtailed, it is necessary that the ministerial contests should be conducted in the legislative bodies, but, in this country, such a course cannot be imitated, without the legislators' assuming an authority that does not belong to them, and without dispossessing the people, in some measure, of their rights. He who will examine the constitution for the powers of congress, will find no authority to pass resolutions on, or to waste the time, which is the property of the public, in discussing the matters, on which, after all, congress has no power to decide. This is the test of legislative authority. Congress cannot properly even discuss a subject, that congress cannot legally control, unless it be to ascertain its own powers. In cases that do not admit of question, this is one of the grossest abuses of the institutions, and ought to be classed with the usurpations of other systems.

There is a feeling connected with this subject, that it behooves every upright citizen cautiously to watch. He may be opposed to the executive, for instance, as a party-man, and yet have an immediate representative in congress, of his own particular way of thinking; and it is a weakness of humanity, under such circumstances, for one to connect himself most directly with his own immediate candidate, and to look on his political opponent with distrust. The jealousy created by this feeling, induces unreflecting men to imagine that curbing their particular representatives, in matters of this nature, is curtailing their own rights, and disposes them to defend what is inherently wrong, on personal motives.

Political systems ought to be, and usually are, framed on certain great and governing principles. These principles cannot be perverted, or lost sight of, without perverting, or rendering nugatory the system itself; and, under a popular government, in an age like this, far more is to be apprehended from indirect attacks on the institutions, than from those which are direct. It is usual to excuse these departures from the right on the plea of human propensities, but human institutions are framed expressly to curb such propensities, and no truth is more salutary than that which is contained in the homely saying, that "law makers should not be law breakers."

It is the duty of the citizen to judge of all political acts on the great principles of the government, and not according to his own political partialities, or prejudices. His own particular representative is no more a representative of the people, than the representative of any other man, and one branch of the government is no more representative than another. All are to keep within their respective spheres, and it may be laid down as a governing maxim of the institutions, *that the representative who exceeds his trusts, trespasses on the rights of the people.*

All comparisons between the powers of the British parliament and those of congress are more than useless, since they are bodies differently constituted, while one is absolute, and the other is merely a special trustee for limited and defined objects.

In estimating the powers of congress, there is a rule that may be safely confided in, and which has been already hinted at. The powers of congress are express and limited. That body therefore, can have no right *to pass resolutions* other than those which affect their own police, or, in a moral sense, even to make speeches, except on subjects on which *they have a right to pass laws.* The instant they exceed these limits, they exceed the bounds of their delegated authority. By applying this simple test to their proceedings, any citizen may, in ordinary cases, ascertain how far the representatives of the nation abuse their trusts.

Liberty is not a matter of words, but a positive and important condition of society. Its great safeguards, after placing its foundations on a popular base, is in the checks and balances imposed on the public servants, and all its real friends ought to know that the most insidious attacks, are made on it by those who are the largest trustees of authority, in their efforts to increase their power.

The government of the United States has three branches. The executive, the legislative and the judicial. These several branches are independent of each other, though the first is intended to act as a check on the second, no law or resolution being legal that is not first submitted to the president for his approval. The check, however, does not render the first an integral part of the legislature, as laws and resolutions may be passed without his approval, by votes of two thirds.

In most constitutional monarchies, the legislatures, being originally secondary powers, were intended as checks on the action of the crown, which was possessed of the greatest, and, by consequence, of the most dangerous authority; whereas, the case is reversed in America, the executive using his veto as a check on congress. Such is the intention of the constitution, though the tactics of party, and bitterness of opposition, have endeavored to interpret the instrument differently, by appealing to the ancient prejudices derived from England.

ON EQUALITY[103]

Equality, in a social sense, may be divided into that of condition, and that of rights. Equality of condition is incompatible with civilization, and is found only to exist in those communities that are but slightly removed from the savage state. In practice, it can only mean a common misery.

Equality of rights is a peculiar feature of democracies. These rights are properly divided into civil and political, though even these definitions are not to be taken as absolute, or as literally exact.

Under the monarchies of the old world, there exist privileged classes, possessed of exclusive rights. For a long period the nobles were exempted from taxes, and many other charges, advantages that are still enjoyed by them, in certain countries. In England, even, the nobles are entitled to hereditary advantages that are denied to those who are of inferior birth. All these distinctions are done away with in principle, in countries where there exists a professed equality of rights, though there is probably no community that does not make some distinctions between the political privileges of men. If this be true, there is strictly no equality of political rights, any where, although there may be, and is, a nearer approach to an equality of civil rights.

By political rights we understand, the suffrage, eligibility to office, and a condition of things that admits of no distinction between men, unless on principles that are common to all. Thus, though a man is not qualified to vote until he has reached the age of twenty-one, the regulation does not effect political equality, since all are equally subjected to the rule, and all become electors on attaining the same age.

With an equality of civil rights, all men are equal before the law; all classes of the community being liable equally to taxation, military service, jury duties, and to the other impositions attendant on civilization, and no one being exempted from its control, except on general rules, which are dependent on the good of all, instead of the exemption's belonging to the immunities of individuals, estates, or families. An equality of civil rights may be briefly defined to be an absence of privileges.

The distinction between the equality of civil and political rights is material, one implying merely equality before the administration of the law, the other, equality in the power to frame it.

An equality of civil rights is never absolute, but we are to understand by the term, such an equality only, as is compatible with general justice and the relations between the different members of families. Thus, women nowhere possess precisely the same rights as men, or men the same rights as women. The wife, usually, can neither sue nor be sued, while the husband, except in particular cases, is made liable to all legal claims on account of the wife. Minors are deprived of many of their civil rights, or, it would be better to say, do not attain them, until they reach a period of life that has been arbitrarily fixed, and which varies in different countries, according to their several policies.

Neither is equality of political rights ever absolute. In those countries where the suffrage is said to be universal, exceptions exist, that arise from the necessity of things, or from that controlling policy which can never be safely lost sight of in the management of human affairs. The interests of women being thought to be so identified with those of their male relatives as to become, in a great degree, inseparable, females are, almost generally, excluded from the possession of political rights.

There can be no doubt that society is greatly the gainer, by thus excluding one half its members, and the half that is best adapted to give a tone to its domestic happiness, from the strife of parties, and the fierce struggles of political controversies. Men are also excluded from political rights previously to having attained the age prescribed by law. Paupers, those who have no fixed abodes, and aliens in law, though their lives may have been principally passed in the country, are also excluded from the enjoyment of political rights, every where. Thus birth-right is almost universally made a source of advantage. These exceptions, however, do not very materially affect the principle of political equality, since the rules are general, and have been made solely with a reference to the good of society, or to render the laws less liable to abuses in practice.

It follows, that equality, whether considered in connection with our civil or political rights, must not be taken as a general and absolute condition of society, but as such an equality as depends on principles that are equitable, and which are suited to the actual wants of men.

ON LIBERTY[104]

Liberty, like equality, is a word more used than understood. Perfect and absolute liberty is as incompatible with the existence of society, as equality of condition. It is impracticable in a state of nature even, since, without the protection of the law, the strong would oppress and enslave the weak. We are then to understand by liberty, merely such a state of the social compact as permits the members of a community to lay no more restraints on themselves, than are required by their real necessities, and obvious interests. To this definition may be added, that it is a requisite of liberty, that the body of a nation should retain the power to modify its institutions, as circumstances shall require.

The natural disposition of all men being to enjoy a perfect freedom of action, it is a common error to suppose that the nation which possesses the mildest laws, or laws that impose the least personal restraints, is the freest. This opinion is untenable, since the power that concedes this freedom of action, can recall it. Unless it is lodged in the body of the community itself, there is, therefore, no pledge for the continuance of such a liberty. A familiar, supposititious case will render this truth more obvious.

A slave holder in Virginia is the master of two slaves: to one he grants his liberty, with the means to go to a town in a free state. The other accompanies his old associate clandestinely. In this town, they engage their services voluntarily, to a common master, who assigns to them equal shares in the same labor, paying them the same wages. In time, the master learns their situation, but, being an indulgent man, he allows the slave to retain his present situation. In all material things, these brothers are equal; they labor together, receive the same wages, and eat of the same food. Yet one is bond, and the other free, since it is in the power of the master, or of his heir, or of his assignee, at any time, to reclaim the services of the one who was not legally manumitted, and reduce him again to the condition of slavery. One of these brothers is the master of his own acts, while the other, though temporarily enjoying the same privileges, holds them subject to the will of a superior.

This is an all important distinction in the consideration of political liberty, since the circumstances of no two countries are precisely the same, and all municipal regulations ought to have direct reference to the actual condition of a community. It follows, that no country can properly be deemed free, unless the body of the nation possess, in the last resort, the legal power to frame its laws according to its wants. This power must also abide in the nation, or it becomes merely an historical fact, for he that was once free is not necessarily free always, any more than he that was once happy, is to consider himself happy in perpetuity.

This definition of liberty is new to the world, for a government founded on such principles is a novelty. Hitherto, a nation has been deemed free, whose people were possessed of a certain amount of franchises, without any reference to the general repository of power. Such a nation may not be absolutely enslaved, but it can scarcely be considered in possession of an affirmative political liberty, since it is not the master of its own fortunes.

Having settled what is the foundation of liberty, it remains to be seen by what process a people can exercise this authority over themselves. The usual course is to refer all matters of choice to the decision of majorities. The common axiom of democracies, however, which says that "the majority must rule," is to be received with many limitations. Were the majority of a country to rule without restraint, it is probable as much injustice and oppression would follow, as are found under the dominion of one. It belongs to the nature of men to arrange themselves in parties, to lose sight of truth and justice in partizanship and prejudice, to mistake their own impulses for that which is proper, and to do wrong because they are indisposed to seek the right. Were it wise to trust power, unreservedly, to majorities, all fundamental and controlling laws would be unnecessary, since they might, as occasion required, emanate from the will of numbers. Constitutions would be useless.

The majority rules in prescribed cases, and in no other. It elects to office, it enacts ordinary laws, subject however to the restrictions of the constitution, and it decides most of the questions that arise in the primitive meetings of the people; questions that do not usually effect any of the principal interests of life.

The majority does not rule in settling fundamental laws, under the constitution; or when it does rule in such cases, it is with particular checks produced by time and new combinations; it does not pass judgment in trials at law, or under impeachment, and it is impotent in many matters touching vested rights. In the state of New York, the majority is impotent, in granting corporations, and in appropriating money for local purposes.

Though majorities often decide wrong, it is believed that they are less liable to do so than minorities. There can be no question that the educated and affluent classes of a country, are more capable of coming to wise and intelligent decisions in affairs of state, than the mass of a population. Their wealth and leisure afford them opportunities for observation and comparison, while their general information and greater knowledge of character, enable them to judge more accurately of men and measures. That these opportunities are not properly used, is owing to the unceasing desire of men to turn their advantages to their own particular benefit, and to their passions. All history proves, when power is the sole possession of a few, that it is perverted to their sole advantage, the public suffering in order that their rulers may prosper. The same nature which imposes the necessity of governments at all, seems to point out the expediency of confiding its control, in the last resort, to the body of the nation, as the only lasting protection against gross abuses.

We do not adopt the popular polity because it is perfect, but because it is less imperfect than any other. As man, by his nature, is liable to err, it is vain to expect an infallible whole that is composed of fallible parts. The government that emanates from a single will, supposing that will to be pure, enlightened, impartial, just and consistent, would be the best in the world, were it attainable for men. Such is the government of the universe, the result of which is perfect harmony. As no man is without spot in his justice, as no man has infinite wisdom, or infinite mercy, we are driven to take refuge in the opposite extreme, or in a government of many.

It is common for the advocates of monarchy and aristocracy to deride the opinions of the mass, as no more than the impulses of ignorance and prejudices. While experience unhappily shows that this charge has too much truth, it also shows that the educated and few form no exemption to the common rule of humanity. The most intelligent men of every country in which there is liberty of thought and action, yielding to their interests or their passions, are always found taking the opposite extremes of contested questions, thus triumphantly refuting an arrogant proposition, that of the exclusive fitness of the few to govern, by an unanswerable fact. The minority of a country is never known to agree, except in its efforts to reduce and oppress the majority. Were this not so, parties would be unknown in all countries but democracies, whereas the factions of aristocracies have been among the fiercest and least governable of any recorded in history.

Although real political liberty can have but one character, that of a popular base, the world contains many modifications of governments that are, more or less, worthy to be termed free. In most of these states, however, the liberties of the mass, are of the negative character of franchises, which franchises are not power of themselves, but merely an exemption from the abuses of power. Perhaps no state exists, in which the people, either by usage, or by direct concessions from the source of authority, do not possess some of these franchises; for, if there is no such thing, in practice, as perfect and absolute liberty, neither is there any such thing, in practice, as total and unmitigated slavery. In the one case, nature has rendered man incapable of enjoying freedom without restraint, and in the other, incapable of submitting, entirely without resistance, to oppression. The harshest despots are compelled to acknowledge the immutable principles of eternal justice, affecting necessity and the love of right, for their most ruthless deeds.

England is a country in which the franchises of the subject are more than usually numerous. Among the most conspicuous of these are the right of trial by jury, and that of the *habeas corpus*.[105] Of the former it is unnecessary to speak, but as the latter is a phrase that may be unintelligible to many, it may be well to explain it.

The literal signification of *Habeas Corpus** is, "thou may'st have the body." In arbitrary governments, it is much the usage to oppress men, under the pretence of justice, by causing them to be arrested on false, or trivial charges, and of subjecting them to long and vexatious imprisonments, by protracting, or altogether evading the day of trial. The issue of a writ of *Habeas*

---

* "*Habeas*," second person singular, present tense, subjunctive mood, of the verb "*Habere*," to have; "*Corpus*," a noun, signifying "body." [*Cooper's note.*]

Corpus, is an order to bring the accused before an impartial and independent judge, who examines into the charge, and who orders the prisoner to be set at liberty, unless there be sufficient legal ground for his detention.

This provision of the English law has been wisely retained in our system, for without some such regulation, it would be almost as easy to detain a citizen unjustly, under a popular government, as to detain the subject of a monarchy; the difference in favor of the first, consisting only in the greater responsibility of its functionaries.

By comparing the privileges of the *Habeas Corpus*, where it exists alone, and as a franchise, with those of the citizen who enjoys it merely as a provision of his own, against the abuses of ordinances that he had a voice in framing, we learn the essential difference between real liberty and franchises. The Englishman can appeal to a tribunal, against the abuse of an existing law, but if the law be not with him, he has no power to evade it, however unjust, or oppressive. The American has the same appeal against the abuse of a law, with the additional power to vote for its repeal, should the law itself be vicious. The one profits by a franchise to liberate his person only, submitting to his imprisonment however, if legality has been respected; while the other, in addition to this privilege, has a voice in getting rid of the obnoxious law, itself, and in preventing a recurrence of the wrong.

Some countries have the profession of possessing a government of the people, because an ancient dynasty has been set aside in a revolution, and a new one seated on the throne, either directly by the people, or by a combination that has been made to assume the character of a popular decision. Admitting that a people actually had an agency in framing such a system, and in naming their ruler, they cannot claim to be free, since they have parted with the power they did actually possess. No proposition can be clearer than that he who has given away a thing is no longer its master.

Of this nature is the present government of France. In that country the ancient dynasty has been set aside by a combination of leaders, through the agency of a few active spirits among the mass, and a prince put upon the throne, who is virtually invested with all the authority of his predecessor. Still, as the right of the last sovereign is clearly derived from a revolution, which has been made to assume the appearance of popular will, his government is termed a government of the people. This is a fallacy that can deceive no one of the smallest reflection. Such a system may be the best that France can now receive, but it is a mystification to call it by any other than its proper name. It is not a government of consultation, but one of pure force as respects a vast majority of Frenchmen.

A good deal of the same objection lies against the government of Great Britain, which, though freer in practice than that of France, is not based on a really free system. It may be said that both these governments are as free as comports with discretion, as indeed may be said of Turkey, since men get to be disqualified for the possession of any advantage in time; but such an admission is only an avowal of unfitness, and not a proof of enjoyment.

It is usual to maintain, that in democracies the tyranny of majorities is a greater evil than the oppression of minorities in narrow systems. Although this evil is exaggerated, since the laws being equal in their action, it is not easy to oppress the few without oppressing all, it undeniably is the weak side of a popular government. To guard against this, we have framed constitutions, which point out the cases in which the majority shall decide, limiting their power, and bringing that they do possess within the circle of certain general and just principles. It will be elsewhere shown that it is a great mistake for the American citizen to take sides with the public, in doubtful cases affecting the rights of individuals, as this is the precise form in which oppression is the most likely to exhibit itself in a popular government.

Although it is true, that no genuine liberty can exist without being based on popular authority in the last resort, it is equally true that it can not exist when thus based, without many restraints on the power of the mass. These restraints are necessarily various and numerous. A familiar example will show their action. The majority of the people of a state might be in debt to its minority. Were the power of the former unrestrained, circumstances might arise in which they would declare depreciated bank notes a legal tender, and thus clear themselves of their liabilities, at the expense of their creditors. To prevent this, the constitution orders that nothing shall be made a legal tender but the precious metals, thus limiting the power of majorities in a way that the government is not limited in absolute monarchies, in which paper is often made to possess the value of gold and silver.

Liberty therefore may be defined to be a controlling authority that resides in the body of a nation, but so restrained as only to be exercised on certain general principles that shall do as little violence to natural justice, as is compatible with the peace and security of society.

ON STATION[106]

Station may be divided into that which is political, or publick, and that which is social, or private. In monarchies and aristocracies the two are found united, since the higher classes, as a matter of course, monopolize all the offices of consideration; but, in democracies, there is not, nor is it proper that there should be, any intimate connexion between them.

Political, or publick station, is that which is derived from office, and, in a democracy, must embrace men of very different degrees of leisure, refinement, habits and knowledge. This is characteristick of the institutions, which, under a popular government, confer on political station more power than rank, since the latter is expressly avoided in this system.

Social station is that which one possesses in the ordinary associations, and is dependent on birth, education, personal qualities, property, tastes, habits, and, in some instances, on caprice, or fashion. Although the latter undeniably is sometimes admitted to control social station, it generally depends, however, on the other considerations named.

Social station, in the main, is a consequence of property. So long as there is civilization there must be the rights of property, and so long as there are the rights of property, their obvious consequences must follow. All that democracies legitimately attempt is to prevent the advantages which accompany social station from accumulating rights that do not properly belong to the condition, which is effected by pronouncing that it shall have no factitious political aids.

They who have reasoned ignorantly, or who have aimed at effecting their personal ends by flattering the popular feeling, have boldly affirmed that "one man is as good as another;" a maxim that is true in neither nature, revealed morals, nor political theory.

That one man is not as good as another in natural qualities, is proved on the testimony of our senses. One man is stronger than another; he is handsomer, taller, swifter, wiser, or braver, than all his fellows. In short, the physical and moral qualities are unequally distributed, and, as a necessary consequence, in none of them, can one man be justly said to be as good as another. Perhaps no two human beings can be found so precisely equal in every thing, that one shall not be pronounced the superior of the other; which, of course, establishes the fact that there is no natural equality.

The advocates of exclusive political privileges reason on this circumstance by assuming, that as nature has made differences between men, those institutions which create political orders, are no more than carrying out the great designs of providence. The error of their argument is in supposing it a confirmation of the designs of nature to attempt to supplant her, for, while the latter has rendered men unequal, it is not from male to male, according to the order of primogeniture, as is usually established by human ordinances. In order not to interfere with the inequality of nature, her laws must be left to their own operations, which is just what is done in democracies, after a proper attention has been paid to the peace of society, by protecting the weak against the strong.

That one man is not deemed as good as another in the grand

moral system of providence, is revealed to us in Holy Writ, by the scheme of future rewards and punishments, as well as by the whole history of those whom God has favored in this world, for their piety, or punished for their rebellion. As compared with perfect holiness, all men are frail; but, as compared with each other, we are throughout the whole of sacred history made to see, that, in a moral sense, one man is not as good as another. The evil doer is punished, while they who are distinguished for their qualities and acts, are intended to be preferred.

The absolute moral and physical equality that are inferred by the maxim, that "one man is as good as another," would at once do away with the elections, since a lottery would be both simpler, easier and cheaper than the present mode of selecting representatives. Men, in such a case, would draw lots for office, as they are now drawn for juries.[107] Choice supposes a preference, and preference inequality of merit, or of fitness.

We are then to discard all visionary theories on this head, and look at things as they are. All that the most popular institutions attempt, is to prohibit that one *race* of men shall be made better than another by law, from father to son, which would be defeating the intentions of providence, creating a superiority that exists in neither physical nor moral nature, and substituting a political scheme for the will of God and the force of things.

As a principle, one man is as good as another in rights. Such is the extent of the most liberal institutions of this country, and this provision is not general. The slave is not as good as his owner, even in rights. But in those states where slavery does not exist, all men have essentially the same rights, an equality, which, so far from establishing that "one man is as good as another," in a social sense, is the very means of producing the inequality of condition that actually exists. By possessing the same rights to exercise their respective faculties, the active and frugal become more wealthy than the idle and dissolute; the wise and gifted more trusted than the silly and ignorant; the polished and refined more respected and sought, than the rude and vulgar.

In most countries, birth is a principal source of social distinction, society being divided into castes, the noble having an hereditary claim to be the superior of the plebeian. This is an unwise and an arbitrary distinction that has led to most of the social diseases of the old world, and from which America is happily exempt. But great care must be had in construing the principles which have led to this great change, for America is the first important country of modern times, in which such positive distinctions have been destroyed.

Still some legal differences, and more social advantages, are produced by birth, even in America. The child inherits the property, and a portion of the consideration of the parent. Without the first of these privileges, men would not exert themselves to acquire more property than would suffice for their own personal necessities, parental affection being one of the most powerful incentives to industry. Without such an inducement, then, it would follow that civilization would become stationary, or, it would recede; the incentives of individuality and of the affections, being absolutely necessary to impel men to endure the labor and privations that alone can advance it.

The hereditary consideration of the child, so long as it is kept within due bounds, by being confined to a natural sentiment, is also productive of good, since no more active inducement to great and glorious deeds can offer, than the deeply seated interest that man takes in his posterity. All that reason and justice require is effected, by setting bounds to such advantages, in denying hereditary claims to trusts and power; but evil would be the day, and ominous the symptom, when a people shall deny that any portion of the consideration of the ancestor is due to the descendant.

It is as vain to think of altogether setting aside sentiment and the affections, in regulating human affairs, as to imagine it possible to raise a nature, known to be erring and weak, to the level of perfection.

The Deity, in that terrible warning delivered from the mount, where he declares that he "will visit the sins of the fathers upon the children, unto the third and fourth generation," does not more than utter one of those sublime moral truths, which, in conformity with his divine providence, pervade nature. It is merely an announcement of a principle that cannot safely be separated from justice, and one that is closely connected with all the purest motives and highest aspirations of man.

There would be a manifest injustice in visiting the offence of the criminal on his nearest of kin, by making the innocent man participate in the disgrace of a guilty relative, as is notoriously done most, by those most disposed to rail at reflected renown, and not to allow of the same participation in the glory. Both depend upon a sentiment deeper than human laws, and have been established for purposes so evidently useful as to require no explanation. All that is demanded of us, is to have a care that this sentiment do not degenerate to a prejudice, and that, in the one case, we do not visit the innocent too severely, or, in the other, exalt the unworthy beyond the bounds of prudence.

It is a natural consequence of the rights of property and of the sentiment named, that birth should produce some advantages, in a social sense, even in the most democratical of the American communities. The son imbibes a portion of the intelligence, refinement and habits of the father, and he shares in his associations. These must be enumerated as the legitimate advantages of birth, and without invading the private arrangements of families and individuals, and establishing a perfect community of education, they are unavoidable. Men of the same habits, the same degree of cultivation and refinement, the same opinions, naturally associate together, in every class of life. The day laborer will not mingle with the slave; the skilful mechanic feels his superiority over the mere laborer, claims higher wages and has a pride in his craft; the man in trade justly fancies that his habits elevate him above the mechanic, so far as social position is concerned, and the man of refinement, with his education, tastes and sentiments, is superior to all. Idle declamation on these points, does not impair the force of things, and life is a series of facts. These inequalities of condition, of manners, of mental cultivation must exist, unless it be intended to reduce all to a common level of ignorance and vulgarity, which would be virtually to return to a condition of barbarism.

The result of these undeniable facts, is the inequalities of social station, in America, as elsewhere, though it is an inequality that exists without any more arbitrary distinctions than are indispensably connected with the maintenance of civilization. In a social sense, there are orders here, as in all other countries, but the classes run into each other more easily, the lines of separation are less strongly drawn, and their shadows are more intimately blended.

This social inequality of America is an unavoidable result of the institutions, though nowhere proclaimed in them, the different constitutions maintaining a profound silence on the subject, they who framed them probably knowing that it is as much a consequence of civilized society, as breathing is a vital function of animal life.

AN ARISTOCRAT AND A DEMOCRAT[108]

We live in an age, when the words aristocrat and democrat are much used, without regard to the real significations. An aristocrat is one of a few, who possess the political power of a country; a democrat, one of the many. The words are also properly applied to those who entertain notions favorable to aristocratical or democratical forms of government. Such persons are not, necessarily, either aristocrats, or democrats in fact, but merely so in opinion. Thus a member of a democratical government may have an aristocratical bias, and *vice versa*.

To call a man who has the habits and opinions of a gentleman, an aristocrat, from that fact alone, is an abuse of terms, and betrays ignorance of the true principles of government, as well as of the world. It must be an equivocal freedom, under which every one is not the master of his own innocent acts and associations, and he is a sneaking democrat, indeed, who will submit to be dictated to, in those habits over which neither law nor morality assumes a right of control.

Some men fancy that a democrat can only be one who seeks the level, social, mental and moral, of the majority, a rule that would at once exclude all men of refinement, education and taste from the class. These persons are enemies of democracy, as they at once render it impracticable. They are usually great sticklers for their own associations and habits, too, though unable to comprehend any of a nature that are superior. They are, in truth, aristocrats in principle, though assuming a contrary pretension; the ground work of all their feelings and arguments being self. Such is not the intention of liberty, whose aim is to leave every man to be the master of his own acts; denying hereditary honors, it is true, as unjust and unnecessary, but not denying the inevitable consequences of civilization.

The law of God is the only rule of conduct, in this, as in other matters. Each man should do as he would be done by. Were the question put to the greatest advocate of indiscriminate association, whether he would submit to have his company and habits dictated to him, he would be one of the first to resist the tyranny; for they, who are the most rigid in maintaining their own claims, in such matters, are usually the loudest in decrying those whom they fancy to be better off than themselves. Indeed, it may be taken as a rule in social intercourse, that he who is the most apt to question the pretensions of others, is the most conscious of the doubtful position he himself occupies; thus establishing the very claims he affects to deny, by letting his jealousy of it be seen. Manners, education and refinement, are positive things, and they bring with them innocent tastes which are productive of high enjoyments; and it is as unjust to deny their possessors their indulgence, as it would be to insist on the less fortunate's passing the time they would rather devote to athletic amusements, in listening to operas for which they have no relish, sung in a language they do not understand.

All that democracy means, is as equal a participation in

rights as is practicable; and to pretend that social equality is a condition of popular institutions, is to assume that the latter are destructive of civilization, for, as nothing is more self-evident than the impossibility of raising all men to the highest standard of tastes and refinement, the alternative would be to reduce the entire community to the lowest. The whole embarrassment on this point exists in the difficulty of making men comprehend qualities they do not themselves possess. We can all perceive the difference between ourselves and our inferiors, but when it comes to a question of the difference between us and our superiors, we fail to appreciate merits of which we have no proper conceptions. In face of this obvious difficulty, there is the safe and just governing rule, already mentioned, or that of permitting every one to be the undisturbed judge of his own habits and associations, so long as they are innocent, and do not impair the rights of others to be equally judges for themselves. It follows, that social intercourse must regulate itself, independently of institutions, with the exception that the latter, while they withhold no natural, bestow no factitious advantages beyond those which are inseparable from the rights of property, and general civilization.

In a democracy, men are just as free to aim at the highest attainable places in society, as to obtain the largest fortunes; and it would be clearly unworthy of all noble sentiment to say, that the grovelling competition for money shall alone be free, while that which enlists all the liberal acquirements and elevated sentiments of the race, is denied the democrat. Such an avowal would be at once, a declaration of the inferiority of the system, since nothing but ignorance and vulgarity could be its fruits.

The democratic gentleman must differ in many essential particulars, from the aristocratical gentleman, though in their ordinary habits and tastes they are virtually identical. Their principles vary; and, to a slight degree, their deportment accordingly. The democrat, recognizing the right of all to participate in power, will be more liberal in his general sentiments, a quality of superiority in itself; but, in conceding this much to his fellow man, he will proudly maintain his own independence of vulgar domination, as indispensable to his personal habits. The same principles and manliness that would induce him to depose a royal despot, would induce him to resist a vulgar tyrant.

There is no more capital, though more common error, than to suppose him an aristocrat who maintains his independence of habits; for democracy asserts the control of the majority, only, in matters of law, and not in matters of custom. The very object of the institution is the utmost practicable personal liberty, and to affirm the contrary, would be sacrificing the end to the means.

An aristocrat, therefore, is merely one who fortifies his exclusive privileges by positive institutions, and a democrat, one who is willing to admit of a free competition, in all things. To say, however, that the last supposes this competition will lead to nothing, is an assumption that means are employed without any reference to an end. He is the purest democrat who best maintains his rights, and no rights can be dearer to a man of cultivation, than exemptions from unseasonable invasions on his time, by the coarse-minded and ignorant.

ON LANGUAGE [109]

Language being the medium of thought, its use enters into our most familiar practices. A just, clear and simple expression of our ideas is a necessary accomplishment for all who aspire to be classed with gentlemen and ladies. It renders all more respectable, besides making intercourse more intelligible, safer and more agreeable.

The common faults of American language are an ambition to effect, a want of simplicity, and a turgid abuse of terms. To these may be added ambiguity of expression. Many perversions of significations also exist, and a formality of speech, which, while it renders conversation ungraceful, and destroys its playfulness, seriously weakens the power of the language, by applying to ordinary ideas, words that are suited only to themes of gravity and dignity.

While it is true that the great body of the American people use their language more correctly than the mass of any other considerable nation, it is equally true that a smaller proportion than common attain to elegance in this accomplishment, especially in speech. Contrary to the general law in such matters, the women of the country have a less agreeable utterance than the men, a defect that great care should be taken to remedy, as the nursery is the birth-place of so many of our habits.

The limits of this work will not permit an enumeration of the popular abuses of significations, but a few shall be mentioned, in order that the student may possess a general clue to the faults. "Creek," a word that signifies an *inlet* of the sea, or of a lake, is misapplied to running streams, and frequently to the *outlets* of lakes. A "square," is called a "park;" "lakes," are often called "ponds;" and "arms of the sea," are sometimes termed "rivers."

In pronunciation, the faults are still more numerous, partaking decidedly of provincialisms. The letter *u*, sounded like double *o*, or *oo*, or like *i*, as in vir*too*, for*tin*, for*tinate;* and *ew*, pronounced also like *oo*, are common errors. This is an exceedingly vicious pronunciation, rendering the language mean and vulgar. "New," pronounced as "*noo*," is an example, and "few," as "*foo;*" the true sounds are "*nu*" and "*fu*," the *u* retaining its proper soft sound, and not that of "*oo*."

The attempt to reduce the pronunciation of the English language to a common rule, produces much confusion, and taking the usages of polite life as the standard, many uncouth innovations. All know the pronunciation of p l o u g h; but it will scarcely do to take this sound as the only power of the same combination of final letters, for we should be compelled to call t h o u g h, thou; t h r o u g h, throu; and t o u g h, tou.

False accentuation is a common American fault. Ensign (insin,) is called en*syne*, and engine (injin,) en*gyne*. Indeed, it is a common fault of narrow associations, to suppose that words are to be pronounced as they are spelled.

Many words are in a state of mutation, the pronunciation being unsettled even in the best society, a result that must often arise where language is as variable and undetermined as the English. To this class belong "clerk," "cucumber" and "gold," which are often pronounced as spelt, though it were better and more in conformity with polite usage to say "clark," "*cow*-cumber," (not cow*cum*ber,) and "goold." For *looten*ant (lieutenant) there is not sufficient authority, the true pronunciation being "*levten*ant." By making a familiar compound of this word, we see the uselessness of attempting to reduce the language to any other laws than those of the usages of polite life, for they who affect to say *looten*ant, do not say "*looten*ant-co-lo-nel," but "*looten*ant-kurnel."

The polite pronunciation of "either" and "neither," is "i-ther" and "ni-ther," and not "eether" and "neether." This is a case in which the better usage of the language has respected derivations, for "*ei*," in German are pronounced as in "height" and "sleight," "*ie*" making the sound of "*ee*." We see the arbitrary usages of the English, however, by comparing these legitimate sounds with those of the words "lieutenant colonel," which are derived from the French, in which language the latter word is called "*co-lo-nel*."

Some changes of the language are to be regretted, as they lead to false inferences, and society is always a loser by mistaking names for things. Life is a fact, and it is seldom any good arises from a misapprehension of the real circumstances under which we exist. The word "gentleman" has a positive and limited signification. It means one elevated above the mass of society by his birth, manners, attainments, character and social condition. As no civilized society can exist without these social differences, nothing is gained by denying the use of the term. If blackguards were to be *called* "gentlemen," and gentlemen, "blackguards," the difference between them would be as obvious as it is to-day.

The word "gentleman," is derived from the French gentil-homme, which originally signified one of noble birth. This was at a time when the characteristics of the condition were never found beyond a caste. As society advanced, ordinary men attained the qualifications of nobility, without that of birth, and the meaning of the word was extended. It is now possible to be a gentleman without birth, though, even in America, where such distinctions are purely conditional, they who have birth, except in extraordinary instances, are classed with gentlemen. To call a laborer, one who has neither education, manners, accomplishments, tastes, associations, nor any one of the ordinary requisites, a gentleman, is just as absurd as to call one who is thus qualified, a fellow. The word must have some especial signification, or it would be synonymous with man. One may have gentlemanlike feelings, principles and appearance, without possessing the liberal attainments that distinguish the gentleman. Least of all does money alone make a gentleman, though, as it becomes a means of obtaining the other requisites, it is usual to give it a place in the claims of the class. Men may be, and often are, very rich, without having the smallest title to be deemed gentlemen. A man may be a distinguished gentleman, and not possess as much money as his own footman.

This word, however, is sometimes used instead of the old terms, "sirs," "my masters," &c. &c., as in addressing bodies of men. Thus we say "gentlemen," in addressing a publick meeting in complaisance, and as, by possibility, some gentlemen may be present. This is a license that may be tolerated, though he who should insist that all present were, as individuals, gentlemen, would hardly escape ridicule.

What has just been said of the word gentleman, is equally true with that of lady. The standard of these two classes, rises as society becomes more civilized and refined; the man who might pass for a gentleman in one nation, or community, not being able to maintain the same position in another.

The inefficiency of the effort to subvert things by names, is shown in the fact that, in all civilized communities, there is a class of men, who silently and quietly recognize each other, as gentlemen; who associate together freely and without reserve, and who admit each other's claims without scruple or distrust. This class may be limited by prejudice and arbitrary enactments, as in Europe, or it may have no other rules than those of taste, sentiment and the silent laws of usage, as in America.

The same observations may be made in relation to the words master and servant. He who employs laborers, with the right to command, is a master, and he who lets himself to work, with an obligation to obey, a servant. Thus there are house, or domestic servants, farm servants, shop servants, and various other servants; the term master being in all these cases the correlative.

In consequence of the domestic servants of America having once been negro-slaves, a prejudice has arisen among the laboring classes of the whites, who not only dislike the term servant, but have also rejected that of master. So far has this prejudice gone, that in lieu of the latter, they have resorted to the use of the word *boss*, which has precisely the same meaning in Dutch! How far a subterfuge of this nature is worthy of a manly and common sense people, will admit of question.

A similar objection may be made to the use of the word "help," which is not only an innovation on a just and established term, but which does not properly convey the meaning intended. They who aid their masters in the toil may be deemed "helps," but they who perform all the labor do not assist, or help to do the thing, but they do it themselves. A man does not usually hire his cook to *help* him cook his dinner, but to cook it herself. Nothing is therefore gained, while something is lost in simplicity and clearness by the substitution of new and imperfect terms, for the long established words of the language. In all cases in which the people of America have retained the *things* of their ancestors, they should not be ashamed to keep the *names*.

The love of turgid expressions is gaining ground, and ought to be corrected. One of the most certain evidences of a man of high breeding, is his simplicity of speech; a simplicity that is equally removed from vulgarity and exaggeration. He calls a spade, a "spade." His enunciation, while clear, deliberate and dignified, is totally without strut, showing his familiarity with the world, and, in some degree, reflecting the qualities of his mind, which is polished without being addicted to sentimentalism, or any other bloated feeling. He never calls his wife, "his lady," but "his wife," and he is not afraid of lessening the

dignity of the human race, by styling the most elevated and refined of his fellow creatures, "men and women." He does not
say, in speaking of a dance, that "the attire of ladies was exceedingly elegant and peculiarly becoming at the late assembly,"
but that "the women were well dressed at the last ball;" nor is
he apt to remark, "that the Rev. Mr. G—— gave us an elegant
and searching discourse the past sabbath," but, that "the parson
preached a good sermon last sunday."

The utterance of a gentleman ought to be deliberate and
clear, without being measured. All idea of effort should be
banished, though nothing lost for want of distinctness. His
emphasis ought to be almost imperceptible; never halting, or
abrupt; and least of all, so placed as to give an idea of his own
sense of cleverness; but regulated by those slight intonations
that give point to wit, and force to reason. His language should
rise with the subject, and, as he must be an educated and accomplished man, he cannot but know that the highest quality of
eloquence, and all sublimity, is in the thought, rather than in
the words, though there must be an adaption of the one to the
other.

This is still more true of women than of men, since the
former are the natural agents in maintaining the refinement of a
people.

All cannot reach the highest standard in such matters, for it
depends on early habit, and particularly on early associations.
The children of gentlemen are as readily distinguished from
other children by these peculiarities, as by the greater delicacy of
their minds, and higher tact in breeding. But we are not to
abandon all improvement, because perfection is reached but by
few. Simplicity should be the first aim, after one is removed
from vulgarity, and let the finer shades of accomplishment be
acquired as they can be attained. In no case, however, can one
who aims at turgid language, exaggerated sentiment, or pedantic
utterance, lay claim to be either a man or woman of the world.

ON THE PRESS[110]

It would seem that providence, for some of its own great ends, has denied to man any particular blessing, which his own waywardness is not destined to lessen, if not entirely to neutralize. In nothing connected with human happiness, is this grave truth more apparent than in the history of the press.

In despotisms, where the weakness of the bodies of nations, is derived from an ignorance of their force, and from the want of means to act in concert, the press is the lever by which the thrones of tyrants and prejudices are the most easily overturned, and, under such circumstances, men often contend for privileges in its behalf, that become dangerous to the peace of society, when civil and political rights are obtained.

In a popular government, so far from according an entire immunity from penalties to the press, its abuses are those which society is required, by its very safety, to visit with its heaviest punishments. In a democracy, misleading the publick mind, as regards facts, characters, or principles, is corrupting all that is dear to society at its source, opinion being the fountain whence justice, honors, and the laws, equally flow.

It is a misfortune that necessity has induced men to accord greater license to this formidable engine, in order to obtain liberty, than can be borne with less important objects in view; for the press, like fire, is an excellent servant, but a terrible master.

It may be taken as rules, that without the liberty of the press, there can be no popular liberty in a nation, and with its licentiousness, neither publick honesty, justice, nor a proper regard for character. Of the two, perhaps, that people is the happiest which is deprived altogether of a free press, since private honesty, and a healthful tone of the publick mind are not incompatible with narrow institutions though neither can well exist under the constant corrupting action of a licentious press.

The governing principle connected with this interest, would seem to depend on a general law, which, under abuses, converts the most beneficial moral agents to be the greatest enemies of the race. The press is equally capable of being made the instrument of elevating man to the highest point of which his faculties admit, or of depressing him to the lowest.

In struggling for liberty and emancipation from errors and prejudices, men have not always paused to reflect on the influence of the agents they have employed, when those agents, from contending with a powerful enemy, shall have become conquerors, and have begun to look about them for the fruits of victory. The press, so efficient as the opponent of tyrants, may become despotic itself; it may substitute new errors for those it has eradicated, and, like an individual spoiled by success, may generally abuse its advantages.

Many false notions have been introduced into society, in the desire to vindicate the rights of so powerful an agent. Of these, one of the worst is the admission of a claim in the press to interfere, in any manner, with private character. The good of such an interference, is at the best but doubtful, and the oppression, in those cases in which injustice is done, is of the most intolerable and irreparable kind.

It would be a proper and a just, though an insufficient atonement, in cases of established libel, to vest a power in the courts to compel the libeller to publish, for a series of weeks, or months, or even years, his own condemnation in his own columns, that the antidote might accompany the poison; though it is to be feared, that the possession of popular rights is still too recent, to permit the majority of men to entertain correct notions concerning an instrument that, they rightly fancy, has been so serviceable in the conflict they have just escaped.

It ought never to be forgotten, that the press, contending for natural but forbidden rights, is no more like the press when these rights are obtained, than the man struggling with adversity, and chastened by misfortune, is like the man flushed with success and corrupted by prosperity.

The history of the press is every where the same. In its infancy it is timid, distrustful, and dependant on truth for success. As it acquires confidence with force, it propagates just opinions with energy; scattering errors and repelling falsehood, until it prevails; when abuses rush in, confounding principles, truths, and all else that is estimable, until it becomes a serious matter of doubt, whether a community derives most good or evil, from the institution.

ON THE AMERICAN PRESS

The newspaper press of this country is distinguished from that of Europe in several essential particulars. While there are more prints, they are generally of a lower character. It follows that in all in which they are useful, their utility is more diffused through society, and in all in which they are hurtful, the injury they inflict is more wide-spread and corrupting.

The great number of newspapers in America, is a cause of there being so little capital, and consequently so little intelligence, employed in their management. It is also a reason of the inexactitude of much of the news they circulate. It requires a larger investment of capital than is usual in this country, to obtain correct information; while, on the other hand, the great competition renders editors reckless and impatient to fill their columns. To these circumstances may be added the greater influence of vague and unfounded rumours in a vast and thinly settled country, than on a compact population, covering a small surface.

Discreet and observing men have questioned, whether, after excluding the notices of deaths and marriages, one half of the circumstances that are related in the newspapers of America, as facts, are true in their essential features; and, in cases connected with party politics, it may be questioned if even so large a proportion can be set down as accurate.

This is a terrible picture to contemplate, for when the number of prints is remembered, and the avidity with which they are read is brought into the account, we are made to perceive that the entire nation, in a moral sense, breathes an atmosphere of falsehoods. There is little use, however, in concealing the truth; on the contrary, the dread in which publick men and writers commonly stand of the power of the press to injure them, has permitted the evil to extend so far, that it is scarcely exceeding the bounds of a just alarm, to say that the country cannot much longer exist in safety, under the malign influence that now overshadows it. Any one, who has lived long enough to note changes of the sort, must have perceived how fast men of probity and virtue are loosing [*sic*] their influence in the country, to be superseded by those who scarcely deem an affectation of the higher qualities necessary to their success. This fearful change must, in a great measure, be ascribed to the corruption of the publick press, which, as a whole, owes its existence to the schemes of interested political adventurers.

Those who are little acquainted with the world are apt to imagine that a fact, or an argument, that is stated publickly in print, is entitled to more credit and respect than the same fact or argument presented orally, or in conversation. So far from this being true, however, in regard to the press of this country, it would be safer to infer the very reverse. Men who are accustomed daily to throw off their misstatements, become reckless of the consequences, and he who would hesitate about committing himself by an allegation made face to face, and as it were on his personal responsibility, would indite a paragraph, behind the impersonality of his editorial character, to be uttered to the world in the irresponsible columns of a journal. It is seldom, in cases which admit of doubt, that men are required to speak on the moment; but, with the compositor in waiting, the time pressing, and the moral certainty that a rival establishment will circulate the questionable statement if he decline, the editor too often throws himself into the breach. The contradiction of to-day, will make a paragraph, as well as the lie of yesterday, though he who sees the last and not the first, unless able to appreciate the character of his authority, carries away an untruth.

Instead of considering the editor of a newspaper, as an abstraction, with no motive in view but that of maintaining principles and disseminating facts, it is necessary to remember that he is a man, with all the interests and passions of one who has chosen this means to advance his fortunes, and of course, with all the accompanying temptations to abuse his opportunities, and this too, usually, with the additional draw-back of being a partisan in politics, religion, or literature. If the possession of power, in ordinary cases, is a constant inducement to turn it to an unjust profit, it is peculiarly so in the extraordinary case of the control of a public press.

Editors praise their personal friends, and abuse their enemies in print, as private individuals praise their friends, and abuse their enemies with their tongues. Their position increases the number of each, and the consequence is, that the readers obtain inflated views of the first, and unjust notions of the last.

If newspapers are useful in overthrowing tyrants, it is only to establish a tyranny of their own. The press tyrannizes over publick men, letters, the arts, the stage, and even over private life. Under the pretence of protecting publick morals, it is corrupting them to the core, and under the semblance of maintaining liberty, it is gradually establishing a despotism as ruthless, as grasping, and one that is quite as vulgar as that of any christian state known. With loud professions of freedom of opinion, there is no tolerance; with a parade of patriotism, no sacrifice of interests; and with fulsome panegyrics on propriety, too frequently, no decency.

There is but one way of extricating the mind from the baneful influence of the press of this country, and that is by making a rigid analysis of its nature and motives. By remembering that all statements that involve disputed points are *ex parte;* that there is no impersonality, except in professions; that all the ordinary passions and interests act upon its statements with less than the ordinary responsibilities; and that there is the constant temptation to abuse, which ever accompanies power, one may come, at last, to a just appreciation of its merits, and in a degree, learn to neutralize its malignant influence. But this is a freedom of mind that few attain, for few have the means of arriving at these truths!

The admixture of truth and falsehood in the intelligence circulated by the press, is one of the chief causes of its evils. A journal that gave utterance to nothing but untruths, would loose [*sic*] its influence with its character, but there are none so ignorant as not to see the necessity of occasionally issuing truths. It is only in cases in which the editor has a direct interest to the contrary, in which he has not the leisure or the means of ascertaining facts, or in which he is himself misled by the passions, cupidity and interests of others, that untruths find a place in his columns. Still these instances may, perhaps, include a majority of the cases.

In a country like this, it is indispensable to mental independence, that every man should have a clear perception of the quality of the political news, and of the political opinions circulated by the press, for, he who confides implicitly to its statements is yielding himself blindly to either the designed and exaggerated praises of friends, or to the calculated abuse of opponents. As no man is either as good, or as bad, as vulgar report makes him, we can, at once, see the value that ought to be given to such statements.

All representations that dwell wholly on merits, or on faults, are to be distrusted, since none are perfect, and it may, perhaps, be added, none utterly without some redeeming qualities.

Whenever the papers unite to commend, without qualification, it is safe to believe in either venality, or a disposition to defer to a preconceived notion of excellence, most men choosing to float with the current, rather than to resist it, when no active motive urges a contrary course, feeding falsehood, because it flatters a predilection; and whenever censure is general and sweeping, one may be almost certain it is exaggerated and false.

Puffs, political, literary, personal and national, can commonly be detected by their *ex parte* statements, as may be their counterpart, detraction. Dishonesty of intention is easily discovered by the man of the world, in both, by the tone; and he who blindly receives either eulogium or censure, because they stand audaciously in print, demonstrates that his judgment is still in its infancy.

Authors review themselves, or friends are employed to do it for them; political adventurers have their dependants, who build their fortunes on those of their patrons; artists, players, and even religionists, are not above having recourse to such expedients to advance their interests and reputations. The world would be surprised to learn the tyranny that the press has exercised, in our own times, over some of the greatest of modern names, few men possessing the manliness and moral courage that are necessary to resist its oppression.

The people that has overturned the throne of a monarch, and set up a government of opinion in its stead, and which blindly yields its interests to the designs of those who would rule through the instrumentality of newspapers, has only exchanged one form of despotism for another.

It is often made a matter of boasting, that the United States contain so many publick journals. It were wiser to make it a cause of mourning, since the quality, in this instance, diminishes in an inverse ratio to the quantity.

Another reason may be found for the deleterious influence of the American press, in the peculiar physical condition of the country. In all communities, the better opinion, whether as relates to moral or scientific truths, tastes, manners and facts, is necessarily in the keeping of a few; the great majority of mankind being precluded by their opportunities from reaching so high in the mental scale. The proportion between the intelligent and whole numbers, after making a proper allowance on account of the differences in civilization, is probably as great in this country, as in any other; possibly it is greater among the males; but the great extent of the territory prevents its concentration, and consequently, weakens its influence. Under such circumstances, the press has less to contend with than in other countries, where designing and ignorant men would stand rebuked before the collected opinion of those who, by their characters and information, are usually too powerful to be misled by vulgarity, sophistry and falsehood. Another reason is to be found in the popular character of the government, bodies of men requiring to be addressed in modes suited to the average qualities of masses.

In America, while the contest was for great principles, the

press aided in elevating the common character, in improving the common mind, and in maintaining the common interests; but, since the contest has ceased, and the struggle has become one purely of selfishness and personal interests, it is employed, as a whole, in fast undermining its own work, and in preparing the nation for some terrible reverses, if not in calling down upon it, a just judgment of God.

As the press of this country now exists, it would seem to be expressly devised by the great agent of mischief, to depress and destroy all that is good, and to elevate and advance all that is evil in the nation. The little truth that is urged, is usually urged coarsely, weakened and rendered vicious, by personalities; while those who live by falsehoods, fallacies, enmities, partialities and the schemes of the designing, find the press the very instrument that the devils would invent to effect their designs.

A witty but unprincipled statesman of our own times, has said that "speech was bestowed on man to conceal his thoughts;" judging from its present condition, he might have added, "and the press to pervert truth."

ON PROPERTY[111]

As property is the base of all civilization, its existence and security are indispensable to social improvement. Were it possible to have a community of property, it would soon be found that no one would toil, but that men would be disposed to be satisfied with barely enough for the supply of their physical wants, since none would exert themselves to obtain advantages solely for the use of others. The failure of all attempts to form communities, even on a small scale, with a common interest, goes to prove this. Where there is a rigid equality of condition, as well as of rights, that condition must necessarily be one of a low scale of mediocrity, since it is impossible to elevate those who do not possess the requisite qualities any higher. Thus we see that the societies, or religious sects, in which a community of property prevails, are content with merely supplying the wants of life, knowing little or nothing of its elegancies, refinements, or mental pleasures. These communities, moreover, possess an outlet for their idle and dissolute, by resorting to expulsion, a remedy that society itself cannot apply.

The principle of individuality, or to use a less winning term, of selfishness, lies at the root of all voluntary human exertion. We toil for food, for clothes, for houses, lands, and for property, in general. This is done, because we know that the fruits of our labor will belong to ourselves, or to those who are most dear to us. It follows, that all which society enjoys beyond the mere supply of its first necessities, is dependant on the rights of property.

It is not known that man exists anywhere without establishing rules for the protection of property. Even insects, reptiles, beasts and birds, have their several possessions, in their nests, dens and supplies. So completely is animal exertion, in general, whether in man or beast, dependant on the enjoyment of this right, under limitations which mark their several conditions, that we may infer that the rights of property, to a certain extent, are founded in nature. The food obtained by his toil, cannot be taken from the mouth of man, or beast, without doing violence to one of the first of our natural rights. We apply the term of robber, or despoiler, to the reptile or bird, that preys on the aliment of another animal, as well as to the human thief. So long as natural justice is admitted to exist, the party assailed, in such cases, has a right to defend his own.

The rights of property become artificial and extended, as society becomes civilized. In the savage state the land is without owners, property consisting in the hut, the food, and the arms used in war and in the chase. In pastoral, or semi-barbarous states, use gives claims, not to individuals, but to tribes, and flocks are pastured on grounds that belong to one entire community, but to that one only. Private property is composed of cattle, sheep, tents, horses, camels, with the common claims to share in the common fields.

Civilization has established various, and in some cases, arbitrary and unjust distinctions, as pertaining to the rights of property. These are abuses, the tendency of man being to con-

vert into curses things that Providence designed to prove benefits. Still, most of the ordinances of civilized society, that are
connected with this interest, are founded in reason, and ought
to be rigidly maintained.

The first great principle connected with the rights of property, is its inviolability in all cases in which the laws leave it in
possession of the proprietor. Every child should be taught to
respect the sanctity of his neighbour's house, garden, fields and
all that is his. On those parts of another's possessions, where it
is permitted to go, he should go with care not to abuse the
privilege, and from those parts which he is forbidden to use, he
should religiously abstain. The child that is properly impressed
in infancy, with the rights of property, is in little danger of
committing theft in after life, or, in any other manner invading
that which is the just possession of another.

The doctrine that any one "may do what he please with his
own," however, is false. One may do with his own, whatever
the laws and institutions of his country allow, and no more. One
may even respect the letter, and yet violate the spirit of those
laws and institutions, committing a moral, if not a legal offence,
in so doing. Thus, he, who would bring his money to bear
upon the elections of a country like this, abuses his situation,
unless his efforts are confined to fair and manly discussions before the body of the people.

In nations where the mass have no political rights, means have
been found to accumulate power by the aid of wealth. The
pretence has been that none but the rich have a stake in society.
Every man who has wants, feelings, affections and character, has
a stake in society. Of the two, perhaps, the necessities of men
are a greater corrective of political abuses, than their surplus
means. Both may lead to evil, beyond a doubt, but, as laws
which are framed by all, must be tolerably impartial and general
in their operation, less danger arises from the rule of the former,
than from the rule of the latter. When property rules, it rules
alone; but when the poor are admitted to have a voice in government, the rich are never excluded. Such is the nature of man,
that all exclusive power is uniformly directed to exclusive pur-

poses. Property always carries with it a portion of indirect political influence, and it is unwise, and even dangerous, to strengthen this influence by adding to it constitutional privileges; the result always being to make the strong stronger, and the weak weaker.

On the other hand, all who love equal justice, and, indeed, the safety of free institutions, should understand that property has its rights, and the necessity of rigidly respecting them. It is the right of the possessor of property to be placed on an equal footing with all his fellow citizens, in every respect. If he is not to be exalted on account of his wealth, neither is he to be denounced. In this country, it is the intention of the institutions, that money should neither increase nor lessen political influence.

There are habits that belong to every condition of life. The man of hereditary wealth, is usually a man of leisure, and he little understands the true spirit of democracy, who supposes that such a man is not to enjoy the tastes and inclinations, which are the fruits of leisure and cultivation, without let or hindrance. Democracy leaves every man the master of his acts and time, his tastes and habits, so long as he discharges his duty to the publick, and respects the laws. He who declaims against another for holding himself aloof from general association, arrogates to himself a power of censure that he does not rightly possess, and betrays his own consciousness of inferiority. Men of really high social station never make this complaint, for they are above jealousy; and they who do, only discover a feeling that is every way removed from the manliness and spirit of true independence.

One may certainly be purse-proud, and of all the sources of human pride, mere wealth is the basest and most vulgar minded. Real gentlemen are almost invariably above this low feeling, and they who attribute habits, that have their rise in sentiment, tastes, knowledge and refinement, to such a cause, usually make the mistake of letting their own ignorance of the existence of motives so elevated, be known. In a word, if the man of property has no more personal legal immunities, than the man who has none, neither has he fewer. He is privileged to use his own means, under the general regulations of society, in the pursuit of his own happiness, and they who would interfere with him, so far from appreciating liberty, are ignorant of its vital principles.

If left to itself, unsupported by factitious political aid, but sufficiently protected against the designs and rapacity of the dishonest, property is an instrument of working most of the good that society enjoys. It elevates a national character, by affording the means of cultivating knowledge and the tastes; it introduces all above barbarism into society; and it encourages and sustains laudable and useful efforts in individuals. Like every other great good, its abuses are in proportion to its benefits.

The possessor of property is not, half the time, as much the object of envy as the needy imagine, for its corrupting influence endangers eternal peace. Great estates are generally of more benefit to the community than to their owners. They bring with them anxiety, cares, demands, and, usually, exaggerated notions, on the part of the publick, of the duties of the rich. So far from being objects of envy, their possessors are often the subjects of commiseration; he who has enough for his rational wants, agreeably to his habits and education, always proving the happier man.

The possessions of new families are commonly exaggerated in the publick mind, while those of long established families are as commonly diminished.

A people that deems the possession of riches its highest source of distinction, admits one of the most degrading of all influences to preside over its opinions. At no time, should money be ever ranked as more than a means, and he who lives as if the acquisition of property were the sole end of his existence, betrays the dominion of the most sordid, base, and grovelling motive, that life offers.

Property is desirable as the ground work of moral independence, as a means of improving the faculties, and of doing good to others, and as the agent in all that distinguishes the civilized man from the savage.

Property has been made the test of political rights, in two distinct forms. It has been *represented*, and it has been established as a *qualification*. The *representation* of property is effected in two modes; first, by giving the proprietor more votes than one, according to the number and situation of his freeholds; and, secondly, by raising the test of qualification so high, as to exclude all but the affluent from the franchise. The first was the English system, previously to the recent changes; the last, is the actual system of France.

A government founded on the representation of property, however direct or indirect, is radically vicious, since it is a union of two of the most corrupting influences to which man is subject. It is the proper business of government to resist the corruptions of money, and not to depend on them.

To a qualification of property, if placed so low as to embrace the great majority of the people, there is no very serious objection, though better tests might, perhaps, be devised. Residence, character, information, and fixed relations with society, ought to be added to this qualification; and it might be better, even, could they be made entirely to supersede it. In local governments, or those of towns and villages, which do little more than control property, a low property qualification is the true test of the franchise, though even in these cases, it might be well to add information and character.

ON UNIVERSAL SUFFRAGE

There is no more a literal universal suffrage, than a literal equality. All these terms must be received in a limited sense, their meaning amounting merely to a comparison with other and older conditions of society. One half of every population is excluded from the suffrage on account of sex, and more than half of the remainder on account of age. From the class that these two great rules do not affect, another, but a small portion, is excluded for their extreme poverty, their crimes, a want of residence or as vagabonds, or for some other cause. The most popularly governed of the American states admits these doctrines.

The policy of adopting a suffrage as wide as that which is commonly called universal, has been much and plausibly contested. Better political tests, perhaps, might be applied than those which now exist, and there can be little doubt that the present system is carried too far in its application and under the particular circumstances of the country, if not too far as a general principle.

The governments of towns and villages, for instance, are almost entirely directed to the regulation of property, and to the control of local interests. In such governments universal suffrage is clearly misplaced, for several grave and obvious reasons, a few of which shall be mentioned.

Towns and villages having no legislative control over the greater interests, such as the general protection of life, the person, the character, and property, there is neither the same necessity for, nor the same justice in, letting in all classes to participate in power. The laws which control the great and predominant interests, or those which give a complexion to society, emanate from the states, which may well enough possess a wide political base. But towns and villages regulating property chiefly, there is a peculiar propriety in excluding those from the suffrage who have no immediate local interests in them. An undue proportion of the dissolute, unsettled, vicious and disorganizing, collect in towns, and that balance of society, which, under other circumstances, might neutralize their influence, is destroyed, leaving, as a consequence, the power to control their governments, under a suffrage that is universal, in the hands of the worst part of [the] community; for, though these persons may not be in sufficient force absolutely to elevate men of their own class to office, they hold a balance between conflicting parties, uniformly act together, and commonly in favor of those who are most disposed to sacrifice principle to expediency. A system must be radically wrong, when the keeper of a tavern, or of a grocery, through his facilities in humoring one of the worst of our vices, can command more votes than a man of the highest attainments, or of the highest character.

The great immigration of foreigners into the country, and the practice of remaining, or of assembling, in the large towns, renders universal suffrage doubly oppressive to the citizens of the latter. The natives of other countries bring with them the prejudices of another and an antagonist state of society; or what is still worse, their reaction; and it is a painful and humiliating fact, that several of the principal places of this country, are, virtually, under the control of men of this class, who have few convictions of liberty, beyond those which arise from a love of licentiousness, who are totally ignorant of its governing principles, and who, in their hearts and language, are hostile to the very people whose hospitality they enjoy. Many of these men cannot even speak the language of the land, and perhaps a majority of them cannot read the great social compact, by which society is held together. Whatever may be said, on general principles, of the necessity of giving to a government the broadest possible base, few will contend that circumstances like these, ought not to qualify the regulation in practice.

Local and limited governments, like those of towns and villages, are best managed in the hands of men who have permanent and fixed interests within their boundaries, and there is little propriety in admitting the more floating part of the population to a participation of an authority that scarcely controls a single right which affects transient persons.

Universal suffrage, in the more extended sense, cannot be received as a naked proposition, without reference to facts. Some nations are totally unqualified to exercise this trust, intelligently and safely, while in others, it may be the best and most sure foundation of society. As a general rule it would be highly dangerous, though the communities that can safely bear it are to be envied and esteemed.

Systems are to be appreciated by their general effects, and not by particular exceptions. Principles also become modified in practice, by facts, and universal suffrage presents very different results in one state of society, from that which it presents in another. So long as the laboring classes of a country can receive high wages, the love of independence that is natural to man, will induce them to give their votes according to their own interests, pleasure, judgment, passions or caprices; for these are equally governing motives of human actions; but when the pressure of society shall become so great as to compel the man of small means to depend on the man of large for his comforts, or even for his bread, as is the natural tendency of all civilized society, the power of money will probably be felt adversely under a suffrage that includes all, or as nearly so, as is practicable. It may then become necessary to liberty, itself, to limit the suffrage.

The representative will necessarily have a direct moral relation to his constituency. In a community that contains many men of character and intelligence, the representation will be of a higher order, than in a community that contains few. We are not to judge of the general effects of the American system, therefore, by the present condition of its representation, though those who have the best means of observation, are of opinion that it will even now sustain a favorable comparison with that of any other country.

There are periods in the histories of all countries, in which entire nations may be said to be on their good behavior. These are the times of struggles and changes, when attention is drawn to the acts of publick men, and principles have unusual influence. Such was the case at the commencement of the American revolution; at one period of the French; and is, in a degree, the present state of the British parliament. At such periods, the same representative acts under impulses very different from those which commonly influence him, and care must be had, in comparing systems, to take into the account all the facts that would be likely to affect them.

Universal suffrage is capricious and uncertain in its minor consequences, often producing results directly contrary to those which were expected.

The transitory nature of the American population renders universal suffrage less advantageous and more injurious, than it would prove to be in a less vacillating condition of society. Thus it is, we see new men, and even strangers, filling offices in places that they entered a year previously, to quit the year that will succeed. The effect of this passing connection with a community is bad, on many accounts, but it becomes seriously so, when the floating and unstable members of society have sufficient interest to unsettle its concerns with their own fluctuating interests.

ON SLAVERY[112]

Domestic slavery is an institution as old as human annals, and probably will continue, in its spirit, through different modifications, as long as man shall remain under the different degrees of civilization that mark his actual existence. Slavery is no more sinful, by the christian code, than it is sinful to wear a whole coat, while another is in tatters, to eat a better meal than a neighbor, or otherwise to enjoy ease and plenty, while our fellow creatures are suffering and in want. According to the doctrines of Christ, we are "to do as we would be done by," but this law is not to be applied to slavery more than to any other interest of life. It is quite possible to be an excellent christian and a slave holder, and the relations of master and slave, may be a means of exhibiting some of the mildest graces of the character, as may those of king and subject, or principal and dependant, in any of the other modifications of human institutions.

In one sense, slavery may actually benefit a man, there being little doubt that the African is, in nearly all respects, better off in servitude in this country, than when living in a state of barbarism at home.

But, while slavery, in the abstract, can no more be considered a sin, than most human ordinances, it leads to sin in its consequences, in a way peculiarly its own, and may be set down as an impolitic and vicious institution. It encourages those faults of character that depend on an uncontrolled will, on the one side, and an abject submission, on the other. It usually limits the moral existence of the slave, too, as there is a necessity of keeping him ignorant, in order that he may be held in subjection.

Slavery is of two kinds; one in which the slave is a chattel, and can be disposed of as such, and one in which he is attached to the soil, like a fixture, and can only be sold with the land. The former is the condition of the American slave; the latter the condition of the European serf. All Europe, formerly, had serfs, or slaves, of the latter class, though their existence is now confined to a few countries in the north and east of that quarter of the world. Still, the consequences of the old system are, more or less, to be traced, in most European countries, and, though differing in degree, their people may as fairly be termed slaves in principle, as those of our own southern states.

ON AMERICAN SLAVERY

American slavery is of the most unqualified kind, considering the slave as a chattel, that is transferable at will, and in full property. The slave, however, is protected in his person to a certain extent, the power of the master to chastise and punish, amounting to no more than the parental power.

American slavery is distinguished from that of most other parts of the world, by the circumstance that the slave is a variety of the human species, and is marked by physical peculiarities so different from his master, as to render future amalgamation improbable. In ancient Rome, in modern Europe generally, and, in most other countries, the slave not being thus distinguished, on obtaining his freedom, was soon lost in the mass around him; but nature has made a stamp on the American slave that is likely to prevent this consummation, and which menaces much future ill to the country. The time must come when American slavery shall cease, and when that day shall arrive, (unless early and effectual means are devised to obviate it,) two races will exist in the same region, whose feelings will be embittered by inextinguishable hatred, and who carry on their faces, the respective stamps of their factions. The struggle that will follow, will necessarily be a war of extermination. The evil day may be delayed, but can scarcely be averted.

American slavery is mild, in its general features, and physical suffering cannot properly be enumerated among its evils. Neither is it just to lay too heavy stress on the personal restraints of the system, as it is a question whether men feel very keenly, if at all, privations of the amount of which they know nothing. In these respects, the slavery of this country is but one modification of the restraints that are imposed on the majority, even, throughout most of Europe. It is an evil, certainly, but in a comparative sense, not as great an evil as it is usually imagined. There is scarcely a nation of Europe that does not possess institutions that inflict as gross personal privations and wrongs, as the slavery of America. Thus the subject is compelled to bear arms in a quarrel in which he has no real concern, and to incur the risks of demoralization and death in camps and fleets, without any crime or agency of his own. From all this, the slave is exempt, as well as from the more ordinary cares of life.

Slavery in America, is an institution purely of the states, and over which the United States has no absolute control. The pretence, however, that congress has no right to entertain the subject, is unsound, and cannot be maintained. Observing the prescribed forms, slavery can be legally abolished, by amending the constitution, and congress has power, by a vote of two thirds of both houses, to propose amendments to that instrument. Now, whatever congress has power to do, it has power to discuss; by the same rule, that it is a moral innovation on the rights of the states to discuss matters in congress, on which congress has no authority to legislate. A constitutional right, and expediency, however, are very different things. Congress has full power to declare war against all the nations of the earth, but it would be madness to declare war against even one of them, without sufficient cause. It would be equal madness for congress, in the present state of the country, to attempt to propose an amendment of the constitution, to abolish slavery altogether, as it would infallibly fail, thereby raising an irritating question without an object.

CONCLUSION

The inferences to be drawn from the foregoing reasons and facts, admitting both to be just, may be briefly summed up as follows.

No expedients can equalize the temporal lots of men; for

without civilization and government, the strong would oppress the weak, and, with them, an inducement to exertion must be left, by bestowing rewards on talents, industry and success. All that the best institutions, then, can achieve, is to remove useless obstacles, and to permit merit to be the artisan of its own fortune, without always degrading demerit to the place it ought naturally to fill.

Every human excellence is merely comparative, there being no good without alloy. It is idle therefore to expect a system that shall exhibit faultlessness, or perfection.

The terms liberty, equality, right and justice, used in a political sense, are merely terms of convention, and of comparative excellence, there being no such thing, in practice, as either of these qualities being carried out purely, according to the abstract notions of theories.

The affairs of life embrace a multitude of interests, and he who reasons on any one of them, without consulting the rest, is a visionary unsuited to control the business of the world.

There is a prevalent disposition in the designing to forget the means in the end, and on the part of the mass to overlook the result in the more immediate agencies. The first is the consequence of cupidity; the last of short-sightedness, and frequently of the passions. Both these faults need be vigilantly watched in a democracy, as the first unsettles principles while it favors artifice, and the last is substituting the transient motives of a day, for the deliberate policy and collected wisdom of ages.

Men are the constant dupes of names, while their happiness and well-being mainly depend on things. The highest proof a community can give of its fitness for self government, is its readiness in distinguishing between the two; for frauds, oppression, flattery and vice, are the offspring of the mistakes.

It is a governing principle of nature, that the agency which can produce most good, when perverted from its proper aim, is most productive of evil. It behooves the well-intentioned, therefore, vigilantly to watch the tendency of even their most highly prized institutions, since that which was established in the interests of the right, may so easily become the agent of the wrong.

The disposition of all power is to abuses, nor does it at all mend the matter that its possessors are a majority. Unrestrained political authority, though it be confided to masses, cannot be trusted without positive limitations, men in bodies being but an aggregation of the passions, weaknesses and interests of men as individuals.

It is as idle to expect what is termed gratitude, in a democracy, as from any other repository of power. Bodies of men, though submitting to human impulses generally, and often sympathetic as well as violent, are seldom generous. In matters that touch the common feeling, they are avaricious of praise, and they usually visit any want of success in a publick man, as a personal wrong. Thus it is that we see a dozen victories forgotten in a single defeat, an irritable vanity in the place of a masculine pride, and a sensitiveness to opinion, instead of a just appreciation of acts.

Under every system it is more especially the office of the prudent and candid to guard against the evils peculiar to that particular system, than to declaim against the abuses of others. Thus, in a democracy, instead of decrying monarchs and aristocrats, who are impotent, it is wiser to look into the sore spots of the only form of government that can do any practical injury, and to apply the necessary remedies, than to be glorifying ourselves at the expense of charity, common sense, and not unfrequently of truth.

Life is made up of positive things, the existence of which it is not only folly, but which it is often unsafe to deny. Nothing is gained by setting up impracticable theories, but alienating opinion from the facts under which we live, all the actual distinctions that are inseparable from the possession of property, learning, breeding, refinement, tastes and principles, existing as well in one form of government, as in another; the only difference between ourselves and other nations, in this particular, lying in the fact that there are no other artificial distinctions than those that are inseparable from the recognised principles and indispensable laws of civilization.

There is less real inequality in the condition of men than

outward circumstances would give reason to believe. If refinement brings additional happiness, it also adds point to misery. Fortunately, the high consolations of religion, in which lies the only lasting and true relief from the cares and seeming injustice of the world, are equally attainable, or, if there be a disadvantage connected with this engrossing interest, it is against those whose lots are vulgarly supposed to be the most desirable.

[PAUL JONES AND THE AMERICAN NAVY]

From *Lives of Distinguished American Naval Officers*[113]

Jones does not appear to have had any connection with the American Navy, until a short time before the passage of the law of December 22, 1775, which, in fact, gave it legal and efficient existence. By this law, a commander-in-chief, four captains, and thirteen lieutenants were appointed. The latter were classed as first, second, and third lieutenants, and of these the name of John Paul Jones takes rank of all others of the highest grade. His commission is said to have been dated the 7th of December, fifteen days before the passage of the law. This, in fact, made him the sixth in rank in the service; though other appointments were shortly after made, and the question of permanent rank was reserved for future consideration.

. . . .

It is worthy of remark, that the very day Congress ordered Jones to the Ranger, it adopted the stars and stripes as the flag of the republic. This was June 14th, 1777. One of the first things Jones did, on reaching his ship, was to hoist this new ensign. He always claimed to have been the first man to hoist the flag of 1775, in a national ship, and the first man to show the present ensign on board a man-of-war. This may be true or not. There was a weakness about the character of the man that rendered him a little liable to self-delusions of this nature, and, while it is probable he was right as to the flag which was shown before Philadelphia, the town where Congress was sitting, it is by no means as reasonable to suppose that the first of the permanent flags was shown at a place as distant as Portsmouth. The circumstances are of no moment, except as they serve to betray a want of simplicity of character, that was rather a failing with the man, and his avidity for personal distinction of every sort.

The Ranger was not ready for sea before the 15th October.

Even then her equipment was very imperfect, the vessel having but one suit of sails, and some of these were made of insufficient cloth. The ship was frigate built, like most of the sloops of that day, and was pierced for twenty-six guns; viz., eighteen below, and eight above. This number was furnished, but he rejected all but those for the main deck, mounting eighteen sixes. Even these guns he considered as three diameters of the bore too short. Of men he had enough, but his stores were very short, and it is a singular fact, that he could obtain but a barrel of rum for his whole crew. Under such difficulties, however, was the independence of this country obtained.

The Ranger sailed from Portsmouth, New Hampshire, for France, Nov. 1st, 1777. This was the first time Jones had left America, or the American waters, since his arrival in Virginia, after the death of his brother. He still went to Europe in expectation of obtaining the Dutch-built frigate, intending to cruise in her with the Ranger in company. On the 2d Dec. the Ranger arrived at Nantes, having made two captures on the passage. She saw a convoy, but got nothing from it, and had a short chase with a two-decked ship. On all occasions, Jones represents his people, who were principally eastern men, as behaving well.

A severe disappointment awaited Jones on reaching France. Owing to the jealousy of England, the commissioners had found themselves under the necessity of transferring the ship building in Holland to the King of France; an arrangement which deprived them of all authority over her.* Jones submitted to this

---

* The *Indien* was subsequently hired to the State of South Carolina, and had her name changed to that of the state. The negotiation was carried on through the agency of the Chevalier de Luxembourg. In his History of the Navy, the writer mentions his belief that this Chevalier de Luxembourg was not a sovereign prince, as has been supposed, but a member of the House of Montmorency. In an *Acte de famille* of this illustrious house, which was made in this century, we find these words—viz.:

"1731. The Duke of Chatillon had but one son, Charles Paul Sigismund, known by the name of Duke of Bouteville; who had an only son, Charles Anne de Montmorency-Luxembourg, Duke of Olonne. The Duke of Olonne had two sons, of which one, known as the *Chevalier de Luxembourg*, is dead without issue."

There is no question that this Chevalier de Luxembourg is the person

defeat of his hopes with a moderation and good sense that are
in his favor; thus proving, we think, that his many previous
complaints were founded on just principles, in his own opinion
at least, and not in querulousness of character, as has been
sometimes alleged; for, in this case, the evil being unavoidable,
he saw no good motive for quarrelling with fortune. He con-
soled himself with the knowledge that Congress thought him
worthy of so important a trust, and says, "I can bear the disappointment with philosophy."

As soon as all hopes of getting another and better ship were
abandoned, Jones took the Ranger round to Quiberon Bay,
convoying some American vessels. Here he met the fleet of
M. Le Motte Picquet, and opened a negotiation for a salute.
His request was acceded to, and salutes were exchanged, not
only with this distinguished officer, but, a few days later, with
the Comte d'Orvillers, the commander-in-chief of the Brest
fleet.[114] In consequence of these proceedings, Jones claimed the
honor of having received the first salute to the American flag,
as he did that of having first hoisted the flag itself. It is certain
he is mistaken as to the former of these claims, unless he means
the particular flag adopted by Congress, June, 1777; for a serious
difficulty occurred in consequence of a Dutch governor's having
saluted an American vessel of war in the West Indies, the year
previously. Still, the motive and the feeling were the same, and
it was certainly a point gained to obtain a salute from a French
commander-in-chief at the time mentioned.

While lying among the French ships, Jones seems to have had
a good deal of communication with its flag officers. He even
went so far as to submit certain plans to them for expeditions
to America, a general war being now certain, and his projects
show an active and fertile mind. These qualities, indeed, form
the great and distinctive features of his character, one military
scheme being no sooner disposed of than he turned his thoughts
to another with untiring ingenuity.

---

who hired the Indien to the State of South Carolina, *on shares*. As the ship
had been given to the king, may not this have been a secret experiment in
royal privateering? [*Cooper's note.*]

April 10th, 1778, the Ranger again went to sea alone, Jones having relinquished all hope of doing any thing, for the present at least, without achieving it with his own limited means. It is usual to ascribe more credit to the great cruise that succeeded than to this of the Ranger, and yet Jones probably never showed more of his real character than in the enterprise which he now undertook. We shall first relate the events as they occurred, and then give a summary of their character and importance.

On the 14th, the Ranger took a vessel, loaded with flaxseed, and bound to Ireland. This prize secured, she shaped her course for St. George's Channel. Off Dublin she captured a London ship. The weather being favorable, Jones now determined to make a descent at Whitehaven, the place out of which he had first sailed, in order to destroy the shipping by fire. With this view, on the evening of the 18th, he was off the port, and, about ten at night, he was on the point of landing himself at the head of a party of volunteers, when the wind shifted, and began to blow so fresh, directly on shore, as to render the descent impracticable. The ship made sail to claw off the land.

The next day the Ranger chased a revenue wherry unsuccessfully, and, though the ship was disguised as a merchantman, it is thought the crew of the boat suspected her of being an enemy. It could not well be otherwise, indeed, since, Jones, in his desire to get the boat, kept up a smart fire on her for some time. The next morning he found himself so near a coaster as to be compelled to sink her, in order to prevent the discovery of his presence. Another attempt inshore was abandoned, the same day, on account of the state of the wind.

All this time Jones was close in with the land, visible from the shore, and looking into the different bays and roadsteads as he passed along the coast. One cutter he chased into the Clyde, going as high as the Rock of Ailsa, and he sunk a Dublin sloop, to prevent intelligence.

On the 20th, the Ranger was off Carrickfergus, and detained a fishing-boat that came alongside. A ship was at anchor in the road, which the prisoners said was the Drake, Capt. Burden, a vessel of about the size, armament and metal of the Ranger;

though she is said to have carried two more guns. This was just such an opportunity as Jones wanted, and though he was alone on an enemy's coast, and might be said to be fighting with a halter round his neck, he at once resolved to attack his enemy at anchor, as soon as it was dark. That night, therefore, the Ranger stood in, with a strong breeze, with the intention of laying the Drake athwart hawse, grappling, and fighting it out. Owing to the darkness, however, and the anchor's hanging, the Ranger brought up about half a cable's length on the Drake's quarter, instead of the position desired, and Jones at once saw the expediency of abandoning the design. He ordered the cable cut, on the instant, so as to give the appearance of its having parted in snubbing, made sail, and began to beat out of the loch. As no warlike demonstration had yet been made, singular as it may seem, this was done without molestation from the Drake. It was Jones' intention to work to windward, and to renew the attempt the same night, but it blew so fresh that he was glad to get an offing on any terms. The wind increased to a gale, and he stood over toward the coast of Scotland to find a lee.

As soon as the weather moderated, Jones determined to renew the attempt on Whitehaven. On the night of the 22nd he got off that port again, though not as close in as he wished, in consequence of the lightness of the wind. At midnight he left the ship, having with him, in two boats, thirty-one volunteers. Day began to dawn just as the party reached the outer pier. Jones now divided his men. One party was sent, under Lieut. Wallingford, to set fire to the shipping on the north side of the harbor, while he went himself with the other to do the same on the south. There was a small fort on Jones' side, with a few men in it as a guard. He scaled the walls, found the men in the guard-house, where he secured them, and spiked the guns. Jones now took a single officer and went a distance of a quarter of a mile to another battery, the guns of which he also spiked.

On his return from the distant battery, Jones expected to find the ships on fire. So far from this, however, nothing material had been done. Mr. Wallingford had altogether abandoned his portion of the enterprise, the candle on which he relied having burnt out just as it was time to use it. The same accident had occurred on his own side of the harbor also. It was now broad daylight, and the alarm had been given, but Jones would not abandon his design. A candle was procured from a house, and a fire was kindled in the steerage of a large ship. As this vessel lay surrounded by a hundred and fifty or two hundred other craft, all high and dry, the tide being out, there is no question that a good fire, fairly kindled, would have destroyed the whole.

The great object of Jones was now to repair the loss of time. The sun had risen, and the people of the place were already in motion, though confused and in alarm. The fire burnt but slowly, and search was made for combustibles to aid it. At length a barrel of tar was found and poured upon the flames. Jones then collected his men, and ordered them to embark from the end of the pier. By this time the inhabitants of the place were out in thousands, and some of the men ran towards the pier. Jones met the last with a presented pistol, ordering them off, at the risk of their lives. Such was the influence of courage and steadiness, that these men retreated, leaving the pier in possession of this handful of enemies. As the flames now burst out of the steerage and began to ascend the rigging, and the sun had been up an hour, Jones thought it prudent to retire. He had remained some time on the pier all alone, and embarked without molestation, though the eminences around were covered with spectators.

The boats retired without difficulty. Attempts were made to fire on them from the batteries, but the guns were all spiked. One or two pieces, however, had escaped, or, as Jones believed, ship's guns were dragged down upon the pier, and began to play upon the adventurers without effect. No person was injured in the affair, and only one man was missing. This person is supposed to have deserted, and to have given the alarm; such a man coming to several houses with the news that a ship had been set on fire. Nor was any material damage done to the shipping, the people of the place succeeding in extinguishing the flames, before they reached the other vessels. Jones took three prisoners, whom he brought off as a sort of trophy.

The same day the Ranger crossed the Solway, and made a landing at St. Mary's Isle, where is the seat of the Earls of Selkirk. Jones had but a single boat on this occasion, and he landed again in person. His object was to seize Lord Selkirk, fancying that a prisoner of his rank might be useful in affecting the treatment of the Americans, who were then in the English prisons. Ascertaining, soon after he had landed, that Lord Selkirk was not at home, Jones returned to his boat. But the men complained of being again disappointed, and, after some discussion, their captain assented that they might go to the house and ask for plate. They were limited to accepting such as was offered. The truth is not to be concealed, that an officer was at the head of this party, but many of the officers of that period were men taken from trading vessels, and were actuated by motives that were little honorable to them. Lady Selkirk received the officers of this party herself, none of the men being suffered to enter the house. Some plate, valued at about £100,* was delivered, and the party retired, doing no other harm.

In the present day, such an act would be entirely unjustifiable. No American officer would dare to be guilty of it openly; and it is to be hoped no one would wish to do it at all. Acts very similar to it, however, have been committed on our own coasts within the last thirty years, if not with the connivance of officers, at least in their presence. If we go back a century earlier, it was the common mode of warfare of the Drakes and other commanders of the English service. As it was, Jones was sensible of its unworthiness, and he subsequently purchased the plate and restored it to its owner. Owing to the difficulties of communication, nearly or quite ten years elapsed before Lord Selkirk actually recovered his property, but he acknowledges that he got it at last, and expressed his satisfaction with the course pursued by Jones.

* The connection of Jones, already mentioned, affirms that the value of the plate taken was more than $5000. Our information was obtained from the present head of the house of Selkirk. Which is right, it is impossible to say, though it strikes us that the smaller sum is most likely to be the true one. If Jones actually paid £1000 sterling out of his own pocket, to redeem this plate, as Miss Taylor seems to think, it greatly enhances the merit of his sacrifices. [*Cooper's note.*]

A letter written by Jones to Lady Selkirk, on this occasion, has been often published, and has been greatly praised. It has much of the exaggerated and false taste of the writer, while it shows creditable sentiments. Its great fault is a want of simplicity, a defect that seems to have pervaded Jones' character. That Jones committed a fault in allowing the plunder at all is undeniable, though he seems to have yielded solely to a temporary expedient, reserving to himself the intention to repair the wrong at the earliest occasion. Sordid he was not; and admitting the redemption to have been an after-thought even, there is no reason for believing that he was any way influenced by a wish to make money. With such an end in view, a man of his enterprise would scarcely have limited his efforts to accepting the little plate that was offered. He would have stripped the house.

The landing at St. Mary's Isle occurred on the 23d April, and the following morning the Ranger once more appeared off Carrickfergus, where Jones saw symptoms that the Drake was preparing to come out. That the character of the American ship was not known, however, is clear from the fact that the Drake sent a boat out to reconnoitre. This boat was decoyed alongside, and her officer and crew captured. From his prisoners, Jones ascertained that intelligence of what had occurred at White-haven reached Carrickfergus the previous night, and no doubt was entertained that the ship which had appeared off the one place was the vessel that had made the attempt on the Drake in the other. The latter vessel had weighed the lost anchor of the Ranger; and it was now ascertained that she had received many volunteers on board, and was coming out in quest of her enemy. The only doubt, therefore, which could exist among the English was whether the vessel now in the offing was the same as that which had made the two previous attempts.

When the Drake got under way, she was accompanied by several boats filled with persons who were disposed to be witnesses of the action. Jones hove-to and waited for his enemy, amid a scene that might well have disturbed the self-confidence of a man of less fortitude. He was in the narrow waters of the most powerful naval power on earth, with the three kingdoms in plain view. Alarm smokes were raised on each side of the channel, in great numbers, showing that his foes were up and doing. He had already given occasion for extraordinary activity, and an enemy that had enjoyed time to get perfectly ready, and which, to say the least, was always his equal in force, was coming out from her moorings purposely to engage him. This, according to a favorite expression of Jones himself, was literally going into "harm's way."

The tide was not favorable, and the English ship came out very slowly. The Ranger's drift was to windward, and her helm was put up several times, in order to run down toward her enemy, when she would throw her main-top-sail aback, and lie with her courses in the brails. As soon as the amateurs ascertained that the boat which was towing astern of the strange ship was that sent out by the Drake, they all bore up and ran back into the loch. At length, long after the turn of the day, the English ship succeeded in weathering the headland, and was enabled to lay a straight course into the offing. She now set her colors, and the Ranger showed what it was then the fashion of England to call the "rebel flag." Jones filled and stood off the land, under easy canvas, to lead his enemy out mid-channel. The Drake followed, gradually closing, until she got within hail.

Jones had at length gained his point, and was in momentary expectation of commencing an action with an enemy's ship of equal force. While he awaited her fire, he was hailed, with a demand to know who and what he was. The answer was given by the master, under Jones' direction—"This is the American continental ship Ranger," he said; "we wait for you, and beg you will come on. The sun is little more than an hour high, and it is time to begin." This cool invitation was scarcely given before the Ranger fell broad off and delivered her fire. The Drake answered this attack, the two ships closing and running off before a light wind. It was soon apparent that the Ranger was getting the best of it; her adversary's spars and sails beginning to suffer. Still the action was animated and well maintained for just one hour and four minutes, when the Drake called out for quarter; her ensign having been previously shot away.

This battle was fairly fought, side by side, and the victory not only gallantly but neatly won. Jones states, in his account of the cruise, that no one on board the Drake placed her people, including the volunteers, at less than one hundred and sixty, while some admitted there must have been one hundred and ninety souls on board. He estimated the loss of the Drake, in killed and wounded, at forty-two, though this exceeds the English statement by nearly half. The volunteers must have rendered the official account of the English very problematical, and there was somewhat of conjecture in that of Jones. Captain Burden fell by a musket-shot in the head, though he was found alive on taking possession of the prize. The English first lieutenant, also, was mortally wounded. The Drake's fore and main-topsail-yards were both down on the cap—main-top-gallant yard and gaff were hanging up and down, the jib was in the water, and, otherwise, the ship had sustained much injury aloft.

The Ranger suffered far less. She had two men killed and six wounded. Mr. Wallingford, the lieutenant who landed at Whitehaven, was one of the former, and a seaman among the wounded subsequently died. The gunner was hurt, and Mr. Powers, a midshipman, lost an arm. Jones remarks, in one of his letters, that he gave the dead a "spacious grave."

The weather continued good, and the repairs proceeded actively. At first Jones intended to steer the direct course for France, but the wind coming foul, he changed his purpose, and passed up channel again. The evening of the 25th, or that of the day after the engagement, the two ships were off the bay of Belfast, once more, and here Jones dismissed the fishermen he had taken. He gave them a boat, money, and other necessaries, and lent them a sail of the Drake's as a hint to those ashore concerning the fate of that vessel.

On the 8th of May, the Ranger, with the Drake in company, arrived safely at Brest. Some bad weather had been encountered on the passage, but no event worthy of being mentioned occurred, unless it be that Jones felt himself bound to arrest his first lieutenant, Simpson, for disobedience of orders, in managing the prize. This affair gave him a good deal of trouble subsequently, though nothing of serious moment grew out of it. The Ranger appears to have been well manned but badly officered, as would be likely to happen with a vessel fitted in an eastern American port, at that early day.

A great sensation was produced by this cruise of the Ranger. It lasted but twenty-eight days; only one week passed between the arrival off the Isle of Man and the action with the Drake. Every hour of this time was passed in ceaseless activity. One enterprise was no sooner ended than another was begun. The reader has only to cast an eye at the map, to understand the boldness with which the ship moved. Her audacity probably caused her impunity, for there was scarcely a more critical position, as to mere localities, in the narrow seas, than that into which Jones carried her. It is true, he knew every foot of the way, but he must have known the dangers of his path, as well as its disadvantages. The attempt on Whitehaven betokened a military mind, though it would scarcely be justified under any other principles of hostility than those so much in vogue with the English themselves. It was merited retaliation, and only failed through the incompetence of subordinates. Throughout the whole of this cruise, indeed, Jones displayed the highest species of courage; that of justly appreciating his own resources, and of not exaggerating dangers, a union of spirit and judgment that ever produces the best commanders.

. . . .

Under the arrangement made, a squadron was finally, though very imperfectly, equipped. It contained five vessels, or three frigates, a brig, and a cutter. The ships were the Duke of Duras,[115] the Alliance, and the Pallas; the brig was called the Vengeance, and the cutter the Cerf, or Stag. Of all these crafts, but two were regularly constructed for war, the Alliance 32, and the Stag 12. The Alliance was an exceedingly fast American-built ship of the class of the large thirty-twos. All the other vessels were French.

. . . .

The orders under which Jones sailed on his next and most remarkable cruise, directed him to go to the westward of Scilly, and to pass the west coast of Ireland, doubling the extremity of Scotland, and remaining some time on the Dogger Bank. By returning to his port of departure, this would have been making the complete circuit of Great Britain and Ireland, most of the time keeping the land aboard. The instructions, however, ordered him to put into the Texel for further orders. It was understood that this last destination was pointed out in the hope of putting the Indien under Jones, that ship still remaining in Holland, in a species of political durance. She was not released, until England declared war against Holland, when the arrangement was made with South Carolina, as already mentioned.

The squadron left the roads of Groix, the second time, early on the morning of August 15th, 1779. One day out, it recaptured a large Dutch ship, laden with French property. In consequence of some misunderstanding with the commander of the Monsieur, which grew out of the disposition of this prize, that ship separated from the other vessels, which saw her no more. The Monsieur was subsequently captured by the enemy, and, as is believed, on this cruise. On the 20th, a brig, from Limerick to London, was taken, and ordered in.

The 23d, the squadron was off Cape Clear, having doubled Scilly, and passed up the west coast of England, in the intervening time. Here it fell calm, and Jones sent several of the Richard's boats to seize a brig that was lying some distance to the north-west. As evening approached, he found it necessary to place his own barge in the water, containing a cockswain and six men, to keep the ship's head off shore. The brig was captured, and towed toward the squadron. Just at this moment, the men in the barge cut the tow-line, and pulled for the shore. Several shots were fired at the fugitives, but without effect. Seeing this, Mr. Cutting Lunt, who appears to have been with the prize, took four soldiers in a boat, and pursued the deserters, becoming lost in a fog. The Richard fired guns, as signals to the master, but he never returned. Counting himself, there were seventeen persons in his boat, making a total loss to the Richard, including the fugitives, of twenty-four men. It is now known that, on the morning of the 23d, (civil time,) the seven men landed at Ballinskellix, in the county of Kerry, and that the other boat landed at the same place, the same day, about one, in pursuit. Mr. Lunt and his people were arrested, and sent to Mill prison. Jones intimates that he understood his master died in that place of confinement, but, in this, he was misinformed. Mr. Lunt was liberated, in the course of a year or two, and was subsequently lost at sea. This was Cutting Lunt, it will be remembered; his kinsman, Henry Lunt, still remaining in the ship, as her second lieutenant. Through the reports of the deserters and prisoners, the character of the squadron, which was plainly visible as soon as the fog dispersed, became known on shore, and its presence created great uneasiness. The linen ships were supposed to be Jones' object, and precautions were taken accordingly. It is worthy of remark, that Jones states, the master saw the Cerf, inshore, whither she had been sent to reconnoitre, and to look for the missing boats, but the cutter showed English colors, and fired at the boat, which induced Mr. Lunt to land, as a last resort. To add to the misfortune, the cutter herself got separated in the fog, and did not rejoin the squadron.

It was at this time, that Jones had a serious quarrel with his second in command, M. Landais. Insubordination soon began seriously to show itself; the conduct of the Cerf being very unaccountable. She went back to France. It is probable that the loss of so many men induced the French officers to distrust the fidelity of the Richard's crew; and it is known that this distrust influenced the conduct of the Pallas, on a most trying occasion, a few weeks later. On the 26th, the Grandeville was sent in, with a prize. This reduced the force of the squadron to four vessels, viz., the Richard, Alliance, Pallas, and Vengeance.

It was the intention of Jones to remain a week longer off Cape Clear, but Capt. Landais seemed so apprehensive of the approach of a superior force, that he yielded to the opinion of his subordinate. On the 26th, it blowed fresh; the commodore accordingly made the signal to stand to the northward, the Alliance parting company the same night. On the 31st, the

Richard, Pallas, and Vengeance, were off Cape Wrath, the northwestern extremity of the island of Great Britain, where the former captured a heavy Letter-of-Marque, of twenty-two guns, laden with naval stores for the enemy's vessels on the American lakes. While this ship was chasing, the Alliance hove in sight, and joined in the chase, having another Letter-of-Marque in company, a prize. These two ships were manned from the Alliance, at Landais' request; and the latter sent them into Norway, contrary to orders, where both were restored to the English by the Danish government. On the night of the 8th, the Alliance again parted company, in a gale of wind.

Jones kept well off the land, the weather being thick, and the wind foul. On the 13th, however, the Cheviot Hills, in the south-eastern part of Scotland, became visible, and the commodore now seriously set about the execution of some of his larger plans. His intention was to land at Leith, the port of Edinburgh itself, and, not only to lay the place under contribution, but to seize the shipping he might find in the Forth. He had hopes that even the Scottish capital might be frightened into a temporary submission. This was a highly characteristic project, and one worthy of the military audacity of the man. Its great merit, in addition to its boldness and importance, was its strong probability of success. The late Com. Dale, who was to act a most important part in the enterprise, and who was a man of singular simplicity and moderation of character and temperament, assured the writer that he never could see any reason why the attack should have been defeated, beyond the obstacle that actually arose. Jones himself intimates that his two *colleagues*, present, (for so he bitterly styled his captains, in consequence of the terms of the *concordat*,) threw cold water on his views, until he pointed out to them the probable amount of the contributions of two such places as Leith and Edinburgh. A delay occurred, moreover, in consequence of the momentary absence of the Pallas and Vengeance, which vessels had given chase to the southward, a circumstance that compelled the Richard to quit the Forth, after she had entered it alone, and this at a moment when she might have secured a twenty-gun ship and two cutters, all of which were lying in Leith roads, unsuspicious of danger; though it would have compelled him to abandon the other and principal objects of the attempt. In order to join his consorts, and consult his captains, therefore, Jones was compelled to quit the Forth, after having once entered it. It appears he had found a man ready to give him information, but the golden opportunity was lost, in consequence of the doubts and misgivings of his subordinates.

Still Jones determined to make the attempt. On the 15th, the Richard, Pallas, and Vengeance, entered the Forth in company, turning up with the tide, against a head wind. By this time the alarm had been given on shore, and guns were mounted at Leith, to receive the strangers. A cutter had been watching the squadron for several hours, also; but Jones deemed all this immaterial. The ships had got up as high as Inchkeith, the island which shelters the roads seaward, and the boats were in the water and manned. Mr. Dale, who was to superintend and command the maritime part of the debarkation, had received his instructions, and was on the point of descending into his boat, when a squall struck the ships, and induced an order to take the people from the boats, to clue up and clue down. Jones held on against the wind as long as he found it possible, but, the squall turning to a gale, he was compelled to bear up before it, and was driven out of the Forth again, at a much faster rate than he had entered it. The gale was short, but so severe that one of the prizes in company foundered. It moderated in the afternoon, but Jones having plainly seen the cutter watching him, conceived it too late to hope for a surprise, his only rational ground for expecting success.

It is a proof how much doubt existed concerning the true character of Jones' vessels, among the people on shore, that a member of parliament sent off, to the Richard, a messenger, to ask for powder and shot; stating that he had heard Paul Jones was on the coast, and that he wished to be ready for him. A barrel of powder was sent in answer, but the "honorable gentleman" was told the vessel had no shot of the size he requested. On this occasion, the ships were seen turning up the Forth, as they stood in quite near to the north shore, and, it being Sunday, thousands were out viewing the scene, which caused a great clamor, and made a deep impression.*

Jones had now fresh projects to annoy the enemy; designs on Hull or Newcastle, as is thought. His captains, however, refused to sustain him, and he was reluctantly obliged to abandon his plans. His object was glory; theirs appears to have been profit. It ought to be mentioned, that all the young officers sustained the commodore, and professed a readiness to follow wherever he would lead. Jones had a respect for the opinion of Capt. Cottineau, of the Pallas, and it is believed he yielded more to his persuasions than to those of all the rest of his commanders. This officer seemed to think any delay of moment would bring a superior force against them. The commodore viewed the matter more coolly, well knowing that the transmission of intelligence, and the collection of three or four vessels, was a matter that required some little time.

Between the 17th and 21st, many colliers and coasters were captured. Most of them were sunk, though one or two were released, and a sloop was ransomed by the Pallas, contrary to orders. On the latter day, the ships were off Flamborough Head, where the Pallas chased to the north-east, leaving the Richard and Vengeance in pursuit of vessels in a directly opposite quarter. Jones overtook and sunk a collier, late in the afternoon. Several craft then hove in sight, and one was chased ashore. Soon after, a brig from Holland was captured, and, at daylight, next morning, a considerable fleet was seen inshore, which kept aloof, on account of the appearance of the Bon Homme Richard. Finding it impossible to decoy them out, Jones used some artifices to delude a pilot, and two boats came alongside. The pilots were deceived, and gave Jones all the information they possessed.

* The Edinburgh Review, in an article on Cooper's History of the Navy, which has been pretty effectually answered,[116] gives its readers reason to suppose that Jones' appearance on the coast produced no uneasiness. Sir Walter Scott told the writer he well remembered the feeling excited by this event, and that it was widespread and general. As Scott was born in 1769, his recollection might be relied on. [*Cooper's note.*]

As it was now impracticable to bring the shipping out of the Humber, on account of the state of the wind and tide, and the Pallas not being in sight, the commodore turned his attention to looking for his consorts. He hauled off the land, therefore, making the best of his way back to Flamborough Head, after passing several hours in endeavoring to entice the ships out of the Humber.

In the course of the night of the 22d, two ships were seen, and chased for several hours, when, finding himself near them, Jones hove-to, about three in the morning, waiting for light. When the day returned, the strangers were found to be the Pallas and the Alliance; the latter of which had not been seen since she parted company off Cape Wrath.

After communicating with his consorts, Jones chased a brig that was lying-to to windward. About meridian, however, a large ship was observed coming round Flamborough Head, when Mr. Henry Lunt, the second lieutenant of the Richard, was thrown into one of the pilot boats, with fifteen men, and ordered to seize the brig, while the Richard made sail toward the strange ship. Soon after, a fleet of forty-one sail was seen stretching out from behind the Head, bearing N. N. E. from the Richard. The wind was light at the southward, and these vessels were a convoy from the Baltic, turning down the North Sea, towards the Straits of Dover, bound to London. This placed Jones to windward and a little in shore, if the projection of the headland be excepted.

As soon as the commodore ascertained that he was in the vicinity of this fleet, he made a signal of recall to the pilot boat, and another of a general chase to his squadron. The first was probably unseen or disregarded, for it was not obeyed: and the officer and men in the pilot boat remained out of their vessel during most of the trying scenes of that eventful day. As twenty-four officers and men had been captured, or had deserted, off Cape Clear, these sixteen increased the number of absentees to forty; if to these we add some who had been sent away in prizes, the crew of the Richard, which consisted of but three hundred and eighty, all told, the day she sailed, was now diminished to little more than three hundred souls, of whom a large proportion were the *quasi* marines, or soldiers, who had entered for the cruise.

Jones now crossed royal yards and made sail for the convoy. He had intelligence of this fleet, and knew that it was under the charge of Capt. Pearson, of the Serapis 44, who had the Countess of Scarborough 20, Capt. Piercy, in company. As the scene we are about to relate is one memorable in naval annals, it may be well to mention the force of the vessels engaged.

That of the Richard has been already given. The Pallas mounted thirty guns, of light calibre, and was perhaps more than a third heavier than the Scarborough, the vessel she subsequently engaged. The Alliance was a large thirty-two, mounting forty guns, mostly twelve pounders. She had a full, but indifferent crew of about 300 souls, when she left the Roads of Groix, of which near, if not quite, fifty were absent in prizes. Of the Vengeance, which had no part in the events of the day, it is unnecessary to speak.

On the part of the enemy, many of the convoy were armed, and, by acting in concert, they might have given a good deal of occupation to the Pallas and Vengeance, while the two men-of-war fought the Richard and Alliance. As it was, however, all of these ships sought safety in flight. The Serapis was a new vessel, that both sailed and worked well, of a class that was then a good deal used in the North Sea, Baltic, and the narrow waters generally; and which was sometimes brought into the line, in battles between the short ships that were much preferred, in that day, in all the seas mentioned. She was a 44, on two decks; having an armament below of 20 eighteens; one of 20 nines, on the upper gun-deck; and one of 10 sixes, on her quarter-deck and forecastle. This is believed to have been her real force, though Jones speaks of her, in one place, as having been pierced for 56 instead of 50 guns. The former was the usual force of what was called a fifty-gun ship, or a vessel like the Leander, which assailed the Chesapeake in 1807. Sands, the most original writer of authority on the subject of Paul Jones, or of any reasoning powers of much weight, infers from some of his calculations and information that the Serapis had 400 souls on board her at the commencement of the action which is now to be related. The English accounts state her crew to have been 320; a number that is quite sufficient for her metal and spars, and which is more in conformity with the practice of the English marine. The Indiamen, stated by Sands to have been obtained by Capt. Pearson, in Copenhagen, may have been 15 Lascars, who are known to have been on board, and to have been included in the 320 souls. It is not probable that the crews of the Richard and Serapis differed a dozen in number. The Countess of Scarborough was a hired ship in the British navy, differing in no respect from a regular man-of-war, except in the circumstance that she belonged to a private owner instead of the king. This was not unusual in that marine, the circumstance being rather in favor of the qualities of the vessel, since the admiralty, on the coast of England, would not be likely to hire any but a good ship. Her officers and people belonged to the navy, as a matter of course. There is a trifling discrepancy as to the force of the Scarborough, though the point is of no great moment, under the circumstances. Jones states that she was a ship mounting 24 guns on *one* deck, while other accounts give her armament as 22 guns in all. She probably had a crew of from 120 to 150 men.

As soon as the leading English vessels saw that strangers, and probably enemies, were to the southward, and to windward, they gave the alarm, by firing guns, letting fly their top-gallant sheets, tacking together, and making the best of their way in toward the land again. At this moment the men-of-war were astern, with a view to keep the convoy in its place; and being near the shore, the authorities of Scarborough had sent a boat off to the Serapis, to apprise her commander of the presence of Paul Jones' fleet. By these means, the two senior officers were fully aware with whom they had to contend. Capt. Pearson fired two guns, and showed the proper signals, in order to call in his leading ships, but, as is very customary with merchant vessels, the warning and orders were unattended to, until the danger was seen to be pressing. While the merchantmen were gathered in behind the Head, or ran off to leeward, the Serapis signaled the Scarborough to follow, and stood gallantly out to sea, on the starboard tack, hugging the wind.

Jones now threw out a signal to his own vessels to form the line of battle. The Alliance, which ought to have dropped in astern of the Richard, paid no attention to this order, though she approached the enemy to reconnoitre. In passing the Pallas, Capt. Landais remarked that if the larger of the enemy's ships proved to be a fifty-gun ship, all they had to do was to endeavor to escape! This was not the best possible disposition with which to commence the action. Soon after the Pallas spoke the Richard, and asked for orders. Jones directed her to lead toward the enemy, but the order was not obeyed, as will be seen by what followed.

The wind being light, several hours passed before the different evolutions mentioned could be carried into execution. As soon as Capt. Pearson found himself outside of all his convoy, and the latter out of danger, he tacked in shore, with a view to cover the merchantmen. This change of course induced Jones to ware and carry sail, with a view to cut him off from the land. By this time it was evening, and this sudden change of course, on the part of the Serapis [Richard], seems to have given rise to a distrust, on the part of Capt. Cottineau, of the Pallas, concerning the control she was under. There were so many disaffected men in the Richard, English and other Europeans, that the security of the ship appears to have been a matter of doubt among all the other vessels. When those on board the Pallas, therefore, perceived the Richard crowding sail inshore, they believed Jones was killed by his own people, and that the mutineers had run away with the ship, intending to carry her into a British port. With this impression, Capt. Cottineau hauled his wind, tacked, and laid the Pallas' head off shore. In consequence of this manœuvre, and of the Vengeance's being far astern, nothing like a line was formed on this occasion.

Jones' object was to cut his enemy off from the land. Keeping this in view, he pressed down in the Richard, regardless of his consorts, passing the Alliance lying-to, out of gun-shot, on the weather quarter of the principal English ship. It was now dark, but Jones watched his enemy with a night-glass, and perceiving that he could cut off the Serapis from getting under the guns of Scarborough Castle, he continued to approach the Englishman under a press of sail. Soon after the Pallas wore round and followed. The Vengeance had directions to order the pilot-boat back, and then to pick up the convoy; but as these last were inshore, and tolerably safe, she seems to have done little, or nothing. In the action that ensued, she took no part whatever.

It was half-past seven, or eight o'clock, when the Richard and Serapis drew near to each other. The former was to windward, both vessels being on the larboard tack. The Serapis hailed, demanding "What ship is that?" "I can't hear what you say," was returned from the Richard. "What ship is that?" repeated the Englishman—"answer immediately, or I shall be under the necessity of firing into you." The Richard now delivered her broadside, which was returned from the Serapis so promptly as to render the two discharges nearly simultaneous. In an instant, the two ships were enveloped in smoke and darkness. The Richard backed her topsails, in order to deaden her way and keep her station to windward. She then filled, and passed ahead of the Serapis, crossing her bows, becalming the Serapis partially. The latter was a short ship, and worked quick. She was, moreover, a good sailer, and Capt. Pearson keeping his luff, as soon as his canvas filled again, he came up on the weather quarter of Jones, taking the wind out of his sails; both vessels fighting the other broadsides, or using the starboard guns of the Serapis and the larboard of the Richard. It will be remembered that the Richard had six eighteens mounted in her gun-room. As the water was smooth, Jones relied greatly on the service of this battery, which, in fact, was his principal dependence with an adversary like the Serapis. Unfortunately two of these old, defective pieces burst at the first discharge, blowing up the maindeck above them, beside[s] killing and wounding many men. The alarm was so great as to destroy all confidence in these guns, which made up eight discharges in all, when their crews abandoned them. This, in addition to the actual damage done, was a most serious disadvantage. It reduced the Richard's armament at once to 32 guns, or, as some authorities say, to 34; leaving her with the metal of a 32 gun frigate, to contend with a full-manned and full-armed 44. The combat, now, was in fact between an eighteen-pounder and a twelve-pounder ship; an inequality of metal, to say nothing of that in guns, that seemed to render the chance of the Richard nearly hopeless.

Half an hour was consumed in these preliminary evolutions, the wind being light, and the vessels nearly stationary a part of the time. When the Richard first approached her adversary, it will be remembered she was quite alone, the Vengeance having been left leagues behind, the Alliance lying-to, out of gun-shot, to windward, and the Pallas not bearing up until her commander had ascertained there was no mutiny on board the commodore, by seeing him commence the action. All this time the Countess of Scarborough was coming up, and she now closed so near as to be able to assist her consort. The Americans affirm that this ship did fire at least one raking broadside at the Richard, doing her some injury. On the other hand, Capt. Piercy, her commander, states that he was afraid to engage, as the smoke and obscurity rendered it impossible for him to tell friend from enemy. It is possible that both accounts are true, Capt. Piercy meaning merely to excuse his subsequent course after having fired once or twice at the Richard. At all events, the connection of this vessel with the battle between the two principal ships must have been very trifling, as she soon edged away to a distance, and, after exchanging a distant broadside or two with the Alliance, she was brought to close action by the Pallas, which ship compelled her to strike, after a creditable resistance of an hour's duration. This vessel fully occupied the Pallas, first in engaging her, then in securing the prisoners, until after the conflict terminated.

When the Serapis came up on the weather quarter of the Richard, as has been mentioned, she kept her luff, passing slowly by, until she found herself so far ahead and to windward, as to induce Capt. Pearson to think he could fall broad off, cross the

Richard's fore foot, and rake her. This manœuvre was attempted, but finding there was not enough room to effect her purpose, the Serapis came to the wind again, as fast as she could, in order to prevent going foul. This uncertain movement brought the two ships in a line, the Serapis leading. It so far deadened the way of the English ship, that the Richard ran into her, on her weather quarter. In this situation neither vessel could fire, nor could either crew board, the collision being necessarily gentle, and nothing touching but the jib-boom of the American. In this state the two vessels remained a minute or two.

While in this singular position, the firing having entirely ceased, and it being quite dark, a voice from the Serapis demanded of the Richard, if she had struck. Jones answered promptly, "I have not yet begun to fight." As the ships had now engaged nearly, or quite, an hour, this was not very encouraging, certainly, to the Englishman's hope of victory, though he immediately set about endeavoring to secure it. The yards of the Serapis were trimmed on the larboard tack, and her sails were full as the Richard touched her; the latter ship bracing all aback, the two vessels soon parted. As soon as Jones thought he had room, he filled on the other tack, and drew ahead again. The Serapis, however, most probably with a view of passing close athwart, either the Richard's fore foot or stern, luffed into the wind, laid all aback forward, and keeping her helm down while she shivered her after sails, she attempted to break round off on her heel. At this moment, Jones seeing his enemy coming down, thought he might lay him athwart hawse, and drew ahead with that object. In the smoke and obscurity, the moon not having yet risen, each part miscalculated his distance, and just before the Serapis had begun to come up on the other tack, her jib-boom passed in over the Richard's poop, getting foul of the mizzen rigging. Jones was perfectly satisfied, by this time, that he had no chance in a cannonade, and gladly seized the opportunity of grappling. He had sent the acting master for a hawser as soon as he perceived what was likely to occur, but it not arriving in time, with his own hands he lashed the enemy's bowsprit to the Richard's mizzen-mast, by means of the Serapis' rigging that had been shot away, and which was hanging loose beneath the spar. Other fastenings soon made all secure.*

* Capt. Mackenzie, in his life of Paul Jones, has the following, in a note, p. 183, vol. 1, viz.: "As considerable difference will be observable between the account of this battle, given in Mr. Cooper's 'Naval History,' and the above, (meaning his own account of the action,) it is proper to state that Mr. Cooper has followed Mr. Dale's description of the manœuvres antecedent to the ship's being grappled; whilst in the present account more reliance has been placed on those of the two commanders who directed the evolutions. Mr. Dale was stationed on the Richard's main-deck, in a comparatively unfavorable position for observing the manœuvres. The evolution of box-hauling his ship, ascribed by Mr. Cooper to Capt. Pearson, would, under the circumstances, have been highly unseamanlike."

In answer to this, the writer has to say, that he nowhere finds any reason for thinking that either of the commanders contradicts his account; and as the late Com. Dale, in a long personal interview, minutely described all the manœuvres of the two vessels, as he has here given them, he feels bound to believe him. The argument that Mr. Dale could not see what he described, is fallacious, since an officer in command of a gun-deck, finding no enemy on either beam, would naturally look for him, and by putting his head out of a forward port, Mr. Dale might have got a better view of the Serapis than any above him. But Com. Dale states a thing *distinctly and affirmatively*, and with such a witness, the writer feels bound much more to respect his direct assertions, than any of the very extraordinary theories in history, of which Capt. Mackenzie has been the propagator. The manœuvres were probably discussed, too, between the younger officers, after the surrender of the Serapis. The writer dissents, also, to Capt Mackenzie's views of seamanship. Bringing ships round *before the wind*, in the manner described, was far more practised in 1779 than it is to-day. It was more practised with the short ships of the narrow seas than with any other. The *river vessels*, in particular, frequently did it twenty or thirty times in a single trip up the Thames, or into the Nore. The writer has seen it done himself a hundred times in those waters. Many reasons may have induced Capt. Pearson to practice what, with a Baltic and London ship, must have been a common manœuvre, especially with a master on board who was doubtless a channel pilot. He might have wished at first to preserve the weathergage; he might not have desired to take the room necessary to ware with his helm hard-a-weather, or might have attempted to tack, and failing on account of the lightness of the wind, or the want of sufficient headway, brought his ship round as described. For the writer, it is sufficient that a seaman and a moralist like Richard Dale has deliberately told him in detail, that this manœuvre was practiced, to upset the vague conjectures of a historian of the calibre of Capt. Mackenzie. A published statement from Com. Dale is given by another writer, in which that truth-loving and truth-telling old officer is made to say, "The Serapis was short round on *her heel*, and her jib-boom ran into the mizzen rigging of the Bon Homme Richard." This is giving in brief what he gave to the writer in detail. [*Cooper's note.*]

The wind being light, the movements of the two vessels were slow in proportion. It was owing to this circumstance, and to the fact that the Serapis was just beginning to gather way as she came foul, that the collision itself did little damage. As soon as Capt. Pearson perceived he was foul, he dropped an anchor under foot, in the hope that the Richard would drift clear of him. The fastenings having been already made, this result was not obtained; and the ships tending to the tide, which was now in the same direction with the wind, the latter brought the stern of the Serapis close in, alongside of the bows of the Richard. In this position the ships became so interlocked, by means of their spars, spare anchors, and other protruding objects, for the moment, as to become inseparable.

As the stern of the Serapis swung round, her lower deck ports were lowered, in order to prevent being boarded. The ships' sides touching, or at least being so close as to prevent the ports from being opened again, the guns were fired inboard, blowing away the lids. This was renewing the action, under circumstances which, in ordinary cases, would have soon brought it to a termination. Wherever a gun bore, it necessarily cleared all before it, and, in reloading, the rammers were frequently passed into a hostile port, in order to be entered into the muzzles of their proper guns. It is evident that such a conflict could be maintained only under very extraordinary circumstances.

The eighteens of the Serapis soon destroyed everything within their range, nor was it long before the main-deck guns of the Richard were, in a great measure, silenced. A considerable number of the men who had been at the eighteens of the Richard's gun-room, had remained below after their pieces were abandoned, but the heavy fire of the Serapis' lower guns soon started them up, and joining some of those who had been driven away from the twelves, they got upon the forecastle. As the Richard was a longer ship than the Serapis, this point was comparatively safe, and thence a fire of musketry was kept up on the enemy's tops and decks. These men, also, threw grenades. The tops, too, were not idle, but kept up a smart fire of muskets, and the men began to resort to grenades also.

In this stage of the action the Serapis had the cannonading nearly to herself. All her guns, with the exception of those on the quarter-deck and forecastle, appear to have been worked, while, on the part of the Richard, the fire was reduced to two nines on the quarter-deck, two or three of the twelves, and the musketry. The consequences were, that the Richard was nearly torn to pieces below, while the upper part of the Serapis was deserted, with the exception of a few officers. Capt. Pearson himself appears to have sent his people from the quarter-deck guns. An advantage of this sort, once gained, was easily maintained, rendering it virtually impossible for the losing party to recover the ground it had lost.

The moon rose about the time the ships came foul. Until this occurred, the Alliance had not been near the principal combatants. She now passed some distance to leeward, and crossed the bows of the Richard and the stern of the Serapis, firing at such a distance as rendered it impossible for her to make sure of her enemy, even if she knew which was which. As soon as her guns ceased to bear, she up helm, and ran a considerable distance farther to leeward, hovering about until the Scarborough submitted. Capt. Landais now spoke the Pallas, when Capt. Cottineau begged him to go to the assistance of the Richard, offering, at the same time, to go himself if the Alliance would take charge of his prize. All these facts appear under oath in the course of the controversy which grew out of the events of this memorable night.

Ashamed to remain idle at such a moment, and in the face of such remonstrances, Capt. Landais hauled up, under very easy canvas, however, for the two combatants, and making a couple of stretches under his topsails, he passed the bows of the Serapis and stern of the Richard, opening with *grape*, the last shot to be used under such circumstances; then keeping away a little, he certainly fired into the Richard's larboard quarter, or that most distant from the enemy. Some of the witnesses even affirm that this fire was maintained until the Alliance had actually passed the Richard's beam, on her way to leeward.

These movements of the Alliance induced Sands aptly to

term that frigate the comet of this bloody system. It is difficult to account for her evolutions, without supposed treachery, or insanity, on the part of her commander. For the latter supposition there are some grounds, his subsequent deportment inducing the government to put him out of employment, as a man at least partially deranged. Still it is difficult to suppose the officers would allow their men to fire into the Richard's quarter, as mentioned, unless they mistook the ship. On the other hand, it is affirmed by the witnesses that three lanterns were shown on the off side of the Richard, the regular signal of reconnoisance; that fifty voices called out, begging their friends to cease firing, and this, too, when so near that the remonstrances must have been heard. By direction of Jones, an officer hailed, too, and ordered Landais to lay the enemy aboard. A question was then put to ascertain whether the order was understood, and an answer was given in the affirmative.

The effect of this transit of the Alliance was very disastrous to the Richard. Her fire dismounted a gun or two on board the latter ship, extinguished several lanterns, did a good deal of mischief aloft, and induced many of the people to desert their quarters, under the impression that the English on board the Alliance had got possession of the ship, and were aiding the enemy. It is indeed, an important feature in the peculiarities of this remarkable cruise, and one that greatly enhances the merit of the man who used such discordant materials, that the two principal vessels distrusted each other's ability to look down revolt, and were distrusted by all the rest, on account of the same supposed insecurity. It may be added as one of the difficulties in explaining Capt. Landais' conduct, that the moon had now been up some time, and that it was very easy to distinguish the ships by their off sides; that of the Serapis having two yellow streaks, dotted as usual with ports, while the Richard was all black.

Not satisfied with what he had done, Capt. Landais shortly after made his re-appearance, approaching the Richard on her off side, running athwart her bows this time, and crossing the stern of her antagonist. On this occasion, it is affirmed, her fire commenced when there was no possibility of reaching the Serapis, unless it were through the Richard; and her fire, of grape especially, was particularly destructive to the men collected on the Richard's forecastle. At this spot alone, ten or twelve men appear to have been killed or wounded, at a moment when the fire of the Serapis could not possibly injure them. Among those slain, was a midshipman of the name of Caswell, who affirmed with his dying breath that he had been hit by the shot of the Alliance. After this last exploit, Capt. Landais seemed satisfied with his own efforts, and appeared no more.

While these erratic movements were in course of execution by the Alliance and her eccentric, if not insane, commander, the two ships engaged lay canopied by smoke, a scene of fierce contention, and of accumulated dangers. The alarm of fire was succeeded by reports that the Richard was sinking. To these sources of apprehension, soon followed that of the dread of a rising within. The accession of water in the hold induced the master-at-arms to release the English prisoners on board, who were more than a hundred in number. As if this were not enough, the ships began to take fire from the explosions of the guns and grenades, and the combatants were frequently called from their quarters, in order to extinguish the flames. Capt. Pearson states, that the Serapis was on fire no less than twelve times, while the ships lay grappled; and, as to the Richard, in addition to several accidents of this nature that were promptly suppressed, for the last hour she was burning the whole time, the flames having got within her ceilings.

Jones was not a little astonished to see more than a hundred English mariners rushing up from below, at a moment when a heavy ship of their country was lashed alongside, and deliberately pouring her fire into his own vessel. Such a circumstance might have proved fatal, with a man less resolute and self-possessed. Lieut. Dale had been below, in person, to ascertain the state of the hold, and it was found that several heavy shot had struck beneath the water line, and that the danger from that source was in truth serious. Profiting by the alarm that prevailed among the prisoners, the commodore set the Englishmen at work at the pumps, where they toiled with commendable zeal near an hour! Had they been so disposed, or cool, most of them might have escaped on board the Serapis.

The precise situations of the two vessels, and of the Richard in particular, are worthy of a passing remark. As for the Serapis, her injuries were far from great. She had suffered from the fire of her opponent at the commencement of the fight, it is true, but the bursting of the Richard's eighteens, and her own superior working and better sailing had given her such essential advantages as, added to her heavier fire, must have long before decided the affair in her favor, but for the circumstance of the two vessels getting foul of each other. The quiet determination of Jones not to give up, might have protracted the engagement longer than usual, but it could hardly have averted the result. The vessels were no sooner square alongside, however, than the English ship's heavy guns swept away every thing in their front. This superiority in the way of artillery could not be overcome, and continued to the close of the engagement. Under any thing like ordinary circumstances, this ascendancy must have given the victory to the English, but Jones was a man calculated by nature, and his habits of thinking, to take refuge against a defeat in extraordinary circumstances. He had succeeded in driving the enemy from above board, and was, in this stage of the action, diligently working two nine-pounders, in the hope of cutting away the Serapis' main-mast. Had he succeeded in this effort, no doubt he would have cut the lashings, and, obtaining a more favorable position on the bow or quarter of his enemy, settled the matter with his main-deck battery. Still, it required many shot, of the weight of his, to bring down so large a spar, with most of its rigging standing, and in smooth water. No one knows what would have been the result, but for the coolness and judgment of a seaman, who belonged to the main-top. As the English had been cleared out of their tops by the greater fire of the Richard's musketry, this man lay out on the main-yard, until he found himself at the sheet-block. Here he placed a bucket of grenades, and began deliberately to throw them upon the Serapis' decks, wherever he saw two or three men collected.

Finding no one on the quarter-deck, or forecastle, to annoy, he tossed his grenades into the hatches, where they produced considerable confusion and injury. At length, he succeeded in getting one or two down upon the lower gun-deck, where one of them set fire to some loose powder. It appears that the powder boys had laid a row of cartridges on the off side of this deck, in readiness for use, no shot entering from the Richard to molest. To this act of gross negligence, Capt. Pearson probably owed the loss of his ship. The lower gun-deck of the Serapis had been perfectly safe from all annoyance, from the moment the ships got foul, no gun of the Richard's bearing on it, while the deck above protected it effectually from musketry. To this security, it is probable, the dire catastrophe which succeeded was owing. The powder that ignited set fire to all these uncovered cartridges, and the explosion extended from the main-mast aft. It silenced every gun in that part of the ship, and indeed nearly stripped them of their crews. More than twenty men were killed outright, leaving on many of them nothing but the waistbands of their duck trowsers, and the collars and wristbands of their shirts. Quite sixty of the Serapis' people must have been placed *hors de combat*, in a moment, by this fell assault. The reader may imagine its effects on a lower gun-deck, choked with smoke, with the ship on fire, amid the shrieks and groans of the living sufferers.

It is now known that the English would have struck, soon after this accident occurred, had not the master of the London Letter of Marque, captured off Cape Wrath, passed out of a port of the Richard into one of the Serapis' and announced that the American ship was in a still worse situation, having actually released her prisoners, as she was on the point of sinking. About this time, too, another incident occurred, that aided in sustaining the hopes of Capt. Pearson. Two or three of the warrant officers of the Richard, when they found the ship in danger of sinking, had looked in vain for Jones, and Mr. Dale being below at that moment, examining into the state of the pumps, they determined that it was their duty to strike the colors, in order to save the lives of the survivors. Luckily, the ensign had been shot away, and the gunner, who had run up on the poop to lower it, called out for quarter. Hearing this, Capt. Pearson demanded if the Richard had struck. Jones answered for himself in the negative, but in such a way that he was not either heard or understood, and the English actually mustered a party of boarders to take possession of their prize. As this was giving Jones' men a better chance with their muskets, the English were soon driven below again, with loss. Some of the latter, however, appeared on the sides of the Richard.

These reverses turned the tide of battle in favor of the Americans. The latter got a gun or two more at work, and, while the fire of their adversaries was sensibly diminishing, their own began to increase. The spirit of the Englishman drooped, and he finally hauled down his colors with his own hands, after the ships had been lashed together nearly, if not quite, two hours and a half. The main-yard of the Serapis was hanging a-cock-bill, the brace being shot away, and the brace pendant within reach. Lieut. Dale seized the latter and swung himself over upon the quarter-deck of the Serapis. Here he found Capt. Pearson quite alone, and received his submission. At this instant, the first lieutenant of the English ship came up from below, and inquired if the Richard had struck, her fire having now entirely ceased. Mr. Dale explained to this officer how the case stood, when, finding his own commander confirmed it, the lieutenant offered to go below, and to stop the guns that were still at work in the Serapis. Mr. Dale objected, however, and these two officers were immediately passed over to the quarter-deck of the Richard. A party of officers and men had followed Mr. Dale from his own ship, and one of them, a Mr. Mayrant, of South Carolina, one of the Richard's midshipmen, was actually run through the thigh by a boarding spike; the blow coming from a party of boarders stationed on the main-deck. This was the last blood spilt on the occasion, the firing being stopped immediately afterward.

Thus ended the renowned conflict between the Serapis and the Bon Homme Richard; one of the most remarkable of naval annals, in some of its features, though far from being as comparatively bloody, or as well fought in others, as many that may be cited.

· · · · · · · · · · · · ·

There can be no question that Paul Jones was a great man. By this we mean far more than an enterprising and dashing seaman. The success which attended exploits effected by very insufficient means, forms the least portion of his claims to the character. His mind aimed at high objects, and kept an even pace with his elevated views. We have only to fancy such a man at the head of a force like that with which Nelson achieved the victory of the Nile—twelve as perfect and well commanded two-decked ships as probably ever sailed in company—in order to get some idea of what he would have done with them, having a peerage or Westminster Abbey in the perspective. No sea captain, of whom the world possesses any well authenticated account, ever attempted projects as bold as those of Jones, or which discovered more of the distinctive qualities of a great mind, if the character of his enemy be kept in view, as well as his own limited and imperfect means. The battle between the Serapis and the Richard had some extraordinary peculiarities, beyond a question, and yet, as a victory, it has been often surpassed. The peculiarities belong strictly to Jones; but we think his offering battle to the Drake, alone in his sloop, in the centre of the Irish Channel, with enemies before, behind, and on each side of him, an act of higher moral courage than the attack on the Serapis. Landais' extraordinary conduct could not have been foreseen, and it was only when Jones found himself reduced to an emergency in this last affair, that he came out in his character of indomitable resolution. But all the cruises of the man indicated forethought, intrepidity, and resources. Certainly, no sea captain under the American flag, Preble excepted, has ever yet equaled him, in these particulars.

That Jones had many defects of character is certain. They arose in part from temperament, and in part from education. His constant declarations of the delicacy of his sentiments, and of the disinterestedness of his services, though true in the main, were in a taste that higher associations in youth would probably have corrected. There was, however, a loftiness of feeling about him, that disinclined him equally to meanness and vulgarity; and as for the coarseness of language and deportment that too much characterized the habits of the sea, in his time, he appears never to have yielded to them. All this was well in itself, and did him credit; but it would have been better had he spoken less frequently of his exemption from such failings, and not have alluded to them so often in his remarks on others.

[SHADOWS OF COMING EVENTS]

From *New York*[117]

New York is essentially national in interests, position, and pursuits. No one thinks of the place as belonging to a particular State, but to the United States. The revenue paid into the treasury, at this point, comes in reality, from the pockets of the whole country, and belongs to the whole country. The same is true of her sales and their proceeds. Indeed, there is very little political sympathy between the places at the mouth of the Hudson, and the interior—the vulgar prejudice of envy, and the jealousy of the power of collected capital, causing the country to distrust the town.

We are aware that the governing motive of commerce, all over the world, is the love of gain. It differs from the love of gain in its lower aspects, merely in its greater importance and its greater activity. These cause it to be more engrossing among the merchants than among the tillers of the soil: still, facts prove that this state of things has many relieving shades. The man who is accustomed to deal in large sums is usually raised above the more sordid vices of covetousness and avarice in detail. There are rich misers, certainly, but they are exceptions. We do not believe that the merchant is one tittle more mercenary than the husbandman in his motives, while he is certainly much more liberal of his gains. One deals in thousands, the other in tens and twenties. It is seldom, however, that a failing market, or a sterile season, drives the owner of the plough to desperation, and his principles, if he have any, may be preserved; while the losses or risks of an investment involving more than the merchant really owns, suspend him for a time on the tenterhooks of commercial doubt. The man thus placed must have more than a common share of integrity, to reason right when interest tempts him to do wrong.

Notwithstanding the generally fallacious character of the

governing motive of all commercial communities, there is much to mitigate its selfishness. The habit of regarding the entire country and its interests with a friendly eye, and of associating themselves with its fortunes, liberalizes its mind and wishes, and confers a catholic spirit that the capital of a mere province does not possess. Boston, for instance, is leagued with Lowell, and Lawrence, and Cambridge, and seldom acts collectively without betraying its provincial mood; while New York receives her goods and her boasted learning by large tranships-ments, without any special consciousness of the transactions. This habit of generalizing in interests encourages the catholic spirit mentioned, and will account for the nationality of the great mart of a great and much extended country. The feeling would be apt to endure through many changes, and keep alive the connection of commerce even after that of the political relations may have ceased. New York, at this moment, contributes her full share to the prosperity of London, though she owes no allegiance to St. James.

The American Union, however, has much more adhesiveness than is commonly imagined. The diversity and complexity of its interests form a network that will be found, like the web of the spider, to possess a power of resistance far exceeding its gossamer appearance—one strong enough to hold all that it was ever intended to inclose. The slave interest is now making its final effort for supremacy, and men are deceived by the throes of a departing power. The institution of domestic slavery cannot last.[118] It is opposed to the spirit of the age; and the figments of Mr. Calhoun, in affirming that the Territories belong to the States, instead of the Government of the United States; and the celebrated doctrine of the equilibrium, for which we look in vain into the Constitution for a single sound argument to sustain it, are merely the expiring efforts of a reasoning that cannot resist the common sense of the nation.

.   .   .   .

But other dangers undeniably beset the country, that have no connection with this question of Slavery. However repugnant it may be to the pride of human nature, or the favorite doc-

trines of the day, there can be little question that the greatest
sources of apprehension of future evil to the people of this
country, are to be looked for in the abuses which have their origin in the infirmities and characteristics of human nature. In a
word, the people have great cause to distrust themselves; and
the numerous and serious innovations they are making on all
sides, on not only the most venerable principles in favor with
men, but on the divine law, must cause every reflecting man to
forbode a state of things, far more serious than even that which
would arise from a separation of the States into isolated parts.

The particular form in which this imminent danger is now,
for the first time seriously since the establishment of the Government, beginning to exhibit itself, is through the combinations
of the designing to obtain a mercenary corps of voters, insignificant as to numbers, but formidable by their union, to hold the
balance of power, and to effect their purposes by practising on
the wilful, blind, wayward, and, we might almost add, fatal obstinacy of the two great political parties of the country. Here,
in our view, is the danger that the nation has most to apprehend.
The result is as plain as it is lamentable. In effect, it throws the
political power of the entire Republic into the hands of the in-
triguer, the demagogue, and the knave. Honest men are not
practised on by such combinations; but, with a fatality that
would seem to be the very sport of the demons, there they stand,
drawn up in formidable array, in nearly equal lines of open and
deriding hostility, leading those who no longer conceive it
necessary to even affect the semblance of respect to many of the
plainest and most important of the principles of social integrity
that have ever been received among men.

Any one familiar with the condition of Europe must know,
that under the pressure of society in that quarter of the world,
and toward which we are fast tending by a rapid accumulation
of numbers, the present institutions of America, exercised under
the prevalent opinions of the day, could not endure a twelvemonth. That which is now seen in France rendering real political liberty a mere stalking-horse for the furtherance of the
projects of the boldest adventurers,[119] would inevitably be seen

here; the bayonet alone would be relied on for the preservation of the nearest and dearest of human rights. There could and would be no other security for the peace of society, and that circle of power which, rising in the masses, ends in the sceptre of the single despot, would once more be made as it might be in derision of all our efforts to be free.

If the existence of nations resembled that of individuals, it would not be difficult to foretell the consequences of this state of things; but communities may be said to have no lives, and are ever to be found occupying their places, and using the means assigned to them by Providence, whether free or enslaved, prosperous or the reverse. No one can foretell the future of this great country, in consequence of the extent and number of its outlets, each a provision of Providence to put a check on revolutions and violence.

The elements of a monarchy do not exist among us; the habits of the entire country are opposed to the reception of such a form of government. Nor do we know, bad as our condition is rapidly getting to be, strong as are the tendencies to social dissolution, and to the abuses which demand force to subdue, that anything would be gained by the adoption of any substitute for the present polity of the country to be found in Europe. The abuses there are possibly worse than our own, and the only question would seem to be as to the degree of suffering and wrong to which men are compelled to submit through the infirmities of their own nature. There is one great advantage in the monarchical principle, when subdued by liberal institutions, as in the case of the government of that nation from which we are derived, which it would seem a republic cannot possess. We allude to the transmission of a nominal executive power that spares the turmoil, expense, and struggles of an election, and which answers all the purposes of the real authorities of the State in designating those who are to exercise the functions of rulers for the time being. It has often been predicted that the periodical elections of the chief magistrate of this country will, at no distant day, destroy the institutions. It would be idle to deny that the danger manifestly increases with the expedients of factions; and that there are very grave grounds for apprehending the worst consequences from this source of evil. As it now is, the working of the system has already produced a total departure from the original intention of the Government; a scheme, probably, that was radically defective when adopted, and which contained the seeds of its own ruin. Recourse to electors has become an idle form, ponderous and awkward, and in some of its features uselessly hazardous. We are in the habit of comparing the cost of government in this country with that of other nations in the Old World. Beyond a question, the Americans enjoy great advantages in this important particular, owing to their exemption from sources of expenses that weigh so heavily on those who rely for the peace of society solely on the strong hand. But confining the investigation simply to the cost of Executives it may well be questioned if we have not adopted the most expensive mode at present known among civilized nations. We entertain very little doubt that the cost of a presidential election fully equals the expenditures of the empire of Great Britain, liberal as they are known to be, for the maintenance of the dignity of its chief magistracy. Nor is this the worst of it; for while much of the civil list of a monarch is usefully employed in cherishing the arts, and in fostering industry, to say nothing of its boons to the dependent and meritorious in the shape of pensions, not a dollar of the millions that are wasted every fourth year among ourselves in the struggles of parties, can be said to be applied to a purpose that has not a greater tendency to evil than to good. The simple publication of documents, perhaps, may form some exception to these abuses; but even they are so much filled with falsehoods, fallacies, audacious historical misstatements, exaggerations, and every other abuse, naturally connected with such struggles, that we are compelled to yield them our respect and credulity with large allowances for caution and truth. Were this the place, and did our limits permit, we would gladly pursue this subject; for so completely has the hurrah of popular sway looked down everything like real freedom in the discussion of such a topic as to render the voice of dissent almost unknown to us. But our purpose is merely to show what probable effects are to flow from the abuses of the institutions on the growth of the great commercial mart of which we are writing.

We certainly think that even the looseness of law, legislation, and justice, that is so widely spreading itself over the land, is not exactly unsuited to sustain the rapid settlement of a country. No doubt men accomplish more in the earlier stages of society when perfectly unfettered, than when brought under the control of those principles and regulations which alone can render society permanently secure or happy. In this sense even the abuses to which we have slightly alluded may be tolerated, which it would be impossible to endure when the class of the needy become formidable from its numbers, and they who had no other stake in society than their naked assistance, could combine to transfer the fruits of the labors of the more industrious and successful to themselves by a simple recurrence to the use of the ballot box. We do not say that such is to be the fate of this country, for the great results that seem to be dependent on its settlement raise a hope that the hand of Providence may yet guide us in safety through the period of delusion, and the reign of political fallacies, which is fast drawing around us. Evil is so much mixed with good in all the interests of life, that it would be bold to pretend to predict consequences of such magnitude in the history of any nation. But we feel persuaded that radical changes must speedily come, either from the powerful but invisible control of that Being who effects his own purposes in his own wise ways, or the time is much nearer than is ordinarily supposed when the very existence of the political institutions of this country are to be brought to the test of the severest practical experiment. The downward tendency can hardly proceed much further with the smallest necessary security to the rights of civilized men. When a legislative body can be brought solemnly to decide by its vote that because the principles of law leave them the control of the rules for the descent of property, therefore, whenever a landlord may happen to die, his tenant shall have the privilege of converting his leasehold estate into a fee on which the debt is secured in the shape of mortgage, there is

little left in the way of security to the affluent and unrepre-
sented.[120] They must unite their means to prevent destruction;
and woe to that land which gives so plausible an excuse to the
rich and intelligent for combining their means to overturn the
liberties of a nation, as is to be found in abuses like those just
named. We very well know that the idea is prevalent among us
of the irresistible power of popular sway; but he has lived in
vain who has seen the course of events in other nations for the
last half century, and has not made the discovery that men in
political matters become the servants of money as certainly and
almost as actively as the spirits of the lamp were made to do the
bidding of Aladdin. To us, it would seem that the future of this
country holds out but three possible solutions of the tendencies
of the present time—viz. the bayonet, a return to the true principles of the original government, or the sway of money. For
the first it may be too soon; the pressure of society is scarcely
sufficient to elevate a successful soldier to the height of despotism, though the ladder has been raised more than once
against the citadel of the Constitution by adventurers of this
character, through the folly and heedless impulses of the
masses. Fifty years hence, and a condition of society will
probably exist among us that would effectually have carried
out the principle of despotic rule which is beginning to show
itself in the bud amongst us, and which is nothing more than
the shadowing out of coming events.

[FICTION AND SOCIAL CRITICISM][121]

PRECAUTION[122]

PREFACE TO THE NEW EDITION

This book originally owed its existence to an accident, and it was printed under circumstances that prevented the usual supervision of the press by the author. The consequences were many defects in plot, style, and arrangement, that were entirely owing to precipitation and inexperience; and quite as many faults, of another nature, that are to be traced solely to a bad manuscript and worse proof-reading. Perhaps no novel of our times was worse printed than the first edition of this work. More than a hundred periods were placed in the middle of sentences, and perhaps five times that number were omitted in places where they ought to have been inserted. It is scarcely necessary to add, that passages were rendered obscure, and that entire paragraphs were unintelligible.

Most of the faults just mentioned have now been corrected, though it would require more labor than would produce an entirely new work, to repair all the inherent defects that are attributable to haste and to the awkwardness of a novice in the art of composing. In this respect the work and its blemishes are probably inseparable. Still, the reader will now be better rewarded for his time, and, on the whole, the book is much more worthy of his attention.

It has been said that PRECAUTION owes its existence to fortuitous circumstances. The same causes induced its English plot, and, in a measure, the medley of characters that no doubt will appear a mistake in the conception. It can scarcely be said that the work was commenced with any view to publication; and when it was finally put into a publisher's hands, with "all its imperfections on its head," the last thought of the writer was any expectation that it would be followed by a series of similar tales from the same pen.

More than this the public will feel no interest in knowing, and less than this the author could not consent to say on presenting to the world a reprint of a book with so few claims to notice.   [1838]

THE SPY[123]

INTRODUCTION

The author has often been asked if there were any foundation in real life, for the delineation of the principal character in this book. He can give no clearer answer to the question, than by laying before his readers a simple statement of the facts connected with its original publication.

Many years since, the writer of this volume was at the residence of an illustrious man, who had been employed in various situations of high trust during the darkest days of the American revolution. The discourse turned upon the effects which great political excitement produce on character, and the purifying consequences of a love of country, when that sentiment is powerfully and generally awakened in a people. He who, from his years, his services, and his knowledge of men, was best qualified to take the lead in such a conversation, was the principal speaker. After dwelling on the marked manner in which the great struggle of the nation, during the war of 1775, had given a new and honorable direction to the thoughts and practices of multitudes whose time had formerly been engrossed by the most vulgar concerns of life, he illustrated his opinions by relating an anecdote, the truth of which he could attest as a personal witness.

The dispute between England and the United States of America, though not strictly a family quarrel, had many of the features of a civil war. The people of the latter were never properly and constitutionally subject to the people of the former, but the inhabitants of both countries owed allegiance to a common king. The Americans, as a nation, disavowed this allegiance, and the English choosing to support their sovereign in the attempt to regain his power, most of the feelings of an internal struggle were involved in the conflict. A large proportion of the emigrants from Europe, then established in the colonies, took part with the crown; and there were many districts in which their influence, united to that of the Americans who refused to lay aside their allegiance, gave a decided preponderance to the royal cause. America was then too young, and too much in need of every heart and hand, to regard these partial divisions, small as they were in actual amount, with indifference. The evil was greatly increased by the activity of the English in profiting by these internal dissensions; and it became doubly serious when it was found that attempts were made to raise various corps of provincial troops, who were to be banded with those from Europe, to reduce the young republic to subjection. Congress named an especial and a secret committee, therefore, for the express purpose of defeating this object. Of this committee Mr. ——, the narrator of the anecdote, was chairman.

In the discharge of the novel duties which now devolved on him, Mr. —— had occasion to employ an agent whose services differed but little from those of a common spy. This man, as will easily be understood, belonged to a condition in life which rendered him the least reluctant to appear in so equivocal a character. He was poor, ignorant, so far as the usual instruction was concerned; but cool, shrewd, and fearless by nature. It was his office to learn in what part of the country the agents of the crown were making their efforts to embody men, to repair to the place, enlist, appear zealous in the cause he affected to serve, and otherwise to get possession of as many of the secrets of the enemy as possible. The last he of course communicated to his employers, who took all the means in their power to counteract the plans of the English, and frequently with success.

It will readily be conceived that a service like this was attended with great personal hazard. In addition to the danger of discovery, there was the daily risk of falling into the hands of the Americans themselves, who invariably visited sins of this nature more severely on the natives of the country than on the Europeans who fell into their hands. In fact, the agent of Mr. ——

was several times arrested by the local authorities; and, in one instance, he was actually condemned by his exasperated countrymen to the gallows. Speedy and private orders to his gaoler alone saved him from an ignominious death. He was permitted to escape; and this seeming, and indeed actual, peril was of great aid in supporting his assumed character among the English. By the Americans, in his little sphere, he was denounced as a bold and inveterate Tory. In this manner he continued to serve his country in secret during the early years of the struggle, hourly environed by danger, and the constant subject of unmerited opprobrium.

In the year —— Mr. —— was named to a high and honorable employment at a European court. Before vacating his seat in Congress, he reported to that body an outline of the circumstances related, necessarily suppressing the name of his agent, and demanding an appropriation in behalf of a man who had been of so much use, at so great risk. A suitable sum was voted, and its delivery was confided to the chairman of the secret committee.

Mr. —— took the necessary means to summon his agent to a personal interview. They met in a wood, at midnight. Here Mr. —— complimented his companion on his fidelity and adroitness; explained the necessity of their communications being closed; and finally tendered the money. The other drew back, and declined receiving it. "The country has need of all its means," he said; "as for myself, I can work, or gain a livelihood in various ways." Persuasion was useless, for patriotism was uppermost in the heart of this remarkable individual; and Mr. —— departed, bearing with him the gold he had brought, and a deep respect for the man who had so long hazarded his life, unrequited, for the cause they served in common.

The writer is under an impression that, at a later day, the agent of Mr. —— consented to receive a remuneration for what he had done; but it was not until his country was entirely in a condition to bestow it.

It is scarcely necessary to add, that an anecdote like this, simply but forcibly told by one of its principal actors, made a deep impression on all who heard it. Many years later, circumstances, which it is unnecessary to relate, and of an entirely adventitious nature, induced the writer to publish a novel, which proved to be, what he little foresaw at the time, the first of a tolerably long series. The same adventitious causes which gave birth to the book, determined its scene and its general character. The former was laid in a foreign country; and the latter embraced a crude effort to describe foreign manners. When this tale was published, it became matter of reproach among the author's friends, that he, an American in heart as in birth, should give to the world a work which aided perhaps, in some slight degree, to feed the imaginations of the young and unpractised among his own countrymen by pictures drawn from a state of society so different from that to which he belonged. The writer, while he knew how much of what he had done was purely accidental, felt the reproach to be one that, in a measure, was just. As the only atonement in his power, he determined to inflict a second book, whose subject should admit of no cavil, not only on the world, but on himself. He chose patriotism for his theme; and to those who read this introduction and the book itself, it is scarcely necessary to add, that he took the hero of the anecdote just related as the best illustration of his subject.

Since the original publication of "The Spy," there have appeared several accounts of different persons who are supposed to have been in the author's mind while writing the book. As Mr. —— did not mention the name of his agent, the writer never knew any more of his identity with this or that individual, than has been here explained. Both Washington and Sir Henry Clinton had an unusual number of secret emissaries; in a war that partook so much of a domestic character, and in which the contending parties were people of the same blood and language, it could scarcely be otherwise.

The style of the book has been revised by the author in this edition. In this respect, he has endeavored to make it more worthy of the favor with which it has been received; though he is compelled to admit there are faults so interwoven with the structure of the tale that, as in the case of a decayed edifice, it would cost perhaps less to reconstruct than to repair. Five-and-twenty years have been as ages with most things connected with America. Among other advances, that of her literature has not been the least. So little was expected from the publication of an original work of this description, at the time it was written, that the first volume of "The Spy" was actually printed several months, before the author felt a sufficient inducement to write a line of the second. The efforts expended on a hopeless task are rarely worthy of him who makes them, however low it may be necessary to rate the standard of his general merit.

One other anecdote connected with the history of this book, may give the reader some idea of the hopes of an American author, in the first quarter of the present century. As the second volume was slowly printing, from manuscript that was barely dry when it went into the compositor's hands, the publisher intimated that the work might grow to a length that would consume the profits. To set his mind at rest, the last chapter was actually written, printed and paged, several weeks before the chapters which precede it were even thought of. This circumstance, while it cannot excuse, may serve to explain the manner in which the actors are hurried off the scene.

A great change has come over the country since this book was originally written. The nation is passing from the gristle into the bone, and the common mind is beginning to keep even pace with the growth of the body politic. The march from Vera Cruz to Mexico was made under the orders of that gallant soldier who, a quarter of a century before, was mentioned with honor, in the last chapter of this very book. Glorious as was that march, and brilliant as were its results in a military point of view, a stride was then made by the nation, in a moral sense, that has hastened it by an age, in its progress toward real independence and high political influence. The guns that filled the valley of the Aztecs with their thunder, have been heard in echoes on the other side of the Atlantic, producing equally hope or apprehension.

There is now no enemy to fear, but the one that resides within. By accustoming ourselves to regard even the people as erring beings, and by using the restraints that wisdom has adduced from experience, there is much reason to hope that the same Providence which has so well aided us in our infancy, may continue to smile on our manhood.

Cooperstown, March 29, 1849.

THE PIONEERS [124]

INTRODUCTION

As this work professes, in its titlepage, to be a descriptive tale, they who will take the trouble to read it may be glad to know how much of its contents is literal fact, and how much is intended to represent a general picture. The Author is very sensible that, had he confined himself to the latter, always the most effective, as it is the most valuable, mode of conveying knowledge of this nature, he would have made a far better book. But in commencing to describe scenes, and perhaps he may add characters, that were so familiar to his own youth, there was a constant temptation to delineate that which he had known, rather than that which he might have imagined. This rigid adhesion to truth, an indispensable requisite in history and travels, destroys the charm of fiction; for all that is necessary to be conveyed to the mind by the latter had better be done by delineations of principles, and of characters in their classes, than by a too fastidious attention to originals.

New York having but one county of Otsego, and the Susquehanna but one proper source, there can be no mistake as to the site of the tale. The history of this district of country, so far as it is connected with civilized men, is soon told.

Otsego, in common with most of the interior of the province of New York, was included in the county of Albany, previously to the war of the separation. It then became, in a subsequent division of territory, a part of Montgomery; and, finally, having obtained a sufficient population of its own, it was set apart as a county by itself, shortly after the peace of 1783. It lies among those low spurs of the Alleghanies which cover the midland counties of New York; and it is little east of a meridional line drawn through the center of the state. As the waters of New York either flow southerly into the Atlantic or northerly into Ontario, and its outlet, Otsego Lake, being the source of the Susquehanna, is, of necessity, among its highest lands. The face of the country, the climate as it was found by the whites, and the manners of the settlers, are described with a minuteness for which the Author has no other apology than the force of his own recollections.

Otsego is said to be a word compounded of Ot, a place of meeting, and Sego, or Sago, the ordinary term of salutation used by the Indians of this region. There is a tradition which says, that the neighboring tribes were accustomed to meet on the banks of the lake to make their treaties, and otherwise to strengthen their alliances, and which refers the name to this practice. As the Indian agent of New York had a log dwelling at the foot of the lake, however, it is not impossible that the appellation grew out of the meetings that were held at his council fires; the war drove off the agent, in common with the other officers of the crown; and his rude dwelling was soon abandoned. The Author remembers it a few years later, reduced to the humble office of a smoke-house.

In 1779, an expedition was sent against the hostile Indians, who dwelt about a hundred miles west of Otsego, on the banks of the Cayuga. The whole country was then a wilderness, and it was necessary to transport the baggage of the troops by means of the rivers—a devious but practicable route. One brigade ascended the Mohawk, until it reached the point nearest to the sources of the Susquehanna; whence it cut a lane through the forest to the head of the Otsego. The boats and baggage were carried over this "portage," and the troops proceeded to the other extremity of the lake, where they disembarked, and encamped. The Susquehanna, a narrow though rapid stream at its source, was much filled with "flood wood," or fallen trees; and the troops adopted a novel expedient to facilitate their passage. The Otsego is about nine miles in length, varying in breadth from half a mile to a mile and a half. The water is of great depth, limpid, and supplied from a thousand springs. At its foot, the banks are rather less than thirty feet high; the remainder of its margin being in mountains, intervals, and points. The outlet, or the Susquehanna, flows through a gorge in the low banks just mentioned which may have a width of two hundred feet. This gorge was dammed, and the waters of the lake collected; the Susquehanna was converted into a rill. When all was ready, the troops embarked, the dam was knocked away, the Otsego poured out its torrent, and the boats went merrily down with the current.

General James Clinton, the brother of George Clinton, then governor of New York, and the father of De Witt Clinton, who died governor of the same state in 1827, commanded the brigade employed on this duty. During the stay of the troops at the foot of the Otsego a soldier was shot for desertion. The grave of this unfortunate man was the first place of human interment that the Author ever beheld, as the smoke-house was the first ruin! The swivel alluded to in this work was buried and abandoned by the troops on this occasion; and it was subsequently found in digging the cellars of the Author's paternal residence.

Soon after the close of the war, Washington, accompanied by many distinguished men, visited the scene of this tale, it is said, with a view to examine the facilities for opening a communication by water with other points of the country. He stayed but a few hours.

In 1785, the Author's father, who had an interest in extensive tracts of land in this wilderness, arrived with a party of surveyors. The manner in which the scene met his eye is described by Judge Temple. At the commencement of the following year the settlement began; and from that time to this the country has continued to flourish. It is a singular feature in American life, that, at the beginning of this century, when the proprietor of the estate had occasion for settlers on a new settlement, and in a remote county, he was enabled to draw them from among the increase of the former colony.

Although the settlement of this part of Otsego a little preceded the birth of the Author, it was not sufficiently advanced to render it desirable that an event, so important to himself, should take place in the wilderness. Perhaps his mother had a reasonable distrust of the practice of Dr. Todd, who must then have been in the novitiate of his experimental acquirements. Be that as it may, the Author was brought an infant into this valley, and all his first impressions were here obtained. He has inhabited it ever since, at intervals; and he thinks he can answer for the faithfulness of the picture he has drawn.

Otsego has now become one of the most populous districts of New York. It sends forth its emigrants like any other old region; and it is pregnant with industry and enterprise. Its manufactures are prosperous; and it is worthy of remark, that one of the most ingenious machines known in European art is derived from the keen ingenuity which is exercised in this remote region.

In order to prevent mistake, it may be well to say that the incidents of this tale are purely a fiction. The literal facts are chiefly connected with the natural and artificial objects, and the customs of the inhabitants. Thus the academy, and court-house, and jail, and inn, and most similar things, are tolerably exact. They have all, long since, given place to other buildings of a more pretending character. There is also some liberty taken with the truth in the description of the principal dwelling: the real building had no "firstly" and "lastly." It was of bricks, and not of stone; and its roof exhibited none of the peculiar beauties of the "composite order." It was erected in an age too primitive for that ambitious school of architecture. But the Author indulged his recollections freely when he had fairly entered the door. Here all is literal, even to the severed arm of Wolfe, and the urn which held the ashes of Queen Dido.*

The Author has elsewhere said that the character of Leather-Stocking is a creation, rendered probable by such auxiliaries as

---

*Though forests still crown the mountains of Otsego, the bear, the wolf, and the panther are nearly strangers to them. Even the innocent deer is rarely seen bounding beneath their arches; for the rifle, and the activity of the settlers, have driven them to other haunts. To this change (which, in some particulars, is melancholy to one who knew the country in its infancy) it may be added, that the Otsego is beginning to be a niggard in its treasures. [*Cooper's note.*]

were necessary to produce that effect. Had he drawn still more upon fancy, the lovers of fiction would not have so much cause for their objections to his work. Still the picture would not have been in the least true, without some substitutes for most of the other personages. The great proprietor resident on his lands, and giving his name to, instead of receiving it from his estates, as in Europe, is common over the whole of New York. The physician, with his theory, rather obtained than corrected by experiments on the human constitution; the pious, self-denying, laborious, and ill-paid missionary; the half-educated, litigious, envious, and disreputable lawyer, with his counterpoise, a brother of the profession, of better origin and of better character; the shiftless, bargaining, discontented seller of his "betterments;" the plausible carpenter, and most of the others, are more familiar to all who have ever dwelt in a new country.

It may be well to say here, a little more explicitly, that there was no intention to describe with particular accuracy any real characters in this book. It has been often said, and in published statements, that the heroine of this book was drawn after a sister of the writer, who was killed by a fall from a horse now near half a century since. So ingenious is conjecture, that a personal resemblance has been discovered between the fictitious character and the deceased relative! It is scarcely possible to describe two females of the same class in life, who would be less alike, personally, than Elizabeth Temple and the sister of the Author who met with the deplorable fate mentioned. In a word, they were as unlike in this respect, as in history, character, and fortunes.

Circumstances rendered this sister singularly dear to the author. After a lapse of half a century, he is writing this paragraph with a pain that would induce him to cancel it, were it not still more painful to have it believed that one whom he regarded with a reverence that surpassed the love of a brother, was converted by him into the heroine of a work of fiction.

From circumstances which, after this introduction, will be obvious to all, the Author has had more pleasure in writing "The Pioneers" than the book will, probably, ever give any of its readers. He is quite aware of its numerous faults, some of which he had endeavored to repair in this edition; but as he has —in intention, at least—done his full share in amusing the world, he trusts to its good nature for overlooking this attempt to please himself.   [1850]

THE PILOT [125]

From the PREFACE

It is probable a true history of human events would show that a far larger proportion of our acts are the results of sudden impulses and accident, than of that reason of which we so much boast. However true, or false, this opinion may be in more important matters, it is certainly and strictly correct as relates to the conception and execution of this book.

The Pilot was published in 1823. This was not long after the appearance of THE PIRATE, a work which it is hardly necessary to remind the reader, has a direct connection with the sea. In a conversation with a friend, a man of polished taste and extensive reading, the authorship of the Scottish novels came under discussion. The claims of Sir Walter were a little distrusted, on account of the peculiar and minute information that the romances were then very generally thought to display. The Pirate was cited as a very marked instance of this universal knowledge, and it was wondered where a man of Scott's habits and associations could have become so familiar with the sea. The writer had frequently observed that there was much looseness in this universal knowledge, and that the secret of its success was to be traced to the power of creating that *vraisemblance*, which is so remarkably exhibited in those world-renowned fictions, rather than to any very accurate information on the part of their author. It would have been hypercritical to object to the Pirate, that it was not strictly nautical, or true in its details; but, when the reverse was urged as a proof of what, considering the character of other portions of the work, would have been most extraordinary attainments, it was a sort of provocation to dispute the seamanship of the Pirate, a quality to which the book has certainly very little just pretension. The result of this conversation was a sudden determination to produce a work which, if it had no other merit, might present truer pictures of the ocean and ships than any that are to be found in the Pirate. To this unpremeditated decision, purely an impulse, is not only the Pilot due, but a tolerably numerous school of nautical romances that have succeeded it.

The author had many misgivings concerning the success of the undertaking, after he had made some progress in the work; the opinions of his different friends being any thing but encouraging. One would declare that the sea could not be made interesting; that it was tame, monotonous, and without any other movement than unpleasant storms, and that, for his part, the less he got of it the better. The women very generally protested that such a book would have the odor of bilgewater, and that it would give them the *maladie de mer*. Not a single individual among all those who discussed the merits of the project, within the range of the author's knowledge, either spoke, or looked, encouragingly. It is probable that all these persons anticipated a signal failure.

So very discouraging did these ominous opinions get to be, that the writer was, once or twice, tempted to throw his manuscript aside, and turn to something new. A favorable opinion, however, coming from a very unexpected quarter, put a new face on the matter, and raised new hopes. Among the intimate friends of the writer, was an Englishman, who possessed most of the peculiar qualities of the educated of his country. He was learned even, had a taste that was so just as always to command respect, but was prejudiced, and particularly so in all that related to this country and its literature. He could never be persuaded to admire Bryant's Water-Fowl, and this mainly because if it were accepted as good poetry, it must be placed at once amongst the finest fugitive pieces of the language. Of the Thanatopsis he thought better, though inclined to suspect it of being a plagiarism. To the tender mercies of this one-sided critic, who had never affected to compliment the previous works of the author, the sheets of a volume of the Pilot were committed, with scarce an expectation of his liking them. The reverse proved to be the case;—he expressed himself highly gratified, and predicted a success for the book which it probably never attained.

Thus encouraged, one more experiment was made, a seaman being selected for the critic. A kinsman, a namesake, and an old messmate of the author, one now in command on a foreign station, was chosen, and a considerable portion of the first volume was read to him. There is no wish to conceal the satisfaction with which the effect on this listener was observed. He treated the whole matter as fact, and his criticisms were strictly professional, and perfectly just. But the interest he betrayed could not be mistaken. It gave a perfect and most gratifying assurance that the work would be more likely to find favor with nautical men, than with any other class of readers.

The Pilot could scarcely be a favorite with females. The story has little interest for them, nor was it much heeded by the author of the book, in the progress of his labors. His aim was to illustrate vessels and the ocean, rather than to draw any pictures of sentiment and love. In this last respect, the book has small claims on the reader's attention, though it is hoped that the story has sufficient interest to relieve the more strictly nautical features of the work.

It would be affectation to deny that the Pilot met with a most unlooked-for success. The novelty of the design probably contributed a large share of this result. Sea-tales came into vogue, as a consequence; and, as every practical part of knowledge has its uses, something has been gained by letting the landsman into the secrets of the seaman's manner of life. Perhaps, in some small degree, an interest has been awakened in behalf of a very numerous, and what has hitherto been a sort of proscribed class of men, that may directly tend to a melioration of their condition.   [1831]

LIONEL LINCOLN [126]

PREFACE

The manner in which the author became possessed of the private incidents, the characters, and the descriptions contained in these tales, will, most probably, ever remain a secret between himself and his publisher. That the leading events are true, he presumes it is unnecessary to assert; for should inherent testimony, to prove that important point, be wanting, he is conscious that no anonymous declaration can establish its credibility.

But while he shrinks from directly yielding his authorities, the author has no hesitation in furnishing all the negative testimony in his power.

In the first place, then, he solemnly declares that no unknown man, or woman, has ever died in his vicinity, of whose effects he has become the possessor, by either fair means or foul. No dark-looking stranger, of a morbid temperament, and of inflexible silence, has ever transmitted to him a single page of illegible manuscript. Nor has any landlord furnished him with materials to be worked up into a book, in order that the profits might go to discharge the arrearages of a certain consumptive lodger, who made his exit so unceremoniously as to leave the last item in his account, his funeral charges.

He is indebted to no garrulous tale-teller for beguiling the long winter evenings; in ghosts he has no faith; he never had a vision in his life; and he sleeps too soundly to dream.

He is constrained to add, that in no "puff," "squib," "notice," "article," or "review," whether in daily, weekly, monthly, or quarterly publication, has he been able to find a single hint that his humble powers could improve. No one regrets this fatality more than himself; for these writers generally bring a weight of imagination to their several tasks, that, properly improved, might secure the immortality of any book, by rendering it unintelligible.

He boldly asserts, that he has derived no information from any of the learned societies—and without fear of contradiction;

for why should one so obscure be the exclusive object of their favors!

Notwithstanding he occasionally is seen in that erudite and abstemious association, the "Bread-and-Cheese Lunch,"[127] where he is elbowed by lawyers, doctors, jurists, poets, painters, editors, congressmen, and authors of every shade and qualification, whether metaphysical, scientific, or imaginative, he avers that he esteems the lore which is there culled, as far too sacred to be used in any work less dignified than actual history.

Of the colleges it is necessary to speak with reverence; though truth possesses claims even superior to gratitude. He shall dispose of them by simply saying, that they are entirely innocent of all his blunders; the little they bestowed having long since been forgotten.

He has stolen no images from the deep, natural poetry of Bryant; no pungency from the wit of Halleck; no felicity of expression from the richness of Percival; no satire from the caustic pen of Paulding; no periods nor humor from Irving; nor any high finish from the attainments exhibited by Verplanck.

At the "soirées" and "coteries des bas bleus" he did think he had obtained a prize, in the dandies of literature who haunt them. But experience and analysis detected his error; as they proved these worthies unfit for any better purpose than that which their own instinct had already dictated.

He has made no impious attempt to rob Joe Miller of his jokes; the sentimentalists of their pathos; or the newspaper Homers of their lofty inspirations.

His presumption has not even imagined the vivacity of the Eastern States; he has not analyzed the homogeneous character of the Middle; and he has left the South in the undisturbed possession of all their saturnine wit.

In short, he has pilfered from no black-letter book, or sixpenny pamphlet; his grandmother unnaturally refused her assistance to his labors; and, to speak affirmatively, for once, he wishes to live in peace, and hopes to die in the fear of God.

[1824]

THE WATER-WITCH [128]

PREFACE

It was a bold attempt to lay the scene of a work like this, on the coast of America. We have had our Buccaneers on the water, and our Witches on the land, but we believe this is the first occasion on which the rule has been reversed. After an experience that has now lasted more than twenty years, the result has shown that the public prefer the original order of things. In other words, the book has proved a comparative failure.

The facts of this country are all so recent, and so familiar, that every innovation on them, by means of the imagination, is coldly received, if it be not absolutely frowned upon. Perhaps it would have been safer to have written a work of this character without a reference to any particular locality. The few local allusions that are introduced, are not essential to the plot, and might have been dispensed with without lessening the interest of the tale.

Nevertheless, this is probably the most imaginative book ever written by the author. Its fault is in blending too much of the real with the purely ideal. Halfway measures will not do in matters of this sort; and it is always safer to preserve the identity of a book by a fixed and determinate character, than to make the effort to steer between the true and the false.

Several liberties have been taken with the usages of the colony, with a view to give zest to the descriptions. If the Dutch of this country ever resorted to the common practice of Holland, in giving such names as the "Lust in Rust" to their villas, it has not only passed out of sight, but out of mind. In the other country, as one moves along the canals, he sees names of this character, painted on different objects, every mile he advances, and admires the contentment which is satisfied with a summer-house, a pipe, a canal, a meadow that is almost under water, and, indeed, with a country that is what seamen term "awash." But nothing of this sort was ever seen here. The fine natural scenery forbade it; and a villa on the banks of the Hudson was a residence that possessed in itself advantages to set at naught such small contrivances of luxury.

Some persons may object to the manner in which we have sketched the conduct and character of Cornbury. We believe, however, that the truth is not exceeded in any thing said of this individual, who would seem to have had neither dignity, self-respect, nor principles. The fact that he remained in this country a prisoner for debt, is historical, his creditors most probably hoping to extort from Anne further concessions in behalf of her worthless relative.

As for the Patroon of Kinderhook, the genus seems about to expire among us. Not only are we to have no more patroons, but the decree has gone forth from the virtuous and infallible voters that there are to be no more estates.

"All the realm shall be in common, and in Cheapside shall my palfrey go to grass."

The collected wisdom of the state has decided that it is true policy to prevent the affluent from investing their money in land! The curse of mediocrity weighs upon us, and its blunders can be repaired only through the hard lessons of experience.

This book was written in Italy, and first printed (in English) in Germany. To the last circumstance, is probably owing the great number of typographical errors that are to be found in it. The American compositor, however, quite likely conceiving that he had a right to correct the blunders of a foreigner, has taken the law into his own hands, and exercised a sovereign power over our labors. That our good old-fashioned mode of spelling should receive the modern improvements, was, perhaps, unavoidable; but surely, we never spelt "coamings" (of a hatch), "combings;" "rullock," "oar-lock," or "row-lock;" or made many other similar, "long-shore" blunders that are to be found in the original editions of this book.

Care has been had to do ourselves justice in these particulars, and we think that the book is more improved, in all these respects, in the present edition than any other work that has passed through our hands.   [1834]

THE BRAVO [129]

PREFACE

It is to be regretted the world does not discriminate more justly in its use of political terms. Governments are usually called either monarchies or republics. The former class embraces equally those institutions in which the sovereign is worshipped as a god, and those in which he performs the humble office of a manikin. In the latter we find aristocracies and democracies blended in the same generic appellation. The consequence of a generalization so wide is an utter confusion on the subject of the polity of states.

The author has endeavored to give his countrymen, in this book, a picture of the social system of one of the *soi-disant* republics of the other hemisphere. There has been no attempt to portray historical characters, only too fictitious in their graver dress, but simply to set forth the familiar operations of Venetian policy. For the justification of his likeness, after allowing for the defects of execution, he refers to the well-known work of M. Daru.

A history of the progress of political liberty, written purely in the interests of humanity, is still a desideratum in literature. In nations which have made a false commencement, it would be found that the citizen, or rather the subject, has extorted immunity after immunity, as his growing intelligence and importance have both instructed and required him to defend those particular rights which were necessary to his well-being. A certain accumulation of these immunities constitutes, with a solitary and recent exception in Switzerland, the essence of European liberty, even at this hour. It is scarcely necessary to tell the reader, that this freedom, be it more or less, depends on a principle entirely different from our own. Here the immunities do not proceed from, but they are granted to, the government, being, in other words, concessions of natural rights made by the people of the state, for the benefits of social protection. So long as this vital difference exists between ourselves and other

nations, it will be vain to think of finding analogies in their institutions. It is true that, in an age like this, public opinion is itself
a charter, and that the most despotic government which exists
within the pale of Christendom, must, in some degree, respect
its influence. The mildest and justest governments in Europe
are, at this moment, theoretically despotisms. The characters of
both prince and people enter largely into the consideration of so
extraordinary results; and it should never be forgotten that,
though the character of the latter be sufficiently secure, that of
the former is liable to change. But, admitting every benefit
which possibly can flow from a just administration, with wise
and humane princes, a government which is not properly based
on the people, possesses an unavoidable and oppressive evil of
the first magnitude, in the necessity of supporting itself by
physical force and onerous impositions, against the natural
action of the majority.

Were we to characterize a republic, we should say it was a
state in which power, both theoretically and practically, is derived from the nation, with a constant responsibility of the
agents of the public to the people—a responsibility that is neither
to be evaded nor denied. That such a system is better on a large
than on a small scale, though contrary to brilliant theories
which have been written to uphold different institutions, must
be evident on the smallest reflection, since the danger of all popular governments is from popular mistakes; and a people of
diversified interests and extended territorial possessions, are
much less likely to be the subjects of sinister passions than the
inhabitants of a single town or county. If to this definition we
should add, as an infallible test of the genus, that a true republic
is a government of which all others are jealous and vituperative,
on the instinct of self-preservation, we believe there would be
no mistaking the class. How far Venice would have been obnoxious to this proof, the reader is left to judge for himself.

[1831]

[THE BRAVO]

From *A Letter to His Countrymen*[130]

The work in question is called the Bravo. Its outline was imagined during a short residence at Venice, several months previously to the occurrence of the late French revolution. I had had abundant occasion to observe that the great political contest of the age was not, as is usually pretended, between the two antagonist principles of monarchy and democracy, but in reality between those who, under the shallow pretence of limiting power to the *élite* of society, were contending for exclusive advantages at the expense of the mass of their fellow-creatures. The monarchical principle, except as it is fraudulently maintained as a cover to the designs of the aristocrats, its greatest enemies, is virtually extinct in christendom; having been supplanted by the combinations of those who affect to uphold it with a view to their own protection. Nicholas may still send a prince to the mines, but even Nicholas keeps not only his crown but his head, at the pleasure of the body of his aristocracy. This result is inevitable in an age when the nobles, no longer shut up in their holds and occupied in warring against each other, meet amicably together, and bring the weight of their united intelligence and common interests to bear upon the authority of the despot. The exceptions to such consequences arise only from brilliant and long continued military successes, great ignorance in the nobles themselves, or when the democratical principle has attained the ascendancy. With these views of what was enacting around me in Europe, and with the painful conviction that many of my own countrymen were influenced by the fallacy that nations could be governed by an irresponsible minority, without involving a train of nearly intolerable abuses, I determined to attempt a series of tales, in which American opinion should be brought to bear on European facts. With this design the Bravo was written, Venice being its scene, and her polity its subject.

I had it in view to exhibit the action of a narrow and exclusive system, by a simple and natural exposure of its influence on the familiar interests of life. The object was not to be attained by an essay, or a commentary, but by one of those popular pictures which find their way into every library; and which, whilst they have attractions for the feeblest intellects, are not often rejected by the strongest. The nature of the work limited the writer as to time and place, both of which, with their proper accessories, were to be so far respected as to preserve a verisimilitude to received facts, in order that the illusion of the tale should not be destroyed. The moral was to be inferred from the events, and it was to be enforced by the common sympathies of our nature. With these means, and under these limitations, then, the object was to lay bare the wrongs that are endured by the weak, when power is the exclusive property of the strong; the tendency of all exclusion to heartlessness; the irresponsible and ruthless movement of an aristocracy; the manner in which the selfish and wicked profit by its facilities, and in which even the good become the passive instruments of its soulless power. In short, I had undertaken to give the reader some idea of the action of a government, which, to use the language of the book itself, had neither "the high personal responsibility that sometimes tempers despotism by the qualities of the chief, nor the human impulses of a popular rule."

In effecting such an object, and with the materials named, the government of Venice, strictly speaking, became the hero of the tale. Still it was necessary to have human agents. The required number were imagined, care being had to respect the customs and peculiarities of the age, and of the particular locality of the subject. Little need be said of the mere machinery of such a plan, as the offence, if offence there be, must exist in the main design. One of those ruthless state maxims which have been exposed by Comte Daru, in his history of Venice, furnished the leading idea of the minor plot, or the narrative. According to this maxim, the state was directed to use any fit subject, by playing on his natural affections, and by causing him to act as a spy, assassin, or other desperate agent of the government, under a promise of extending favors to some near relative who might happen to be within the grasp of the law. As the main object of the work was to show the manner in which institutions that are professedly created to prevent violence and wrongs, become themselves, when perverted from their legitimate destination, the fearful instruments of injustice, a better illustration could not have been wished, than was furnished by the application of this rule. A pious son assumes the character of a Bravo, in the hope of obtaining the liberation of a father who had been falsely accused; and whilst the former is blasting his own character and hopes, under the delusion, and the latter is permitted to waste away his life in prison, forgotten, or only remembered as a means of working on the sensibilities of his child, the state itself, through agents whose feelings have become blunted by practice, is seen, forgetful of its solemn duties, intent alone on perpetuating its schemes of self-protection. This idea was enlarged upon in different ways. An honest fisherman is represented as struggling for the release of a grandson, who had been impressed for the galleys, while the dissolute descendant of one of the inquisitors, works his evil under favor of his rank. A noble, who claims an inheritance; an heiress; watermen; females of low condition, and servants, are shown as contributing in various ways to the policy of the soulless state. On every side there exist corruption and a ruthless action. That some of the faces of this picture were peculiar to the Venitian polity, and to an age different from our own, is true; this much was necessary to the illusion of the tale; but it was believed that there remained enough of that which is eternal, to supply the moral. [1834]

THE HEADSMAN[131]

INTRODUCTION

Early in October, 1832, a travelling carriage stopped on the summit of that long descent where the road pitches from the elevated plain of Moudon, in Switzerland, to the level of the lake of Geneva, immediately above the little city of Vévey. The postilion had dismounted to chain a wheel, and the halt enabled those he conducted to catch a glimpse of the lovely scenery of that remarkable view.

The travellers were an American family, which had long been wandering about Europe, and which was now destined it knew not whither, having just traversed a thousand miles of Germany in its devious course. Four years before, the same family had halted on the same spot, nearly on the same day of the month of October, and for precisely the same object. It was then journeying to Italy, and as its members hung over the view of the Leman, with its accessories of Chillon, Châtelard, Blonay, Meillerie, the peaks of Savoy, and the wild ranges of the Alps, they had felt regret that the fairy scene was so soon to pass away. The case was now different, and yielding to the charm of a nature so noble, and yet so soft, within a few hours the carriage was in remise, a house was taken, the baggage unpacked, and the household gods of the travellers were erected, for the twentieth time, in a strange land.

Our American (for the family had its head) was familiar with the ocean, and the sight of water awoke old and pleasant recollections. He was hardly established in Vévey as a housekeeper, before he sought a boat. Chance brought him to a certain Jean Descloux (we give the spelling at hazard), with whom he soon struck up a bargain, and they launched forth in company upon the lake.

This casual meeting was the commencement of an agreeable and friendly intercourse. Jean Descloux, besides being a very good boatman, was a respectable philosopher in his way; possessing a tolerable stock of general information. His knowledge of America, in particular, might be deemed a little remarkable. He knew it was a continent, which lay west of his own quarter of the world; that it had a place in it called New Vévey; that all the whites who had gone there were not yet black, and that there were plausible hopes it might one day be civilized. Finding Jean so enlightened on a subject under which most of the eastern savans break down, the American thought it well enough to prick him closely on other matters. The worthy boatman turned out to be a man of singularly just discrimination. He was a reasonably good judge of the weather; had divers marvels to relate concerning the doings of the lake; thought the city very wrong for not making a port in the great square; always maintained that the wine of Saint Saphorin was very savory drinking for those who could get no better; laughed at the idea of there being sufficient cordage in the world to reach to the bottom of the Genfer Sea; was of opinion that the trout was a better fish than the fêrà; spoke with singular moderation of his ancient master, the bourgeoisie of Berne, which, however, he always affirmed kept singularly bad roads in Vaud, while those around its own city were the best in Europe, and otherwise showed himself to be a discreet and observant man. In short, honest Jean Descloux was a fair sample of that homebred, upright common sense, which seems to form the instinct of the mass, and which it is greatly the fashion to deride in those circles in which mystification passes for profound thinking, bold assumption for evidence, a simper for wit, particular personal advantages for liberty, and in which it is deemed a mortal offence against good manners to hint that Adam and Eve were the common parents of mankind.

"Monsieur has chosen a good time to visit Vévey," observed Jean Descloux, one evening that they were drifting in front of the town, the whole scenery resembling a fairy picture rather than a portion of this much-abused earth; "it blows sometimes at this end of the lake in a way to frighten the gulls out of it. We shall see no more of the steamboat after the last of the month."

The American cast a glance at the mountain, drew upon his memory for sundry squalls and gales which he had seen himself, and thought the boatman's figure of speech less extravagant than it had at first seemed.

"If your lake craft were better constructed, they would make better weather," he quietly observed.

Monsieur Descloux had no wish to quarrel with a customer who employed him every evening, and who preferred floating with the current to being rowed with a crooked oar. He manifested his prudence, therefore, by making a reserved reply.

"No doubt, monsieur," he said, "that the people who live on the sea make better vessels, and know how to sail them more skilfully. We had a proof of that here at Vévey" (he pronounced the word like v-*vais*, agreeably to the sounds of the French vowels), "last summer, which you might like to hear. An English gentleman—they say he was a captain in the marine—had a vessel built at Nice, and dragged over the mountains to our lake. He took a run across to Meillerie one fine morning, and no duck ever skimmed along lighter or swifter! He was not a man to take advice from a Swiss boatman, for he had crossed the line and seen water-spouts and whales! Well, he was on his way back in the dark, and it came on to blow here from off the mountains, and he stood on boldly toward our shore, heaving the lead as he drew near the land, as if he had been beating into Spithead in a fog"—Jean chuckled at the idea of sounding in the Leman—"while he flew along like a bold mariner, as no doubt he was!"

"Landing, I suppose," said the American, "among the lumber in the great square?"

"Monsieur is mistaken. He broke his boat's nose against that wall; and the next day, a piece of her, big enough to make a thole-pin, was not to be found. He might as well have sounded the heavens!"

"The lake has a bottom, notwithstanding?"

"Your pardon, monsieur. The lake has no bottom. The sea may have a bottom, but we have no bottom here."

There was little use in disputing the point.

Monsieur Descloux then spoke of the revolutions he had seen. He remembered the time when Vaud was a province of Berne. His observations on this subject were rational, and were well seasoned with common sense. His doctrine was simply this: "If one man rule, he will rule for his own benefit and that of his parasites; if a minority rule, we have many masters instead of one" (honest Jean had got hold here of a cant saying of the privileged, which he very ingeniously converted against themselves), "all of whom must be fed and served; and if the majority rule, and rule wrongfully, why, the minimum of harm is done." He admitted that the people might be deceived to their own injury, but then he did not think it was quite as likely to happen, as that they should be oppressed when they were governed without any agency of their own. On these points the American and the Vaudois were absolutely of the same mind.

From politics the transition to poetry was natural, for a common ingredient in both would seem to be fiction. On the subject of his mountains, Monsieur Descloux was a thorough Swiss. He expatiated on their grandeur, their storms, their height, and their glaciers, with eloquence. The worthy boatman had some such opinions of the superiority of his own country as all are apt to form who have never seen any other. He dwelt on the glories of an Abbaye des Vignerons, too, with the gusto of a Vévaisan, and seemed to think it would be a high stroke of state policy, to get up a new *fête* of this kind as speedily as possible. In short, the world and its interests were pretty generally discussed between these two philosophers during an intercourse that extended to a month.

Our American was not a man to let instruction of this nature easily escape him. He lay hours at a time on the seats of Jean Descloux's boat, looking up at the mountains, or watching some lazy sail on the lake, and speculating on the wisdom of which he was so accidentally made the repository. His view on one side was limited by the glacier of Mount Vélan, a near neighbor of the celebrated col of St. Bernard; and on the other, his eye could range to the smiling fields that surround Geneva. Within this setting is contained one of the most magnificent pictures that Nature ever drew, and he bethought him of the human actions, passions, and interests, of which it might have been the scene. By a connexion that was natural enough to the situation, he imagined a fragment of life passed between these grand limits, and the manner in which men could listen to the never-wearied promptings of their impulses in the immediate presence of the majesty of the Creator. He bethought him of the analogies that exist between inanimate nature and our own wayward inequalities; of the fearful admixture of good and evil of which we are composed; of the manner in which the best betray their submission to the devils, and in which the worst have gleams of that eternal principle of right, by which they have been endowed by God; of those tempests which sometimes lie dormant in our systems, like the slumbering lake in the calm, but which excited, equal its fury when lashed by the winds; of the strength of prejudices; of the worthlessness and changeable character of the most cherished of our opinions, and of that strange, incomprehensible, and yet winning *mélange* of contradictions, of fallacies, of truths, and of wrongs, which make up the sum of our existence.

The following pages are the result of this dreaming. The reader is left to his own intelligence for the moral.

A respectable English writer observed: "All pages of human life are worth reading; the wise instruct; the gay divert us; the imprudent teach us what to shun; the absurd cure the spleen."

[1833]

HOMEWARD BOUND[132]

PREFACE

In one respect, this book is a parallel to Franklin's well-known apologue of the hatter and his sign. It was commenced with a sole view to exhibit the present state of society in the United States, through the agency, in part, of a set of characters with different peculiarities, who had freshly arrived from Europe, and to whom the distinctive features of the country would be apt to present themselves with greater force, than to those who had never lived beyond the influence of the things portrayed. By the original plan, the work was to open at the threshold of the country, or with the arrival of the travellers at Sandy Hook, from which point the tale was to have been carried regularly forward to its conclusion. But a consultation with others has left little more of this plan than the hatter's friends left of his sign. As a vessel was introduced in the first chapter, the cry was for "more ship," until the work had become "all ship;" it actually closing at, or near, the spot where it was originally intended it should commence. Owing to this diversion from the author's design—a design that lay at the bottom of all his projects—a necessity has been created of running the tale through two separate works, or of making a hurried and insufficient conclusion. The former scheme has, consequently, been adopted.

It is hoped that the interest of the narrative will not be essentially diminished by this arrangement.

There will be, very likely, certain imaginative persons, who will feel disposed to deny that every minute event mentioned in these volumes ever befell one and the same ship, though ready enough to admit that they may very well have occurred to several different ships; a mode of commenting that is much in favor with your small critic. To this objection, we shall make but a single answer. The caviller, if any there should prove to be, is challenged to produce the log-book of the Montauk London packet, and if it should be found to contain a single sentence to controvert any one of our statements or facts, a frank recantation shall be made. Captain Truck is quite as well known in New York as in London or Portsmouth, and to him also we refer with confidence, for a confirmation of all we have said, with the exception, perhaps, of the little occasional touches of character that may allude directly to himself. In relation to the latter, Mr. Leach, and particularly Mr. Saunders, are both invoked as unimpeachable witnesses.

Most of our readers will probably know that all which appears in a New York journal is not necessarily as true as the Gospel. As some slight deviations from the facts accidentally occur, though doubtless at very long intervals, it should not be surprising that they sometimes omit circumstances that are quite as veracious as any thing they do actually utter to the world. No argument, therefore, can justly be urged against the incidents of this story, on account of the circumstance of their not being embodied in the regular marine news of the day.

Another serious objection on the part of the American reader to this work is foreseen. The author has endeavored to interest his readers in occurrences of a date as antiquated as two years can make them, when he is quite aware, that, in order to keep pace with a state of society in which there was no yesterday, it would have been much safer to anticipate things, by laying his scene two years in advance. It is hoped, however, that the public sentiment will not be outraged by this glimpse at antiquity, and this the more so, as the sequel of the tale will bring down events within a year of the present moment.

Previously to the appearance of that sequel, however, it may be well to say a few words concerning the fortunes of some of our *characters*, as it might be *en attendant*.

To commence with the most important: the Montauk herself, once deemed so "splendid" and convenient, is already supplanted in the public favor by a new ship; the reign of a popular packet, a popular preacher, or a popular anything-else, in America, being limited, by a national *esprit de corps*, to a time materially shorter than that of a lustre. This, however, is no more than just; rotation in favor being as evidently a matter of constitutional necessity, as rotation in office.

Captain Truck, for a novelty, continues popular, a circumstance that he himself ascribes to the fact of his being still a bachelor.

Toast is promoted, figuring at the head of a pantry quite equal to that of his great master, who regards his improvement with some such eyes as Charles the Twelfth of Sweden regarded that of his great rival Peter, after the affair of Pultowa.

Mr. Leach now smokes his own cigar, and issues his own orders from a monkey rail, his place in the line being supplied by his former "Dickey." He already speaks of his great model, as of one a little antiquated, it is true, but as a man who had merit in his time, though it was not the particular merit that is in fashion to-day.

Notwithstanding these little changes, which are perhaps inseparable from the events of a period so long as two years in a country so energetic as America, and in which nothing seems to be stationary but the ages of Tontine nominees and three-life leases, a cordial esteem was created among the principal actors in the events of this book, which is likely to outlast the passage, and which will not fail to bring most of them together again in the sequel.   [April, 1838]

HOME AS FOUND[133]

PREFACE

Those who have done us the favor to read HOMEWARD BOUND will at once perceive that the incidents of this book commence at the point where those of the work just mentioned ceased. We are fully aware of the disadvantage of dividing the interest of a tale in this manner; but in the present instance, the separation has been produced by circumstances over which the writer had very little control. As any one who may happen to take up this volume will very soon discover that there is other matter which it is necessary to know, it may be as well to tell all such persons, in commencement, therefore, that their reading will be bootless, unless they have leisure to turn to the pages of Homeward Bound for their cue.

We remember the despair with which that admirable observer of men, Mr. Mathews the comedian, confessed the hopelessness of success, in his endeavors to obtain a sufficiency of prominent and distinctive features to compose an entertainment founded on American character. The whole nation struck him as being destitute of salient points, and as characterized by a respectable mediocrity, that, however useful it might be in its way, was utterly without poetry, humor, or interest to the observer. For one who dealt principally with the more conspicuous absurdities of his fellow-creatures, Mr. Mathews was certainly right; we also believe him to have been right in the main, in the general tenor of his opinion; for this country, in its ordinary aspects, probably presents as barren a field to the writer of fiction, and to the dramatist, as any other on earth; we are not certain that we might not say the most barren. We believe that no attempt to delineate ordinary American life, either on the stage or in the pages of a novel, has been rewarded with success. Even those works in which the desire to illustrate a principle has been the aim, when the picture has been brought within this homely frame, have had to contend with disadvantages that have been commonly found insurmountable. The latter being the intention of this book, the task has been undertaken with a perfect consciousness of all its difficulties, and with scarcely a hope of success. It would be indeed a desperate undertaking, to think of making anything interesting in the way of a *Roman de Société* in this country; still, useful glances may possibly be made even in that direction, and we trust that the fidelity of one or two of our portraits will be recognized by the looker-on, although they will very likely be denied by the sitters themselves.

There seems to be a pervading principle in things, which gives an accumulating energy to any active property that may happen to be in the ascendant at the time being: money produces money; knowledge is the parent of knowledge; and ignorance fortifies ignorance. In a word, like begets like. The governing social evil of America is provincialism; a misfortune that is perhaps inseparable from her situation. Without a social capital, with twenty or more communities divided by distance and political barriers, her people, who are really more homogeneous than any other of the same numbers in the world perhaps, possess no standard for opinion, manners, social maxims, or even language. Every man, as a matter of course, refers to his own particular experience, and praises or condemns agreeably to notions contracted in the circle of his own habits, however narrow, provincial, or erroneous they may happen to be. As a consequence, no useful stage can exist; for the dramatist who should endeavor to delineate the faults of society, would find a formidable party arrayed against him, in a moment, with no party to defend. As another consequence, we see individuals constantly assailed with a wolf-like ferocity, while society is everywhere permitted to pass unscathed.

That the American nation is a great nation, in some particulars the greatest the world ever saw, we hold to be true, and are as ready to maintain as any one can be; but we are also equally ready to concede, that it is very far behind most polished nations in various essentials, and chiefly that it is lamentably in arrears to its own avowed principles. Perhaps this truth will be found to be the predominant thought, throughout the pages of "Home as Found."   [1838]

THE DEERSLAYER[134]

This series of Stories, which has obtained the name of "The Leather-Stocking Tales," has been written in a very desultory and inartificial manner. The order in which the several books appeared was essentially different from that in which they would have been presented to the world, had the regular course of their incidents been consulted. In the Pioneers, the first of the series written, the Leather-Stocking is represented as already old, and driven from his early haunts in the forest, by the sound of the axe, and the smoke of the settler. "The Last of the Mohicans," the next book in the order of publication, carried the readers back to a much earlier period in the history of our hero, representing him as middle-aged, and in the fullest vigor of manhood. In the Prairie, his career terminates, and he is laid in his grave. There, it was originally the intention to leave him, in the expectation that, as in the case of the human mass, he would soon be forgotten. But a latent regard for this character induced the author to resuscitate him in "The Pathfinder," a book that was not long after succeeded by "The Deerslayer," thus completing the series as it now exists.

While the five books that have been written were originally published in the order just mentioned, that of the incidents, insomuch as they are connected with the career of their principal character, is, as has been stated, very different. Taking the life of the Leather-Stocking as a guide, "The Deerslayer" should have been the opening book, for in that work he is seen just emerging into manhood; to be succeeded by "The Last of the Mohicans," "The Pathfinder," "The Pioneers," and "The Prairie." This arrangement embraces the order of events, though far from being that in which the books at first appeared. "The Pioneers" was published in 1822; "The Deerslayer" in 1841; making the interval between them nineteen years. Whether these progressive years have had a tendency to lessen the value of the last-named book by lessening the native fire of its author, or of adding somewhat in the way of improved taste and a more matured judgment, is for others to decide.

If anything from the pen of the writer of these romances is at all to outlive himself, it is, unquestionably, the series of "The Leather-Stocking Tales." To say this, is not to predict a very lasting reputation for the series itself, but simply to express the belief it will outlast any, or all, of the works from the same hand.

It is undeniable that the desultory manner in which "The Leather-Stocking Tales" were written, has, in a measure, impaired their harmony, and otherwise lessened their interest. This is proved by the fate of the two books last published, though probably the two most worthy an enlightened and cultivated reader's notice. If the facts could be ascertained, it is probable the result would show that of all those (in America, in particular) who have read the three first books of the series, not one in ten has a knowledge of the existence even of the two last. Several causes have tended to produce this result. The long interval of time between the appearance of "The Prairie" and that of "The Pathfinder," was itself a reason why the later books of the series should be overlooked. There was no longer novelty to attract attention, and the interest was materially impaired by the manner in which events were necessarily anticipated, in laying the last of the series first before the world. With the generation that is now coming on the stage this fault will be partially removed by the edition contained in the present work, in which the several tales will be arranged solely in reference to their connexion with each other.

The author has often been asked if he had any original in his mind, for the character of Leather-Stocking. In a physical sense, different individuals known to the writer in early life, certainly presented themselves as models, through his recollections; but in a moral sense this man of the forest is purely a creation. The idea of delineating a character that possessed little of civilization but its highest principles as they are exhibited in the uneducated, and all of savage life that is not incompatible with these great rules of conduct, is perhaps natural to the situation in which Natty was placed. He is too proud of his origin to sink into the condition of the wild Indian, and too much a man of the woods not to imbibe as much as was at all desirable, from his friends and companions. In a moral point of view it was the intention to illustrate the effect of seed scattered by the way side. To use his own language, his "gifts" were "white gifts," and he was not disposed to bring on them discredit. On the other hand, removed from nearly all the temptations of civilized life, placed in the best associations of that which is deemed savage, and favorably disposed by nature to improve such advantages, it appeared to the writer that his hero was a fit subject to represent the better qualities of both conditions, without pushing either to extremes.

There was no violent stretch of the imagination, perhaps, in supposing one of civilized associations in childhood, retaining many of his earliest lessons amid the scenes of the forest. Had these early impressions, however, not been sustained by continued, though casual connexion with men of his own color, if not of his own caste, all our information goes to show he would soon have lost every trace of his origin. It is believed that sufficient attention was paid to the particular circumstances in which this individual was placed to justify the picture of his qualities that has been drawn. The Delawares early attracted the attention of missionaries, and were a tribe unusually influenced by their precepts and example. In many instances they became Christians, and cases occurred in which their subsequent lives gave proof of the efficacy of the great moral changes that had taken place within them.

A leading character in a work of fiction has a fair right to the aid which can be obtained from a poetical view of the subject. It is in this view, rather than in one more strictly circumstantial, that Leather-Stocking has been drawn. The imagination has no great task in portraying to itself a being removed from the every-day inducements to err, which abound in civilized life, while he retains the best and simplest of his early impressions; who sees God in the forest; hears him in the winds; bows to him in the firmament that o'ercanopies all; submits to his sway in a humble belief of his justice and mercy; in a word, a being who finds the impress of the Deity in all the works of nature, without any of the blots produced by the expedients, and passion, and mistakes of man. This is the most that has been attempted in the character of Leather-Stocking. Had this been done without any of the drawbacks of humanity, the picture would have been, in all probability, more pleasing than just. In order to preserve the *vrai-semblable*, therefore, traits derived from the prejudices, tastes, and even the weaknesses of his youth, have been mixed up with these higher qualities and longings, in a way, it is hoped, to represent a reasonable picture of human nature, without offering to the spectator a "monster of goodness."

It has been objected to these books that they give a more favorable picture of the red man than he deserves. The writer apprehends that much of this objection arises from the habits of those who have made it. One of his critics, on the appearance of the first work in which Indian character was portrayed, objected that its "characters were Indians of the school of Heckewelder,[135] rather than of the school of nature." These words quite probably contain the substance of the true answer to the objection. Heckewelder was an ardent, benevolent missionary, bent on the good of the red man, and seeing in him one who had the soul, reason, and characteristics of a fellow-being. The critic is understood to have been a very distinguished agent of the government, one very familiar with Indians, as they are seen at the councils to treat for the sale of their lands, where little or none of their domestic qualities come in play, and where, indeed, their evil passions are known to have the fullest scope. As just would it be to draw conclusions of the general state of American society from the scenes of the capital, as to suppose that the negotiating of one of these treaties is a fair picture of Indian life.

It is the privilege of all writers of fiction, more particularly when their works aspire to the elevation of romances, to present the *beau-idéal* of their characters to the reader. This it is which constitutes poetry, and to suppose that the red man is to be represented only in the squalid misery or in the degraded moral state that certainly more or less belongs to his condition, is, we apprehend, taking a very narrow view of an author's privileges. Such criticism would have deprived the world of even Homer.

[1850]

THE WING—AND—WING [136]

PREFACE

It is difficult to say of which there is most in the world, a blind belief in religious dogmas, or a presumptuous and ignorant cavilling on revelation. The impression has gone abroad, that France was an example of the last, during the height of her great revolutionary mania; a charge that was scarcely true, as respects the nation, however just it might be in connection with her bolder and more unquiet spirits. Most of the excesses of France, during that momentous period, were to be attributed to the agency of a few, the bulk of the nation having little to do with any part of them, beyond yielding their physical and pecuniary aid to an audacious and mystifying political combination. One of the baneful results, however, of these great errors of the times, was the letting loose of the audacious from all the venerable and healthful restraints of the church, to set them afloat on the sea of speculation and conceit. There is something so gratifying to human vanity in fancying ourselves superior to most around us, that we believe few young men attain their majority without imbibing more or less of the taint of unbelief, and passing through the mists of a vapid moral atmosphere, before they come to the clear, manly, and yet humble perceptions that teach most of us, in the end, our own insignificance, the great benevolence as well as wisdom of the scheme of redemption, and the philosophy of the Christian religion, as well as its divinity.

Perhaps the greatest stumbling-block of the young is a disposition not to yield to their belief unless it conforms to their own crude notions of propriety and reason. If the powers of man were equal to analyzing the nature of the Deity, to comprehending his being, and power, and motives, there would be

some little show of sense in thus setting up the pretence of sat-
isfying our judgments in all things, before we yield our credence
to a religious system. But, the first step we take brings with it
the instructive lesson of our incapacity, and teaches the wholesome lesson of humility. From arrogantly claiming a right to
worship a deity we comprehend, we soon come to feel that the
impenetrable veil that is cast around the God-head is an indispensable condition of our faith, reverence, and submission. A
being that can be comprehended, is not a being to be worshipped.

In this book, there is an attempt to set these conflicting
tendencies in a full but amicable contrast to each other. We
believe there is nothing in the design opposed to probability;
and it seems to us, that the amiable tenderness of a confiding but
just-viewing female heart might, under the circumstances, be
expected to manifest the mingled weakness and strength that
it has here been our aim to portray.

We acknowledge a strong paternal feeling in behalf of this
book, placing it very high in the estimate of its merits, as compared with other books from the same pen: a species of com-
mendation that need wound no man. Perhaps some knowledge
of Italian character is necessary to enjoy the *vice-governatore*
(veechy-gover-na-*to*-re), and the *podestà;* but we confess they
have given us, in reading over these pages for the first time
since they were written, quite as much amusement as if they
were altogether from an unknown hand.

As for the Mediterranean, that unrivalled sea, its pictures
always afford us delight. The hue of the water; the delicious
and voluptuous calm; the breathings of the storm from the
Alps and Apennines; the noble mountain-sides basking in the
light of the region, or shrouded in mists that increase their
grandeur; the picturesque craft; the islands, bays, ricks, vol-
canoes, and the thousand objects of art, contribute to render it
the centre of all that is delightful and soothing to both the mind
and the senses.

The reader will recollect the painful history of Caraccioli.
We have taken some liberties with his private history, admitting

frankly that we have no other authority for them than that which we share in common with all writers of romance. The granddaughter we have given the unfortunate admiral, is so much in accordance with Italian practices, that no wrong is done to the *morale* of Naples, whatever may be the extent of the liberty taken with the individual.

Nelson seems to have lived and died under the influence of the unprincipled woman who then governed him with the arts of a siren. His nature was noble, and his moral impressions, even, were not bad; but his simple and confiding nature was not equal to contending with one as practised in profligacy as the woman into whose arms he was thrown, at a most evil moment for his reputation.

There is nothing more repugnant to the general sense of rights, than the prostitution of public justice to the purposes of private vengeance. Such would seem to have been the reason of the very general odium attached to the execution of Admiral Prince Caraccioli, who was the victim of circumstances, rather than the promoter of treason. The whole transaction makes a melancholy episode in the history of modern Europe. We have made such use of it as is permitted to fiction, neither neglecting the leading and known facts of the event, nor adhering to the minuter circumstances more closely than the connection of our tale demanded.   [1842]

AFLOAT AND ASHORE [137]

PREFACE

The writer has published so much truth which the world has insisted was fiction, and so much fiction which has been received as truth, that, in the present instance, he is resolved to say nothing on the subject. Each of his readers is at liberty to believe just as much, or as little, of the matter here laid before him, or her, as may suit his or her notions, prejudices, knowledge of the world, or ignorance. If anybody is disposed to swear he knows precisely where Clawbonny is, that he was well acquainted with old Mr. Hardinge, nay, has often heard him

preach—let him make his affidavit, in welcome. Should he get
a little wide of the mark, it will not be the first document of
that nature which has possessed the same weakness.

It is possible that certain captious persons may be disposed
to inquire into the *cui bono?* of such a book. The answer is this.
Every thing which can convey to the human mind distinct and
accurate impressions of events, social facts, professional peculiarities, or past history, whether of the higher or more familiar
character, is of use. All that is necessary is, that the pictures
should be true to nature, if not absolutely drawn from living
sitters. The knowledge we gain by our looser reading often
becomes serviceable in modes and manners little anticipated in
the moments when it is acquired.

Perhaps the greater portion of all our peculiar opinions have
their foundation in prejudices. These prejudices are produced
in consequence of its being out of the power of any one man to
see, or know, every thing. The most favored mortal must receive far more than half of all that he learns on his faith in others;
and it may aid those who can never be placed in positions to
judge for themselves of certain phases of men and things, to get
pictures of the same, drawn in a way to give them nearer views
than they might otherwise obtain. This is the greatest benefit
of all light literature in general, it being possible to render that
which is purely fictitious even more useful than that which is
strictly true, by avoiding extravagances, by portraying with
fidelity, and, as our friend Marble might say, by "generalizing"
with discretion.

This country has undergone many important changes since
the commencement of the present century. Some of these
changes have been for the better; others, we think out of all
question, for the worse. The last is a fact that can be known to
the generation which is coming into life by report only, and
these pages may possibly throw some little light on both points,
in representing things as they were. The population of the
republic is probably something more than eighteen millions and
a half to-day; in the year of our Lord one thousand eight hundred, it was but a little more than five millions. In 1800, the

population of New York was somewhat less than six hundred thousand souls; to-day it is probably a little less than two millions seven hundred thousand souls. In 1800, the town of New York had sixty thousand inhabitants; whereas, including Brooklyn and Williamsburg, which then virtually had no existence, it must have at this moment quite four hundred thousand. These are prodigious numerical changes, that have produced changes of another sort. Although an increase of numbers does not necessarily infer an increase of high civilization, it reasonably leads to the expectation of great melioration in the commoner comforts. Such has been the result, and to those familiar with facts as they now exist, the difference will probably be apparent in these pages.

Although the moral changes in American society have not kept pace with those that are purely physical, many that are essential have nevertheless occurred. Of all the British possessions on this continent, New York, after its conquest from the Dutch, received most of the social organization of the mother country. Under the Dutch, even, it had some of these characteristic peculiarities in its patroons; the lords of the manor of the New Netherlands. Some of the southern colonies, it is true, had their caciques and other semi-feudal and semi-savage noblesse, but the system was of short continuance; the peculiarities of that section of the country arising principally from the existence of domestic slavery on an extended scale. With New York it was different. A conquered colony, the mother country left the impression of its own institutions more deeply engraved than on any of the settlements that were commenced by grants to proprietors, or under charters from the crown. It was strictly a royal colony, and so continued to be, down to the hour of separation. The social consequences of this state of things were to be traced in her habits until the current of immigration became so strong as to bring with it those that were conflicting, if not absolutely antagonist. The influence of these two sources of thought is still obvious to the reflecting, giving rise to a double set of social opinions; one of which bears all the characteristics of its New England and puritanical origin, while the other may be said to come of the usages and notions of the middle states, proper.

This is said in anticipation of certain strictures that will be likely to follow some of the incidents of our story, it not being always deemed an essential in an American critic that he should understand his subject. Too many of them, indeed, justify the retort of the man who derided the claims to knowledge of life set up by a neighbor, that "had been to meetin' and had been to mill." We can all obtain some notions of the portion of a subject that is placed immediately before our eyes; the difficulty is to understand that which we have no means of studying.

On the subject of the nautical incidents of this book, we have endeavored to be as exact as our authorities will allow. We are fully aware of the importance of writing what the world thinks, rather than what is true, and are not conscious of any very palpable errors of this nature.

It is no more than fair to apprise the reader that our tale is not completed in the first part, or the volumes that are now published. This the plan of the book would not permit; but we can promise those who may feel any interest in the subject, that the season shall not pass away, so far as it may depend on ourselves, without bringing the narrative to a close. Poor Captain Wallingford is now in his sixty-fifth year, and is naturally desirous of not being hung up long on the tenter-hooks of expectation so near the close of life. The old gentleman having seen much and suffered much, is entitled to end his days in peace. In this mutual frame of mind between the principal and his editors, the public shall have no cause to complain of unnecessary delay, whatever may be its rights of the same nature on other subjects.

The author—perhaps editor would be the better word—does not feel himself responsible for all the notions advanced by the hero of this tale, and it may be as well to say as much. That one born in the Revolution should think differently from the men of the present day, in a hundred things, is to be expected. It is in just this difference of opinion that the lessons of the book are to be found.   [1844]

SATANSTOE [138]

PREFACE

Every chronicle of manners has a certain value. When customs are connected with principles, in their origin, development, or end, such records have a double importance; and it is because we think we see such a connection between the facts and incidents of the Littlepage Manuscripts, and certain important theories of our own time, that we give the former to the world.

It is perhaps a fault of your professed historian, to refer too much to philosophical agencies, and too little to those that are humbler. The foundations of great events are often remotely laid in very capricious and uncalculated passions, motives, or impulses. Chance has usually as much to do with the fortunes of states, as with those of individuals; or, if there be calculations connected with them at all, they are the calculations of a power superior to any that exists in man.

We had been led to lay these manuscripts before the world, partly by considerations of the above nature, and partly on account of the manner in which the two works we have named, "Satanstoe" and the "Chainbearer," relate directly to the great New York question of the day, ANTI-RENTISM; which question will be found to be pretty fully laid bare, in the third and last book of the series. These three works, which contain all the Littlepage Manuscripts, do not form sequels to each other, in the sense of personal histories, or as narratives; while they do in that of principles. The reader will see that the early career, the attachment, the marriage, etc., of Mr. Cornelius Littlepage are completely related in the present book, for instance; while those of his son, Mr. Mordaunt Littlepage, will be just as fully given in the "Chainbearer," its successor. It is hoped that the connection, which certainly does exist between these three works, will have more tendency to increase the value of each, than to produce the ordinary effect of what are properly called sequels, which are known to lessen the interest a narrative might otherwise have with the reader. Each of these three books has its own hero, its own heroine, and its own picture of manners, complete; though the latter may be, and is, more or less thrown into relief by its *pendants*.

We conceive no apology is necessary for treating the subject of anti-rentism with the utmost frankness. Agreeably to our views of the matter, the existence of true liberty among us, the perpetuity of the institutions, and the safety of public morals, are all dependent on putting down, wholly, absolutely, and unqualifiedly, the false and dishonest theories and statements that have been boldly advanced in connection with this subject. In our view, New York is, at this moment much the most disgraced state in the Union, notwithstanding she has never failed to pay the interest on her public debt; and her disgrace arises from the fact that her laws are trampled underfoot, without any efforts, at all commensurate with the object, being made to enforce them. If *words* and *professions* can save the character of a community, all may yet be well; but if states, like individuals, are to be judged by their actions, and the "tree is to be known by its fruit," God help us!

For ourselves, we conceive that true patriotism consists in laying bare every thing like public vice, and in calling such things by their right names. The great enemy of the race has made a deep inroad upon us, within the last ten or a dozen years, under cover of a spurious delicacy on the subject of exposing national ills; and it is time that they who have not been afraid to praise, when praise was merited, should not shrink from the office of censuring, when the want of timely warnings may be one cause of the most fatal evils. The great practical defect of institutions like ours, is the circumstance that "what is everybody's business, is nobody's business;" a neglect that gives to the activity of the rogue a very dangerous ascendency over the more dilatory correctives of the honest man.   [1845]

THE CRATER[139]

PREFACE

The reader of this book will very naturally be disposed to ask the question, why the geographies, histories, and other works of a similar character, have never made any mention of the regions and events that compose its subject. The answer is obvious enough, and ought to satisfy every mind, however "inquiring." The fact is, that the authors of the different works to which there is any allusion, most probably never heard there were any such places as the Reef, Rancocus Island, Vulcan's Peak, the Crater, and the other islands of which so much is said in our pages. In other words, they know nothing about them.

We shall very freely admit that, under ordinary circumstances, it would be *prima facie* evidence against the existence of any spot on the face of this earth, that the geographies took no notice of it. It will be remembered, however, that the time was, and that only three centuries and a half since, when the geographies did not contain a syllable about the whole of the American continent; that it is not a century since they began to describe New Zealand, New Holland, Tahiti, Oahu, and a vast number of other places, that are now constantly alluded to, even in the daily journals. Very little is said in the largest geographies, of Japan, for instance; and it may be questioned if they might not just as well be altogether silent on the subject, as for any accurate information they do convey. In a word, much as is now known of the globe, a great deal still remains to be told, and we do not see why the "inquiring mind" should not seek for information in our pages, as well as in some that are ushered into public notice by a flourish of literary trumpets, that are blown by presidents, vice-presidents, and secretaries of various learned bodies.

One thing we shall ever maintain, and that in the face of all who may be disposed to underrate the value of our labors, which is this: there is not a word in these volumes which we now lay before the reader, *as grave matter of fact*, that is not entitled to the most implicit credit. We scorn deception. Lest, however, some cavillers may be found, we will present a few of those reasons which occur to our mind, on the spur of the moment, as tending to show that every thing related here *might* be just as true as Cook's voyages themselves. In the first place, this earth is large, and has sufficient surface to contain, not only all the islands mentioned in our pages, but a great many more. Something is established when the possibility of any hypothetical point is placed beyond dispute. Then, not one half as much was known of the islands of the Pacific, at the close of the last, and at the commencement of the present century, as is known to-day. In such a dearth of precise information, it may very well have happened that many things occurred touching which we have not said even one word. Again, it should never be forgotten that generations were born, lived their time, died, and have been forgotten, among those remote groups, about which no civilized man ever has, or ever will hear anything. If such be admitted to be the facts, why may not *all* that is here related have happened, and equally escape the knowledge of the rest of the civilized world? During the wars of the French Revolution, trifling events attracted but little of the general attention, and we are not to think of interests of this nature, in that day, as one would think of them now.

Whatever may be thought of the authenticity of its incidents, we hope this book will be found not to be totally without a moral. Truth is not absolutely necessary to the illustration of a principle, the imaginary sometimes doing that office quite as effectually as the actual.

The reader may next wish to know why the wonderful events related in these volumes have so long been hidden from the world. In answer to this we would ask if any one can tell how many thousands of years the waters have tumbled down the cliffs at Niagara, or why it was that civilized men heard of the existence of this wonderful cataract so lately as only three centuries since. The fact is, there must be a beginning to every thing; and now there is a beginning to the world's knowing the history of Vulcan's Peak, and the Crater. Lest the reader, however, should feel disposed to reproach the past age with having been negligent in its collection of historical and geological incidents, we would again remind him of the magnitude of the events that so naturally occupied its attention. It is scarcely possible, for instance, for one who did not live forty years ago to have any notion how completely the world was engaged in wondering at Napoleon and his marvellous career, which last contained even more extraordinary features than any thing related here; though certainly of a very different character. All wondering, for near a quarter of a century, was monopolized by the French Revolution and its consequences.

There are a few explanations, however, which are of a very humble nature compared with the principal events of our history, but which may as well be given here. The Woolston family still exists in Pennsylvania, and that, by the way, is something toward corroborating the truth of our narrative. Its most distinguished member is recently dead, and his journal has been the authority for most of the truths here related. He died at a good old age, having seen his three-score years and ten, leaving behind him, in addition to a very ample estate, not only a good character—which means neither more nor less than what "the neighbors," amid their ignorance, envy, love of detraction, jealousy, and other similar qualities, might think proper to say of him—but the odor of a well-spent life, in which he struggled hard to live more in favor with God, than in favor with man. It was remarked in him, for the last forty years of his life, or after his return to Bucks, that he regarded all popular demonstrations with distaste, and, as some of his enemies pretended, with contempt. Nevertheless, he strictly acquitted himself of all his public duties, and never neglected to vote. It is believed that his hopes for the future, meaning in a social and earthly sense, were not very vivid, and he was often heard to repeat that warning text of Scripture which tells us, "Let him that thinketh he standeth, take heed lest he fall."

The faithful, and once lovely partner of this principal personage of our history is also dead. It would seem that it was not intended they should be long asunder. But their time was come, and they might almost be said to have departed in company. The same is true of Friends Robert and Martha, who have also filled their time, and gone hence, it is to be hoped, to a better world. Some few of the younger persons of our drama still exist, but it has been remarked of them, that they avoid conversing of the events of their younger days. Youth is the season of hope, and hope disappointed has little to induce us to dwell on its deceptive pictures.

If those who now live in this republic, can see any grounds for a timely warning in the events here recorded, it may happen that the mercy of a divine Creator may still preserve that which he has hitherto cherished and protected.

It remains only to say that we have endeavored to imitate the simplicity of Captain Woolston's journal, in writing this book, and should any homeliness of style be discovered, we trust it will be imputed to that circumstance.   [1847]

THE OAK OPENINGS [140]

PREFACE

It ought to be matter of surprise how men live in the midst of marvels, without taking heed of their existence. The slightest derangement of their accustomed walks in political or social life shall excite all their wonder, and furnish themes for their discussions, for months; while the prodigies that come from above are presented daily to their eyes, and are received without surprise, as things of course. In a certain sense, this may be well enough, inasmuch as all which comes directly from the hands of the Creator may be said so far to exceed the power of human comprehension, as to be beyond comment; but the truth would show us that the cause of this neglect is rather a propensity to dwell on such interests as those over which we have a fancied control, than on those which confessedly transcend our understanding. Thus is it ever with men. The wonders of creation meet them at every turn, without awakening reflection, while their minds labor on subjects that are not only ephemeral and illusory, but which never attain an elevation higher than that the most sordid interests can bestow.

For ourselves, we firmly believe that the finger of Providence is pointing the way to all races, and colors, and nations, along the path that is to lead the east and the west alike, to the great goal of human wants. Demons infest that path, and numerous and unhappy are the wanderings of millions who stray from its course; sometimes in reluctance to proceed; sometimes in an indiscreet haste to move faster than their fellows, and always in a forgetfulness of the great rules of conduct that have been handed down from above. Nevertheless, the main course is onward; and the day, in the sense of time, is not distant, when the whole earth is to be filled with the knowledge of the Lord, "as the waters cover the sea."

One of the great stumbling-blocks with a large class of well-meaning, but narrow-judging moralists, are the seeming wrongs that are permitted by Providence, in its control of human events. Such persons take a one-sided view of things, and reduce all principles to the level of their own understandings. If we could comprehend the relations which the Deity bears to us, as well as we can comprehend the relations we bear to Him, there might be a little seeming reason in these doubts; but when one of the parties in this mighty scheme of action is a profound mystery to the other, it is worse than idle, it is profane, to attempt to explain those things which our minds are not yet sufficiently cleared from the dross of earth to understand. Look at Italy, at this very moment. The darkness and depression from which that glorious peninsula is about to emerge, are the fruits of long-continued dissensions and an iron despotism, which is at length broken by the impulses left behind him by a ruthless conqueror, who, under the appearance and with the phrases of Liberty, contended only for himself. A more concentrated egotism than that of Napoleon probably never existed; yet has it left behind it seeds of personal rights that have sprung up by the way-side, and which are likely to take root with a force that will bid defiance to eradication. Thus is it ever, with the progress of society. Good appears to arise out of evil, and the inscrutable ways of Providence are vindicated by general results, rather than by instances of particular care. We leave the application of these remarks to the intelligence of such of our readers as may have patience to peruse the work that will be found in the succeeding pages.

We have a few words of explanation to say, in connection with the machinery of our tale. In the first place, we would remark, that the spelling of "burr-oak," as given in this book, is less our own than an office spelling. We think it should be "bur-oak," and this for the simple reason, that the name is derived from the fact that the acorn borne by this tree is partially covered with a bur. Old Sam Johnson, however, says that "burr" means the lobe, or lap of the ear; and those who can fancy such a resemblance between this and the covering of our acorn, are at liberty to use the two final consonants. Having commenced stereotyping with this supernumerary, for the sake of uniformity that mode of spelling, wrong as we think it, has been continued throughout the book.

There is nothing imaginary in the fertility of the west. Personal observation has satisfied us that it much surpasses anything that exists in the Atlantic states, unless in exceptions, through the agency of great care and high manuring, or in instances of peculiar natural soil. In these times, men almost fly. We have passed over a thousand miles of territory within the last few days, and have brought the pictures at the two extremes of this journey in close proximity in our mind's eye. Time may lessen that wonderful fertility, and bring the whole country more on a level; but there it now is, a glorious gift from God, which it is devoutly to be wished may be accepted with due gratitude and with a constant recollection of His unwavering rules of right and wrong, by those who have been selected to enjoy it.

June, 1848.

THE WAYS OF THE HOUR [141]

PREFACE

The object of this book is to draw the attention of the reader to some of the social evils that beset us; more particularly in connection with the administration of criminal justice. So long a time has intervened since the thought occurred, and so many interruptions have delayed the progress of the work, that it is hoped that enough has been done to cause a few to reflect on a matter of vital importance; one that to them may possess the interest of novelty.

A strange indifference exists as to the composition of the juries. In our view, the institution itself, so admirable in a monarchy, is totally unsuited to a democracy. The very principle that renders it so safe where there is a great central power to resist, renders it unsafe in a state of society in which few have sufficient resolution to attempt even to resist popular impulses.

A hundred instances might be given in which the juries of this country are an evil; one or two of which we will point out. In trials between railroad companies and those who dwell along their lines, prejudice is usually so strong against the former, that justice for them is nearly hopeless. In certain parts of the country, the juries are made the instruments of defeating the claims of creditors who dwell at a distance, and are believed to have interests opposed to the particular community where the debtor resides. This is a most crying evil, and has been the source of many and grievous wrongs. Whenever there is a motive for creating a simulated public opinion, by the united action of several journals, justice is next to hopeless; such combinations rarely, if ever, occurring in its behalf. In cases that are connected with the workings of political schemes, and not unfrequently in those in which political men are parties to the suits, it is often found that the general prejudices or partialities of the out-door factions enter the jury-box. This is a most serious evil too; for, even when the feeling does not produce a direct and flagrant wrong, it is very apt so far to temper the right as to deprive it of much of its virtue. In a country like this, in which party penetrates to the very bottom of society, the extent of this evil can be known only to those who are brought into close contact with the ordinary workings of the institution.

In a democracy, proper selections in the material that are necessary to render juries safe, become nearly impossible. Then, the tendency is to the accumulation of power in bodies of men; and in a state of society like our own, the juries get to be much too independent of the opinion of the court. It is precisely in that condition of things in which the influence and authority of the judge guide the juror, and the investigation and substantial power of the juror react on the proceedings of the court, that the greatest benefits have been found to accrue from this institution. The reverse of this state of things will be very likely to produce the greatest amount of evil.

It is certain that the juries are falling into disrepute throughout the length and breadth of the land. The difficulty is to find a substitute. As they are bodies holding the lives, property and character of every member of the community, more or less, in their power, it is not to be supposed that the masses will surrender this important means of exercising their authority voluntarily, or with good will. Time alone can bring reform through the extent of the abuses.

The writer has not the vanity to suppose that any thing contained in this book will produce a very serious impression on the popularity of the jury. Such is not its design. All that is anticipated is to cause a portion of his readers to reflect on the subject; persons who probably have never yet given it a moment of thought.

There is a tendency, at the present time, to court change for its own sake. This is erroneously termed a love of reform. Something very like a revolution is going on in our midst, while there is much reason to apprehend that few real grievances are abated; the spurious too exclusively occupying the popular mind, to render easy a just distinction between them. When an American prates about aristocracy, it is pretty safe to set him down as knavish or ignorant. It is purely cant; and the declaimers would be puzzled to point to a single element of the little understood and much decried institution, the country being absolutely without any, unless the enjoyment of the ordinary rights of property can be so considered. But the demagogue must have his war-cry as well as the Indian; and it is probable he will continue to whoop as long as the country contains minds weak enough to furnish him with dupes.   [1850]

stances would be increased (in which one, one single holding
high and narrow and inadequate assessment of the estate) by
Salisbury, without any, unless the enjoyment of the immediate
vested property can be so considered. But the immediate
circumstances his way as well as the testator, and it is probable he
and promise to share as long as the colony subsists, if need
were enough to furnish him with these.   [1834]

NOTES

1. The title-page of the first American edition reads: NOTIONS/ OF THE/AMERICANS:/PICKED UP BY A/TRAVELLING BACHELOR./IN TWO VOLUMES./VOL.I.[II.]/[rule]/Philadelphia:/ CAREY, LEA & CAREY./CHESNUT-STREET./[dotted rule]/ 1828. It was published first in London by Henry Colburn on June 20, 1828; the American edition followed in August of the same year. There was at least one subsequent English edition, and eight American, by the year 1852; and it was translated into French and German immediately upon its first appearance. It does not seem to have been reprinted since 1852 except in the collected edition of Cooper's novels published in New York, 1857–1860. This is the only collected edition, except the German translation of Sauerländer, to include it.

Letter XXIII: [Learning and Literature]

2. Stephen Day set up the first press in this country at Cambridge in 1639, and by 1723, when Franklin went to Philadelphia, there were printers established in most of the seaboard cities. The *Boston News-Letter*, the first successful paper, was started in 1704. The *American Magazine* and the *General Magazine*, the earliest ventures of their kind, appeared simultaneously in 1741. Nevertheless, until Cooper's time, American authors had great difficulty in gaining a hearing because of the practice of reprinting English works, both in books and in the periodical press.

3. The correct dates are as follows: Harvard, 1636; William and Mary, 1693; Yale, 1701; University of Pennsylvania, 1740; Princeton (Nassau Hall), 1746; Columbia, 1754. The educational level of the curricula of these institutions was approximately that of such English schools as Eton and Rugby.

4. It was a fairly general practice for the sons of Virginia gentlemen before the Revolution to study law at the Inns of Court in London.

5. Between 1760 and 1766 the first group of Americans, including Morgan, Shippen, Rush, and others, went to London and Edinburgh to study medicine, and returned to found the Pennsylvania Hospital in Philadelphia and other early medical schools. For many years the practice of spending a year or two in European centers persisted in the medical profession.

6. Cooper constantly repeats this point and it furnishes him with his justification for a distinction between himself and Scott. Approaching the novel from the point of view of ideas rather than forms, he did not hesitate to use the same material as that of Scott, as in *The Pilot* and *The*

Bravo, laying his claim to originality in the democratic as contrasted with the feudalistic bases of his social theories.

7. An illustration of the fallacy of reasoning from a single instance to a generalization.

8. Cooper's cordial feeling toward both the press and the jury system at this stage of his development is in marked contrast to his later attitudes, the one illustrated in his long series of libel suits in defense of his personal immunity against the attacks of the Whig press, the other in *The Ways of the Hour*, his last novel.

9. Cooper, perhaps more than any other author of his day, freed American literature from this handicap. Whereas Brockden Brown had to finance his own novels in a market flooded with cheap reprints of English works, the authors of which received no American royalties, Cooper invaded the English market and received sufficient remuneration to allow him adequate support as a writer. (See Introduction, pp. lxxii–lxxvi)

10. Similarly, Cooper, perhaps more than anyone else, helped American authors to overcome this obstacle by showing them the resources of a primitive life for literary expression. But even he was under the spell of the English authors who served as models for American writers. English novels and plays were about a settled society and its manners; America had no such society; hence a literature was impossible. Paulding was aware of this difficulty but went boldly ahead; Irving chose European themes; Tyler and other dramatists did the best they could with American social problems, flaunting their patriotism and apologizing for their materials in the same breath. With *Home as Found*, Cooper accepted this problem as his own and devoted much of his later fiction to its discussion.

11. Fitz-Greene Halleck (1790–1867) was, next to Bryant, the most widely-read American poet of his day. With Joseph Rodman Drake, he started the "Croker" verses in the *New York Evening Post* and the *National Advocate* in 1819. His longer social satire, *Fanny*, appeared the same year, but after a short visit to Europe, he turned to a more robustious type of lyric romanticism in *Marco Bozzaris* and later verses.

12. Charles Brockden Brown (1771–1810), author of *Wieland*, *Edgar Huntly*, and other novels in the mode of Gothic romance.

13. Cooper is here discussing his own work. Even so early as this he has developed the idea of disguising social commentary as romance.

14. Prescott and Sparks were contemporary; Everett, Webster, Motley, Bancroft, and Parkman were slightly later.

15. By this time Dunlap, Barker, Payne, Tyler, and Bird had contributed original plays, but such works were still in a substantial minority in the repertory of the "American" company.

Letter XXIV: [*Science and the Arts*]

16. Benjamin West, P.R.A. (1738–1820), was born near Philadelphia, but lived, painted, and taught painting in London from 1763 to the year

of his death. His prestige in his adopted country stimulated that at home and attracted many young Americans to London to study with him. Among these was C. W. Peale, who founded the Pennsylvania Academy of Fine Arts in 1809. So great was the interest in painting by 1834 that William Dunlap published a *History of the Rise and Progress of the Art of Design in the United States*, in two volumes. Cooper was much interested in this work.

17. The Charter of 1814.

18. The square brackets here are Cooper's.

19. The first edition of Noah Webster's *Dictionary*, 1828, and of Lindley Murray's *Grammar*, 1795 (5th ed., the last to be corrected by the author, 1824), mark the beginnings of interest in modern linguistic scholarship in America. Cooper was theoretically a purist and constantly attacks dialectic variations in his writings.

20. In 1930, a century after Cooper wrote this passage, the population of the United States was 122,775,046.

21. Cooper's antipathy to New England and New Englanders is a constantly recurring note in his writings. It frequently takes the form of criticism of their ways of speech, but there are deeper roots than this. Essentially, the feeling which Cooper shared with most inland New York landowners of the early days was based on social difference. New York was aristocratic in feeling, New England middle class and democratic. Undoubtedly this antipathy was fostered and sustained by such historical circumstances as the contention of the governors of New York and of New Hampshire for property rights in Vermont, claims which resulted in the creation of an independent republic after the Revolution and delayed Vermont's entry into the Union until 1791. Furthermore, New England squatters set up sawmills in New York during these days and were a constant source of irritation to the landowners with whom Cooper sympathized (see *The Chainbearer* and other novels). A more immediate source of irritation in Cooper's case was the personality of the typical New Englander who settled in Cooperstown and similar posts when inland New York was first being developed by William Cooper and others. The semi-ignorant and self-seeking settler followed the backwoodsman across the continent, and made himself disagreeably aggressive in the town in which Cooper grew up. He appears first in *The Pioneers*, but soon becomes a typical Cooper character.

22. Cooper was educated in the local schoolhouse in Cooperstown. He was prepared for college by an Anglican clergyman in Albany (*Gleanings in Europe: England*, New York, 1930, pp. 196–197). His elder brothers had been sent to Nassau Hall (Princeton), but he was sent to Yale.

23. A "cracker" was a lower-class white of the southern states.

Letter XXXVII: [*Economic Resources*]

24. Cooper is here speaking as a liberal English gentleman of Whig political sympathies, warring with Tory interests at home, and gradually becoming aware of the ultimate importance of America in commerce, industry, and world politics.

25. William Cooper had early agitated for the building of a canal to connect the Lakes with the Hudson. He died in 1809; the Erie Canal was started in 1817 and completed in 1825.

26. Cooper's use of the word "intelligence" is similar to our use today of "education."

27. Cooper's position on the slavery issue was very nearly nonpartisan. On humanitarian grounds, he admitted that it was a social evil. As an established institution, however, it seemed to him to be a necessary evil, not to be abolished except by a slow and natural process. While writing his *Notions*, he prepared an article on the subject for the *Revue Encyclopédique*, published in French in April, 1827 (translated in the *American Historical Review*, XXXV, 575–582, April, 1930). See also, *The American Democrat, New York*, and *The Oak Openings*.

28. Cooper's arithmetic is apparently at fault. His figures total $63,913,-347, not $61,913,541; and his figure of $10,596,963 should apparently be $10,636,997.60.

29. Protective tariff for American industries first became a political issue with the Revenue Act of 1792, fathered by Hamilton. The Tariff Bill of 1816, proposed by the South, actually benefited the North. A juggling of the issue was a feature of the first Jackson campaign and led to revisions in 1828, 1832, and 1833. The problem was, therefore, of active public interest at the time when Cooper wrote this passage.

Letter XXXVIII: [*Political Ideals*]

30. The *Notions* was written on the eve of the passage of the Reform Bill of 1832, with which Cooper was in active sympathy. The gradual rise of Whig doctrine to which he here refers formed the motivation of Macaulay's *History of England* (1849–1855).

31. This passage is characteristic of the laissez faire optimism of political thinkers of the period. They saw no reason why competition and altruism should not co-exist. Cooper accepted this doctrine without question.

32. The cornerstone of Cooper's theory about America was the indestructibility of the idea of union. On this idea he based his optimistic view of the future, an evidence of the survival of his father's Federalism in his own political and social thought.

33. For example, the British held Detroit until 1787.

34. Napoleon sold the Louisiana Territory to the United States in 1803.

35. 1819.

36. The title-page of the first American edition reads: GLEANINGS/ IN EUROPE. / [rule] / IN TWO VOLUMES. / VOL. I. [II.] / PHIL-ADELPHIA: CAREY, LEA & BLANCHARD./[rule]/1837. It is the third of his travel books in point of date of publication, the first in terms of the chronology of his European trip. It was published first by Bentley in London, January 24, 1837, and was republished by Carey in Philadelphia on March 4. It was translated into French and German (three separate editions in 1837), and was issued in English in Paris, 1837. It was not re-published again until the appearance of the edition of 1928, with notes and introduction by R. E. Spiller.

Volume II, Letter VII: [Paris under the Bourbons]

37. Cooper arrived in Paris July 18, 1826, with his wife, his daughters, his young son, and his nephew William, then acting as his secretary. The family rented an apartment in the Hôtel de Jumilhac, on the "narrow, gloomy rue St-Maur," in the Latin Quarter. Downstairs was a girls' school which the daughters attended, next door a convent. Lafayette and Walter Scott were among the first visitors, but Cooper soon began to move in French society through the introduction of James Brown, then American envoy. These were exciting days in the French capital. The Bourbon Charles X was still on the throne, but his days were numbered. Already when the Coopers arrived there were rumblings of popular discontent, and during his stay he witnessed an actual outbreak with street fighting. When summer came, a house was rented at St-Ouen, just outside the walls of Paris, overlooking the Seine.

38. N. P. Willis, John Neal, and other American travelers of this period made free use of letters of introduction to European celebrities. Cooper tells us that many such letters were given to him before his departure from America, but that his pride would not allow him to use them.

39. Mrs. Cooper seldom accompanied her husband on his social adventures.

40. Villèle resigned in June, 1827. The Martignac ministry, which succeeded his, made an attempt at mild compromise between King and people, caused dissatisfaction on both sides, and fell in its turn in July, 1829.

41. Cooper's French is invariably bad, but in this instance the spelling is correct though now old-fashioned.

42. It is impossible to identify all the personages whom Cooper leaves anonymous in this account, but his intimate friendship with the emigrèe Russian Princess Galitzin would suggest that he might be here referring to her.

43. Asmodeus, in Jewish demonology, was an evil spirit.

Volume I, Letter VIII

44. "Deployed" [?]

45. The restoration of the Bourbons after the fall of Napoleon led to a violent reaction.

46. Caroline, daughter of the King of Naples, married Charles Ferdinand, Duc de Berri, son of Charles X of France. The Duc was assassinated in 1820. His son, the Dauphin, known as "Henri V," was the hope of the Bourbon party in the July revolution of 1830.

47. "Industrial" [?].

Volume II, Letter X

48. Cooper's meaning obviously is: "The popular notion that American travelers in Europe generally favor liberty is singularly erroneous." A review of the records of impressions of these travelers would seem to bear out his observation. Most of them were exceedingly uncritical of European social and political ideas. On quests for the romance of antiquity, they were inclined to accept governments and societies as they found them. Furthermore, they felt somewhat defensive about their own country and its ideals, and their natural attitude was one of day-by-day conciliation of manner and idea.

49. The order of the Knights Templars was dissolved in 1312.

GLEANINGS IN EUROPE: ENGLAND

50. The title-page of the first American edition reads: GLEANINGS IN EUROPE./[double rule]/ENGLAND:/BY/AN AMERICAN./ IN TWO VOLUMES./Vol. I.[II.]/*PHILADELPHIA:*/CAREY, LEA, AND BLANCHARD./1837. It is the fourth of his travel books in point of date of publication, the second in terms of the chronology of his European trip. It was published first by Bentley in London on May 29, 1837, and was republished by Carey in Philadelphia on September 2. It was translated into French and German (two editions), and was issued in English in Paris in 1837. It was not republished again until the appearance of the edition of 1930, with notes and introduction by R. E. Spiller.

Volume I, Letter XI:
[*London on the Eve of the Reform Bill*]

51. "Demand" here means "summon for a hearing."

52. "Translation" here means removal to another bishopric.

Volume I, Letter XIV

53. This is the logical point of view for Cooper to absorb in his conversations with his Whig friends. Agitating as they were for the Reform Bill, they naturally assumed its desirability. Cooper, however, understood more than the superficial meanings of the social movement then in process

in England. He realized that the industrial revolution had already brought about a shift in the balance of power between the English aristocracy and the middle class. He believed that England was moving slowly toward a social philosophy which he defined as American democracy. Views such as these were liberal and far-sighted in the England of that day; but they were also conservative to the point of reaction in terms of the movement of the democratic idea in America. Cooper's Jeffersonian ideals of democracy were therefore being emphasized in his mind as liberal principles at the time that his friends at home were being stamped as conservatives in contending for them against Jacksonian equalitarianism.

54. The Parliamentary leadership of William Pitt, the younger, at the turn of the century was marked by many reforms but also by suppressive measures aimed at Jacobinism at home.

Volume II, Letter XXVIII

55. Agitation for reform of Parliament during these years caused feeling to run high in the lower as well as in the upper classes. The "Manchester Massacre," a mass meeting which was broken up by the cavalry in 1819, caused wide dissatisfaction in the people and more repressive measures in Parliament. By 1824, the Trade Union movement was legally recognized by a bill (modified the next year) which repealed the laws forbidding their existence. With his background of American political ideals, Cooper naturally interpreted these events as evidences of the coming of democracy to England.

56. *A Journey through India*, by Bishop Reginald Heber, appeared in the year this passage was written. Although English power had dominated ever since the Battle of Plassey in 1757, there were many uprisings of the natives during the period when Europe was disturbed by the revolutionary movements and the Napoleonic conquests. Nevertheless, the prevailing tendency was toward extension of British control, even though the direction of the movement of conquest remained in the hands of the East India Company until Queen Victoria was made Empress of India in 1858. When Bishop Heber wrote, British imperialism was in its infancy, and his pride is in full accord with the spirit of the day. St. John Chrysostom, one of the four fathers of the Greek Church, and a man of great influence, was famed for his humility; the reference to St. Polycarp, an early Christian martyr and friend of St. Sebastian, is meant likewise to point out the inevitability of pride in even the most humble.

57. Cooper reveals little actual knowledge of the Utilitarians and their political economy. Like Carlyle, he was temperamentally opposed to any system of thought which attempted to reduce the amenities of life to materialistic terms. The Utilitarians, under the leadership of Jeremy Bentham, laid down the principle of "the greatest good for the greatest number" as the basis of their social philosophy, and attempted to set up accurate and determinable measures of pleasure and pain as guides for

individual and social conduct. A distinction must therefore be made between the concept of liberty of Bentham and John Stuart Mill on the one
hand and Cooper on the other. The doctrine of the former led directly to
a laissez faire social philosophy, whereas that of the latter led to conservatism and regulatory law. The difference is in part accountable by the
contrasting situations in England and America: in the former the old laws
and social institutions were in a process of breakdown through reform; in
the latter they were in the process of formulation.

58. Again, Cooper's reaction to English social developments is to be
explained in terms of a background very different from that of England.
To an Englishman, with his memories of an absolute monarchy, the trans-
ference of power from the throne and the House of Lords to the House of
Commons was a movement toward democracy. Cooper, with his background of American distribution of power between the legislative, judicial,
and executive branches of the government, saw it rather as a shift of dominance.

59. The sirocco is a hot, dust-laden wind blowing from the Libyan
desert. In southern countries the term is applied to any wind from the
south, and is associated with habits of lassitude and indolence.

SKETCHES OF SWITZERLAND

60. The title-page of the first American edition reads: SKETCHES/
OF/SWITZERLAND./[rule]/BY AN AMERICAN./[rule]/IN TWO
VOLUMES./VOL. I. [II.]/[French rule]/PHILADELPHIA:/CAREY,
LEA & BLANCHARD./[rule]/1836. It is the first of his travel books in
point of date of publication, the third of the *Gleanings* in terms of the
chronology of his European trip. It was republished in the same contemporary English, French, and German editions as the other volumes in
the series, but has never been reprinted since.

Volume II, Letter XVI: [*The Alps*]

61. At Einseideln, in the Canton of Schwyz. Cooper was at this time
on the most extensive of his trips about Switzerland, traveling usually on
horseback, but occasionally by coach or on foot. He had brought his
family from Paris to Berne in July, 1828, and settled them in a house not
far from the town.

62. Cooper studied Picot's *Statistique de la Suisse* (1819) and Ebel's
Manuel du voyageur en Suisse (1826), as well as Keller's *Carte itinéraire de
la Suisse*. For a mere traveler, he was unusually well informed on the
geography, history, and folk tradition of the country of his visit. His comments on political conditions are based on more than guesses. By this time
Swiss independence and unity had been asserted, but the struggles of
Austria and France were still too recent to allow the republic to feel secure
in its future. It was undergoing an even more severe test of permanence
than that which the United States was experiencing, and Cooper observed

the clash of new ideas and old forms with intense interest, reserving his adverse criticism for those aspects of the present and past of the nation definitely associated with tyranny and oppression.

63. In 1388, the Austrians were defeated at Näfels by the army of the Canton of Glarus, which threw a torrent of stones from the mountains.

GLEANINGS IN EUROPE: ITALY

64. The title-page of the first American edition reads: GLEANINGS IN EUROPE/[double rule]/ITALY:/BY AN AMERICAN./IN TWO VOLUMES./VOL. I. [II.]/*PHILADELPHIA:*/CAREY, LEA, AND BLANCHARD./1838. It was published by Bentley in London, February 28, 1828, and by Carey in Philadelphia on May 28. Like the other *Gleanings*, it was published contemporaneously in French and German, but has not since been reprinted.

Volume I, Letter III: [*Liberal Florence*]

65. Cooper took his family by coach direct from Berne to Florence, arriving in the latter city on October 20. The winter was spent in an apartment on the street floor of the Palazzo Ricasoli, near the Duomo, the spring and early summer in a villa just outside the city. At the time Florence was the refuge for the liberal expatriates of Europe. Grand Duke Leopold was friendly to the fine arts and broad in his political sympathies. His city-state provided a haven for the ex-kings of the family of Napoleon, for Russian and Polish emigrés, and for American gentlemen. Cooper found its society altogether congenial.

66. By this time his long residence in Europe had developed Cooper's feeling for tradition. Compare his comment on Netley Abbey when he first arrived in Europe: "Had we seen Netley Abbey, just as far advanced towards completion as it was, in fact, advanced towards decay, our speculations would have been limited by a few conjectures on its probable appearance." (*France*, New York, 1928, p. 37.)

67. The walls have since been removed.

68. From the end of the French rule, 1808–1814, Tuscany was an independent duchy. In 1860 it was incorporated into the kingdom of Italy.

69. Boston, New York, Philadelphia, Baltimore, and probably Washington, although Cooper may have had Charleston or one of the other southern towns in mind rather than the last. Washington was as yet pretty much of a capital in the wilderness.

THE HEIDENMAUER

70. The title-page of the first American edition reads: THE/HEIDEN-MAUER;/OR,/THE BENEDICTINES./A LEGEND OF THE RHINE./BY THE AUTHOR OF "THE PRAIRIE," "RED ROVER," "BRAVO,"/&c. &c./[rule]/"From mighty wrongs to petty perfidy,/Have I not seen what human things could do?" BYRON./[rule]/IN TWO

VOLUMES./VOL. I. [II.]/[French rule]/Philadelphia:/CAREY &
LEA–CHESTNUT STREET/[dotted rule]/1832. It was first published
by Bentley in London, July 19, 1832; then by Carey in Philadelphia on
September 25. It was one of the least popular of Cooper's novels. Before
1852 there were only one English and five other American editions. It was
translated into French, German, and Italian, and published in Paris in English. It was the second of Cooper's novels on European themes, the one
which carries his most direct attack on Scott's ideals of the feudal state.
After extended residences in Naples and Rome, the Cooper family returned
to Paris in the fall of 1830. Late the following summer they made a circular
tour through Belgium and Germany, and revisited the Rhine, pausing at
Dürckheim, the scene of this novel.

Introduction

71. One of the minor adjustments following the realignment of Europe
after the Congress of Vienna in 1815. In 1826 the ducal line of Saxe-Gotha
became extinct, and a new grouping of the Saxon duchies became necessary.

72. Belgium had become a part of the Kingdom of the Netherlands by
the first Treaty of Paris, 1814. She became independent again by revolution in August, 1830.

73. Once capital of the empire of Charlemagne.

74. Cooper's occasional comparisons of the natural scenery of the two
continents is evidence of his defensive national pride. The habit of American travelers to accept the superiority of everything European to everything American irritated him, with some justice, when applied to the works
of nature.

75. The romantic spirit of the art of the day is nowhere more apparent
than in the then fashionable steel engravings, particularly those of natural
scenes.

76. Cooper's nephew, William.

77. "Shall I not take mine ease in mine inn but I shall have my pocket
picked?" (*King Henry IV*, Part I, Act III, Scene 3.) Susan Cooper tells us
that her father was accustomed to carry copies of Shakespeare's plays
about with him in his travels (Preface to *The Wept of Wish-ton-Wish*).

78. His son, Paul, then about seven years old.

79. The Benedictine Abbey of Limburg, which Cooper made the scene
of his novel, the theme of which is the destruction of the old orders in both
church and state by the coming of Lutheranism. The novel takes its title
from the Pagan's Wall. To Cooper, the ruins were evidence of a sixteenth-
century movement toward popular rights which had meaning in terms of
the advance of democratic principles in the Europe and the America of his
own day.

80. Cooper usually protected himself against the possible charge of in-
accuracy on the part of the historian and antiquary. He did not believe it
the province of historical fiction to hold too strictly to literal truth.

SKETCHES OF SWITZERLAND: PART SECOND

81. The title-page of the first American edition reads: SKETCHES/OF /SWITZERLAND./[rule]/PART SECOND./[rule]/IN TWO VOL-UMES./ VOL. I. [II.]/[French rule]/PHILADELPHIA: CAREY, LEA & BLANCHARD./[rule]/1836. It was published first by Bentley in London on September 16, 1836; then by Carey in Philadelphia on October 8. There were the usual contemporary French and German translations and the edition in English published at Paris. It has not been reprinted. It is the final volume of the five dealing with Cooper's European travels, even though it was the second to appear. It falls into three sections: that dealing with Cooper's life in Paris after February, 1832, (Letters I–VII); that dealing with his visit to the Rhine and the Bernese Oberland (Letters VIII–XVI) on his summer vacation trip; and that dealing with a month's residence at Vevey on the Lake of Geneva.

Volume I, Letter I: [Paris after the July Revolution]

82. The "July Revolution" of 1830 broke out on July 28 and lasted three days. Charles X, the last of the Bourbon French kings, abdicated in favor of the posthumous son of the late Duc de Berri, the Duc de Bordeaux spoken of by Cooper and others as "Henri V." On August 3, however, the Chamber of Deputies reorganized itself and called to the throne Louis Philippe, of the house of Orléans, a younger branch of the royal family. The revolution represented a compromise between traditional ideas of absolute monarchy and the newer republican ideas, but it was a step in the direction of the doctrine of sovereignty of the people. Lafayette gave it his sanction at the start, but later became the leader of the opposition party.

83. Lafayette was then spending most of his time at his Paris apartment in the rue d'Anjou. His power was slipping away as the government became more and more reactionary. Even before the end of 1830 he resigned under pressure as Commander of the National Guard. On March 13, 1831, the ministry of Casimir Périer came into power and the issue between liberalism and reaction became clearly defined. The finance controversy of 1832, in which he summoned Cooper to his aid in defending the low cost of a republican form of government, brought the two men into intimate contact, as did their joint work in behalf of the refugees of the Polish Revolution, 1830–1832. This friendship, more perhaps than any other single influence, shaped Cooper's liberalism into a definite form of republican political philosophy, equally antagonistic to absolute monarchy and to the Jacksonian form of equalitarian democracy which was then developing in the United States. Lafayette died in 1834, shortly after Cooper's return to America.

84. In 1832, a convention in South Carolina nullified the tariff as unconstitutional.

85. The royal Château de St-Cloud, *i.e.*, "gossip of the Court."

86. Gouverneur Morris was American minister to France, 1792–1794.

87. William H. Crawford was American minister to France, 1813–1815. In 1824, he was a candidate for President of the United States against Jackson and Adams.

88. The original spy upon whom Cooper modeled the character of his novel has always been a subject of dispute, and many candidates have been advanced, among them one Enoch Crosby, for the honor. Cooper, however, always insisted that the character was a typical and fictional creation of his own, suggested by an anecdote told to him by his friend, Judge William Jay, rather than by any one of the numerous spies who operated in the "neutral ground" during the war. See McDowell's article, "The Identity of Harvey Birch," listed in Bibliography, p. xcviii.

89. Cooper wrote of this incident to Captain W. B. Shubrick, "I wanted no more than this to forsee the fate of Lafayette's power, the moment the King could get secure in his seat" ("New Letters," *American Literature*, I, 139, May, 1929).

90. Louis McLane was American envoy to Great Britain, 1829–1831.

91. William C. Rives was American envoy to France, 1829–1833.

92. A reception to American ladies then in Paris was held on September 23 at the Palace and attended by Mr. and Mrs. Cooper.

93. On February 24, 1848, Louis Philippe abdicated and was succeeded, not by his son as he wished, but by the Second Republic under Louis Napoleon.

A LETTER TO HIS COUNTRYMEN

94. The title-page of the first American edition reads: A/LETTER/TO /HIS COUNTRYMEN,/BY/J. FENIMORE-COOPER./[rule]/NEW-YORK:/JOHN WILEY, 22 NASSAU-STREET./[rule]/1834. It was published in New York in June, and reprinted by Miller in London the same year. Bentley published it in 1837. It has not since been reprinted, and there are no foreign translations.

95. The substitution of a taxpaying for a freehold qualification for voting was a slow but inevitable process in the original colonies. Pennsylvania was first, in 1776; Vermont entered the Union in 1791 with a taxpaying qualification; Delaware, Maryland, and Massachusetts followed; New York joined the list in 1821, Virginia in 1830, and North Carolina not until 1856.

96. Between 1815 and 1848, Germany was a loose confederation of states.

97. The basic compromise was, of course, what A. C. McLaughlin (*Confederation and Constitution*, pp. 176–177) has called "an equitable distribution of authority between the center and the parts." There were also the interests of the states with aristocratic and those with democratic political and social organizations to be reconciled; and the issue between the

larger and the smaller states on the matter of representation occupied much of the debate which kept the convention in session for sixteen weeks during the summer of 1787.

98. Chief Justice Marshall, perhaps more than anyone else, laid the basis for the development of constitutional law in the United States in terms of strict interpretation of the Constitution. In 1803, he gave it as his opinion that "A legislative act contrary to the Constitution is not law. . . . It is emphatically the province and duty of the judicial department to say what the law is."

99. I. e., since the accession of William and Mary in 1688.

100. English constitutional law rests on court decisions and is therefore far more flexible than that of the United States.

THE AMERICAN DEMOCRAT

101. The title-page of the only edition published during Cooper's lifetime reads: THE/AMERICAN DEMOCRAT,/OR/HINTS ON THE SOCIAL AND CIVIC RELATIONS/OF THE UNITED STATES OF AMERICA./[rule]/BY/J. FENIMORE COOPER./[rule]/COOPERS-TOWN:/H. & E. PHINNEY./1838. It appeared in April, 1838. The only subsequent edition is that edited by H. L. Mencken (New York, 1931).

1. *On Distinctive American Principles*

102. The significant point is that Cooper's statement of the doctrines of constitutional government based on popular sovereignty were liberal when applied to the contemporary status of England or of almost any of the continental countries, but when applied to that of America, they were conservative and reactionary.

2. *On Equality*

103. The ideas of theoretical equality of human beings contained in the Declaration of Independence are not repeated in the Constitution. Amendment XIV prohibits any state from denying "to any person within its jurisdiction the equal protection of the laws." Cooper's doctrine on this point is therefore not in accord with Jefferson's original theories, but is in accord with the theories implicit in the Constitution.

3. *On Liberty*

104. Similarly, Cooper's ideas on the subject of liberty are far more limited than those of the earlier theorists, but are not out of accord with the constitutional theories.

105. A common-law writ having for its object to bring a party before a court or judge. Amendment VI of the Constitution provides that "in all criminal prosecutions, the accused shall . . . have compulsory process for obtaining witnesses in his favor."

4. *On Station*

106. Cooper's theories on liberty and equality are further limited by his acceptance of the principle of property rights. His principal modification of the European caste system is in the direction of flexibility. He retains most of its elements, but attacks its rigidity.

107. Compare the Preface to *The Ways of the Hour*, Selections preceding, pp. 323–325.

5. *An Aristocrat and a Democrat*

108. In this section, Cooper reasons, on the basis of the earlier sections, that a type of American gentleman is not inconsistent with the principles of democracy. Compare John Cadwallader, of the *Notions*, Edward Effingham, of *Home as Found*, etc., etc. This is perhaps the key to his entire social theory.

6. *On Language*

109. Throughout his work, Cooper makes occasional reference to the pronunciation and use of words, particularly by New Englanders. In this, as in most other matters, his point of view is conservative.

7. *On the Press*

110. This section is of particular interest because, at this time, Cooper's differences with the American, particularly the Whig, press, were acute, but had not yet crystallized in his long series of suits on libel. His first suit, of September, 1837, was against local Cooperstown editors; those against New York City editors began in 1839 and continued through 1845 (see The *"Effingham" Libels on Cooper*, by Ethel R. Outland, Madison, Wis., 1929).

111. For discussions of property, suffrage, etc., see Introduction, pp. lii–lv above.

112. See note 27.

LIVES OF DISTINGUISHED AMERICAN NAVAL OFFICERS

113. The essays of which this volume is composed were published serially in *Graham's Magazine* between May, 1843, and June, 1845. The title-page of its first appearance in book form reads: LIVES / OF / DISTINGUISHED AMERICAN / NAVAL OFFICERS. / BY / J. FENIMORE COOPER, / AUTHOR OF "THE SPY," "THE PILOT," &c. &c / VOL. I. / BAINBRIDGE, SHAW, / SOMERS, SHUBRICK, / PREBLE. / [VOL. II. / JONES, PERRY, / WOOLSEY, DALE.] / PHILADELPHIA: / CAREY AND HART. / 1846. The only reprint appeared in Auburn, N. Y., the same year.

[*Paul Jones and the American Navy*]

114. Paul Jones had established his base at Brest. The French, with an

excellent navy, were prepared to co-operate with him. The British fleet at the time, under Lord Sandwich, was in very poor condition.

115. Jones changed the name to *Le Bonhomme Richard*.

116. The *Edinburgh Review* compared Cooper's *History* to that of James. Cooper replied in the *United States Magazine and Democratic Review* in May and June, 1842.

NEW YORK

117. For the second time in his literary career, Cooper decided to give up the writing of novels after the failure of *The Ways of the Hour* (1850). At the time of his death the next year, he had in manuscript a large part of a work on the towns of New York state. It was apparently to have been a summary of the state of civilization or decay then reached by the society to the study of which he had devoted his thought for many years, a fitting conclusion to the task which he had set himself a quarter century before in the *Notions of the Americans*. The greater part of the manuscript was burned; the remaining fragment published posthumously in *The Spirit of the Fair*, April 5–15, 1864. The parts were assembled and published for the first time in book form under the title (which was not Cooper's) of *New York* (New York, 1930).

[Shadows of Coming Events]

118. Cooper was tolerant of slavery only because he believed that it would eventually die out. Compare note 27.

119. Cooper was no more deceived by the republicanism of Louis Napoleon than he was by that of Louis Philippe.

120. On the new economic issue between the capitalists of the North, with Webster as their spokesman, and the slave-owning agrarians of the South, with Calhoun as spokesman, Cooper was unable to take sides. There was no place in either picture for a planned economy based on protection of property and other rights, modified and liberalized by the Jeffersonian ideal of equality of opportunity. Whichever way a man of Cooper's theories turned, he was confronted with "the politics of economic drift." The only choice was dismay, tempered by a final warning.

PREFACES AND INTRODUCTIONS TO THE NOVELS

121. Cooper wrote his prefaces and introductions at various periods in his career, not all of them at the time of the first appearance of the work. Before 1831, they have little significance. In that year, the first three volumes of the revised edition were published by Richard Bentley in London as a part of his numbered series of "Standard Novels" by popular authors on his list. Twenty-one of Cooper's novels were eventually included in the series, and for each he wrote an introduction, with his English readers primarily in mind. These introductions, after 1831, usually ap-

peared also in the first editions in both England and America. The only
other edition for which he did special editorial work was that projected by
Putnam in New York in 1849. For this he wrote his introduction to the
Leather-Stocking series and several to individual volumes. The edition
included only twelve volumes and was absorbed into that of Townsend,
with illustrations by F. O. C. Darley, published in New York, 1859–1861.
In this edition were reprinted those introductions which Cooper himself
apparently wished to retain.

1. *Precaution*

122. Cooper's first novel (1820) was his thirteenth to be included by
Bentley in his popular reprints, the seventy-fourth novel in the series as a
whole. The first edition had been pretty well mangled as to text by an
inexperienced printer and contained a brief introduction by the author.
In the intervening eighteen years, Cooper had come to be ashamed of his
inexperience with respect to both his art and his methods of publication.
He revised his text thoroughly and wrote a new preface; but he allowed
the book to stand otherwise essentially as it had been written, with "all
its imperfections on its head." Although brief, this preface reveals as
many of Cooper's ideas about his art as does any statement from him. His
criticisms of his choice of an English plot and of his "medley of characters"
are particularly noteworthy as revealing his beliefs that he was under
obligation to use American materials and to distinguish and develop his
characterizations.

2. *The Spy*

123. This was the second of Cooper's novels (1821), the first on an
American theme. The Bentley reprint was based on the fifth American
edition (1827). It contained the fourth introduction which Cooper wrote
for this work, the earlier ones, here dropped, having appeared in the editions of 1821 and (two editions in the same year) 1822. The text was drastically revised, principally in the interests of an improved style and an
expansion of incidental comments of a social nature. There was a further,
but apparently not drastic, revision for the Putnam edition of 1849, with a
new (fifth) introduction. The introduction to the Putnam reprint is of
further interest because it gives in detail the anecdote upon which the plot
is founded, and lays at rest the supposition that, in the character of Harvey
Birch, Cooper was depicting a spy of whom he had first-hand knowledge.
His attitude in this case toward the use of real people for fictional characters
may be applied to other similar problems in his work. The author's con-
fession that he wrote his final chapter some time before he had planned
out a number of earlier episodes reveals at least two things: that the main
outlines of his plots were presumably in mind when he began writing a
book, and that the elaboration of detail was comparatively adventitious,
in response to a fluent and careless habit of writing.

3. *The Pioneers*

124. The third of Cooper's novels (1823) contains more autobiographical material than any others of his works. With a substitution of fictional names, and the usual liberty which he demanded in the treatment of both characterization and events, it is a record of his father's experiences in settling Cooperstown. At the time it was written, the idea of a Leather-Stocking series had not occurred to him, but the character of Natty Bumppo was so popular that he crowded Judge Temple from the position of central interest in the tale, and suggested further stories of more definite concern with the lives of Indians and trappers. Although written first, *The Pioneers* is the third novel in the series as it finally developed. The introduction here quoted was written for the Putnam edition of 1850. It is of special interest because it states its author's belief that he had not, in 1823, perfected his fictional method and that in retrospect he felt that he had held too closely to facts except for the character of Leather-Stocking. The relationship between fact and fancy can be checked with fair accuracy by a comparison of the account in Cooper's own *Chronicles of Cooperstown* (1838; reprinted 1929). The Rev. Ralph Birdsall discusses the original of Leather-Stocking in his *The Story of Cooperstown* (1917), pp. 161–167. In spite of Cooper's protest to the contrary, there is no reason to believe that the heroine of the novel was less dependent upon an original than any other of the characters.

4. *The Pilot*

125. The fourth of Cooper's novels (not counting *Tales for Fifteen*, 1823) appeared in 1824. It was his first sea tale, and like the others, its theme was suggested quite by accident. A discussion of Scott's *The Pirate* with some New York friends (among them the poet Fitz-Greene Halleck) led to a criticism by Cooper of the author's nautical knowledge. With so little artistic a motive, he set about a sea tale of his own, and created the type in English. His was the first through and through novel of the sea to be written in the language. Although his desire to "illustrate vessels and the ocean, rather than to draw any pictures of sentiment and love" would seem today an obvious and legitimate aim for a realistic type of adventure novel, in Cooper's day it was heresy. Again he had stumbled upon a new function for literature because of his deliberately unliterary intentions. Marryat's success owes much to Cooper's experiment. This novel was selected by Bentley to inaugurate his "Standard Novels" series, a testimony to its vogue in 1831 in England; and the preface here quoted was written at that time.

5. *Lionel Lincoln*

126. The use of the plural, "these tales," is explained by the fact that *Lionel Lincoln* (1825) was planned as the first of a series of "Legends of

the Thirteen Republics," and was so announced on the half-title of the
first edition. The step in Cooper's literary development which it marks is
obvious from this fact: He had written two historical tales of his own state
and was gradually developing a curiosity about the antecedents of the
forms of life in neighboring colonies of the early days. Two objectives
therefore led to the choice of theme for the next novel. He would reveal
the life of colonial Massachusetts at the time when the colonial period came
to an end and the foundations of the American nation were being laid;
and he would study the problem of the American of loyalist sympathies
during this crisis. He had many friends of loyalist tendency and his wife's
family furnished him with much material. Susan Cooper tells us in her
preface that her father journeyed to Boston in order to study locations and
documents for the scene dealing with the Battle of Bunker Hill. But in
spite of its author's care and the validity of his purpose, the novel was not
a success. During the writing, the theme grew cold; it was too far removed
from Cooper's immediate knowledge and interest to hold at a pitch necessary for creative power the enthusiasm which the project at first aroused.
The novel never "came alive" to its author, and it was the last as well as
the first of the series. His facetious treatment of the problem of sources is
a comment on the literary device used by Irving in his *Knickerbocker's
History of New York* (1809) and by Paulding in his *John Bull in America*
(1825), that of setting up the character of a fictitious historian and surrounding him with mystery. There is a suggestive parallel between the
work of Cooper and that of Paulding at this period. After *Koningsmarke*
(1823), a tale of the Swedes on the Delaware, Paulding wrote a series of
books defending the American character against the attacks of English
travelers. His next novel, *The Dutchman's Fireside* (1831), pictured the
New York Dutch at the time of the French and Indian Wars, and in 1832,
he published *Westward Ho!*, a story of Virginia and Kentucky. There is
an intense and provincial nationalism in the work of both men, and in
both it turned on the one hand to direct attacks on English criticism, and
on the other to examination of American origins in the social and political
life of the late colonial period. This preface is from the first American
edition.

127. The informal club of prominent New Yorkers of all walks of life,
of which Cooper was the rallying point up to the time of his departure for
Europe in 1826.

6. *The Water-Witch*

128. Several important novels intervened before the publication of
The Water-Witch (1830), Cooper's only experiment with a fanciful theme.
Written principally at Sorrento, on the Bay of Naples, it has, as Susan
Cooper remarks, "a carnival aspect" about it. Although laid in and about
New York harbor and peopled by the early Dutch, it has the borrowed
spirit of Italian sunlight and is somewhat alien to Cooper's genius. His

criticism that it blends too much of the real with the ideal is sound. He was struggling with the notion of legendary lore for the first time, and had not yet adapted it to a social purpose, as he was to do later in *The Heiden-mauer*. His hand was that of the man of action rather than of fancy, and it was too heavy. His realistic passages, dealing with Dutch characters, anticipate the material of which he was to make such excellent use more than a decade later in the Littlepage series. This preface is from the Bentley edition (1834).

7. *The Bravo*

129. *The Bravo* (1831) was Cooper's first attempt to deal with Euro-pean material. In spite of its ulterior purpose, it is an excellent adventure romance, dealing with the career of a professional assassin. But Cooper's mind was now growing more capable of the theoretical formulation of his social and political ideas, and for the first time he wrote a book with a clearly defined thesis. A residence of a few weeks in Venice, a reading of Daru's *Histoire de la république de Venise*, and a growing feeling that America had little to learn, except by contrast, from the political ideals of medieval Europe were probably the principal factors which determined him to confront Scott on his own ground and to use the latter's material to set up a contrary social and political doctrine, of Whig rather than Tory color. The distinction here made between the traditional forms of govern-ment in their bearing upon social states was developed in *The American Democrat*. In 1831, Cooper was still feeling his way. He was still using his romantic formula for the depiction of society at a given time and place, in as realistic a fashion as possible, in order to point his moral empirically rather than dogmatically. His plea for "a history of the progress of politi-cal liberty" is a new note in his comment on his own work, and marks his theoretical turn to an acceptance of the problem novel as his medium. This and his two other novels on European themes contribute to this purpose, yet only *The Heidenmauer* escapes from the habit of romantic narrative, and escapes to its cost in interest. This preface appeared in the first edition.

8. From *A Letter to His Countrymen*

130. This passage from Cooper's *Letter* (see note 94) contains his de-fense of *The Bravo*.

9. *The Headsman*

131. *The Headsman* (1833) is the third of Cooper's trilogy on European themes, and carries his examination of false republican institutions to a setting in Vevey and the Hospice of St. Bernard. The early chapters follow closely a short story by Balzac, "Jesus-Christ en Flandres" (cf. T. R. Palfrey, "Cooper and Balzac," *Modern Philology*, XXIX, 335–341, Febru-ary, 1932), but the greater part of the story seems to be original. The introduction, published in the first edition, reveals by a narrative method

Cooper's approach to his theme, his progress from a contemplation of the scenes about him to a questioning of the ideals of the past.

10. *Homeward Bound*

132. With the exception of *The Monikins* (1835), Cooper's work for five years had been in the field of direct social commentary when *Homeward Bound* (1838) appeared. We judge from his preface to the first edition that his return to romance was accidental, the result of a temperamental love of action. *The Monikins* had contrasted allegorically the civilizations of England, France, and America; the *Gleanings* and *The American Democrat* had stated his views on the same subject more explicitly. He now planned to present the reactions of a typical American family upon its return from a residence in Europe. But when he had placed his family on shipboard, the author of *The Red Rover* and *The Last of the Mohicans* reasserted himself and that of *The Heidenmauer* was forgotten. The long chase and capture again became the theme. Although a relatively good adventure story, *Homeward Bound* is not important in the history of Cooper's literary development except as revealing the duality of his interests and pointing to his return to romance in *The Pathfinder* (1840). Again, in this preface, Cooper returns to his old problem of the relationship between fact and fancy in fiction, this time to treat his fictional characters with mock seriousness as actual people.

11. *Home as Found*

133. In this tale, which appeared in the same year as *Homeward Bound*, Cooper carried out his original purpose and wrote his first admittedly social problem novel on an American theme. The scene is that of *The Pioneers*, but the time is contemporary, and the central character, a typical American gentleman, is, in spite of his own denials, a self-portrait. Having revealed the falsity of the pseudo-republican institutions of medieval Europe, he set about the task now of revealing the degeneracy of the republican ideal in America. The lack of a settled society (see note 10) had always seemed to Cooper to be one of the principal obstacles to an American social literature, but in this novel he overcomes the objection by dealing frankly with American deficiencies. The result was not popular. By the time the novel appeared, Cooper had already made himself unpopular with the press by his attitude toward his fellow townsmen in the "Three Mile Point Controversy," and his war with the local newspapers had begun. With *Home as Found*, the battleground was transferred to New York City by the Whig press, and the attack was taken up by James Watson Webb in the New York *Courier and Enquirer* for November 22, 1838. Stone, Benjamin, Weed, and Greeley were soon drawn into the fray, Cooper's version of which was summed up in a series of letters to *Brother Jonathan*, which included the famous "lost chapter" of the novel in the issue of January 1, 1842. (Ethel R. Outland presents a detailed his-

tory of the controversy in her *The "Effingham" Libels on Cooper*, Madison, Wis., 1929. Her facts are well marshalled, but her conclusions as to the results of the controversy are subject to question.)

12. The Deerslayer

(Preface to the Leather-Stocking Tales)

134. Apparently the earliest mention by Cooper of a possible Leather-Stocking series occurs in a letter to his English publisher, Henry Colburn, dated from Paris, October 17, 1826. (Spiller and Blackburn, *Descriptive Bibliography*, p. 224.) The novels were arranged by Cooper according to the sequence of events in Natty Bumppo's life in the Putnam edition (Nos. 4–8 inclusive), and this special introduction written for the series. The "resuscitation" of Leather-Stocking in 1840 cannot be explained wholly on financial grounds, even though it inaugurated a period in which Cooper returned to fiction as a means of support. Cooper had meanwhile repurchased Otsego Hall, the family mansion in Cooperstown, and had returned to the scenes and the ideals of his youth. The liberalism of the European and post-European period had become a set of fixed principles, and the natural conservatism of middle age had been built up about the symbol of the American gentleman. The transition from political and social doctrine to a more elemental morality was a natural consequence of his settled way of life. Leather-Stocking had always been his model for human conduct, "a character that possessed little of civilization but its highest principles." The recurrence of a moral God in this novel, a primary factor in his early thought (*Precaution* contains an attack on deism) but somewhat lost sight of in the years of travel and observation, set the key of most of his later work. His social and political idealism from this time on tends to establish its bases on moral and religious grounds.

135. *An Account of the History, Manners, and Customs of the Indian Nations who once Inhabited Pennsylvania and the Neighboring States*, by the Rev. John Heckewelder, a Moravian missionary, appeared in 1819, and was Cooper's chief source of knowledge about the Indians. Heckewelder idealized the Delawares, whom he knew, and accepted their enemies, the Iroquois, as diabolical. Cooper knew no Indians at first hand, as they had been driven out of central New York state long before the time of his boyhood. He therefore accepted Heckewelder's point of view as his own and made it the basic motivation of the series.

13. The Wing-and-Wing

136. An eddy rather than a part of the current of Cooper's literary development, *The Wing-and-Wing* (1842) is chiefly interesting for its sentimental morality. The material was drawn from a voyage from Leghorn to Naples in a Genoese felucca in the spring of 1829 (*vid. Gleanings in Europe; Italy*, I, 136–155), and the characters are based on memories of

people he had met at that time and during his residence at Sorrento. Prince Francesco Caraccioli, who occupies an important part of the story, was an admiral in the small fleet of the Parthenopian republic which was established at Naples in 1798. He repulsed the Anglo-Sicilian fleet in 1799 and was arrested and hanged by the order of Nelson. With this historical background, Cooper wrote a simple and moralistic love tale, the theme of which is the religious devotion and loyalty of a Neapolitan girl. The novel takes its title from the peculiar crossed arrangement of the sails on an Italian felucca; it also was published under the title *Le Feu-Follet*, and its English equivalent, *The Jack O'Lantern*, the name of the boat in question. This preface appeared in the first edition, 1842.

14. *Afloat and Ashore*

137. All of the materials and ideas with which Cooper had been experimenting throughout his career as a writer of fiction seemed to come to a focus in his five novels of the Dutch-English landed arristocracy of the Hudson and Mohawk valleys: *Afloat and Ashore* (two parts, 1844); *Satanstoe* (1845); *The Chainbearer* (1845); and *The Redskins* (1846). In them we find the sea, the Indians, New York City society, the Dutch-English landed proprietors; we find the American gentleman from youth to old age, the conventional heroine, the primitive man of heart, the noble savage and the savage villain; we find the chase and capture on land and sea, the battles of the backwoods and of the drawing-room, the stereotyped love story, the reward of virtue, the rediscovery of lost relatives; but most important of all, we find the romance of adventure finally synthesized if not harmonized with the social problem novel, the novel of manners. *Afloat and Ashore* deals with the career of Captain Miles Wallingford, a member of one of the older New York families of English blood. It was published in two parts, the second of which variously appeared under the original title and as *Lucy Hardinge* and *Miles Wallingford*. Although a large part of the tale deals with adventures at sea, the part in which Cooper was obviously most interested was that which "can convey to the human mind distinct and accurate impressions of events, social facts, professional peculiarities, or past history." His ground was firmer, his ideas clearer, his perspective better in these novels than in *Home as Found*. He had finally decided to take his stand for the traditional and aristocratic social philosophy under which he had formed his character in his youth, and to expound rather than to protest. The result is the most accurate and thorough study of colonial society that we have in early American fiction. What he had hoped to do for all the colonies at the time of writing *Lionel Lincoln*, he finally succeeded in doing for his own New York in five novels. In all of these novels, he assumed the role of editor rather than author. He felt himself the historian of morals and manners rather than the writer of fiction. This preface appeared in the first edition of the first part of the story in 1844.

15. *Satanstoe*

138. The opening paragraph of this preface, which appeared in the first edition in 1845, is perhaps Cooper's most succinct statement of his matured literary theory, and the novel which follows is the best example of that theory. It is the first of the trilogy dealing with the Anti-Rent War in New York State during the forties and fifties. A disturbance of little more than local interest and now almost forgotten by the historians, this "war" seemed to Cooper to be conclusive evidence of the decay of American ideals. The reason for his attitude lies in his theory of property (see note 106). The Anti-Rent War was waged by the tenants of the Manor of Rensselaerwyck against "the last of the patroons," Stephen Van Rensselaer. They demanded the right to purchase land which had been worked by members of their family for many generations; they were refused. Cooper was on the side of the patroon, in the interest of the right of holding property. To support his case, he followed a typical English land-owning family, the Littlepages, back to Revolutionary times, and traced their history through four generations. The first two novels present excellent pictures of life in past times, based on a deep understanding of the principles upon which the feudal and agrarian social system of the state was developed. The third, *The Redskins*, deals with the "war" itself, and is more controversial and less vital. This preface appeared in the first edition.

16. *The Crater*

139. Cooper wrote two allegories to illustrate his social theories in satirical terms: *The Monikins* (1835) and *The Crater* (1847). The preface to the latter is interesting principally as an illustration of Cooper's manner when in a facetious mood, and of his growing desire to point his moral directly. This preface appeared in the first edition.

17. *The Oak Openings*

140. *The Oak Openings* (1848) was the last of Cooper's Indian stories. It was suggested by two incidents, both of which Susan Cooper relates in *Pages and Pictures* (1861). In June, 1847, Cooper took his first trip west to Michigan. He was gone only a few weeks. Shortly after his return he saw a man rowing across the lake. When he drew up to the shore he told Cooper that he had lost some bees and asked the latter to help him hunt for them. Cooper was much interested in the method used in luring the bees by the use of honey and flowers, and by the character of the man, who, as a "bee-hunter," he made the central figure of his new work. His purpose was to represent, in the character of this man, the essential qualities of the Christian ideal. In the early days of his marriage, when he was living at Angevine Farm, near Mamaroneck, New York, he used to drive on Sundays to the Episcopal Church at Rye or New Rochelle; in his last

years, his intense interest in religion returned to him. He was a confirmed Trinitarian, and most of the novels of his last five years preach the acceptance of this faith as the only means of rectifying a world that had lost all others in its mad search for money and democratic power.

18. *The Ways of the Hour*

141. In his last novel (1850), Cooper's social purpose became more specific than was his custom. He directed his attack against the jury system on the ground of prejudice. The story shows much of his old power, but his last word is a criticism of democracy in fictional form. The final paragraph of this preface is a summary of his position on public questions during the declining years. Since the more objective social studies of New York State, he had further developed his fictional form in the direction of the pulpit. His latter novels, without losing their narrative power, had become instances of the value of specific doctrines.